HOPELESS WARS

Yakov (Yasha) Kedmi

Hopeless Wars

Yakov (Yasha) Kedmi

Senior Editors & Producers: Contento
Translators: Diana File and Lenn Schramm
Editor: Melanie Rosenberg
Illustration on Cover: Revital Kedmi
Cover and Book Design: Liliya Lev Ari

ISBN: 978-965-550-483-5

International sole distributor: Contento
22 Isserles Street, 6701457, Tel Aviv, Israel
www.ContentoNow.com
Netanel@contento-publishing.com

HOPELESS WARS

Yakov (Yasha) Kedmi

Foreword

Efraim Halevy

The story of Yakov (Yasha) Kedmi's life and personal battles is interwoven with many important chapters in the history of the State of Israel and the Jewish people in the second half of the twentieth century. In some, he was a supporting player, watching events with a sharp and extremely critical eye. In others he had a central role—a trailblazer who, by virtue of his force of personality and talents, reached a very senior rank in the Israeli civil service as head of the government agency responsible for bringing Jews from the former Soviet Union to Israel.

But this book is much more than the story of one man's life. It is a panoramic account of a fateful period in the history of the Jewish people and the State of Israel, as reflected in the experiences of a resolute nonconformist, a Jewish and Israeli patriot who held his own against everyone.

Kedmi, a Jew born in Moscow, fought a vigorous one-man campaign for the right to move to Israel, braving all odds and defying the norms of the mid- and late nineteen-sixties—a struggle made all the more difficult by the fact that the Soviet Union severed diplomatic relations with Israel right after the Six Day War. The first chapters of the book recount this struggle. Kedmi's success in overcoming all the obstacles by himself, thanks to his intelligence and courage, endowed him with dauntless faith in his abilities and gave him the knowledge that one can win even "hopeless" wars; thus he chose that title for his autobiography.

Soon after his arrival in Israel, Kedmi enlisted in the IDF where he completed Officer's Candidate School in the intelligence track. But the most significant episode of his service came during the Yom Kippur War, when he was attached to a reserve armored battalion commanded by Ehud Barak. Kedmi spent the entire war in the battalion commander's tank. His observations about those weeks and his perspective on the battles, the brave deeds of the fallen (some of them his close friends), as well as his view of the failures, fiascos, and mistakes made by so many—all make this book an important document produced by a fighter in the field, affording a broad canvas of topics and aspects that go far beyond a bare recitation of the events. Through it all we see the dominant figure of the battalion commander, Ehud Barak, as described by Lieut. Yasha Kedmi. This is rare testimony to the man who rose in the pyramid of command to become Chief of Staff and then Prime Minister and Defense Minister. Anyone who is looking for authentic evidence about Ehud Barak, the man and the leader, will find a font of information and unique insights here.

Kedmi has harsh criticism for the IDF and the establishment—the ruling elite on both the right and the left. From the description of his first encounter with them at Training Base 1, continuing through his survey of episodes in Israel's military and political history, the book offers us the perspective of a new immigrant who quickly assimilated into Israeli society but nevertheless missed no opportunity to compare how things work in Israel and in the Soviet Union.

A few years after the war, Kedmi found work as a temporary employee in Nativ (the clandestine Israeli government liaison organization that maintained contact and worked to encourage national sentiment among Jews living in the Eastern Bloc). Kedmi was referred there by no less than Prime Minister Menachem Begin. From the day of its founding by David Ben-Gurion, Nativ was the inner sanctum of the ruling establishment in Israel. Its first director was Shaul Avigur, Ben-Gurion's personal and political intimate. A heavy veil of secrecy was imposed on the organization's activities and missions, and its operatives were chosen with great care and expected to display maximum loyalty to the country's political leadership. Nativ's mission of bringing Jews to Israel from behind the Iron Curtain and especially from the Soviet Union demanded the greatest sensitivity. This was at the height of the Cold War between the West, headed by the United States, and the Eastern Bloc, headed by the Soviet Union. In those days, Israel identified with the West, ideologically and politically, even though it was the Eastern Bloc that had provided it with weapons in critical stages of the War of Independence.

Nativ had three main missions at its birth. The first was to develop and maintain the strongest possible ties with the large Jewish population of Eastern Europe and the Soviet Union, estimated at some five million persons. The second was to conduct appropriate operations to bring Jews to Israel. The third was to initiate and develop comprehensive political activity in the West, especially the United States, which would generate heavy political pressure on Moscow to allow Soviet Jews to emigrate.

In the view of the Israeli political leadership in the first quarter-century after independence, the diplomatic arena in which Israel operated demanded special sensitivity in this matter. After two decades of independence, Israel had managed to build a strong strategic relationship with the United States (of which the first fruits appeared just after the Six Day War). For this reason, the political echelons felt a need for caution in all actions vis-à-vis the Soviet Union, so that Israel would not be seen as interfering with Washington's policy towards Moscow. The leaders of the Soviet Communist Party, aware of the rapprochement between Israel and the United States, would not allow

Jews to leave the country if they had even the slightest connection to sensitive domains of Soviet security. Moreover, Israel of the 1950s and 1960s, especially its defense and political establishment, was a priority objective of Soviet intelligence. The espionage cases uncovered in those years involved Israeli scientists and senior members of the country's strategic and political elite.

Consequently, the methods for bringing Jews from Eastern Europe to Israel were saturated with complex national, international, and Zionist considerations. In the view of the Israel leadership of that time, everyone dealing with the matter had to be supremely loyal to the state, both with regard to security and with regard to their political orientation.

This was the situation that the "temporary employee" Yasha Kedmi found himself in. He came to Nativ shortly after the first and most significant change of regime in Israel—the *mahapach* or "reversal" that brought Menachem Begin to power. Begin, of course, did not adhere to his predecessors' ideas that Nativ employees must be loyal to the ruling party. Yet he did feel that the director of Nativ should owe him political allegiance and thought that extraordinary diplomatic caution was still required for dealing with the Jews behind the Iron Curtain.

Kedmi had a totally different approach and believed that there had to be revolutionary changes in how Israel perceived the Soviets and their power as well as in all aspects of the information campaign and political pressure that should be developed in the West, especially in the United States. He fought for his truth and was able to effect significant changes in this policy and to play an important role in the process that led to the opening of the gates for *aliyah* in the 1990s.

In the many chapters devoted to Nativ, readers are exposed not only to the details of events in which Kedmi took part but also to his perception of the Israeli political culture. It is an insider's view of the Israeli administration through Kedmi's prism: tales of the interagency wars and descriptions of the many persons who passed in the nonstop parade before Kedmi, the civil servant who piled up promotions until, despite his lack of political backing and patrons, he reached the pinnacle of the agency whose task was to promote *aliyah*—the same *aliyah* he had achieved as a lone fighter.

The many battles waged in the last quarter of the twentieth century to open the gates of the Soviet Union for Jewish emigration went far beyond Israeli foreign and defense policy. They were also inextricably linked to Israel's relations with American Jewry and to fierce internal quarrels within the American Jewish community. Should the campaign to open the gates focus exclusively on bringing the emigrants to Israel? Or should those escaping from behind the crumbing Iron Curtain be allowed to immigrate to the United States, that is, to "drop out" en route and select destinations other than Israel?

Kedmi had a strong opinion and clear practical policy aimed at preventing dropouts, by every possible means. His approach was not always in tune with that of the political echelons in Israel and of some American Jewish leaders.

But Yasha Kedmi fought stubbornly for his views. Readers will learn how he views the leaders of Israel and American Jewry in those years.

The Jews who came to Israel from the former Soviet Union in the last great wave of *aliyah* have drastically changed the face of Israel in the last two decades. Yasha Kedmi, who was the director of Nativ at the start of that period but later resigned his post, sketches out a clear and novel profile of the members of this *aliyah*, including its leaders, unique character, and self-image. Anyone who is looking for a first-hand source to help understand the behavior of the members of this *aliyah* since their arrival in Israel will find information and insights here that perhaps no one else could commit to paper.

What factors have shaped the complex relations between the immigrants from the former Soviet Union and the Israelis whom they met when they reached this country? How do the immigrants see Israel and Israelis? How do the immigrants react to their reception? What is the result of the collision between the pride of Jews who hail from a vast empire that covered thousands of kilometers, from Moscow and St. Petersburg and Kiev all the way to Vladivostok in the Far East, and the proud Israel that won its independence in bloody battle? How does Yasha Kedmi—the proud Russian Jew—relate to the behavior of law enforcement agencies that, in their perception (or perhaps gross misperception) of the immigrants, identify signs of a strategic threat posed by "organized crime"? Kedmi has a clear and pointed view on this issue, to which he gives unvarnished expression here.

The concluding chapters are under the sign of Yasha Kedmi's last war, as the head of Nativ—a conflict with strong forces in the corridors of Israeli power, who aspired to terminate the organization on the grounds that since its goals were fulfilled, it had no further raison d'être—or, at least, to sharply curtail its size and mission. As the head of the Mossad (the Israeli national intelligence agency) in those years, I was privy to various aspects of this last battle and remember my meetings with Yasha Kedmi, which always took place in a cordial atmosphere. At the height of this campaign he resigned his position and Prime Minister Netanyahu appointed his replacement. I am sure that Yasha Kedmi would agree with me that Nativ has changed greatly since his departure; some would say its luster has been tarnished.

The decision to publish this book stemmed from two main considerations: first, to allow Israeli readers a glimpse of the soul of a Jewish freedom fighter, a lone wolf who realized his dream of *aliyah* and was then able to return to the arena of his personal battle as the head of a national organization with no parallel anywhere in the world, equipped with his own insights and extraordinary abilities, to fulfill his mission. Second, to permit Jewish readers of Russian origins to contemplate their community's *aliyah* enterprise with immense pride, through the eyes of a hero, while at the same time allowing non-Russian Israeli readers to look in the mirror and see themselves in previously unknown hues. Anyone who reads this book carefully cannot remain indifferent to its message.

I close on a personal note. Some of the individuals described in this book in unflattering terms are well known to me from our joint endeavors. I see them in a very different way than Kedmi does, and my experiences of them involve glorious chapters in the history of Israel. My impression of people like Simcha Dinitz, whose important posts included service as the Israeli Ambassador to the United States during the Yom Kippur War, and Zvi Barak, the head of the Finance Department of the Jewish Agency during the daring campaigns for aliya from countries of distress, is not the same as Kedmi's. My experience of working alongside Supreme Court Justice Elyakim Rubinstein on many and diverse matters, is very different from the picture presented by Kedmi and I am happy to be numbered among Rubinstein's many friends. But this is Yakov Kedmi's book, not mine, and the style is his style. Kedmi's contribution and merits justify (some might even say require) that his story see the light of day and be read with all due respect.

Introduction

This book is not autobiographical. It should be described instead as a collection of memories that I have chosen to set down on paper. Over the course of my life I became accustomed to saying only what was essential and permitted, and that is what I have done in my book.

I wrote strictly from memory. I have never kept a diary, nor did I rely on documents or other written material to produce this book. So it is possible that inaccuracies have crept in here and there. I preferred not to draw on the archives of Nativ or of other agencies or individuals.

Although I wrote this book in Hebrew, which is not my native language, I found it easy to express myself on most topics. My goal has been to describe how a young Soviet Jew from Moscow, part of the generation born right after the most terrible of all wars, discovered his Jewish identity and himself, decided to make *aliyah (immigration to Israel)*, and fought to turn this resolution into reality, all alone, against the entire world and against all odds. And how his fight for the truth, which he made his way of life, continued.

Because I had the good fortune to be involved in important and meaningful events—not only in my personal life, but also in the history of my people and my country—I thought it appropriate to recount what happened, and especially the reasons and circumstances and how I saw and understood them as they were taking place. Some of this information is known only in part to the public.

I also wanted to present certain matters from my own perspective, which is uncommon, to say the least. What is unique about my perspective derives from my biography, from the fact that for almost forty years, I was involved in the life of the Jewish people in almost every way possible. I was among the first activists at the dawn of the struggle for *aliyah* from the Soviet Union. After I reached Israel, I enlisted in the public struggle, outside the establishment and against the establishment, to change official Israeli policy, in accordance with my own outlook and perceptions. Finally, I pursued this as my life's work for twenty-two years within one of the most wonderful and successful government agencies—which I had the honor not only to be associated with, but also to run. This gave me the opportunity not only to determine the nature and fate of *aliyah*, but also to exert significant influence on the destiny of the State of Israel and the Jewish people.

Because of security constraints and my focus on the main issues, I have described only events I was directly involved in, with no intention to analyze in depth any of the topics covered in the book. Nor do I claim to have written a full survey of the history of the struggle of Soviet Jewry, but only, as stated, my personal account of the events I took part in.

The title of the book—*Hopeless Wars*—expresses, I believe, the motto of my life. Here I tell how it was born and in what circumstances.

I would like to thank Reuven Miran, Dubi Shiloah, and Yonadav Navon, whose advice was of great assistance while I was writing the book. I am eternally grateful to my family and relatives who encouraged me, assisted in the writing, and supported me throughout the life I have described here.

Yasha Kedmi
August 2008

Chapter 1

A black dog, giant, immense and terrifying, much larger than me. A dog everyone's afraid of. But I am not afraid of the dog—we're friends. We're both three years old. His name is Julbers and he's my dog. I don't understand why people are afraid of him. He does anything I tell him to. I even ride him.

These are my first memories. I guess it's from that memory that I derived the feeling, or the ability, not to be afraid of what frightens other people. I can control it, just as I controlled my Caucasian dog.

Julbers was taken from me suddenly. They said he was dangerous and would make a good watchdog. I cried and felt very sad, so my dad brought me a different dog. We called him Pirate. He was a beautiful German shepherd, as big as Julbers, and he, too, quickly became my friend. I rode and harnessed him to my small sled, and everyone but me was afraid of him, too. To this day, big dogs are my great love and perhaps even part of my personality.

Another vivid childhood memory is of the first time I was cursed for being a Jew. I was small, so of course I didn't understand what it meant, but I sensed it was something bad. When I got home, I asked my parents, "What's a Jew? The children cursed me and said I'm a Jew. Why are they cursing only me?"

My dad looked at me, looked at my mom. Mom looked at Dad and sighed heavily. And then he explained it to me. "It's not a curse. The children simply have no manners and are trying to insult you. 'Jew' is the name of a people, and we belong to that people. Just like there are Russians, Ukrainians, French, there is also a people like that." What else could he have said to a three-year-old child? Should he have explained what a Jew is and how I was supposed to deal with anti-Semitic slurs? After all, I had no clue what anti-Semitism was.

Later, I kept running into my Judaism in a way that was unique to the Moscow of those years. I was almost six, and Stalin was ill. A few months before my birthday, on the anniversary of the October Revolution, my dad took me to a demonstration in Red Square. He put me on his shoulders and walked with me past the mausoleum where I saw Stalin and the entire Soviet leadership. Like any son of intelligent parents, I recognized most of the people standing on the mausoleum balcony—Molotov, Beria, Budyonny with his walrus moustache. But one person in particular caught my attention: "Who's that funny man, the bald one, who keeps waving his hat?" My dad looked around. "No, no, he is not funny," he told me. "He, too, is an important man. His name is Nikita Khrushchev." All the while, Stalin stood and looked at us from the mausoleum balcony. That's how I remember him.

I also remember my preschool and the two women there, Russians in white smocks. I remember one of them telling her friend, "The Jews are killing us, murdering our Stalin—it's all because of them. The Jews and the Jewish doctors are a plague and will bring disaster upon us."

I have remembered this episode ever since; even then I understood that their words referred to me as well, and I was filled with a sense of danger and fear. A few days later, I was talking with one of the other children in the preschool, a Russian boy, and he said, "Maybe Stalin will die?"

"Stalin can't die!" I burst out furiously. "He will live forever. We will all die, but he will go on living, because he's Stalin." That was what many believed. A total belief in the cosmic order of the country and the environment in which we lived. A truly religious belief in an orderly and organized system, more just than any other, with Stalin at its head. Despite the atheism of the Soviet Union, he was its God.

Stalin died two days later. It was the first time, but not the last, that the worldview I had constructed and thought was correct and perfect, which I believed in with complete and absolute faith, with extraordinary passion, collapsed. It was an important lesson for a six-year-old child. Stalin died on my sixth birthday, March 5, 1953.

I was born to a typical Soviet Jewish family. My mother was a Muscovite whose parents had moved to Moscow from the Ukraine in the late nineteenth century. Moscow was outside the Pale of Settlement (the region where Jews were permitted to live in Imperial Russia), but her family received permission to settle there. My father was born in Smolensk. His father, my grandfather, came to Smolensk from the Samara region of Russia. His mother, my grandmother, came from western Belorussia. In 1945, my father finished the foreign language school for officers, majoring in German. He had to pass through Moscow on his way to his unit which was stationed in Austria. Among the passengers on the crowded Metro, he spotted a beautiful young Jewish girl. She was just nineteen years old. He started talking to her and they made a date. Within a few weeks they were married and my father went on to his unit.

I attended the same school that my uncle, my mother's brother, had. A third of the students in his class were Jewish. All but one of the boys who graduated with him on June 21, 1941 (the day before the Nazi armies invaded the Soviet Union), were killed in the war. My uncle volunteered for the armored corps and served as a tank crewman. Barely twenty, he was killed in battle not far from Moscow. My brother Shurik was named for him. My paternal grandfather, Jacob, for whom I am named, was also killed in the war. His widow, my grandmother, had four sisters who remained in Russia (the rest of the family immigrated to the United States during the First World War). My grandmother and her sisters didn't manage to get out while they could. All of them married Jews, and none of their husbands came home from the war. They all had sons. All those who were of age served in the army. My mother's father, my other grandfather, was a captain.

My mother, of blessed memory, joined in the defense of Moscow at age fifteen. As the Germans neared the city, hundreds of thousands of residents fled on foot. My mother and grandmother stayed behind; they never considered leaving, even if the Germans managed to conquer the city. When I asked my mother about this, she explained that they hadn't known about the Nazi atrocities. At night, my mother ran around the rooftops with other teenagers to put out the fires started by incendiary bombs dropped during the German air raids. They also tried to locate German agents who signaled the bombers and directed them towards their targets. My mother earned the Moscow Defense medal for her activities.

About a year and a half later in 1943, when she was almost seventeen, my mother was called in for an interview at the special school of the NKVD, the Soviet secret police, and offered a chance to enlist. The recruiters wanted to train her in explosives and wireless communications and to parachute her behind the German lines as part of an intelligence and sabotage commando. She considered the proposal and rejected it. When I asked her why, she said she didn't think she was suited for that kind of work.

This is the environment I was raised in. This was my family heritage.

The next strange story in my mother's life took place just before I was born. One day, when she was pregnant with me, a group of gypsies passed the house. A woman came up to her and said, "Let me tell you your future." My young mother, a member of the Komsomol who did not believe in such superstitions, said no.

"Don't go," the gypsy coaxed her. "Listen. What do you care?" In the end, my mother gave in.

"You're pregnant," the gypsy told her. "You will have a boy. If he survives his first year and grows up, this boy will take all of you to a distant land across the sea."

My mother listened in total disbelief and dismissed her: "What utter nonsense!" This was the USSR of 1946, where it was enough for someone to inform on you for the mere thought of leaving the country to get you sentenced to ten years in prison.

My mother remembered the gypsy woman when I began my struggle to leave for Israel, but she didn't tell me the story until after she reached Israel herself.

Chapter 2

Mine was a typical childhood in an assimilated Jewish family in Moscow of the 1950s.

My mother understood but did not speak Yiddish, but my father was fluent and spoke it to her on occasion. I was raised in Soviet Russian society. I knew that I was Jewish, but my Judaism and the State of Israel were far in the background.

In 1957, my father told me that he had seen the Israeli delegation to the World Festival of Youth and Students and was strongly impressed by its members' young, confident, and cheerful appearance. The State of Israel had also been in the news previously, during the Sinai Campaign of 1956. Other than that, I encountered no references to it until the Adolph Eichmann trial.

As I grew older, I became curious about Judaism. I met very few Jews in my school, and if Jews were mentioned in newspapers it was usually in a negative context. I was nineteen when, in a conversation with a Jewish acquaintance as we were walking to our exams in the institute where we were studying, he said, "I have a pamphlet—maybe you'd like to see it?" And without waiting for my answer, he handed me a small booklet with information about Israel and a Hebrew calendar on its cover. The calendar was in Russian, printed in the State of Israel, and brought to the Soviet Union by Nativ (also known as the "Liaison Bureau," a clandestine Israeli government agency responsible for maintaining contacts with Jews behind the Iron Curtain), with the goal of stimulating national sentiment among the Jews.

Flipping through the pamphlet, I was particularly intrigued by the pictures of people, some of them my age, and was overcome by a strange emotion—the feeling of belonging to what I was reading about. When I finished reading the "calendar," I went for a walk. I always loved thinking while walking, and this time I started wondering why they were there and I was here. If I was Jewish, and there was a Jewish state, why wasn't I there? This was part thought and part feeling, and it possessed me in a very strange way that I could not comprehend.

I found it hard to be calm after that. Another day of thoughts that drifted onto the same topic led me to something that was part decision and part bewilderment: Could I allow myself not to take part in what was happening in the Jewish state or to the Jewish people? Could I waste my life on other things that were trivial in comparison with that? I felt that I had no way back.

I have no explanation, at least not a logical one, for what happened that day. Everything that had been important to me until then lost all meaning. Apparently, all the emotions that had been building up inside me for years, ever since the first time I heard the word "Jewish" applied to me with disgust, were bursting forth. Everything I had tried to repress and ignore, all the half-statements, the attempt to attach no importance to my Jewishness, all of these had been simmering inside me, waiting for the right moment. For the first time, I felt proud of my Jewishness and proud to be connected to the State of Israel. I felt, more than understood, that if I wanted to be a proud man, at peace with myself and my identity, I could only do so in the Jewish state. In any alternative, I would have to compromise with my truth and live a lie. The decision was made even before I fully understood it and all its implications. I no longer had any choice.

A few days later, in early February 1967, I went to the synagogue. I had never been there before. Once, when we were riding the bus, Dad pointed out the window towards a building and said, "Do you see the people standing there? They are Jews who have come here for the Jewish Rosh Hashanah, the new year." His words left no impression on me then, but I remembered the place. I went to the synagogue now, walked up to an old man, and asked him, "Maybe you know the address of the Israeli Embassy?" The man was taken aback. He looked at me, and then to both sides, and gave me the address. Back then in the Soviet Union, you could not just walk up to the municipal information booth and receive the address of the embassy. Soviet citizens did everything they could to keep their distance from any foreign embassy, certainly a Western embassy, and all the more so the Israeli Embassy—particularly if they were Jewish.

I decided to go and take a look at the Israeli Embassy, even though I didn't know what I would do when I got there. I walked past the embassy, on the other side of the street. I saw the building, unusual in terms of Soviet architecture, with an open gate and a sign in Hebrew letters. A policeman was patrolling back and forth in front of the entrance. Suddenly I made my decision. I crossed the road and walked with measured steps, like any normal citizen, towards the embassy gate and the policeman. He cast a glance towards me and continued to scan the street with his eyes. He apparently did not see anything suspicious about me. I counted my steps, calculated how long it would take me to get past the gate and the policeman behind me, and then sprang in the direction of the gate and walked in. The policeman sensed something and turned around, but didn't manage to catch me. I was already in the embassy compound. He stared at me for several seconds and ran over to his booth to call in a report. I had implemented Julius Caesar's famous maxim and crossed my Rubicon. "Breaking in" to the embassy was a step from which there was no return.

In the courtyard, on the left, there was a garage. A short man came out of it and walked briskly towards me. At first glance, it was apparent that he was a Soviet citizen and not Jewish. The man walked up and told me with the vulgarity that was the norm in Russia, "Get the f-out of here!" I looked at him and told him quietly that this was the territory of the State of Israel, that he was not the proprietor here, and that it would be better for him to get the hell back to his stinking garage and stay there. I was a graduate of the "school" of the Moscow streets, where I had learned this special and not-very-delicate (to say the least) lexicon. I had internalized the rule that one cannot show weakness to people like him and that they must be spoken to in the language of command and vulgarity. This manner of speaking—body language, facial expression, the way you look at people—means a great deal. I saw that the man was on the brink of exploding, but knew he couldn't hurt me. And indeed, he understood that there was nothing he could do and headed back towards the garage. I looked around. At the edge of the courtyard, I saw a door with a curtain, and someone peering out from behind it. Because this was the only door I saw, I walked towards it.

As I approached the door, it opened. Standing before me was a well-dressed man. His appearance, the way he looked at you, and his expression were not typically Soviet. He spoke to me in a foreigner's Russian: "Welcome. Please come in." I entered the building.

"How can I help you?" he asked. "What are you looking for?"

I told him that I was a Jew and wanted to know how I could immigrate to Israel. A second before the words had left my mouth I had no idea what I was going to tell him.

"Okay, come into the office," he said. I did so and the man asked me who I was, what I was, what I did, and who I had in Israel. I said I had no relatives in Israel; perhaps my grandmother had sisters in the United States, but I had no contacts with Israel.

"Fine," he said. "I can't tell you anything now. If you are really serious, come back to me in a week or two and we'll talk." Before I left, I asked him for materials about Israel. He led me to the table in the corner, which was covered with Russian-language pamphlets about Israel. I picked up one of each, along with a Hebrew textbook, and stuffed them into my overcoat pockets.

The man was Herzl Amikam, a veteran of Lehi (the Stern Group) who had immigrated to mandatory Palestine from Latvia in 1938. He was a close friend of Yitzhak Shamir from their days in the Lehi underground. When Shamir was recruited to join the Mossad, he took Amikam ("Herzke" to his friends) along with him. Among other things, Amikam worked on tracking down Nazi criminals. Later, Herzke was seconded by the Mossad to Nativ and stationed in Moscow.

The story of his posting to Moscow was interesting. Herzke's brother David Warhaftig, a Prisoner of Zion and veteran of the Beitar youth movement, had been released from the Soviet prison camps after many years and returned to Riga. In early 1966, after many applications, he received permission to leave for Israel. In one conversation, a KGB man told him that instead of dispatching all kinds of people to serve in the Moscow embassy, Israel would do better to send his brother, who was hunting for Nazi criminals in South America on behalf of Israeli intelligence. I should note that Amikam had already been asked to accept a posting as the Nativ representative in the Soviet Union, but had said, and rightly so, that he would be willing to serve in Moscow only after his brother immigrated to Israel.

After I joined Nativ, many years after the day I broke into the Israeli Embassy, I read Amikam's report of our first meeting. At its end, he noted: "I looked at the lad who was leaving the embassy and thought that I would never see him again, and then I had another thought: He's a fine fellow and would have made a good officer in the IDF."

When I left the embassy, there was a group of police officers waiting for me, boiling with rage, cursing and yelling. They led me to the guardroom and started questioning me. I gave them my ID card. When I walked into the embassy, I knew that if I were given the once-over by the police, the stupidest thing would be to be caught without documents. I told the officers the story of my grandfather, who disappeared in World War II, and said I thought that maybe he had somehow found his way to Israel. I said I had left his particulars in the embassy, hoping that perhaps they would locate him in Israel.

The officer told me that I should go to the Red Cross. After half an hour of exchanges and phone calls, during which they waited for their superiors to decide what to do with me, they released me with a warning not to sneak into the embassy again and to obey the law. It was clear they were surprised and confused and didn't even think to search me. I did not believe they would arrest me just for visiting the embassy. In the Soviet bureaucracy, every decision was a slow and cumbersome affair. The response was always delayed, and if your initiative was quick enough and unexpected, you had a margin of response time.

After that day, I started having various thoughts, which I tried to repress, until they returned with even greater clarity. During that period, I could not allow myself to think about what I was doing. Today, years later, I am quite able to analyze the events of that period and what was bothering me. When I argued with the Soviet functionary in the embassy courtyard, Amikam was watching us through the window. He didn't dare come out and intervene or show me off the premises. His heart ached for the fate of the Jewish boy who had dared to break into the embassy. But his orders, his mentality, and his operating method at the time did not allow him to escort me, to show the regime that I was not alone and that he, a representative of the State of Israel, was protecting me. I had subconsciously expected him to do so and was disappointed when it didn't happen. In the end, though, I suppressed the experience. It surfaced many years later, when I was already in Israel and could allow myself to think in a more objective manner.

Because of this incident, when I reached a senior position in Nativ, I instructed its agents to protect Jews in every situation, to escort them if there was any suspicion of government abuse. Both the authorities and the Jews needed to know that we were protecting the Jews and would not stand quietly by. I repeated this motto in my briefings, time after time, even when there was no real possibility of implementing it and when I knew that I would not be backed up by my superiors or the state and was quite aware that this deviated from all the ground rules of diplomatic relations. This was my prime directive: Never leave a Jew alone, as I had been left.

When I returned home that day, I hid the books and didn't say a word to anyone. I read them late at night. To avoid questions, I didn't want anyone in the house to see the books. After a week, I went back to the embassy, unsure whether I would be allowed to enter. Again I walked on the opposite side of the street and examined the policeman's behavior before deciding to act in the same way as before. It was not the same policeman, but like the other one he was a captain. I again sprang through the open gate. When I entered the courtyard, no one came out of the garage to intercept me and I turned towards the entrance to the offices. I rang the doorbell. A good-looking woman opened the door. In heavily-accented Russian, she asked me what I wanted. I responded that I had come to see Herzl Amikam. She said he was out of Moscow and would return in a few days, and then asked who I was and what I wanted. After I told her my name, she told me to wait while she called someone else. She turned out to be Esther Bartov. Within a few minutes, her husband, David Bartov, the head of Nativ in the Soviet Union, came down to see me. At the time, of course, I had no idea of his affiliation. In fact, the actual embassy staff was limited to the ambassador, a security guard, and a logistics officer. Everyone else was a Nativ operative.

By profession, David Bartov was a lawyer and had previously served as the registrar of the Israeli Supreme Court. In the late 1980s, he was appointed director of Nativ. No less important, he was the brother of Haim Israeli, the confidant of every defense minister from the establishment of the state to the early twenty-first century, starting with Ben-Gurion, and was also a close friend of Shaike Dan who effectively founded Nativ. Bartov was born in western Belorussia, which had been part of Poland until 1939. He had lived in the Soviet Union during the Second World War and was fluent in Russian. Our conversation in the embassy was courteous and straightforward. He knew of me from Amikam's report and suggested that I come back in another week, when he returned. I asked for and received more books and pamphlets.

When I left this time, I was not afraid. There were several people standing by the gate, in addition to the policeman. He had already reported on me and knew who he was dealing with. After he wrote down my particulars, he asked me why I had snuck in. "I wasn't sure you'd let me enter," I replied.

"According to the law," he said, "I cannot prevent you from entering the embassy. I must let you do so. If you show me your ID card, I have to let you in. But if you sneak in, you only cause me problems. They could cut my salary, deny me a bonus, or put a negative comment in my personnel file. So please, ask like a human being and I'll let you enter."

I apologized, thanked him, and left.

I went back to the embassy a week later. There was yet another policeman on duty this time, also a captain. I went up and showed him my ID card. He looked at me in surprise. "What do you want?"

"I want to enter the embassy."

"Why on earth? What do you mean?" he answered. "Get out of here."

I gave him a look and slowly said, "Take my ID card and write down my particulars. I am not asking you for permission to enter. You cannot prevent me from entering. If you want, call your superiors, report me. But I will enter the embassy. Is that clear?" This was not the way Soviet policemen were used to being spoken to, certainly not by a boy of nineteen. It was clear that the policeman was astounded. He mumbled something, went to call, and returned, flushed with anger, and saluted me. A policeman must salute a civilian when he addresses him. He returned my ID card and motioned with his head that I could go in. I thanked him and walked in to the compound. After that, I almost never had problems entering the embassy, and when I did, they were always resolved after I put the policemen in their place, bluntly and crudely.

Amikam greeted me warmly and asked whether I still wanted to immigrate to Israel. I responded that this was my reason for coming. "Okay," he said, "maybe I can do something for you. In another week, I will prepare a document that you can use." In the meantime, I was interested in the situation in Israel, particularly on the northern border, where there was tension with Syria. When he explained the situation to me, I saw a completely different picture than that painted by Soviet propaganda. As before, I took books and pamphlets with me when I left the embassy. This time, no one was waiting for me outside. I said goodbye to the policeman, who responded by saluting me, and went home. On the way, I thought that perhaps the regime was much weaker than we thought and that we imposed most of the restrictions on ourselves, because of fears that were already outdated. In any case, I felt satisfied—my first confrontation with the authorities had ended in a quick victory.

A week later, I entered the embassy without any problems. Amikam was waiting for me and passed me a sheet of paper, on the letterhead of the embassy. The document, in Russian, was headed "Request-Invitation." According to the text, the Israeli government pledged to give me an immigrant's visa if I received permission to leave the Soviet Union. I took the document and asked what I needed to do now. Amikam explained that I should go to the offices of OVIR (the Visa Department in the Ministry of the Interior) and apply for an exit visa. To my question of whether the document was sufficient, he explained that only people with first-degree relatives abroad received permission to leave the Soviet Union. "If you are allowed to leave," he noted, "the State of Israel will be happy to accept you. But getting permission to leave is your problem. We cannot help you with that." I thanked him and left the embassy. I understood that I would have to fight, all on my own, against the might of the Soviet Union. The official Israeli document in my pocket, with my name blazoned on it, gave me power, but I was still filled with fear. That sense of tremendous tension and stress, as before a battle, would follow me for many years to come.

When I went to the OVIR office and approached the receptionist, he looked at me with astonishment and asked whether I had an invitation from a family member. Instead of responding, I showed him the document I had received from the embassy. "This is just a piece of paper, which tells us nothing," he responded jeeringly. "You need an invitation from a first-degree relative. If you don't have such an invitation, you have nothing to do here. We cannot grant your request." I didn't argue with him, but only asked where and to whom I could appeal.

This was not unusual in the Soviet Union. A state with a Byzantine bureaucracy always has channels for appeals and complaints. Soviet immigrants to Israel were astonished that when they ran into a bureaucratic snag and asked where they could complain, the clerks just stared at them uncomprehendingly. "What are you talking about? There is no one you can complain to." In Israel, the bureaucrat and his decisions are usually the highest level, from which there is no appeal. A Soviet citizen always knew that he could complain to higher authority, even the head of state. The response I received was that this was the district office and I had the right to appeal to the municipal level.

When I went to the OVIR office for the city of Moscow, they wouldn't even speak to me. They told me them that my case was a matter for the district authority. "We do not deal with applications from private individuals. You have nothing to do here," they dismissed me. I asked where the All-Union office of OVIR was and received an address. I wrote a letter of complaint that my application was not being processed, attaching the document I received in the embassy, and submitted it to the national offices of OVIR. It was in response to my complaint, rather than a normal application, that my request to leave Russia was granted.

Chapter 3

After I submitted my request to the national office of OVIR, I was ready to tell my parents what I had done. They came home from work and we all sat down in the kitchen. I announced that I had been to the Israeli Embassy that day. If I had said that in five minutes an alien from outer space would enter our house and we were going to be married, I could not have surprised them more.

"Say that again?" my dad asked in utter disbelief. So I repeated what I had just said: I had gone to the Israeli Embassy today.

"Why?" he asked.

"It wasn't my first time," I said. "I'd already been there before."

"Who let you in?" my dad continued. I explained that they had tried to keep me out a few times, but now they were letting me enter.

"And what did you want?" he asked. I said I had inquired about the possibility of immigrating to Israel.

Now my parents' shock was complete. All my dad could find to say was, "And what would you do there?" I said that I would live like all other Israelis.

"What do you know about Israel? Would you be able to continue your studies there? Would you work? You don't know the language, you don't know anything. How would you live there?" my dad continued, close to despair. I told him I didn't know any details yet.

"This is the answer of a serious man?" he demanded. "You want to go to a foreign land, one that you know nothing about, and when you're asked for details, you say you don't know?!"

"That's not important to me, and I'll live there however I can manage. There are other people living there, more than two million, and I will live the way they live."

The rest of the conversation was calmer, albeit still quite tense—the conversation of a confused Soviet Jewish family, shocked that their son was going to destroy his life with his own hands. I showed them the pamphlets I'd picked up, and this only added fuel to the fire.

"Isn't it dangerous to hold on to this material?" my parents asked. I replied that there was nothing anti-Soviet in it and that the Soviet Union wasn't even mentioned. Was it a crime to possess a Hebrew textbook?

They asked whether I was studying Hebrew. "Yes, from a book." And I did start learning Hebrew. I had never heard the language and it was rather difficult to learn it without hearing it. The prayers in synagogue, which I attended a few times over the course of the next several weeks, were incomprehensible, in part because of the Ashkenazi pronunciation.

After this conversation, life at home changed. My parents tried to convince me that I was doing something stupid, making a mistake that would cause incredible damage to me and to the family, particularly to the future of my younger brother and sister. As far as I was concerned, life was going in one direction, spinning around a single axis—the Israeli Embassy on one side, the Soviet authorities on the other, and me in the middle. During that period, in addition to my university studies, I was working in a research institute as a junior engineer to help support the family. I couldn't go to school if I didn't also have a job. My family of six, three of them children, plus a grandmother, was pretty exceptional in Moscow, especially among the Jews.

After a short while, I was summoned to the All-Union Office of OVIR, where they explained that my request was against all the rules and procedures. The authorities could not approve my application because I had no relatives in Israel, and only those with a first-degree relative in Israel could immigrate there. I had been born in the Soviet Union and my family was here, so the State had no reason to let me leave.

I wracked my brains trying to figure out what to do next and what steps I should take in the future. I even considered drastic measures, but knew the authorities would retaliate with brutal force. I essentially came to the conclusion that I would never get out of the USSR through normal channels. I would have to manipulate the authorities to a point where they could no longer ignore what I was doing and were forced to do one of two things—let me go or send me to jail. If I was smart enough to develop the scenario in a way that it would be difficult and not worth their while to imprison me, there was a chance they'd let me leave. I decided to devote my energies to creating a safety net.

In the meantime, the appeals process dragged on, yielding one negative response after another. It became clear that without drastic measures, I would not manage to break the cycle. I began thinking about renouncing my Soviet citizenship. I saw this as the most efficient course of action, both in terms of principle and public interest. On the one hand, it wasn't against the law, while on the other hand it would be an act of public protest on an unprecedented level. There had been only one case of someone renouncing his citizenship: In the 1930s, a Soviet diplomat, Raskolnikov, had done so when recalled to Moscow. He also published an open letter about it in the French press, but he was beyond the Soviet authorities' grasp at the time. I decided to do so while still inside the Soviet Union, thereby augmenting its effectiveness. I was only waiting for the right moment.

The Middle East was on the brink of war. In Moscow, an international food exhibition was in progress. I went to visit the Israeli pavilion every day. The day I arrived, there was a reception in honor of the Israeli delegation during which I heard that President Nasser of Egypt had imposed a blockade on the Straits of Tiran. My instinctive response was that this was tantamount to a declaration of war. I asked Herzl Amikam whether the report was true, and he confirmed it. I asked him whether this meant that there was going to be a war. He said that he hoped not, but there might be no way to avoid it. In my previous conversations with him, he had told me about the IDF and about the military capabilities of the State of Israel, so I wasn't worried or afraid that the Arabs might win. My faith in the State of Israel had made me overconfident in the Jewish state. Incidentally, the guest of honor at the reception was Minister of Labor Yigal Allon, who was visiting the Soviet Union.

The war broke out a few days later and forged a link between two developments—one on the national level and the other on the personal. The war severely worsened the friction between the Soviet Union and Israel, and I came to the conclusion that I could not avoid more extreme action against the authorities. On June 11, 1967, after the IDF conquered the Golan Heights, the USSR severed diplomatic relations with Israel. I decided that the day the Soviet Union broke ties with Israel was the day I would break my ties with the Soviet Union. I went to the Public Petitions Office of the Supreme Soviet—the parliament. Under the constitution, it was the only body authorized to annul Soviet citizenship. The reception hall was filled with petitioners. Most of them were submitting requests for pardons for imprisoned family members. I sat over to the side and spent an hour and a half writing a letter asking to renounce my Soviet citizenship. Then I made a copy, sealed and placed the letter in an envelope, and handed it to the clerk. I put my copy in a separate envelope and went off in the direction of the Israeli Embassy.

Outside the embassy, Arab university students and a few Soviet citizens were holding a demonstration. There were also many policemen, some of whom I knew from my visits to the embassy. When I asked to enter the compound, I was told that no one could go inside today: Diplomatic relations had been severed, the embassy was closed, and the Israelis were leaving. I asked who would represent

Israel, but the policemen could not give me an answer. "We don't know. Ask us again in a few days."

I decided to proceed to the American Embassy and ask that they pass along the copy of the letter renouncing my citizenship to the United Nations Human Rights Commission. My goal was to make the West aware of my situation in case something happened to me. I thought that it might help, that maybe the UN would decide to get involved. When they are cut off from the world, people tend to cultivate naïve beliefs in the ability or willingness of agencies outside their countries to work on behalf of human rights. I had only one small problem: getting inside the US Embassy. I knew that the security there was much tighter, but nonetheless decided to follow the method that had worked when I first sneaked into the Israeli Embassy: a preliminary survey from the other side of the street.

The sidewalk by the US Embassy was broad—a good twenty-two yards. I managed to figure out the entry arrangements. The embassy compound had two entrances, on driveways that were separated from the sidewalk by a garden area. The distance between the part of the sidewalk where civilians walked and the embassy entrance and gate was eleven to twelve yards. The driveways were about a yard wider than a car. The distance the policeman patrolled back and forth, from one end of the gate to the other, was therefore shorter, only about a third of the distance I would have to run. To sneak into the embassy, I had to take off like a shot, whereas the policeman had only to turn around and take two or three steps to catch me. But I decided to take the risk.

I walked on the sidewalk with the idea of reaching the edge of the driveway just when the police officer was at the far side with his back towards me. In school, I had enjoyed light sports, including sprints, and I was good at taking off from the starting points. I made my move. As I ran, I could see the policeman turn around and jump in my direction. I managed to get inside the embassy grounds and could feel the wind from the motion of his arm as he tried to catch hold of my back. I stopped. The officer stood there and let out a juicy curse in Russian, then barked, "Get out of there right now, or I'll come and drag you out."

I looked at him and smiled. In a quiet voice I told him that I knew he was an idiot, but not so stupid that he didn't know the law and realize he was not allowed to enter the embassy. This was a childish approach. Maybe in the back of my mind, I was trying to be impudent to stave off my fear. The police officer said he would settle accounts with me when I left the embassy. I dismissed him with a wave of my hand and walked towards the embassy building. After I entered, I had no idea which way to turn. I saw a man, apparently a foreigner, and asked him in English where the consular department was. He looked at me in amazement and directed me towards it.

When I got there, I asked to speak with the consul. The security and all the arrangements inside the embassy were much more relaxed than they are today. I entered the consul's office and briefly told him about my request to immigrate to Israel and my application to renounce my Soviet citizenship. I asked him to pass on my letter to the Secretary General of the UN and the Human Rights Commission. The consul looked surprised, but took my letter and promised to forward it to the UN. He wished me luck, and I walked back outside.

When I left the embassy, I was greeted by a large delegation of police officers, including the one who had promised to "settle accounts" with me. He said that he would soon have the pleasure of breaking my bones. Although he was almost twice my size, I apparently had more bravado and told him, with a show of indifference, that I didn't know who would break whose bones. I was calm now that I had carried out my mission, and of course didn't want to show him that I was afraid.

They took me into a room in a booth next to the embassy and spoke roughly to me. I answered them quietly and politely. Several officers hammered at me in a chorus: "What were you doing in the embassy? Why did you break in? Now we have no choice but to throw you in to jail and have you tried for hooliganism."

I told them I only wanted to find out who was representing the State of Israel now that diplomatic relations had been severed, and a few other bits of choice nonsense that sounded like a plausible story. They didn't believe a word of it, of course, and stripped-searched me. They checked for materials, slips of paper, something incriminating. When they came up empty-handed, they said, "Okay, go sit in the corner. Soon we'll take you to a judge and you'll get thirty days in jail." The criminal code did include an article like that. A breach of public order was an offense for which you could be imprisoned for up to thirty days. I told them to do whatever they wanted, asked for a newspaper, and went to sit in the corner. I ignored all of them and acted as if they didn't exist, sinking into my reading. After a few hours, they came over to me, gave me back my ID card, and told me to go home. They gave me what was called a "last warning"—one more act of this kind and I would be sent to jail or banished from Moscow. According to the law, the authorities could banish a citizen from Moscow for one or two years and forbid him from coming within 63 miles of the city. This provision was frequently applied to anti-social types, opponents of the regime, or simply people whose existence they found inconvenient.

When I left, I wondered what had happened. Why wasn't I arrested? I could understand why I was held there for a few hours—the police officer lacked the authority to decide on his own and was only a cog in the bureaucratic system. It took time to complete the inquiry: they had to find my KGB file, start considering and investigating who this was, what this was, what reason he could have had, why he entered the embassy, what should be done with him. For this, two different departments had to decide which of them was responsible for the case: the counter-espionage division, which dealt with foreign embassies and their contacts with Soviet citizens (the Second Directorate), or the department responsible for political dissidents, subversion, and Jews (the Fifth Directorate). What did they know about me? What didn't they know about me? In the end, they reached the conclusion that no disaster had taken place and that it wasn't worth pursuing me just for breaking into the embassy. Or maybe they still hadn't decided what to do with me, didn't know how to digest this strange fellow, and were leaving the matter hanging for now.

This marked the end of the process of renouncing my Soviet citizenship and the start of the next stage. Now I had to figure out how to live in a country whose citizenship I no longer held, how to battle with the authorities, and how to behave vis-à-vis the world around me and the State of Israel.

Chapter 4

After I renounced my Soviet citizenship, I began waiting for the authorities to respond. At the same time I increased my contacts with dissidents, even though I had no intention of participating in dissident activities or trying to change the nature of the Soviet regime. I listened to the Voice of America as well as to German and British radio stations in Russian. The broadcasters talked about dissidents and read out their letters and public statements. The open letters they read over the air included the writers' addresses and phone numbers. I decided to contact some of them. Going to an address I had written down, I went to the home of Pavel Litvinov, grandson of Soviet foreign minister Maxim Litvinov, a Jew. Litvinov was one of the most prominent and active dissidents. I also met with Pyotr Yakir, son of Iona Yakir, the Jewish Red Army general who was executed during Stalin's purges. Pyotr himself, only fourteen at the time, was shipped off to the Gulag.

At our meetings, I told them about the steps I was taking against the Soviet regime. They did not show much interest. Apparently they weren't sure who I was, why I was doing what I was doing, and what I really wanted from them. They had relations with Zionist activists like David Khavkin, but I wasn't involved with that group. The dissidents treated me with caution and even a measure of suspicion. Provocateurs are the favorite tool of the security services throughout the world, particularly the Soviets, and the most effective way of countering every sort of subversive activity. What was more, everyone was paranoid and suspicious of everyone else, suspicion that the secret services encouraged and that eroded the solidarity and effectiveness of the dissident movement. So it was only natural for them to treat me, the outsider no one knew or had ever met, with suspicion. From the beginning I made clear to the people I talked with that I sympathized with their acts. Yet because I did not want to live in this country, I had no moral or legal right to interfere in what was going on in the Soviet Union, aside from the issue of the Jews' conditions and right to emigrate. On the other hand, it was their obligation to promote human rights in their country, including the right of Jews to immigrate to their own state. So far as I was concerned, the purpose of my meetings with them was to show the security services that I was in contact with the dissidents and that they knew who I was. The dissidents had contacts with foreign journalists and the staffs of foreign embassies.

During that time, the trial of Yuri Galanskov and his associates was under way in Moscow. They had published documents from the show trial of the prominent dissident writers Yuri Daniel and Andrei Sinyavsky. When I went to the courthouse, I discovered that although the trial was officially open to the public, only family members could enter the courtroom. The rest of us had to wait outside in the corridors, where they updated us during the recesses. My goal was to walk around the area so they would know I existed and that I was meeting with various people. I saw KGB men secretly trying to photograph everyone there, particularly the unfamiliar faces. After they had taken my picture a few times, I came up to the KGB man and arrogantly and insolently asked him where I could go to receive the photos. I told him I was willing to pay for them. Taken aback, the man mumbled, "I'm not a photographer, I'm not taking pictures. Where did you get that idea?" and quickly beat a retreat.

An interesting incident happened during the trial, whose meaning I would understand only much later. During one of the recesses in the proceedings, I went outside and walked down the street towards the Metro station. As I approached it, a policeman came up and asked me to step aside with him. He said that someone's pocket had been picked in the nearby Metro station and I matched the pickpocket's description. He just wanted to check my documents, in case they needed me as a witness or for interrogation. I gave him my ID card, which I always had on me. He looked around, and a young woman in her twenties came up to him and took my ID card from him. After checking it, she told him, "Write it down." The officer recorded my details and gave her the piece of paper, and she went away. Then he returned my documents to me and told me I was free to go. Later, I realized that because I was not familiar to the operatives who were tracking those present at the trial, they decided they had to discover the identity of the person who kept showing up at the courthouse. I was tailed simply to find out who I was.

From time to time, usually near the synagogue and particularly on the holidays, I also met a group of Jews, among them David Khavkin and Tina Brodetskaya, whose presence made a strong statement. They were among the dozens of Jews from all over the Soviet Union who had been arrested in 1958, sentenced to various prison terms for their Zionist activities which were defined as "anti-Soviet," and sent to special camps. After their release, they returned to their Zionist activities—keeping a slightly lower profile, but having greater impact. They decided to do things that would keep their campaign alive but would not look too daring or dangerous, so as not to scare new people from joining them. I understood their tactic because they were working among the Jewish community, whereas I was fighting an individual, almost private battle, which was therefore different in nature. I think that if one of them had broken off from the group to work on his own, he, too, could have allowed himself to carry out more radical activities, as I did. But they were already part of a group and everything they did would affect all its members. So I considered that their caution was understandable and justified. I found no fault with it, neither then nor now. We all played our roles in accordance with our own situations and the goals we set for ourselves. Nonetheless, the value of what was done by these and similar groups cannot be overstated. These groups—in Riga, Kishinev, Minsk, and several in the Ukraine—engaged in Zionist activities. Most of their members were tried and convicted in the 1950s and the early 1960s; some were sentenced to long prison terms. But after their release, they went back to their activities with even greater vigor. They made Zionism their life's goal.

Chapter 5

From the first time I broke into the Israeli Embassy, I began looking for ways to learn more about Judaism, the State of Israel, and Zionism. The normal Soviet channels provided no helpful information other than various defamatory screeds in the classic style of Soviet propaganda. But I had the good fortune of living in Moscow, where it was still possible to reach many and varied sources of information.

I began to look in libraries, including the Lenin State Library (the largest in the Soviet Union), the Moscow Central Library, and the Library of History. I discovered that the History Library had many books about Judaism, including the writings of Herzl, Ahad Ha'am, Pinsker, and Max Nordau, as well as anti-Semitic literature, of course. The books about Judaism had not yet been relegated to a classified department that required special permission to enter. I sat in the library for entire days and late into the night, plowing through everything there was on the topic in Russian, even the anti-Semitic books. I also read opponents of Zionism, including Lenin and Marx, and everything published as part of their debates. Soviet citizens were not allowed access to modern literature. I knew the material was there because I saw the titles in the catalogue, but when I requested such a volume they showed me the symbol that meant that this book could not be accessed without special authorization that it was needed for academic research. Over the course of about a year, I managed to deepen and strengthen my ideological foundations and amass many arguments in favor of my desire to make *aliyah*, which, of course, had not been born of any familiarity with Judaism or Zionism. First came the inexplicable, illogical, and incomprehensible desire, and only later did I find an explanation and ideological basis for it.

The authorities' response to my renunciation of Soviet citizenship was about one month in coming. I was invited to a meeting with the director of the Moscow branch of OVIR. The director, who held the rank of deputy-commissioner, invited me into his office and introduced me to two men in their forties, both in civilian garb— standard Russian faces, stolid expressions—whose profession was unmistakable. They were the type of people whose appearance you forget the moment you say goodbye to them. They looked straight at you—not typical of the average Soviet citizen—with an inquisitive gaze, penetrating and cold. Not a single spark of informality. Men in full control of themselves throughout any conversation and quick to understand what they heard. Their speech was Muscovite and intelligent; their language was pure and correct, but somewhat standard. Their questions were short, to the point, and deep. They listened closely to my answers and jotted things down. I felt rather tense and nervous, but I wasn't afraid. Adrenaline soared through my veins and filled me with confidence in my ability to cope with the situation. Throughout my life, I have met many members of secret services and intelligence operatives in various situations, and have always felt the same tension and adrenaline racing through me in anticipation of the challenge, accompanied by a feeling of inner power and lightness. I have never had a feeling of fear or worry, but only the taut expectation before the event that a hunter feels.

The conversation went on for half a day. Almost every exchange took place between me and the two civilians, who behaved in a courteous but haughty manner. This combination of emphatic courtesy, confidence, concealed aggressiveness in their words, alertness, and rapid response was typical of KGB men only. Bureaucrats could not be bothered with courtesies and didn't listen very closely. It was more important for them to give orders and demonstrate their authority. But it was very important for these two "civilians" to understand me and my motives, so they barraged me with question after question. They asked me to clarify the reasons for my request and to explain my perspective on various topics. They asked about my attitude towards the Soviet Union, Soviet society, Communist ideology, and national and international problems. They also asked about personal and family matters and the like. The exchange remained calm, but they slipped in warnings from time to time. For example, they said that my behavior was atypical and abnormal, which sometimes was an indicator of mental imbalance. Such deviant behavior might lead to a diagnosis that my true problem was mental and I might have to be treated in an appropriate institution. They said these things in a quiet voice, as though offering me a tour of a museum. They both drilled into me with their eyes and followed my every response; the hint was perfectly clear. I replied in an utterly calm tone, half-smiling, that if they had the power and were sure they would succeed, let them try; as far as I was concerned, I would do what I thought was right.

"We're asking you not to take unconsidered steps, such as trying to burn your internal passport in Red Square," they warned me. "We would not be able to overlook such a thing and it would not do you any good." I said that I would weigh my steps in accordance with the situation and my goals, but I didn't think I would want to burn my passport in the Red Square, because destroying a passport was a criminal offense and I had no intention of providing them with stupid grounds for a useless criminal charge.

The conversation moved on to other topics. "One day you'll have to do military service. What do you think of that?"

My response surprised them. "I will not serve in your army," I said. The words "your army" from the mouth of a Soviet citizen certainly rankled them. The shock on their faces was the best indicator of this. I continued, "There is only one army in the world that I will serve in, the Israel Defense Forces. I will not serve in any other army."

They didn't back off. "Look," they said, "And if there's a war between China and the Soviet Union, you won't go to the army then, either?" There were serious tensions between the Chinese and the Soviets at the time, even border incidents.

"I renounced my Soviet citizenship," I told them. "I don't want to be your citizen, I don't want to live here, and your problem with China has nothing to do with me. What happens to your country is a problem for the Soviet Union and its citizens. Perhaps it will interest me, but as a bystander, not as a Soviet citizen. I will not join the Soviet army even if you go to war with China."

Then one of them asked, "What if there is a war between Israel and the Soviet Union?" I responded that if the Soviet Union attacked Israel, then, as someone who wants to live in Israel and sees himself as an Israeli citizen, I would defend my country against them. "And if Israel attacks the Soviet Union?"

"There is a limit to wild imagination," I said. "I don't think Israel has any interest in attacking the Soviet Union—but in any case I will not serve in your army."

They said that should this problem arise, they would act in accordance with the law. "Fine," I responded. "You will act according to the law and I will act according to my own considerations."

At the end of the conversation they said, "Your request has not been approved. There are no grounds for giving you permission to leave or for nullifying your Soviet citizenship. As far as we are concerned, you remain a Soviet citizen and will behave in the appropriate manner. We suggest that you abandon this madness and return to normal life. You will never get to Israel and will only have problems here." With that we parted.

I tried to recap the conversation for myself later on. I left the meeting feeling confident and encouraged. My assumptions were being confirmed. Instead of putting an end to the matter once and for all, the authorities had opened negotiations and argued with me. I interpreted this as the weakness of the regime. In contrast to the average citizen, who trembled with dread of the all-powerful regime, I concluded that the authorities were not omnipotent. I also saw that they did not wield any serious arguments in our discussion. I recalled Prime Minister Kosygin's declaration during his visit to Europe that the Soviet Union did not prevent its citizens from emigrating to the West if they desired. I thought that if Kosygin was forced to make this statement, it must mean that the government was afraid of Western public opinion and was trying to hide the fact that it did block emigration. I grasped the regime's main vulnerability—fear for its standing in the West.

I recalled a story about Lenin we had been taught in school. In his youth, Lenin was interrogated by the Czar's secret police. "Who are you fighting, young man?" the interrogator demanded of Lenin. "There's a wall in front of you."

"True, there is a wall," Lenin responded. "But it's rotted through. Give it one good blow, and it will fall down."

I believed that the wall I was fighting, too, was rotted, but that few were aware of this. I understood that the way to succeed was to confront the Soviet Union with the possibility of damage to its international standing. Thus, I began looking for a way to bring the story of my struggle to the attention of the Western public, as the most effective manner of getting out of the Soviet Union. I was aware of the danger involved, but I had passed the point of no return and no longer had any alternative to making my campaign more extreme. I interpreted the conversation at OVIR as an attempt by the authorities to understand what was going on, to find out where a phenomenon like me had come from and how best to deal with it. On one hand, they knew of my contacts with the Jews, but they saw that the phenomenon was not spreading. On the other hand, how could a law-abiding family like mine have produced a young man with such a strong urge to go to Israel? I was barely twenty years old; KGB agents did not often conduct candid conversations with civilians. The fact that they interviewed me demonstrated the extent of their bewilderment.

I obtained indirect evidence of this when I finally received my exit visa. I was handed the document I had received at the embassy, a sort of entry permit to Israel, which I had submitted with my application. I noted a handwritten number at the top left of the document, which I took to be the page number—107. That is, there were 106 pages of documents preceding it in my file—testimonies, opinions, and various kinds of certificates. All told, 107 pages in the file of a boy who was not quite twenty years old. This demonstrated the serious work invested in me and the huge headache I had given them. Later, I heard from one of the heads of the Komsomol (the Soviet Communist youth organization) that he had attended a closed forum of Komsomol leaders that fall, where they had discussed my case, trying to fathom this aberration of nature and decide what to do. They assessed whether there was significant risk of similar cases arising in the future and their ramifications.

Time passed. I submitted appeal after appeal, each time to a higher authority. I thought that before I took my case to the West I should go through the full range of conventional channels for solving my problem. I did not have great hopes that my petitions would be granted, but it was important to collect as many facts as possible about the authorities' conduct. In the meantime one year passed, and I decided to move on to the next and decisive level.

Chapter 6

The year was 1968, and I decided to take steps so that my case would gain recognition abroad. When I resubmitted my request to renounce my Soviet citizenship, I made nine copies of my application. I distributed them to three groups, with a cover letter attached. Each letter was addressed to a different newspaper. My impression from the Voice of Israel broadcasts was that the most important newspaper in Israel was *Davar*. (I assume it really was the most important paper for those who were broadcasting on the Voice of Israel in Russian in those days.) Every press review began with *Davar*, followed by *Lamerchav* and then *Hazofeh*. *Maariv* and *Yedioth Ahronoth* were rarely mentioned, and *Ha'aretz* almost never. I didn't know back then that Nativ determined the broadcasts and their content. So my first letter was addressed to *Davar*. The second letter was addressed to the *Times of London* and the third to *The New York Times*. I decided to give these three letters to Westerners in Moscow, in the hope that they would agree to smuggle them out and send them to their destinations abroad.

First I tried my luck with diplomats. I spent about a month observing cars with diplomatic license plates and got to the point that I could identify those of the most important embassies. Once I identified a car from the Greek Embassy and followed the diplomat into a store. Inside I approached him.

"Are you from the Greek Embassy?"

Taken aback, he looked at me and mumbled in a tremulous whisper, "Yes."

I told him that I had several letters I wanted to send to the West and asked whether he would be willing to take them.

"No, no, no," he replied hurriedly, and beat a hasty retreat. I understood that I had acted not only naively, but also stupidly. It must certainly have looked like a set-up. A Soviet citizen comes up to you on the street, seemingly innocent, associates you with the staff of a particular embassy, and asks you to take an envelope with unknown content and smuggle it abroad! I was angry at myself for being such an idiot. Years later, when I served in Nativ, I gave my agents in the Soviet Union clear and unequivocal instructions, which I repeated ad nauseam: never accept any material from people on the street, not in any case, not in any place, no matter what. I warned the operatives that anyone who violated this order would be recalled immediately. My fear of provocation by security agents was more than simply well-founded. It was bound up with personal, professional, and political complications.

Putting the first package away for the time being, I decided to send the second parcel of letters through the British Embassy. I again observed the embassy procedures and entry arrangements. This time, however, I decided not to infiltrate it but to pretend to be a foreigner. To begin with, I walked to one of the main hotels in Moscow, the Metropol. Tourists, mostly foreigners, frequented this hotel. As part of the Soviet propaganda efforts, foreign newspapers, mainly those of Communist parties, were on sale at the kiosk nearby. I knew that the Sunday editions included color inserts on special paper, whose appearance contrasted sharply with the grey of Soviet newspapers. I had to go there several times over a period of a few weeks until the newspaper was available, because whenever an issue contained something the censor considered inappropriate for the eyes of Soviet citizens, the "banned" issues were not sold. In the end, I was able to buy a Sunday edition of the French Communist newspaper *Humanité.*

I wore a foreign-made raincoat to the British Embassy, wrapped my neck in a scarf, and raised my collar. This made me look somewhat different than the average Soviet citizen. I also polished my shoes to a high shine. I held the newspaper supplement under my arm, so that the language and color pictures were clearly visible. I approached the gate confidently, without looking at the police officer or even paying attention to him, and entered the embassy. From the corner of my eye, I saw that the policeman had glanced at me and immediately turned away. Apparently, the newspaper and my confident manner in ignoring him had done the trick. The police were instructed not to check foreigners entering an embassy. After I entered the building, I approached a clerk behind a counter in the center of the lobby and asked her where I could leave materials for the *Times* reporter. She pointed to the journalists' cubbyholes and I slipped my package of three envelopes into the one marked *Times.* I lingered there for a few more minutes and left the building without looking in the police officer's direction. For a long time, I thought that the Soviets didn't know I had visited the British Embassy. In the end, though, I learned that the KGB tracked everyone who entered an embassy and was caught on their surveillance cameras; the authorities had studied the photos and learned about my visit.

I walked the streets of Moscow with the other bundle of letters for a few weeks, looking for my chance. One night I saw a group of German-speaking students next to the Aragvi Restaurant in the center of Moscow. I walked up to them and asked them in English where they were from. They said they were from Germany. I asked what city, and one said Hamburg, which I knew was in West Germany. I picked out a young man who seemed more self-confident, more independent, and sharper-witted than the rest. I told him I wanted to speak with him and asked him to step aside. He followed me and I told him that I was a Jew trying to immigrate to Israel and that the authorities would not allow me to do so. I had letters I wanted to send to the West—to the United States, to Israel, and to Great Britain. Was he willing to help me and take them?

"No problem," he replied. "Give them to me." I handed him the package. Later, after I reached Israel, I learned in Nativ that the letters they received were posted in Germany. The student had been true to his word.

A few weeks later, I received a notice that I had a package from Israel. I ran like a crazy man to the post office. The package contained a recording of Geulah Gil singing children's songs. She was listed as the return address, so I interpreted the record as an indication that the letters I sent had been received. This boosted my confidence, after more than a year of being cut off from the Israeli Embassy, which had closed.

After the Soviet Union severed relations with Israel, I would visit the Dutch Embassy from time to time. The first time, I broke in as usual and was again interrogated on my way out by the policeman stationed at the gate. I recognized him: the policeman who had formerly been posted at the Israeli Embassy and had become my acquaintance had been reassigned to the Dutch Embassy. After that, I entered the Dutch Embassy just as I had the Israeli mission: show up, go in, walk out, and sometimes converse with them. In the Dutch Embassy, I met with the Dutch consul, whom I updated about my situation and asked to pass on the information to the relevant parties in Israel.

After I renounced my Soviet citizenship, I decided to apply for Israeli citizenship. I thought that if Israel gave me citizenship, this would strengthen my position vis-à-vis the authorities and boost my confidence. I thought that in Israel, as in the Soviet Union, it was the Knesset that conferred citizenship. I gave the Dutch Embassy a petition to the Israeli Knesset, requesting Israeli citizenship. When I returned to the embassy a month later, the Dutch consul conveyed Israel's response to me: "Under Israeli law, it is not possible to confer citizenship on a person who is not in the territory of the State of

Israel." I was very angry. I realized that there was a difference between my understanding of our situation in the Soviet Union and how the people in Israel saw us and formulated policy to deal with us. Once again I concluded that I could rely only on myself. I finally understood that aside from moderate and cautious signs of encouragement, it was doubtful that I could rely on any action, petition, or official intervention by the State of Israel.

During those months, I came to the conclusion that Israel ought to pass a law extending citizenship to Jews in the Soviet Union whose immigration was being blocked by the regime. When I brought up the idea after I reached Israel, I was at first ridiculed, but I didn't lose hope. When Binyamin Halevy resigned from the Supreme Court and joined the Herut movement, I met with him and presented my idea. After he was elected to the Knesset, he submitted a bill to that effect and had it passed into law. The government of Israel, Nativ, and the Foreign Ministry tried but failed to block its passage. Over the years, more than a hundred Jews—Prisoners of Zion and refuseniks— received Israeli citizenship under its provisions, despite the resistance of the Israeli bureaucracy and some reservations on the part of Nativ (at least until I achieved a senior position there). The citizenship was purely formal, of course, but it encouraged the refuseniks and gave them a good feeling. The Israeli authorities did not respond to the refuseniks' attempts to use their Israeli citizenship. They did not take advantage of it in international forums, even for propaganda and public relations. But this idea crystallized as part of my battle against the Soviet authorities, and ultimately was realized and forced on the Israeli establishment after my *aliyah*.

Chapter 7

In the meantime, an additional development had taken place. Some six months before I admitted to myself that I was a Zionist, the research institute where I worked pressed me to join the Komsomol. I was not a member, even though I was already nineteen, and it was unusual for anyone over fifteen not to belong to the Young Communist League. The young woman who was secretary of the Komsomol branch at the institute told me that she was being harassed on my account: One of the employees at "her" institute was not a Komsomol member! This upset her, detracted from her status, and would probably harm her career. Please, would I register, if only for her sake. I couldn't see why I shouldn't do this cute girl a favor, so I signed up. Later, after I began my struggle to leave the Soviet Union, I understood that my worldview was incompatible with membership in the Communist youth organization. I wanted to make *aliyah*, but I had joined a movement whose leadership supported an anti-Semitic and anti-Israel policy. I realized that if I had renounced my citizenship, and all the more so for the reasons that I had cited, there was no way I could remain a member of the Komsomol, even if only formally. By then I was working at a different think tank. I went to the Komsomol office there and submitted a request to resign from the organization: "In light of my desire to immigrate to Israel and my renunciation of Soviet citizenship, I request to leave the Communist Youth League and to no longer be considered a member." The shock was absolute. You have to understand that in 1968, in the Soviet Union, anti-Israel propaganda had reached a new zenith and was accompanied by traditional anti-Semitism. In form and content, it resembled the propaganda in *Der Stürmer* during the Nazi period. And suddenly, one of "our members" wanted to immigrate to that fascist country, Israel, and was even throwing away his Komsomol membership card. The municipal and district Party offices sent instructions to convene a general assembly of Komsomol members and denounce this anti-Soviet character for all to see, as a deterrent to others who might be tempted to do the same.

A date and time were set for the meeting, and announcements were posted. Neither I nor Israel was mentioned in the notice. Knowledge of the meeting spread like wildfire and the auditorium was packed. I estimate that several hundred people attended. A fair number of Jews came, but most of those present were Gentiles. To start the proceedings, the Komsomol leaders came and spoke about the disgrace that I had brought upon them. They read a few passages from the press and the Party about Israel, Zionism, and the like. Afterwards, I was allowed to speak to explain myself. Over the course of an hour, I explained my position and my Zionist worldview in a fairly cogent manner. It was the first time these people had heard a well-organized and carefully reasoned lecture about Judaism and Zionism. The hall was completely silent. Afterwards, the floor was opened for questions, which I answered. I stood alone on the stage before a packed auditorium, with standing room only. For the organizers, the result was fatal. Several hundred people, including Jews, spent three hours hearing me expound on ideas they had never heard of—Zionism, the Jewish people's struggle for national rebirth and independence, the Six Day War, the Soviet involvement, the anti-Semitic policy of their country, the cultural and national suppression of the Jews in the Soviet Union. I was an excellent speaker in Russian. My interest in and penchant for mathematics shaped and honed the logical aspect of my presentation. The facts, carefully formulated, with no use of fossilized, official propaganda, did their part. All the arguments raised against me sounded pathetic and merely added to the effectiveness of my speech. Finally, someone in the audience moved that the meeting denounce my anti-Soviet behavior and request that the authorities kick me out of the Soviet Union to Israel.

That was going too far. The Party overseers understood that the passage of such a resolution would threaten their own status. One of them jumped on the stage and said that although he completely agreed with the feeling in the auditorium, it was completely forbidden to interfere with the work of the authorities and the procedures of the government, and they should be allowed to determine their course of action in a free and professional manner. He proposed that a letter be sent to the authorities at the institution where I was enrolled, telling them the truth about this student of theirs and of the decision to kick him out of the Komsomol. The implications were clear.

When the letter reached my school, the administration recommended that I pack up and leave voluntarily. Otherwise, I would fail my coming examinations. I was just about to sit for the examination in economics, based on Karl Marx's *Das Kapital*. *Das Kapital* has two parts: the first is an analysis of capitalist economy and society, while the second discusses socialist theory. I had already been tested on capitalism but not on socialism. Half in jest, I told them that I had already studied the part I needed for my future life and would leave the theory of socialism to those who were staying behind. I asked for my file, to make sure they wrote that I had left my studies of my own free will and was not thrown out for behavior unbecoming a Soviet citizen. I applied to a different school, also related to the construction industry, noting that I had changed my employment profile and wanted to study a subject closer to the field I would be working in. This was not an unusual request and they were glad to accept me at once.

I continued my studies in my new school. Then, without warning, I received a draft notice. I sent back proof that I was a student and received a second call-up notice. I went to the draft office to find out what was going on, given that students had the right to defer conscription until they completed their studies. They explained to me that, by law, the deferment was valid only as long as one did not change schools. The minute I transferred to a different school, I had lost my right to a deferment and was now required to report for military service. I could continue my studies after I was discharged.

I understood that I was in hot water, but decided that come what may, I would not serve. The punishment for refusing to serve in the military was three years in prison, one year longer than the length of compulsory service. I thought that I would rather go to jail than serve in a foreign army, and began a game of cat and mouse with the authorities. I kept getting draft notices and throwing them out. I warned my family that if a messenger showed up with a notice, none of them should accept it or sign any form. I told them to say they didn't know where I was and not to sign; a signature on the notice made it impossible to evade it, and failure to report for duty after confirming receipt of a draft notice was grounds for the miscreant's immediate arrest.

I began planning how I could evade my army service. One way I considered, however strange it may sound, was to break my arm. I had once broken my arm playing ball and knew it would not be so bad. I even consulted with a Jewish doctor, the father of one my friends, on how to do this and whether he would help. He was unwilling to break my arm deliberately, but explained what to do and how to do it. This option seemed like a last resort. Still, a broken arm would allow me to defer my conscription for at least six months.

I began to have minor problems at the institute where I worked, which conducted research throughout the Soviet Union. My job meant I had to travel to various places, including, on one occasion, to Vladivostok on the Pacific Ocean. I traveled by train. One night, when the train stopped in Birobidzhan, I jumped off to look around. Like a sleepwalker, I stared at the signs, which were in Yiddish, in Hebrew letters. I bought newspapers and was surprised to hear the saleswomen speaking to each other in Yiddish. It was a profound emotional experience. Soon, however, the security unit at the institute informed me that all border districts, including ports, were now off-limits for me and they could not send me to any of those places.

The military draft took place twice a year, in the spring and in the fall. I had managed to make it through the spring draft without being called, but the fall draft was on the horizon. But in August 1968, the Soviet Army invaded Czechoslovakia. Strangely enough, the invasion of Czechoslovakia played a decisive role in my future. It led to the postponement of the discharge of some half a million soldiers who were supposed to complete their service in August or September. When the fall draft came, it became clear that the army had too many soldiers and could not absorb an additional several hundred thousand until it discharged those who had completed their service. But as noted, it was impossible to release soldiers stationed in Czechoslovakia. As a result, the entire fall draft was cancelled and deferred to the spring of 1969. All the open files were carried over to the next year, with no attention to the particulars of any specific case. Bureaucracy had triumphed! The KGB, which had orchestrated the attempt to draft me, had not placed this mission at the top of its agenda. They knew that the machine was still working and that sooner or later I would have to enter the army or stand trial. The draft notices stopped coming. When it became clear that the autumn draft was cancelled, I breathed a sigh of relief. I told myself that many things could happen before the spring of 1969.

Chapter 8

On one of my walks past the synagogue, I saw a man, who looked to be around thirty, conversing with two Jewish tourists from the West. To judge by his clothes, the man was a Soviet citizen, but his Hebrew sounded very good to me. I followed him when he walked away. After a few blocks, I overtook him and addressed him in Hebrew. At first, he recoiled. We shifted into Russian and I noticed that his Russian was marked by a very slight foreign accent that I couldn't identify. His name was Avigdor Levitt. He was born during the war years in Kazakhstan. His mother was Russian (non-Jewish). His father was a Polish Jew who was a member of General Anders' Free Polish Army and allowed to leave the USSR with his family when his unit was posted to the Middle East. Avigdor grew up in Israel and married there; Hebrew was his first language. His mother remarried after his father died, but within a few years divorced her second husband and returned to the Soviet Union with her son. In Israel, Avigdor's parents joined the Communist Party and he had been a member of the Young Communists League. We began meeting on a regular basis and kept up our friendship until I made *aliyah*. We conversed in Hebrew, which was of great help to me. I had never before spoken with a native Hebrew speaker. Thanks to him, my command of the language increased by leaps and bounds.

He was homesick for Israel and dreamed of going back, but his employment by Soviet government agencies that exploited his knowledge of Hebrew left him with no chance of ever getting out. In addition, he was entangled in family complications because of certain weaknesses in his character. All in all, he was a wretched man. In the eyes of the Soviets, he was a Jew and an Israeli; for Israel and America, he was a non-Jew (because of his Russian mother) and a traitor. At that time, he was working for the Soviet Hebrew radio station, *Shalom ve-kidma* ("Peace and progress"). From time to time, he would pass me classified information that was distributed to the staff at the station—reports of the so-called Red TASS (the Telegraphic Agency of the Soviet Union)—which included a detailed and uncensored overview of the entire Western press. So, for example, I read all of the Western publications and descriptions of the Soviet invasion of Czechoslovakia. He told me a great deal about the Communist Party in Israel, its activities and leaders, most of whom he had known as a child and whom he continued to meet on their visits to Moscow. I found it interesting to meet a leftist, a Western Communist, who believed in these principles not out of careerism but pure faith. I had never met anybody in the Soviet Union who genuinely held such opinions.

My grandfather, my mother's father, once saw me wearing a chain with the Star of David. He became very grave, looked at me quietly, sighed, and asked if I understood the meaning of the Star of David. I told him it was a Jewish and Israeli symbol. Somewhat warily, he asked why I wore it. I told him that I was fighting to make *aliyah* and was hoping to succeed. My grandfather was silent a bit longer. Then he said sadly that he didn't want to argue with me.

"My dear boy," he continued, "you do not know what it is when a Jew exploits another Jew and squeezes him dry. I know the Jews; you'll find out sooner or later."

We spoke of it no more. When I received my exit visa and told him goodbye, my grandfather asked me to remember what he had said and wished me luck. At the time, I didn't understand the meaning of his words. After my decades in Israel, I still recall, with sorrow and sadness, my grandfather's sage remark, and more and more so with each passing year.

In August of 1968, at another one of our meetings, the director of OVIR rejected my application once more and told me that the policy on emigration to Israel had changed. The Soviet government was now issuing exit visas to those who had received them before the Six Day War but whose departure had been delayed because of it. He also noted that they were once again processing requests to allow first-degree relatives—parents and children—to make *aliyah*. However, the changes did not apply to my case and he encouraged me to abandon my delusions. I immediately went to the Dutch Embassy, spoke with the consul, and asked him to relay a message to Israel about the modification of the *aliyah* policy. The Dutchman was skeptical, but promised to convey the message. Although the changes in policy ostensibly did not apply to me, I concluded that changes were in the offing and that the very fact of change was a good sign.

My workplace asked for a certificate from my new school that I was actually enrolled there. I realized that after I brought it in, my superiors would inform the institute of my "anti-Soviet" behavior and my education would be at risk again. I decided to quit my job and begin working as a simple laborer in a cast-concrete factory, where they had had never had Jewish workers. I was surprised to discover that my salary there would be more than double what I was making as a junior engineer, but assumed that this was just another expression of the Soviet economic and social worldview. The work was in shifts; my first shift was scheduled for the night between December 31, 1968, and January 1, 1969.

The shift began at 11 PM. Just when I was ready to leave my house, I was struck with fierce abdominal pains. In the ambulance, they discovered it was appendicitis. I was operated on by dawn. When I woke from surgery, my mother told me that a friend of mine had called.

It was the fellow whose father I had consulted for advice about how to break my arm. He told her that his father had heard my name on the Yiddish broadcasts of the Voice of America, mentioned in connection with some letter.

My body trembled. I felt waves of cold and heat passing over me. My mother asked what it meant for my name to be mentioned on the Voice of America.

"Mama, the trick worked!" I told her. I thought to myself that I had managed to push the Soviet authorities to the point of decision, as I had planned. Now they had to decide whether to respond with force or give up. The way I put it to my mother was, "Mama, now it's certain that I'll be going to the East. The question is whether it will be the Middle East or the Far East."

It was clear to me that the something was about to change. My mother grew pale and silent, overcome by fear and sorrow, all the more so because my entire family had long ago resigned itself to their oldest son's mania. People often told them, "Well, let's hope they'll let him out—otherwise he'll end his life here in prison. Whatever our misgivings about Israel, it would be better for him to live there."

Years later, when I was already working for Nativ in Israel, I heard from Nehemiah Levanon, its director, how my letter came to be published in the United States. At the time, Levanon was head of the Nativ mission in North America and the organization's representative in Washington. When he received a copy of my letter from headquarters in Israel, he tried to get it published but met with resistance. The *New York Times* refused to publish it, claiming it was "too militant." The head of an American Jewish organization that Levanon begged to publish the letter refused on the grounds that it was "too Zionist"! And all the while, the Jews in the Soviet Union were risking their lives in the belief that world Jewry would immediately run to their rescue! But Levanon was stubborn and refused to give up. After great effort, and thanks to the assistance of several Jews and non-Jews, he finally managed to have the letter published simultaneously in the

Washington Post, the *Los Angeles Times*, and the *Chicago Tribune*. Its impact forced the Soviets to throw in the towel and let me leave. Who know how things would have gone had someone less obstinate, less sensitive, and less devoted to our struggle been in Nehemiah Levanon's place. I have had many arguments with him, some of them quite bitter, about the appropriate methods of action and support for the struggle by Soviet Jewry, but I always knew the matter was close to his heart and important to him. Even if every possible mistake was made, his efforts made a tremendous contribution to the opening of the gates of the Soviet Union for Jewish emigration. But then, in Moscow, I knew nothing of this.

Chapter 9

I was discharged from the hospital after a few days. Two weeks later, when I went downstairs to bring in the evening paper from the mailbox as I did every night, there was a postcard lying next to the paper. I read it immediately and a deafening roar escaped my throat, shaking the building entranceway, penetrating the walls and doors, and echoing as far as our apartment. A rush of exhilaration ran through me; I felt like I was about to float away. The postcard was a summons to the OVIR office to receive my exit documents. All the stress, all the anticipation, all the battles, all the suffering I had been through dissipated in a second. For two years I had felt alone, prey to constant tension and fear. And even though I never surrendered to despair, I felt that I was waging a solitary battle against the whole world. I had fought a superpower, a great and cruel machine, which had arrayed all its forces against me. Even the few who supported me were dubious and skeptical. In that second, I felt I had vanquished a giant. I had overcome the Soviet Union, which only six months ago had crushed Czechoslovakia, while the rest of the world was mute with fear! I recalled a line from Isaac Babel's *Odessa Stories*, which described my feelings exactly: "You are twenty-five years old. If heaven and earth had rings attached to them, you would seize hold of those rings and pull heaven down to earth."[1]

---

1   Isaac Babel, "How It Was Done in Odessa," in *Red Cavalry and Other Stories*, editor: Efraim Sicher, translator: David McDuff (London: Penguin, 2005), p. 244.

I bounded up the stairs and found my family in a panic. "What happened? What was that roar?"

"It's over, I won!" I responded with unrestrained glee. "I'm getting an exit visa! I'm making *aliyah!*"

My parents were astounded. My mother started crying. It was a heartrending cry, the lament of a mother who knows that her son is going away and she may never see him again. That was how people felt about those who left for Israel. My father stepped away and I saw that he was crying too. I gnashed my teeth, sorry for the pain I was causing the people I loved most. But at the same time, I was bursting with joy.

On the designated date I showed up at OVIR. The official who received me was extremely, perhaps emphatically cordial, and apologized that it had taken so long to review my application. He justified the delay by saying that they had engaged in serious deliberations about how I, a young man who had been educated in a Communist society, would manage in a foreign, cruel, and capitalist country, without family or friends. It was only "out of worry and concern" for my sake and "the state's responsibility for a young citizen who is making a mistake" that the process of considering my request had dragged on for two long years. The official gave me questionnaires to fill out, along with a request for an exit visa to Israel. I looked at him with obvious surprise.

Somewhat perplexed, he smiled and said, "Forget it. You don't have to fill out any questionnaires. We have everything." So it was that in the end I never submitted a formal application or filled out any questionnaires. I was told that I had to leave the Soviet Union within two weeks and that I could never return, not even for a visit. I grinned and said that I would get over that somehow. Then another official joined us and both of them warned me not to engage in anti-Soviet propaganda in Israel. Here I became tense. In a dry and somewhat aggressive tone, I told them that my behavior in Israel would depend on how they treated my friends and family.

I received the exit documents and went to the Dutch Embassy to obtain an immigration visa to Israel. The embassy staff affixed it to my exit visa, booked me a flight to Vienna, and asked me how many days I would be needing to stay in a Moscow hotel, so they could make me a reservation. I said that I didn't need a hotel and would simply stay at home. The secretary, a Soviet citizen, was astonished and asked if I had relatives in Moscow. I responded that I was a Muscovite and was living with my family. She and her colleagues were stunned, because, as they told me, I was the first Muscovite to receive an *aliyah* permit. Before I left, I said goodbye to the Dutch consul with whom I had been in contact and thanked him for all the embassy's assistance.

On February 15, 1969, almost two years from the day I first stole into the Israeli Embassy in Moscow, I boarded an Aeroflot plane to Vienna. During the customs inspection at the airport, I was stripped completely naked and meticulously searched. My baggage consisted of a single suitcase half-filled with books, which also contained two bottles of vodka, a jar of caviar, two spare shirts, and underwear. The officers who checked me asked if this was all I had and I told them that it was all I thought I could take out of their country. Everything else was in my head and heart, and I was leaving them the rest.

My farewell to my family was, of course, emotional and difficult. It was only many years later that I finally understood what my mother and father had gone through when they embraced their son, their first-born, for what they thought would be the last time. Their whole world contracted into their last few minutes with their son, who was going off to a terra incognita at the end of the world, to a country in a frightening state of war, and there was almost no chance we would ever see each other again. My younger sister Vera held me tight and wept. My younger brother Shurik stood to the side choking back his tears, because after all, men don't cry.

I boarded the plane at the last possible moment, and it took off a few minutes later. All my thoughts were focused on the future, on the State of Israel, on my first encounter with the crazy dream that, against all odds, had come true.

Chapter 10

Until the Second World War, the Jewish problem was not one of the most serious nationality issues for the Soviet Union, neither for the security forces nor for the heads of the regime. Lenin, and Stalin even more so, saw assimilation as the natural and preferred solution to the Jewish problem. In essence, the entire Communist leadership, particularly its Jewish members, viewed assimilation as the appropriate and voluntary solution.

The persecution of the Jewish national movement during the years between October Revolution and the Second World War was based on ideological quarrels. The persecution, imprisonment, and even liquidation of members of the Zionist and non-Zionist movements (such as the Bund) were not motivated by anti-Semitism, but by the campaign against a rival and overly nationalist ideology. The same held true for other movements with a national bent. In fact, the persecution and attempt to destroy Zionism in the Soviet Union was instigated and led by the Jewish Bolsheviks.

The gravest national problem before the Second World War, one that the authorities saw as far more important and dangerous, was that of the German minority. In the Soviet Union then, ethnic Germans' representation in science, society, culture, and many key domains was very high, almost a critical mass, far greater than the number of Jews. Hitler's rise to power and his policy of inciting extreme German nationalism troubled the Soviet authorities, who feared its influence on a sizeable minority whose members occupied key positions. The Nazis engaged in sophisticated and effective attempts to exploit the German minority in the Soviet Union.

Stalin was more aware than anyone of the Soviet Union's weakness. His fear of real and imagined enemies was very strong and merely increased with the years. The sense of external and internal threats was the foundation and most distinctive feature of the Soviet regime, both in Stalin's time and afterwards.

The authorities began to wake up to the Jewish problem during the Second World War and its immediate aftermath. Stalin and the rest of the Soviet leadership saw the United States as their most dangerous enemy. The United States was home to the largest and most powerful concentration of Jews anywhere in the world, and this contingent was growing stronger. The fact was that a majority of American Jews had emigrated there from the territories of the Russian Empire. During the war, the Soviets decided to exploit this Jewish power by establishing the Jewish Anti-Fascist Committee.

The Soviet leadership assumed that an increased Jewish awareness would necessarily produce a closer relationship between Jewish Soviet citizens and Jewish citizens of the United States. The Anti-Fascist Committee amassed great prestige among Soviet Jews, who came to it with all kinds of problems, both personal and national. The Committee consolidated and bolstered Jewish consciousness. It also developed its own independent contacts with the West, the United States, and American Jewish organizations. Stalin and the Soviet leadership believed this situation had become dangerous and was at odds with the policy of assimilating the Jews. The solution was to stifle the awakening of Jewish nationalism in the Soviet Union. Here there was not one iota of the anti-Semitic views of Stalin and his associates, even if some of them held anti-Semitic opinions. This was a cold political calculation.

The result was the liquidation of the Jewish Anti-Fascist Committee. Every link, however small, between Soviet Jewry and Jews abroad was cruelly suppressed. The regime decided to solve the Jewish problem with the same determination it had applied to the case of the Germans, who had been deported to Soviet Asia at the beginning of the war, while the German Autonomous Republic was disbanded. Both the Jewish and German problems weighed on the regime primarily because of their international significance. That is, the greatest peril for the regime was the existing or potential involvement of hostile foreign states in dealing with the nationalities issue in the Soviet Union and exploiting it to their advantage. There was no difference between Germany, with its radically nationalist Nazi ideology, and the United States or Israel.

The outcome of the Second World War left the Soviet Union in possession of new territories that were home to many Jews who had been active in Zionist organizations or youth movements in the 1920s and 1930s. Groups of young Jews, most of them in their early twenties, began organizing even before the war was over, united by national sentiment and sympathy for the Jewish struggle in Palestine. They were arrested and imprisoned for their "anti-Soviet activities." In the camps, they encountered the surviving members of Zionist organizations who had been imprisoned in the 1920s and 1930s. Thus, Zionist activity in the Soviet Union was renewed (in fact, it had never really stopped). The prisoners of the 1920s and 1930s had battled alone, without hope, driven by their faith in the Jewish people and their dream of creating a Jewish state. Most of them are anonymous and have been totally erased from our national memory. But as in every revolution, the Jewish movement always spawned a new generation that joined the fight.

The groups that centered around Meir Gelfand, Vitaly (Vilia) Svechinsky, and others were an astonishing phenomenon in the history of the Soviet Zionist movement. They began their activities during Stalin's reign of terror. Jewish students, most of them born and educated after the Revolution, raised their heads and dared to work for their people, which almost nobody thought possible in those dark days. After Stalin's death, groups organized to study Hebrew; the one in Riga was headed by Yosef Schneider, who had survived the Riga ghetto. This group became the foundation of the Zionist movement that developed in Riga afterwards. Schneider was a marksman; when he organized the Hebrew study group he also taught the members to use firearms. "When we make *aliyah*," he used to say, "in addition to speaking Hebrew we'll also have to know how to shoot." Schneider was arrested after the Israeli "Sinai Campaign" on various charges, including one of an utterly fantastical nature: planning to assassinate Egyptian president Nasser. The shipyard in Riga was building submarines for the Egyptian navy, so Nasser came to the city during his visit to the Soviet Union in 1958. Everyone laughed at the absurd charge, but when I spoke with Schneider in Israel many years later, he told me that "despite the laughter, they were right—I really did think about assassinating Nasser." This was an example of the young Jews' passion and willingness to sacrifice themselves for the Jewish state.

There were always new recruits to the cause of Zionist activity who enlisted in the campaign in some form or another. Boys and girls in their late teens joined as individuals or in groups, and usually more vigorously and more blatantly than the members of the previous generation. What this movement lacked, however, was an obsession for *aliyah*. Stalin's terror and his successors' response created the sense that under a totalitarian regime, there was no chance of leaving the country. The State of Israel, too, sinned by misunderstanding—though perhaps less grossly than others—the situation of the Jews in the Soviet Union and the possibility of a campaign on behalf of *aliyah*. As a result, no one inside or outside the Soviet Union, recognized that it might be possible to fight the Soviet authorities for the right to make *aliyah*.

The penny dropped in 1967. The open campaign for *aliyah*, which I had the privilege of launching, started before the Six Day War and had nothing to do with it. This was a new phase. What worried the Soviet authorities and frightened Western Jews, too, was the very demand for *aliyah*, which was aggressive, uncompromising, and militant. It was only a matter of chance that I was the first. From the moment I managed to leave, the Soviet authorities and the Jews, both in the USSR and the West, understood that it was possible.

The Six Day War had two main consequences for the Jewish struggle in the Soviet Union. One was related to the Israel Defense Forces' capture of the Golan Heights. The IDF did this without serious advance planning, with no deep strategic thinking, and against the reigning political wisdom of that period.

In the present context, what is important is that the capture of the Golan Heights, which left open the possibility of an attack on Damascus and the fall of the pro-Soviet regime in Syria, led the Soviet Union to cut off diplomatic ties with Israel. Along with the severing of relations, the Soviet authorities halted *aliyah* to Israel, which had only just begun and was slowly increasing. No one in Israel had given serious thought to the political consequences of the attack on Syria, the Soviet Union's most important client-state in the Middle East, and the occupation of the Golan: the cessation of *aliyah*. It is possible that had diplomatic relations not been severed, the entire *aliyah* process would have developed in a different way and on a different scale. As it happened, the isolation from Israel and its institutions left Soviet Jews greater freedom to assert their identity without subordinating themselves to Israeli interests. This stimulated their motivation and capacity for independent action in the struggle for *aliyah*, which became steadily more radical and more aggressive.

The second consequence of the Six Day War is that it put Israel at the center of the Jewish world. The war led world Jewry to focus its efforts on Israel, and eventually put an end to the debate among the Jewish organizations about Israel and *aliyah*. As a result, the Soviet

Jews' struggle for *aliyah* garnered ever-increasing support in the Diaspora. The exalted spirits, powerful emotions, and heightened national pride produced by the Israeli victory inspired Jews the world over, as well as those in the Soviet Union, to more ardent activity on Israel's behalf.

For the Zionist movement in the Soviet Union, it was the start of a new era—the era of the struggle for *aliyah*, which swept over Soviet Jewry like a tidal wave. There is no doubt that what I did in 1967 would not have been possible in 1954 or 1955, but by the early 1960s, the stage was set for the *aliyah* struggle to begin in earnest.

Chapter 11

Due to bad weather in Vienna, my plane leaving Russia at last landed in Budapest. To put it mildly, I was not happy about this. When the plane had taken off, I felt that in just two hours, I would be a free man—but suddenly I had to wait another day. I could not relax until I was totally outside the borders of Soviet control. I had to finish my journey by train. After a while, I asked the conductor when we would reach the border.

"In another twenty minutes," he said.

I stood by the window, waiting excitedly for the moment I would once and for all leave the Soviet world and my old life behind to enter a new and better world and a new life. When we crossed the border, I smiled to myself. This is it, I told myself. I am finally safe. I'm over the border and nothing can catch me or bring me back. I am a free man. All the tension disappeared in an instant, and even my breathing came easier. The first of my hopeless wars was over. Now I know that this was the most difficult war of all.

We arrived in Vienna. Aboard the train were several more Jewish families from Georgia and Riga who had been on the plane from Moscow with me. At the railway station, we were approached by an older man. His appearance was clearly and unmistakably Jewish. In broken Russian with a heavy Polish accent, he asked, "Who is going to Israel?" I answered him in Hebrew.

The man was surprised. I gave him my exit visa for Israel. His surprise grew. Not only was I speaking Hebrew, but I was young and on my own. He took me to a hostel outside Vienna where they put up the *olim* (immigrants). I looked around in curious excitement, because this was my first time outside the Soviet Union. They took down my particulars and told me that I would have to wait a few days until my turn came to board the plane for Israel. There were dozens of families in the hostel, most of them from Georgia, some from Latvia and western Ukraine, and a few from Poland. I was the only one who was by himself. I asked permission to go into Vienna and they told me when I had to be back. I wanted to visit the city because my father had been stationed there during and after the war and I had heard a lot about Vienna from him. I wanted to write and tell him about the city where he had served, and I also wanted to see a Western city for the first time. No less important to me was to find a bookstore with Russian books. I bought a few volumes by Solzhenitsyn and other authors forbidden in Russia. Then I walked around the city and found the monument for the Soviet soldiers who had fallen in the liberation of Vienna. Looking at the monument and inscriptions, I felt that I no longer belonged to it; it was no longer mine, but belonged to another country. Although it was familiar, this was a foreign country. The feeling was strange and liberating, without the slightest tinge of sadness.

A day or two later, I was informed I would be flying that night. I remember the mounting sense of tension and excitement I felt as we approached Israel. Suddenly, in the darkness, on the horizon we saw a sea of lights. The passengers cried out in excitement. People wept. I choked up, too. What I felt was impossible to describe, because these lights approaching in the darkness were Israel. My life's dream was to come to Israel, and in a few minutes that dream would come true. Since then I have landed in Israel hundreds of times, but each time I am moved when I first catch sight of the city lights or coastline. I am always overwhelmed by a sense of warmth and elation.

The plane landed and the doors opened. I walked out of the cabin, stood on the ramp, and looked to the left and right. A sweet scent wafted towards me—citrus blossoms. That aroma is still with me today. It is the aroma of my homeland, the scent of Israel. This is my Israel—a warm night, darkness, people murmuring, and the strong sweet aroma of citrus blossoms.

I came down the ramp. I was so overcome by emotion that I don't remember the moment my foot first touched Israeli ground. I did not prostrate myself on the tarmac or kiss it. I stood there for a few seconds, trying to feel the ground of my homeland with both feet. "This is it, I'm home," I told myself, and walked off. I went up to the immigration control desk and showed the officer my Soviet exit visa.

"What is this?" the officer asked in surprise.

I explained to him in Hebrew that I was a new immigrant and these were the documents people use to leave the Soviet Union.

"All right, go on through," he said. After two minutes, I was already outside the passenger terminal at Lod airport and seeing the State of Israel for the first time—the noise, the tumult, the screaming taxi drivers, people in shorts and sandals, and the strong smells that engulfed me. I tried to find out where the Ministry of Absorption was, but nobody knew. I went back to the terminal and looked there. No one knew what I was talking about. I walked past the same officer again and left the building. In the end, another officer gave me directions and I found the hut. There were many people around me, waiting for their family members who were still inside. I managed to make my way through and push open the door. A few minutes passed before somebody poked out his head and asked "What do you want?" I told them that I was a new immigrant and that I had got off a plane from Vienna an hour ago.

"We've been looking for you all this time," he told me, almost accusingly. It turns out that I had caused quite a commotion. The people in Vienna had reported that I boarded the plane, but I had not disembarked with the other immigrants. I was supposed to stand to the side, like everyone else who didn't know where to go, until a representative of the Ministry of Absorption came to escort us. But because I had no problem with Hebrew—I had studied the language on my own for two years and could explain myself and communicate with those around me—I went with the rest of the passengers. In the end, they found the lost immigrant—rather, I found them—and I began the process of registration and absorption. I was put up for a night in a small hotel next to the airport. They told me that the next morning they would send me to a Hebrew language *ulpan (intensive language course)* on Kibbutz Revivim.

In the morning the Ministry of Absorption workers put me in a taxi and told the driver to take me to Revivim. We drove through various cities and towns. The driver picked up passengers on the way and turned off the main highway to stop off at his passengers' destinations. I actually enjoyed this. I saw more places and was able to meet lots of people, because I spoke with all the passengers. When we reached Revivim they told me there was a change of plans—I was being sent to the ulpan in Carmiel instead. We drove back to Lod on the same road. The office there told me that I would not be leaving for Carmiel until the next morning, so I decided to go to Tel Aviv. One of the staff was driving to Tel Aviv and gave me a ride. First I walked to the beach and stood there on the shore, filling my lungs with the sea air and trying to digest the fact that I was actually in Israel. Feeling hungry, I went into a cafe. The young woman sitting by the entrance escorted me inside cordially and sat me down at a table. I thought it strange that she sat down next to me. When I asked for a menu, she tried to explain something to me. It took me a few minutes to realize that this was not exactly a place to order coffee and a roll. I apologized and left. In the Soviet Union, I had heard and read about prostitution in the West—but I never expected to run into it so quickly in Israel, and in such a vulgar manner. But now I understood that a "coffee shop" with a young woman lounging by the entrance was not a place you went for a meal. In the end, I made do with a kiosk.

I wanted to find Geula Gill, the singer in whose name they had sent me the phonograph record. I thought that perhaps someone had told her about me and she had sent the album herself. I wanted to thank her for her attention. I asked passersby how to get to Savyon, where she lived. At first no one could give me directions, but finally one man stopped and tried to explain it to me. Then he asked if I was from Argentina, because my accent sounded a little South American to him. No, I answered, I was from the Soviet Union. The man was astonished.

"When did you make *aliyah*?"

"Yesterday," I replied.

The man was in shock. He looked at me as though I was a Hebrew-speaking creature from outer space. He said a few cautious words in Russian and I immediately picked up that he was from Ukraine. When I answered him in Russian, he was even more astonished. We continued our conversation. He told me that he had been born in Ukraine and had made *aliyah* in the 1940s, after surviving the war. He invited me to his home. That's how I saw my first Israeli house on my first day in the country. His warmth gave me a very good feeling, a feeling of being at home. Later we drove to Savyon, but it turned out that Geula Gill was abroad. At my request, he took me back to Lod. When we met many years later, I learned that he was Pinhas Sapir's driver (Sapir was finance minister at the time).

Now I was free until the next morning and decided to go to Jerusalem. Back in Moscow after my letter had been published in American newspapers, I received a letter in Hebrew from an American who had made *aliyah* and was studying at the Hebrew University in Jerusalem. He wrote that he had read about my case and would be delighted to meet me. He told me that he himself had renounced his American citizenship in protest against the Vietnam War. I didn't really understand this. Soviet Jews' attitude towards the United States, and in general to many things in the world, tended to be different, naive, rather simplistic or even primitive, like many ideas that Soviet citizens had of the world back then—particularly those having to do with criticism of the state and the regime. At the time I could not comprehend the opposition to the Vietnam War. After all, the Americans were fighting against Communism, which made it a legitimate war for me. Only years later did I understand the criminal folly of the Vietnam War. In the 1990s, I visited the border region between Laos and Thailand. When I saw the Laotians leading their primitive and quiet life, two thoughts came to my mind. First, what on earth were the Americans looking for there? These people, scarcely out of the Stone Age, did not pose any danger to the United States. My second thought was that these people had defeated the strongest and richest power on Earth!

I wanted to find my correspondent and I wanted to go to Jerusalem. I went to the student dormitories on Mount Scopus, found his address, and knocked on the door. A voice called out, "Who's there?" I stated my name and added that he had sent me a letter in Moscow. He was in shock. Sitting in his room were a few students from Czechoslovakia, still feeling the brunt of the Soviet invasion of their country. We sat and talked for a long time.

Later that night, I went to the Western Wall, and then returned to my hotel in Lod. In the morning, I set off for Carmiel with the same driver. First we made a detour to Rosh HaNikra to drop off the other passengers, giving me a chance to stand on the border between Israel and Lebanon. By night, I was settled into a room in the Carmiel ulpan. But I found it hard to fall asleep—after all, just a few days beforehand I had still been in Moscow.

Chapter 12

The next day, after I completed my registration in the Absorption Center, they sent me to have lunch in the cafeteria where several immigrants from Riga were already sitting and eating. One of the women came up to my table.

"We heard that you are from the Soviet Union," she said in Russian.

"That's right."

"What city?"

"Moscow."

"Perhaps, then," she continued, "you've heard about the case of a Jewish boy, Yasha Kazakov? Do you know what happened to him? Did they arrest him?"

"Yes, I've heard about him," I answered quietly. "I don't think they arrested him." "Are you sure?" she asked me excitedly.

I smiled at her. "Yes, I'm sure."

But she wasn't satisfied and went on impatiently, "Do you know where he is? What's going on with him?"

I smiled again. "Yes, I know where he is. He's sitting right here in front of you." The people were stunned. They were sincerely worried and never imagined that the young man speaking to them was the person they were asking about.

That's how my new life in Israel began, in the absorption center in Carmiel, a new town which had about 2,000 residents back then. The absorption center housed immigrants from several countries including a small group from the Soviet Union, members of the activist group in Riga with whom I had many things in common. The ulpan classes didn't interest me very much. I preferred to learn Hebrew on the streets, by conversing with Israelis. I made great progress with my Hebrew outside the ulpan, and within a month had already begun reading newspapers. My fluency in spoken Hebrew was more than sufficient to carry on a conversation or argument.

This period was marked by spontaneous initiatives by activists and Prisoners of Zion who had been allowed out of the Soviet Union. They tried to explain to the authorities in Israel, particularly the officials of Nativ, what was really going on—what was happening to the Jews in the USSR, what problems they faced, and what policies we thought would contribute to the success of the struggle to open the gates. We were surprised to discover that there was a real need to make the decision-makers aware that a handful of Jews were fighting for the right to make *aliyah* and that organized activities were being conducted to that end. The Nativ staff met with all of us. I was among those invited to its offices, where I met all its senior officials, including the director Shaul Avigur.

My impression, which was shared by other *aliyah* activists, was that the heads of Nativ had a distorted and faulty understanding of the situation of Soviet Union Jewry. They did have a fair amount of information about the activists and what they were doing, but their basic assumptions and comprehension of Soviet policy were flawed. Although Nativ personnel had more expertise on the Soviet issue than others whose knowledge bordered on utter ignorance, it was still insufficient. One reason for this was a lack of professionalism, both among individuals and in the system as a whole, which worked to the organization's detriment. Its staff was chosen on the basis of personal acquaintance and political loyalty. For example, until the 1960s, even members of the leftist Ahdut Ha'avoda party were blacklisted from Nativ, to say nothing of Revisionists. Binyamin Eliav, who was head and shoulders above everyone else both as a person and in his knowledge, was hired by Nativ only after "he sobered up" from his Revisionist opinions and publicly admitted his youthful error. Most Nativ staffers had lived in Eastern European countries and in the Soviet Union and also had a background of Zionist activity and operations in the field. But this background, unaccompanied by careful study and professional work habits, was inadequate and even liable to get in the way. Events in the Soviet Union were characterized by a rapid and complex dynamic. Nativ operatives did not understand the changes and remained frozen in their old ideas, which were irrelevant to the new age. The biggest discrepancy was in their understanding of the Jews, especially the younger generation.

Nativ's operatives had grown up in Zionist youth movements—mainly socialist ones—in the countries of Eastern Europe. They were not raised in Soviet society and did not know or understand how young people who grew up under the Soviet regime could be fired up by Zionism and join its ranks. They also found it hard to comprehend the Soviet Jews' passion, stubbornness, and willingness to take risks. Several Nativ members had been in Soviet prison camps. The experience left them traumatized and with an almost physical dread of the Soviets. For all these reasons, they failed to properly assess the power, capability, and weakness of the Soviet regime, nor the strength, willingness, courage, and potential of Soviet Jewry.

We newly-immigrated *aliyah* activists certainly did not know of all of this. It was only after I myself joined Nativ that I arrived at these conclusions. Nonetheless, we felt and understood the gap between us and the Israeli establishment on all matters related to Soviet Jewry and their struggle to make *aliyah*. It was essentially a conflict between two worldviews. On one side were the Zionist-minded *aliyah* activists, some of whom had spent years in prison for their efforts. They believed, and rightly so, that they could and should help their country—Israel—with their knowledge, experience, and contacts with

Jews, especially their friends who were still in the Soviet Union. The senior echelons of Nativ in those years thought precisely the opposite. After the *aliyah* activists had reached Israel, Nativ officials thought, there was no need for their continued involvement in any efforts on behalf of Soviet Jews. The Nativ line was that it was a bad idea to wage an open battle against the Soviet Union over *aliyah*, because that country was so strong and cruel that it could afford to ignore world opinion and international pressure. An overt campaign would only put Soviet Jewry at greater risk. Moreover, Nativ operated on the assumption that only some Soviet Jews would want to make *aliyah*—no more than a few thousand over the course of many years, perhaps ten or twenty thousand, and that was only in Nativ's wildest dreams. It could not understand how masses of Jews who had been cut off from Judaism for two generations and raised under the Communist regime could even conceive of *aliyah* as an option.

For our part, we thought—knew—that the Soviet Union was much weaker and would not always be able to hold out against the West. We believed that serious international pressure, exerted in a cogent and coordinated manner, would instill the Jews with greater confidence and ultimately force the Soviet Union to throw open its gates for *aliyah*. We saw that the majority of the Israeli establishment was afraid of the Soviet Union and its power. Our hopes of helping those we had left behind were quickly dissipated, and those of us who had made it out of the Soviet Union began seeking new and indirect ways to help our friends remaining there to make *aliyah*.

The people at Nativ hoped to elude the activists' pressure on the cheap, and in a show of fulfilling their obligations, to "buy off" a few of them with promises of assistance in finding a place to live or a job. I was not involved in this game. I had an advantage over all the others, who were ten to twenty years my senior. Everyone, without exception, had come with their families, with parents or a wife and children. They had to be concerned with issues of employment, financial security, and so on. I was young, alone, and with no family obligations—much freer, much more mobile. I had much more leeway to take risks. My background and worldview were also very different from theirs. I was a member of the younger generation, freer and more daring. Another important factor was the place where I had grown up—Moscow, the real Russia—as opposed to the others, who came from the Baltic States or outlying districts and had absorbed their Judaism from their home and surroundings. I came from an assimilated family and had not been exposed to the traditional Jewish outlook, including the Diaspora willingness and tendency to "get by" to adapt to the environment. I was free of the traits, habits, and complexes of the Jews from the provinces, for better or for worse.

It must be confessed that some of the activists were influenced by their political outlook and later by their political ambitions. Those from the Baltic States included members of the Revisionist youth group Beitar or had relatives or friends who were. This influenced both their behavior and the way the establishment, dominated by the opposing left wing (Mapai and the other socialist parties), related to them. Political overtones, new and old accounts that were yet to be settled, and frustrations percolated into the disputes between the two sides and diverted attention from the main issues of the struggle. Some of the activists declared outright that the hostility or cluelessness of the Israeli bureaucrats stemmed from their socialist ideology—that they were not really dedicated to Zionist ideas. Some went so far as to assert that the bureaucrats' socialist sympathies prevented them from acting against the Soviet Union, which was of course a socialist state. In retrospect, I know that the allegation of ideological motives was incorrect. Now that I know the Israeli system from the inside, I realize that the main problem was the lack of professionalism of those involved. I would never claim they were disloyal or not committed to the idea of *aliyah* from the Soviet Union; quite the contrary.

One controversial issue had to do with the content of the Voice of Israel radio broadcasts in Russian and Yiddish. Nativ was responsible for the propaganda content. It also handled the funding for the Voice of Israel transmitters that broadcast to the Soviet Union. We all complained about the anemic content of the programs, the poor quality of the material broadcast, the suppression of everything related to the struggle for *aliyah*, and the substandard Russian. The dominant view in Israel was that nothing should be said aloud about *aliyah* from the Soviet Union, on the premise that the Soviet Union was concerned about Arab pressure: if it became public knowledge that Jews were being let out of the country, the Soviets would put an immediate halt to *aliyah*. In fact, there was no basis for the idea that the Soviets wanted to keep things under wraps; a professional investigation and assessment would have clarified the issue. This flawed hypothesis informed and guided Israeli policy for years. Even three decades later, I encountered this unprofessional belief based on erroneous ideas about the Soviet Union among members of the Israeli intelligence community. The truth is that whenever the Arab representatives brought up the subject of *aliyah* from the USSR, the Soviet response was, "The Arab states gave Israel a million *olim*. You haven't a leg to stand on with the claim of a few hundred per year."

Nativ personnel and the Israeli intelligence community simply did not understand the essence of the relations between the Soviet Union and the Arab states. They brought up the example of the suspension of immigration from Romania after David Ben-Gurion mentioned it in public. But that *aliyah* resumed soon afterwards because it was just as important to the Romanians as it was to the Israelis. Moreover, it also seemed to escape the people at Nativ that Romania was not the Soviet Union and the Soviet Union was not Romania. There was indeed a Soviet-style Communist regime in both countries, but the aliyah from Romania was, quite simply, a financial transaction. The Romanians set a price for each Jew as a function of his or her education and professional training, family demographics, and so on. The price ranged from a thousand or two thousand dollars per head to as much as six, seven, or eight thousand dollars, and in some exceptional cases, even ten thousand for those with an advanced education who were members of the scientific elite. The agreement was made with the Romanian intelligence services, who received the money—part of which was siphoned off into Ceausescu's private bank account. The rest provided the foreign currency budget of Romanian intelligence. So the senior echelons in Romania had a personal interest in the continuation of *aliyah*. In my opinion, this arrangement allowed the State of Israel and the Jewish people to express a supreme moral value: the rescue of their coreligionists at any cost. In talks conducted shortly before 1967, Nativ personnel tried to find out, though not in so many words, whether the Soviets would be willing to apply the Romanian model to their own Jews. The Soviet response was crude and blunt, dripping with scorn and disgust, though totally untrue: "We aren't Romanians; we don't traffic in human beings." Later things took on a different dimension regarding both *aliyah* and the emigration of ethnic Germans from the USSR. But it was never so blatant and crude as with the Romanians.

Some of the earliest activists to reach Israel launched a campaign aimed at rousing public opinion in order to influence and force the Israeli establishment to modify its policy with regard to the *aliyah* campaign by Soviet Jewry. Some of them spoke by phone with their friends in the Soviet Union. Communications grew more and more intensive, with letters, telegrams, and messages conveyed by immigrants. At first these efforts ran into a brick wall at Nativ. These interchanges were not under its control; what was worse, so was their outcome, which, of course, was quite intolerable. Nativ had become accustomed to having a monopoly on the issue and felt that this was slipping from its grasp. Some officials simply could not comprehend that the times had changed. Nehemiah Levanon (who became the head of Nativ in 1970) was among the few who understood the changes and tried to modify the organization's operating methods, but with only minimal success.

In 1969, the first public demonstration in Israel on behalf of Soviet Jewry was organized by activists who had made *aliyah*. It was motivated by the news that a young Jewish mathematics student, Ilya (Eliyahu) Rips, had tried to set himself on fire in a public plaza in Riga and that he was committed to a mental ward after his release from the hospital. The motives behind his solo protest were unclear, but some of the activists wanted to publicize the incident immediately. They asserted that inasmuch as Rips was from Riga, he must have been trying to call attention to his battle to make *aliyah*. In this case, at least, Nativ's response was professional and balanced. It officially maintained, and rightly so, that there was no indication that the incident was related to Israel or to *aliyah*, and the fact that he was Jewish was not enough to justify that claim. Nativ's concern was that if it turned out that Rips was not protesting a refusal to let him leave the Soviet Union for Israel, the credibility of the reports about the genuine struggle was apt to be dealt a serious blow. In contrast, the activists who called for holding a demonstration to support Rips held that the precise facts of the case didn't really matter and it was important to portray the act as related to the campaign for *aliyah* (employing the method of Soviet propaganda, in fact). After all, the incident took place a few months after the suicide-by-fire of Jan Palach in Prague, who had immolated himself to protest the invasion of Czechoslovakia by the Warsaw Pact countries. It is hard to find fault with the activists, given the atmosphere in which they grew up. And because Nativ did not want or was simply unable to find a common language with the activists, it could not influence them. Moreover, the activists dismissed the Nativ approach as unworthy of trust and interpreted it as an attempt to elude an open battle.

So the demonstration took place anyway, despite the reservations of Nativ and the Israeli establishment. Quite a few people, mainly university students, joined the protest as part of the opening phase of a public campaign for Soviet *aliyah*. Other Israelis, too, participated in the demonstration, which was funded largely by people who had been in the country for years, including supporters of the Revisionist Movement. Although the truth was that Rips had set himself on fire to protest the invasion of Czechoslovakia and had no thought of *aliyah* at the time, this information did not emerge till much later and did not affect the demonstration. The protest did its part and inspired some Israelis to enlist in the campaign for Soviet Jewry. Rips himself was released from the mental hospital several years later, made *aliyah* in 1972, completed his studies in mathematics, joined the faculty of the Hebrew University, and became an observant Jew (one of his papers laid the basis for the "Bible Codes" theory).

This case taught me to be suspicious about facts and their interpretations, especially when the interpretation is compatible with your own perspective. I did not accept the idea that the truth doesn't matter and that the main objective is to take advantage of any report that may be convenient and useful. I saw this as a Bolshevik-Soviet approach and did not think we had come to Israel to transplant Bolshevism and employ Bolshevik methods with a Jewish accent. I also had an advantage over the others. In those days, Jews who were allowed out to Israel, activists and Prisoners of Zion alike, did so under the rubric of "family reunification." As long as they were in the Soviet Union, they engaged in Zionist activity but did not conduct an open campaign on behalf of *aliyah*. So the Israeli establishment and Nativ tried to counter their claims with the true observation that "back there in the Soviet Union, you sat quietly and never did any of the things that you are demanding we do now. You've made it here, so you can allow yourselves to do whatever you want and speak loudly, but in doing so, you are endangering your friends remaining there and behaving irresponsibly."

No one could say that to me. I was the first and at the time the only Jew who had waged an open fight for *aliyah* back in Russia and been allowed to leave for Israel. My entire family was still there. I had taken a risk myself and was willing to take a risk for my family as well. So it was difficult to argue with me when I asserted, citing my own example, that a public campaign was the appropriate strategy.

However, we all agreed on one thing. Despite people's political inclinations and the Revisionist background of the more militant activists, it was out of the question for us to join political parties. We were afraid that the struggle for Soviet Jewry would be painted in partisan colors and diverted to political disputes. I had no political ambitions, though some of us did, especially those who came from Riga and were followers of Jabotinsky.

Soon after I reached Israel I contacted Herzl Amikam, who had been the first Israeli I encountered in the Moscow embassy. Through him I was introduced to his former commander in Lehi, Yitzchak Shamir. I visited Shamir's home, where he impressed me as a reasonable and serious man who viewed our struggle with great warmth and understanding. But a more significant introduction was to Geula Cohen. My friendship with her has exerted a major influence on my life and outlook.

Geula Cohen, a member of my mother's generation, was then a relatively young and lively woman. At the time, she worked as a journalist for the *Maariv* newspaper. Although she had already become interested in *aliyah* from the Soviet Union, Cohen was strongly influenced by her encounters with *aliyah* activists who had come to Israel and she enlisted in their struggle with a passion. She saw this as a direct continuation of her activity in the pre-State Lehi underground. Thanks to her contacts, we were able to reach many Israeli public figures—including politicians, military men, and intellectuals—and acquaint them with the struggle and situation of Soviet Jews. Through her I got to know Shimon Peres, as well as Ariel Sharon and other senior officers in the IDF, including Ze'ev Almog.

It became clear that individual encounters and salon meetings would not be enough to explain the problem of Soviet Jewry and their struggle to the Israeli public. We had to reach out to the media, but reports about *aliyah*, *olim* and the situation of the Jews in the Soviet Union were censored. Nativ was responsible for this censorship and nixed every item. The heads of the Student Union at the Technion-

Israel Institute of Technology who had heard my story, got in touch with me when I enrolled in the Chemistry Department. A short interview with me later appeared in the student newspaper. After this, a senior Nativ official phoned Yona Yahav, the chairman of the Student Union (today mayor of Haifa), screaming that he would have him sent to jail. That was just what we needed to prove our credibility. This affair made waves, and student protests on behalf of Soviet Jewry were organized on several campuses.

Many public figures took up the cudgels against the censorship of information on the struggle for *aliyah*. One of them was Shulamit Aloni, then an Alignment member of Knesset. She took the bold step of standing up at the Knesset rostrum and reading out a letter from the Soviet Union, calling on the authorities to permit *aliyah*. This stratagem allowed her to get around the censor. Prime Minister Golda Meir, never wild about Aloni in the first place, was fuming. This may have been the straw that broke the camel's back and pushed Aloni far down the Alignment list for the next Knesset elections. Aloni quit the Alignment in 1973 and established the Citizens' Rights Movement (known as "Ratz") with a group of like-minded friends. The rest is history. And thus, albeit indirectly, the immigrants from the Soviet Union began to influence Israeli politics.

Thanks to the activities of the immigration campaign, the public exerted strong pressure on the establishment and Prime Minister Meir. The result was the start of changes—albeit slow and insufficient—in national policy. More open letters by Jews insisting on their right to make *aliyah* were published. Addressing the Knesset in November 1969, the prime minister referred to the open letter by eighteen families from Soviet Georgia in which they demanded to be allowed to immigrate to Israel. This was a tremendous achievement for us. For the first time, the demand that Soviet Jews be permitted to make *aliyah* was voiced publicly in Israel, in Jerusalem, by the prime minister herself. Encouraged by the success of the open letters, requests, and official Israeli support for their wide distribution, Soviet Jews turned more and more to the path of an overt campaign for *aliyah*, calling for assistance from Israel, the Jewish people, and public opinion in the West.

The National Union of Israeli Student Unions organized a large protest in Kings of Israel Square (today Rabin Square) in Tel Aviv. Prime Minister Meir agreed to address the crowd. She made only one request to the organizers: that Yasha Kazakov not be allowed to speak from the platform. This was apparently in response to things I had said in various meetings and interviews in which I criticized the "silent diplomacy" of the Soviet Union and Israel. The fact that like other activists who demanded changes, I was supported by such people on the right as Geula Cohen, Menachem Begin, and Yitzhak Shamir, merely fanned the establishment's displeasure with me and my colleagues. When the demonstration organizers somewhat reluctantly told me about Golda's condition, I told them that I had no problem with it. It was more important that the Prime Minister of Israel take part in the rally and address the crowd. I was even willing to stay away from the demonstration, because its very existence had achieved the goal—the first large and almost government-sanctioned rally on behalf of Soviet Jewish *aliyah*. And when the evening came, I stayed home.

Chapter 13

Geula Cohen decided to interview me for *Maariv.* We met several times, after which her text was submitted to the censor, as was standard in those days, because it focused on the sensitive topic of *aliyah.* A representative of Nativ who checked it approved only a few vague sentences for publication, which left it impossible to tell who was speaking, what about, and where the interview was conducted. Geula went to see him.

After much unpleasant haggling and a threat to appeal to the High Court of Justice, the interview was approved for publication with almost no cuts. Covering two full pages in two successive Friday editions, it made a strong impression on the Israeli public. For the first time, Israelis were exposed to an unfamiliar picture. Suddenly they learned that there was immigration from the Soviet Union and that Jews were coming to Israel, despite all the obstacles. The interview included criticism of the Israeli government for its wishy-washy policy, inadequate support for the struggle, and fear of public protest.

In the meantime, a small group of veteran Israelis had coalesced. Most of them had belonged to Lehi or the Irgun, including Yitzhak Shamir, Geula Cohen, and Herzl Amikam. A number of recent immigrants who had been prominent activists in the Soviet Union were also involved—notably Dov Sperling and Leah Slovin. In the late fifties, Sperling had been tried and sentenced to a long prison term for "anti-Soviet activity." This was the catch-all "crime" for which all Soviet Zionist activists were hauled into court and convicted. The Israeli group set for itself the goal of supporting the campaign by Jews in the Soviet Union in several ways: preparing information material and somehow getting it to reach them, and producing reports about their struggle for distribution in Israel and the world at large. This was not the only group. Others coalesced as well, largely because of the total lack of national action on the issue and the faulty communication and collaboration with the activists who had made it to Israel.

As so often happens, each group worked separately and competed with the others. Personal interests and old accounts among the activists played a significant role in the tensions between the different factions—though they did cooperate on occasion. I was not part of this rivalry, mostly because I had not been affiliated with any group in the Soviet Union and knew few, if any, of them until I immigrated to Israel. I was not a member of any organization and was willing to talk to any group that showed interest in the Jews' struggle.

Geula Cohen organized a meeting for us with a well-to-do American Jew, Bernard (Bernie) Deutsch. Drawing on our personal experiences, Dov Sperling and I told him about the Jews' efforts to escape the Iron Curtain. Impressed by our story, Deutsch said that it was important to bring it to the attention of American Jewry. One of his initiatives, in cooperation with Geula, was an English translation of her *Maariv* interview with me and its distribution to American Jews. In late 1969, Geula notified me that Deutsch was ready to organize a series of meetings for us (herself, Sperling, and me) with influential Jews and non-Jews in the United States, so we could spread the story of Soviet Jewry and its struggle. The idea, which was revolutionary at the time, struck me as important and I agreed to it at once.

One of my reasons was my parents' decision in the late summer of 1969 to immigrate to Israel. They came to the conclusion, fairly logical as far as they were concerned, that they had no future in the Soviet Union. There was no future there for them, and certainly not for their children—my younger brother and sister, who were still in school. It was with great joy that I sent them the required invitation. My father went to OVIR to submit his request with an invitation in hand from a son, a first-degree relative, as the regulations required. When we talked by phone, I asked him to make sure to give the director of OVIR my fondest regards and to tell him, word for word, that if his country's good name and standing were dear to him, I recommend that he not repeat the mistake he had made with me but instead approve my family's request without delay. Nonetheless, my family soon received a resounding *nyet,* with no explanation. I saw my parents' case as evidence of the Soviet Union's deceitful propaganda and policy: Here my parents were trying to leave, and the regime had turned down their request for no reason, even though they had a son in Israel. This concrete example exposed the falsity of the Soviet authorities' claim that they would not make problems for those wishing to emigrate.

The three of us—Geula, Dov, and myself—planned to depart for the United States in mid-December 1969. Nativ learned of our tour, apparently from its North American office, and decided to stop us from leaving. Its bureaucracy saw us as a threat to the policy of quiet diplomacy and the total censorship it had imposed on everything related to immigration from the Soviet Union. That summer, Nehemiah Levanon had replaced Shaul Avigur as the director of Nativ. Levanon asked Menachem Begin (then serving as a minister without portfolio in Golda Meir's government) to try to persuade us to call off our trip. Begin responded with a firm "no" and told Levanon that he couldn't tell these people what to do. They'd made their way to Israel on their own and were old enough to know how to conduct their fight. No one had the right to try to deter them from what they wanted to do.

One higher-up in Nativ decided to take care of the "problem" in his own way. When we landed in the United States in late December and began our round of meetings there, we soon realized that an official representative of the State of Israel, an employee of Nativ, had contacted all the Jewish organizations, as well as many non-Jews, asking them on behalf of the Israeli government to refrain from all meetings and contact with us. He supplemented the usual arguments about the potential "danger to Jews" with the information that Dov and I were probably KGB agents. Most of the Jewish organizations took this at face value and cancelled their meetings with us. But the non-Jews and non-Jewish organizations, including members of Congress, met with us anyway. They heard what we had to say and were very impressed. I remembered the perplexity of a reporter for the *Christian Science Monitor*, obviously a non-Jew: "I don't understand what's going on here. What you are saying is incredibly important for the Jewish people, for *aliyah*, for the State of Israel. Why did they slander you?"

In retrospect, Nativ's entire conception of the possible impact on *aliyah* and harm to Jews from our meetings and publicity about the immigration struggle exploded into smithereens. There was no Soviet reaction. On the contrary, the Jews drew encouragement from the public exposure of their struggle, and under the pressure of international public opinion, the Soviet regime started to cave in.

During that same visit, we met a young Jew, not part of the establishment, who at the time was famous only for his opposition to the Black Panthers. His name was Meir Kahane. Our meeting took place in his small office. He made a positive impression on me: a fine Jew who said all the right things about the *aliyah* campaign and American Jewry's duty to support it. He took an uncompromising line and displayed quite healthy opinions about the struggle on behalf of the Jews. Unlike the heads of most Jewish organizations in the West, as well as the Israeli leadership, Kahane immediately adopted our perspective that the crux of the struggle was the demand for freedom to make *aliyah*. Everyone else was hard pressed to give up the idea of polite requests to the Soviet authorities that they allow Jews freedom to obtain religious paraphernalia and *matza* (unleavened bread for Passover) and engage in Jewish cultural activities. Kahane also had the reputation of someone who had defended the honor of the Jewish people; we had already heard stories about his war against anti-Semitism in the United States. For us, Jews from a country with a long tradition of anti-Semitic violence and not-so-distant memories of pogroms, our time with Kahane was an interesting and moving encounter.

Something happened when we returned to Israel that still reverberates for me today, the incident that essentially began the process of my disillusionment with Israel's security and intelligence agencies. When we landed at Lod airport, we were supposed to hold a press conference. Right after passport control, a man whom I knew to be a member of the General Security Service (because he had interviewed me in the past) approached me and said we had to speak right away, without a moment's delay. As a Jew who had come to Israel, I was full of respect for its security and intelligence agencies. Not suspecting anything, I told Geula Cohen and Dov Sperling that something urgent had come up. I followed the man to his office and didn't take part in the press conference. As he questioned me about some trivial matter, I quickly realized, despite my naïveté and unwillingness to doubt the good intentions of the General Security Service, that there was nothing urgent here and our conversation could have easily taken place a half hour or hour later, perhaps even the next day. The real reason for the interview was to prevent "real and present harm to state security." For a long time I repressed the obvious conclusion that taking advantage of the good relations between the organizations—and there were always good relations, even on my watch at Nativ decades later—someone from Nativ had asked the GSS for a favor: to keep me, with my positive image among the Israeli public, from taking part in the press conference. In other words, the GSS, against all rules and regulations, acceded to a request by its colleagues in Nativ and prevented an Israeli citizen from appearing at a press conference for no good reason.

During our visit in the United States, I floated the idea of staging a hunger strike outside the UN building to make the world aware that the Soviet Union had a problem with Jewish emigration. The hope was that this would lead to international pressure on the Soviet authorities with regard to my own family as well. Geula Cohen and Bernie Deutsch told me that even though the idea was intriguing, this trip was not the proper time for it. If I decided to do it at some point in the future, they would help me. I didn't know then that as a condition for my receiving a visa, Deutsch had to promise that we would not organize any political demonstrations during the visit, and back this with a financial guarantee. Deutsch, an American citizen, did not want to break his commitment to the American authorities, and rightly so.

I have immense respect for Bernie Deutsch and he has a warm place in my heart, as do his wife and the rest of his family. For me, they came to symbolize the Jewish solidarity of American Jews and their willingness to help us. Deutsch was a special man, a warm, observant Jew who devoted himself to helping the Jewish struggle in the Soviet Union. I remember how his children looked at us, their jaws gaping, enthusiastic about what we were saying. Later, they immigrated to Israel. One son served as an officer in the regular army; his daughter settled in Kfar Darom.

After our return to Israel, I saw the beginnings of a change in official policy towards our struggle. This was due in part to Nehemiah Levanon's taking over as head of Nativ and getting settled in the job—but mainly because of the pressure exerted by Jews in the West. Golda Meir, who only months earlier had expressed reservations about joining me in a demonstration on behalf of Soviet Jewry, publicly read the open letter that my parents had signed. My parents kept me updated on the refuseniks' activities. Then, one sunny day in February 1970, Geula Cohen called to tell me that she had heard a report on the news that my father had been roundly attacked in *Izvestia*, the official Soviet government newspaper. It was more than possible that the attack was laying the groundwork for harsh steps against my family. If so, Geula said, she was willing to support me in a hunger strike outside the United Nations, if I was still open to that idea. Naturally, I responded in the affirmative. Bernie Deutsch quickly arranged whatever was necessary. In mid-March I flew off to New York, this time by myself. My goal was clear and well-defined, because I had planned it out in my mind for months.

The day before I was supposed to launch the hunger strike, a group of us sat in Deutsch's home and planned the strike down to the last detail. We wanted to keep the plan a secret to prevent unexpected interference by various agencies. That evening, I phoned my girlfriend back in Israel, Alla Woloch. I asked the neighbor whose number I had dialed (her family didn't have a phone) to call Alla to the phone so I could reassure her that everything was fine. The neighbor then told me that Alla had been severely injured in a traffic accident in the Negev and that I should come home at once, if at all possible. In utter shock, I packed my bags and went straight to the airport. Before boarding the plane, I called again and was told that Alla had passed away. I suddenly understood that all of us, no matter how strong or self-confident we seem, are just human beings, and our capabilities are much more limited than we think. For the first time in my life, I felt powerless. Since then I have had many encounters with death and have always been overwhelmed by this feeling of incredible pain and helplessness.

Until that day, it seemed to me that there was nothing I couldn't do. Just a short while earlier, I had vanquished the mightiest and most intimidating empire in the world. I had come to the State of Israel. With a group of friends, I had managed to stir up Israeli public opinion. I had been able to demonstrate the validity of my worldview and influence the world around me. And suddenly, when I was certain there was nothing I could not do, fate had shown me in a flash that I was no more significant than a tiny insect. All my plans and dreams had come crashing down around me. The person dearest to me was dead, and there was nothing I could do about it, despite all my pride and arrogance. I flew back to Israel but was too late for the funeral, and found Alla's family deep in intense mourning. She had been a young student at Tel Aviv University, only twenty years old. I had gotten to know her and her amazing family in the ulpan in Carmiel, a few weeks after their *aliyah* from Poland.

When I landed in Israel, I saw newspaper headlines that Yasha Kazakov had gone to New York to conduct a hunger strike but had called it off and flown home because of his fiancée's death. I didn't pay much attention to the accuracy of the report, but noted that the premature exposure of my plan by a journalist who had been in on the secret was unfortunate and liable to complicate matters.

After the week of mourning, I returned to New York in early April and launched my hunger strike. We had chosen the best possible location for my vigil: the "Isaiah Wall" in the park across the street from the UN complex. Anyone who came to the UN would see me and the placards I had set up. So would the tens of thousands of people making their way along the bustling avenue. The response to my hunger strike, which continued for nine days, was extraordinary.

For the first few days, the Jewish establishment kept its distance, in accordance with instructions from Israel. Most of those who came to show their support were members of the Student Struggle for Soviet Jewry, members of Beitar, students at Yeshiva University, and various people I had met during my visit with Geula Cohen and Dov Sperling several months earlier. Members of Meir Kahane's Jewish Defense League also turned out. The buzz in both the American and Israeli media increased from day to day.

During the strike, I experienced a few truths that I had only heard of before. For example, on the second day a policeman showed up. Although he made sure to tell me that he was Jewish, he didn't cut me any slack. He said that because I didn't have a permit to park a trailer there, I had to move it at once and couldn't spend the night in the trailer as I had planned. It is still cold in New York in April, particularly at night. We made various excuses to stall for time until the officer had gone off duty and was replaced by one of New York's many Irish policemen. When we asked him if he had a problem with the trailer and my lack of a permit, he smiled warmly—"What's the big deal? It's a holy matter. Forget about it"—and wished me luck. I am sorry to say that Jews frequently try to be more Catholic than the Pope when some Jewish matter is on the table. In order to avoid suspicions of dual loyalty, and as part of the familiar Diaspora Jewish complex, they show greater hostility and rigidity than non-Jews do. Moreover, I have often heard even Israelis and Israeli bureaucrats make anti-Semitic remarks in a conscious or unconscious attempt to curry favor with non-Jews: "We're not like *those* Jews—we're different, we're better."

During my hunger strike in New York, the Israel Students' Union organized a mass demonstration in sympathy with me outside the Knesset, demanding that the government publicly express its identification with my protest and with the struggle of Soviet Jewry. While the rally was in progress, a Cabinet meeting was taking place inside the building. Politicians from every part of the spectrum addressed the students, including Geula Cohen, Zevulun Hammer, Shulamit Aloni, and Yehuda Ben-Meir. Afterwards, someone told me that during the cabinet meeting, Golda Meir had said, with unwonted quietness, "I can't keep this up any longer. This kid has broken me. We must show support for him." After that demonstration, the dam burst. Official Israeli agencies and Jewish organizations in New York were given explicit permission to express their solidarity with me. Joseph Tekoa, the Israeli ambassador to the UN, visited me in the park, and I realized that the Foreign Ministry had instructed him to do so.

Tekoa had previously served as the Israeli ambassador in Moscow. He was one of the few to hold that post whose fervor and willingness to work with Nativ and support its activities on behalf of Soviet Jews were sometimes even more pronounced than those of the organization's own operatives. He devoted his life to the problems of Soviet Jewry and offered them unqualified support. Tekoa told me that he had spoken with UN Secretary General U Thant, who had been promised during a meeting with members of the Soviet mission that my family would receive an exit visa within a year if I called off the hunger strike. It was the eighth day of the hunger strike and I was totally exhausted, not so much from the protracted lack of food as from everything that had led up to it, particularly Alla's tragic death. I decided that I had achieved my goal and nine days was long enough. If Alla had lived, though, I think I would have carried on the strike until my family received their exit visas, certain that it was possible to achieve that.

One day during my hunger strike, a man came up and asked me to step aside with him. When we were alone, he switched to Russian.

"I can't tell you my name," he said. "But is your father's name Iosif?"

When I said that it was, he was overwhelmed with emotion. Only after he recovered his composure did he continue that when he saw my picture in the newspaper he felt sure I must be the son of his friend, Iosif Kazakov, who had served with him in Vienna at the end of the war. The two young Jewish officers became friends. One day, he went on, he ran away to the American Zone and later immigrated to the United States. He did not conceal his fear of conversing with me, but confessed he could not help himself—he wanted to see his friend's son so badly. He told me stories about my father and asked me to convey his fondest regards to him. "He'll know who I am." And indeed, when I hinted over the phone that I had regards for him from an old friend, my father immediately knew who I was talking about.

After the hunger strike, my father was invited to OVIR. The director was annoyed and aggravated. "Why? Why is Yasha doing this to us?"

"Didn't he warn you?" my father answered proudly. "But you didn't listen. You yourself caused these problems for your country. You should have taken his words more seriously. You were warned."

One way or another, though, the strike ended successfully and I returned to Israel, where I began a new life, quite different from my routine and way of thinking before I'd launched the hunger strike. At the same time, the problem that lay at the root of my campaign had been placed on the agenda of American Jewry and the world community. What ensued was a period of stormy demonstrations to push the demand that Soviet Jews be permitted to make *aliyah*, led in large part by Jews who were recent *olim* or who had refusenik relatives back in the Soviet Union.

My return to Israel marked the end of my second hopeless war. It was a war I had not expected—not a war with an enemy, but a war against my country's establishment on behalf of my own country and people. It was a war I was forced to fight against my will, since I would not otherwise have been able to advance the goals for which I had made *aliyah*. If I didn't oppose the Israeli establishment, I would be betraying my friends left behind in the Soviet Union, as well as those who had given their lives for the country in the past—for a country that didn't even know they existed.

I remember a meeting in Tel Aviv one summer day. I was walking down Kaplan Street and saw Zvi Netzer coming towards me. Netzer was a senior official of Nativ and the source of the instruction to the representative in the United States to keep us from meeting with Jews by dragging our name in the mud with the claim that we were Soviet spies.

Netzer stopped and addressed me angrily. "What do you think you're doing? Of course you fought against the Soviet Union. But now that you're here, why are you fighting the State of Israel?"

My Muscovite impudence got the better of me. I stared back at him derisively and spat out my words: "*You* are not the State of Israel. I am not fighting against the State of Israel, but against people like you, to make the country a better place."

In fact, Netzer had accomplished much for Israel. His name is prominent in the story of immigration from Poland and the *aliyah* of Soviet Jews through Poland as part of the repatriation campaign of the 1950s and 1960s. He really and truly believed that his methods were the right ones and devoted his whole life, along with everyone else at Nativ, to the Jews and their *aliyah*.

In fact, everyone at Nativ showed unlimited commitment to the cause. Theirs was a total and pure devotion that was preserved within the organization until the end of the century. The trouble was that their mindset and habits, the environment in which they grew up, and their worldview, which were mainly shaped between the two world wars and during the Second World War—other places, other times, and other battles—simply were not appropriate for the real problems that Nativ faced in the late 1960s and early 1970s. This same phenomenon could be seen in other arenas of Israeli life, where good and loyal people whose worldviews were outmoded fought to their last ounce of strength to defend themselves and their outdated perspective. The most tragic expression of this, of course, was the Yom Kippur War.

When my parents made *aliyah*, my mother told me that in the late spring of 1970 she was called in by herself for an interview with the KGB. A senior official greeted her cordially and told her that he knew exactly what was going on in my life, down to the smallest details, including the tragic death of my girlfriend and all my problems and clashes I had with the authorities and the Israeli establishment. He suggested that she come visit me during what he referred to as "my difficult time" in Israel. They were even willing to pay her way! While she was in Israel, he suggested, she should try to persuade me to return to the Soviet Union. If I came home, the regime was willing to forgive everything I had done. I could apply to any university I wanted and he guaranteed I would be accepted, with a full scholarship. He promised my mother that they would give me an apartment in Moscow.

To corroborate what he had said, the KGB official showed my mother the thick files full of material on me. When she asked, they let her leaf through a binder full of photographs. My mother told me that she had never seen so many pictures of me. They had been taken in Israel and the United States. As the interview continued, she turned the pages of the album, trying to soak in all the images of her dear firstborn son. She turned down the official's proposal; she said such a trip would be tantamount to betraying me.

The man abruptly changed his tone. "The KGB will find your Yasha wherever he is and settle accounts for all the harm he has done to the Soviet Union. He will not escape his punishment."

My mother pretended not to be impressed by these threats. Although her heart was racing with fear for me, she steadfastly continued to reject the offer. The interview ended after about two hours. My mother went home drained and shaken, but ecstatic that she had seen my pictures and held her own against the KGB. They left her alone after that, until she left the country.

When I came back from New York after the hunger strike, I felt a void inside, which Alla's death had only intensified. I was increasingly preoccupied by a thought that had begun to take shape several months before the hunger strike. I was finding it hard to sit in the classroom listening to learned explanations of the problems of polymers or solve differential equations. All of my peers and classmates were reserve soldiers or officers. They had fought in the Six Day War and told many stories about their experiences. From time to time they were called up for reserve duty. Deep inside, I realized that until I discharged my obligation and served in the army, too, I would never feel like a full citizen. Now that I had ensured my family's *aliyah* and, in my opinion, done enough for the cause of *aliyah* in general, I could and should enlist in the IDF.

When I went to the enlistment office in Haifa, the commander tried to persuade me to drop the idea and stay where I was, in the academic reserve, and complete my degree before carrying out my military service. All my friends and acquaintances also tried to deter me. Not a single person supported the idea of my enlisting. But I insisted. I wanted to be inducted as soon as I returned from the United States. In the end, though, the enlistment office persuaded me to pass up the May induction and wait for August, on the grounds that the boys and girls with the highest potential were called up at the end of the summer, so a wider range of jobs and opportunities would be available at that time.

Chapter 14

In August 1970, I reported to the IDF intake base to begin the standard three-year tour of conscript duty. All the other new recruits were five years my junior. For me, enlisting in the IDF was an emotionally complex event. On one hand, it was the fulfillment of my dream: I was joining the Jewish army of the Jewish state. For the first few minutes after I put on my uniform, I felt as if I were floating in mid-air. I was proud to be joining the best army in the world; I had a total and absolute belief that the IDF was the finest army on earth. On the other hand, I couldn't help but worry that I would not be able to integrate into an army of young Israelis, new Jews who had grown up in the Jewish state. Would I be as worthy a soldier as they were? My thoughts were full of naïveté: the pure naïveté of a Jew who had grown up in the Diaspora, yearning for his country, for his army—in brief, yearning to be just like everyone else. I yearned to feel I was not a foreigner, not a minority, to be a person with a homeland who does not have to fight for equal treatment because he is Jewish. This natural condition is almost inconceivable for a Jew not born in Israel, and utterly fantastic for a Jew who grew up in the Soviet Union, with its pervasive, widespread, and palpable anti-Semitism, which continued to influence our thoughts, feelings, and perceptions many years later.

At the intake base, I stubbornly insisted on being assigned to the Armored Corps. I wanted to be part of a tank crew. I saw the Armored

Corps as the embodiment of military power due to its nature, the intense experience of storming the enemy, of the fire, of the fighting on the front line. Subconsciously, perhaps, I was also influenced by the fact that my uncle was a tank crewman who had been killed in battle against the Nazis.

My army service was typical. I quickly adjusted to the new life, having no real problems with the language, although I didn't always understand the technical concepts. Because I was a new immigrant having arrived only a year and a half earlier, I was assigned to a Hebrew language class as part of my basic training. I soon learned that there were other recent immigrants in the battalion, but I was the only one from the Soviet Union. The others were from Western Europe and North Africa and all of them had been in Israel for several years. In the first class, the teacher, a sergeant, gave us a test, checked the papers, and then called me over and irately threatened to have me court-martialed for trying to evade training drills by pretending not to know Hebrew. She said that with my command of Hebrew, there was no reason for me to be in her class. I was taken aback by her accusation of fraud, and told her that it was not my decision to attend Hebrew lessons, and I was not malingering. This level of suspicion—expecting every action to be an attempt to evade and deceive—was new and incomprehensible to me.

During basic training, I had a run-in with the mess hall sergeant, sparked, no doubt, by my personality. I was doing kitchen duty one day when they told me that one of the squads was delayed in the field and would not make it back for lunch, so I should be sure to ask the kitchen staff to leave food for the latecomers. I passed on the request to the kitchen and was told it would be taken care of. The squad arrived about an hour later and I led them to the mess hall. But when we got there, there was no food for them. Apparently, the mess hall sergeant had told the cooks to ignore the special request. I was livid. I had heard from my friends who served in the Soviet Army that soldiers there sometimes went without food—but here, in the

Jewish army?! I went up to the sergeant, saluted him, and asked why there was no food for the soldiers, despite the advance notice and agreement to provide it. The sergeant replied that latecomers could go hungry. He didn't care what I had told the cooks; I should take the squad back to their tents. I told him that was unacceptable: The soldiers had come back from a training exercise, they were famished and should be fed.

The sergeant looked at me in amazement and hollered that I should get the hell out of there if I didn't want to end up in jail. Then he added a few curses for good measure. My temper got the better of me and I said what should never be said, certainly not by a raw recruit to a sergeant. I told him, in a quiet but threatening tone, that I didn't give a fig about the stupidity he was spewing and that he would see to it that these soldiers got food, whether he wanted to or not. For a good two minutes, I bombarded him with curses in good Russian, as I had learned to do on the streets of Moscow. The sergeant didn't understand most of what I said, but he apparently figured out that these were curses of a higher register.

It is the nature of sergeants to explode when a buck private insults them. He turned bright red and bawled, "Report to the base commander's office in ten minutes. From there, have no illusions, you will go straight to jail."

I did as ordered and reported to the base commander's office. The sergeant went in first. When he came out, I was invited in. The commander asked me to explain my conduct. I told him what had happened. The commander smiled. "You're not allowed to curse out sergeants in this army. The next time it happens, you'll face charges, even if the sergeant is in the wrong."

I saluted and walked out. The sergeant was astonished to see me coming out without an escort to lead me off to the prison tent. "Where do you think you're going?" he asked in disbelief.

"Back to my platoon, sir, on the orders of the base commander," I replied, saluted, and beat a hasty retreat. It was clear to me that the matter had ended as it had not because the commander accepted my conduct, but because I was a minor celebrity in Israel.

After my enlistment in the IDF, I naturally avoided the media and simply disappeared from public view. Israel is fundamentally a provincial society where people rely on connections and personal loyalties, and gossip is the leading news agency. When I withdrew from the public eye, rumors quickly spread throughout the country that the reason Yasha Kazakov was no longer being heard from was that he was a Soviet spy. Day in, day out, almost everywhere they went, my friends heard that the "Soviet spy" had been locked up. There was something pathological about the Israeli public's obsessive belief in this crazy rumor. Apparently it's hard to swallow someone unusual, so people have to debunk the myth and cut him down to size. I wasn't bothered by the rumors, but my friends, especially Idit, my girlfriend and future wife, took them very hard.

Geula Cohen asked Zevulun Hammer to submit a parliamentary question about my disappearance from public view. The response to his inquiry was an official statement that I had enlisted in the IDF. When this failed to kill the rumor, Geula Cohen contacted Chief of Staff Haim Bar-Lev and asked him to authorize my presence at the celebration on the night after the Simhat Torah holiday in Tel Aviv. The idea was for the public to see me on the podium with the Chief Rabbi of Tel Aviv, Rabbi Yitzchak Yedidya Frankel, and for the press to note my presence at the event. The request was granted. The base commander's office received an order from the chief of staff to give me a twenty-four-hour furlough, despite the state of alert. Although this exercise did quiet the rumors somewhat, they persisted with varying intensity until my parents made *aliyah*.

After that, my military service followed the usual path: basic training and then a specialization course in tanks. The commander of the gunnery section at the Armor School was Avigdor Kahalani, a young major. When he rolled up his sleeves, you could see the burn scars on his skin. He was a gentle young man and a superb tank commander, crowned with the aura of a hero of the Six Day War. Having read Shabtai Teveth's *Exposed in the Turret*, about the exploits of the Armored Corps in 1967, I was familiar with names like Gorodish and Kahalani. Kahalani was the polar antithesis of a Red Army officer. He was a quiet man who never raised his voice, modest, intelligent, and refined.

I remember the wrap-up session with Kahalani at the end of the gunnery course. He looked at us and said, "You think you're tank crewmen? The fact that you have shot off a few shells means nothing. When you reach the battalion and feel that the tank is your home, that this is your family, that the tank is your entire life, when you feel that the tank is an inseparable part of your body, when you sleep in it, eat in it, and merge with it, only then will you be tank crewmen—and I'm sure you will be!"

I frequently recalled his words throughout my service. He was right; the tanks really did become part of us. I loved my tank: I loved its armored body, its quiet and gentle power. I felt as though the tank was an extension of my body and that every millimeter of my body and every gram of those fifty-one tons were merged into a single being.

During the course, I had another unique experience. It was in my first gunnery practice, on the night I fired my first shell from a tank. Although I fired many shells after that, I will never forget that occasion. After I fired the first volley, I climbed down out of the tank. I was behind the tanks with everyone else, waiting for the second volley. We were allowed to turn on our transistor radios. On the Army Radio newscast, I heard that several refuseniks had staged a demonstration in the center of Moscow and that two women had been arrested—one of them my mother—but had been released after a few hours. It is difficult to describe the experience and emotion this news evoked in me. Here I was in Israel, firing my first shell as an Israeli tank gunner, and at the same time my mother was continuing her fight, going out to protests and being arrested. Besides my concern and love for my mother, I was filled with exceptional pride.

I got into yet another scrap with the military system during the course. We were given a furlough and I went to Haifa. On the way, I heard that a group of new immigrants was staging a demonstration by the Western Wall to call attention to the plight of the refuseniks. I changed course and proceeded to Jerusalem. When I got there, I went straight to the Western Wall and joined the demonstrators, most of whom I knew. I didn't notice that someone took my picture. When I returned to the base after my furlough, I was called in by the tank school commander Col. Mordechai (Motke) Tzipori. I had met him before I enlisted in the IDF, when Geula Cohen, Dov Sperling, and I spoke with the instructors at the armor school about the struggle of Soviet Jewry. Now Tzipori told me that I would be facing disciplinary charges. He showed me a newspaper with a picture of me in uniform, standing with the demonstrators by the Western Wall. He explained that soldiers were absolutely forbidden to be interviewed or photographed by the press or to participate in demonstrations. I replied that I hadn't known that. Tzipori let me off with a severe reprimand, but cautioned me that I would be put on trial if it happened again. Today, every time I read about senior IDF commanders boasting or leaking information, I remember what the commander of the armor school, Col. Motke Tzipori, one of the outstanding IDF officers of all time, told me in 1970.

After the tank course, we were all assigned to operational battalions. Once again, fate, blind or not so blind, delivered a surprise that affected the rest of my life. I was assigned to Battalion 79, Company B, of the Fourteenth Armored Brigade. We went down to Sinai at night, in pouring rain, and arrived at battalion headquarters where we were welcomed with a festive meal. When we finished eating, we went outside and stood in the requisite threesomes. "Summer camp is over," announced the platoon sergeant. "You're in the army now!"

And we were indeed. Tanks positioned not far from the Suez Canal, drills, constant maintenance of our vehicles, six or seven hours of sleep a week at best. The strain was immense and the exhaustion beyond belief, but the satisfaction, too, was immense. Every day, I felt more and more like a tank crewman, more in control of my weapon, the situation, and the military mindset. I enjoyed every moment. I loved firing my cannon. All in all, I was having a great time.

But the person who influenced my destiny was my company commander, a young, baby-faced major, quiet and not particularly tall. He introduced himself to the company: "Ehud Brog—I'm your company commander." (This was before he changed his name to Barak.) We had a normal relationship. What kind of relationship can a young corporal have with his company commander? I didn't speak with him more than any soldier would speak with a company commander. A rumor passed among the soldiers that our company commander was going to be named commander of the elite and storied General Staff Commando Unit.

We knew that Ehud had retrained to serve in the Armored Corps, like every IDF officer who wanted to climb up the command ladder. In the past, the IDF maintained the doctrine (since forgotten) that an officer who wanted to command large formations needed to have experience in tanks. He had to be familiar with the force that spearheads the attack and delivers the decisive blow. Ehud, like the many officers I met in the Armor School and later in the tank commanders' course, had never served in tanks, so he switched to the Armored Corps and mastered all the subjects relevant to field maneuvers and the command of armored units. Ehud's first Armored Corps position was company commander. When he completed that assignment, he went back to his regular unit and was appointed commander of the General Staff Commando Unit. To this day he is considered to have been one of the most successful, dynamic, and creative commanders in the history of that elite unit. As soldiers, we never had the chance to appreciate him and his talents as a tank company commander. I did see that he had extensive knowledge of tanks and how to maneuver them, but we never learned anything about his capacity as a commander on the ground. We were too young.

One sunny day, in the middle of a drill, I was called to the battalion commander's office and informed that headquarters had granted me leave for twenty-four hours. I was to go to Tel Aviv for a meeting with Nehemiah Levanon. At the time, we were on Red Alert at the Canal. I was the only soldier heading back to Israel, certainly the only one from the front line at the Canal. I didn't know the reason for the summons and was fairly tense. In uniform, carrying my gun, I made my way to the Nativ office in Tel Aviv. An unfamiliar man was sitting in Nehemiah Levanon's office. From his clothes and appearance, it was obvious that he was fresh off the plane from the Soviet Union.

"Meet Vilya Sobchinsky," Levanon introduced us. I knew the name: He was a former Prisoner of Zion, one of the most prominent activists in those years. Levanon told me that Vilya had news from my parents and that he wanted me to treat what I heard with the utmost seriousness. Sobchinsky told me that he knew my family and that he had come to tell me what had happened to my younger brother. He asked me not to get too agitated and informed me that my brother had been hurt while playing ice hockey—he had fractured a vertebra in his neck and was in a cast. Sobchinsky and Levanon wanted to be sure that I knew it had happened in a hockey game and that my brother had not been assaulted by the authorities. No one had hit him; it was an accident during a game. I should keep my cool and not respond in some drastic or unpredictable way. I believed Sobchinsky and trusted him. Had it come from anyone else, I'm not sure I would have believed the report. Levanon told me that they were concerned that when I heard the news about my brother, I would assume that the Soviet authorities were responsible and do something rash. My love and concern for my younger brother and sister bordered on madness. This incident showed that Levanon and his people were concerned that if I thought the Soviets had hurt my brother, I would be capable of going too far. As luck would have it, I did not have to pass this test. I thanked Levanon and Sobchinsky and returned to my battalion. Before I left, I asked Sobchinsky not to tell my parents that I had come to our meeting from the army. My parents did not know that I had enlisted and I didn't want them to worry about me.

A short while afterwards, I was informed that my parents had been granted an exit visa. Brigade HQ in Tasa set up a phone call to Moscow. When my father asked where I was speaking from, I told him, "slightly south of Tel Aviv" and smiled to myself. If my father only knew that his son was just a few kilometers from the Suez Canal and much closer to Cairo than Tel Aviv... This thought cheered me and added what I thought was a fairly significant dimension to my conversation with my parents in Moscow after they received their exit visa.

I was granted a 24-hour furlough to meet my family at the airport and accompany them to the absorption center. On my way to the airport, I stopped off at the Nativ office to change into civilian clothes. I put my Uzi in the bag with my uniform and slung the bag on my shoulder. That's how I traveled to the airport to meet my family. I met them at the foot of the plane and we went into a special VIP lounge. Everybody who was anybody had arrived at the airport in honor of the special event. Everyone wanted to be seen at my reunion with my family. The folks at Nativ had put together a list of those to be allowed in. When I looked around, I saw that Geula Cohen wasn't there. I asked where she was and was met with a dead silence. I asked again, obviously agitated but trying to control my anger: "Where is Geula Cohen?!" All of the distinguished guests and hosts began glancing about, anywhere but at me. Livid, I left the room and went outside to look for her. I saw her almost immediately. Geula had tried to enter the lounge but found her path barred, because Nativ had left her name off the list. The person who had worked harder than anyone else and moved heaven and earth for me, for my parents' aliyah, and for the struggle of Soviet Jewry for aliyah, had been excluded by petty people with petty accounts to settle—bureaucracy always has the upper hand. I hugged her and brought her into the lounge, where I introduced her to my parents and told them about her. Amazingly, almost everyone in the room now came up to greet her and thank her, feigning shock that she had not been allowed in. Still, the mishap did not cast a pall on our good cheer. Most of the Israelis were overjoyed and celebrated this new victory, a victory for us all in the struggle for Soviet *aliyah*.

I accompanied my parents to the absorption center in Haifa. En route, I told them that I had enlisted in the IDF and had come especially from Sinai, from the Canal, to meet them. My parents were somewhat shocked. That was not what they had expected, and they didn't quite understand what it meant at first. They weren't the only ones: Most people didn't comprehend the situation. But they quickly got used to the idea. The next morning, I returned to the battalion.

At the end of the squad/platoon/company training, we became tank crewmen in every sense of the term, qualified in every form of armored combat. Ehud Brog went back to his unit, a new company commander arrived, and we were posted to the rear positions along the Suez Canal. Once again, I encountered an unsavory side of IDF commanders, which taught me yet another lesson about life in Israel. Like all combat soldiers on the frontline in Sinai, we received a furlough one weekend a month. As fate would have it, our squad was rewarded for its excellence twice during the course by being granted an extra leave. This meant I had enjoyed two more furloughs, in addition to the short leave I had been given when my parents arrived in Israel. The new company commander decided to punish me for having had so much time off. When my company was due for its weekend off, the week after my parents' *aliyah*, he told me that I'd received quite enough leave. "What's the difference between the immigrants from Morocco and the immigrants from Russia or another country?" I would not be allowed to go home until the next regularly scheduled leave for my company.

I told him I hadn't seen my family in two years and asked him to cancel my next leave instead of this one. But some IDF commanders simply say "no" to any request that would require them to change a decision they've already made, apparently to protect their dignity. I wasn't really angry with the company commander. In fact, I felt sorry for him. But I asked myself what kind of officer in a Jewish army didn't know the difference between the possibility of making *aliyah* from the Soviet Union and from Morocco and other countries. I just had to find a way to explain to my parents why, after not seeing them for two years, I wouldn't be home for the next six weeks.

When we completed our stretch at the Canal, I was sent to a tank commanders' course. At its start, we were given various tests to determine whether we had officer potential. I was surprised by the very high grade I received. I hadn't realized that I had the qualities they were looking for, particularly as compared to all the other soldiers. Yes, I was older than the rest and more emotionally mature, and perhaps this had an impact. But my image of the Israeli soldier was still very high. To me, the test results were formal confirmation that my military capacity was not inferior to that of native-born Israelis. It marked the beginning of the full internalization of my identity as an Israeli, an equal among equals. From that moment, I no longer looked up to Israeli officers and soldiers as if I were a Diaspora Jew lost in wonder at the sight of some superman. The army was responsible for that.

The second surprise was that I passed the Hebrew-language test, even though I had never formally studied Hebrew. This achievement was especially remarkable because even some of the Israelis failed the test. When I completed the tank commanders' course, I reported to Training Base 1 for the IDF officer's course.

Chapter 15

After my parents made *aliyah*, my own chapter in the struggle against the Soviet Union essentially came to an end. Other relatives made *aliyah* later, including my grandmother's sister and the children of her other sisters. None of my extended family was left in the Soviet Union.

As is customary in Israel, many people, including public figures, tried to hitch a ride on the wave of natural sympathy set off by my family's *aliyah*. Although they were a minority, they were a vocal minority. As in many similar cases, most people treated the situation with sincere warmth and joy, without petty attempts to settle personal accounts. Some organized gatherings in honor of my family; others tried to drag my parents to various meetings, such as one between my father and Shimon Peres (then the Minister of Transportation and Communications), which enjoyed wide media coverage. Peres, in his typical manner, waxed passionate in his speech. Among other things, the honorable minister said that the State of Israel was delighted that professionals were making *aliyah*, because it needed men like my father. The result of all of the festivities, greetings, and self-congratulation was that my father did not find work. The usual excuse was that he was overqualified. Many *olim*, particularly those who came in the mass *aliyah* of the 1990s, couldn't find jobs despite their outstanding professional qualifications, supposedly for this reason. I kept my distance from all the hoopla. I was in the army and there were many things I knew nothing of. The politicians got their time in the limelight and that completed their mission—according to the worldview of the rank-and-file Israeli politician.

My father's efforts to find a job, which lasted several years, were unsuccessful, so in the end he decided to leave Israel and seek his luck elsewhere. In 1974, after the Yom Kippur War, he went abroad, first to Europe and then to Canada. My younger brother, concerned for his health (my father was a severe diabetic), joined him. My brother is extraordinarily talented, much more than me, particularly in his extraordinary capacity for learning. Accepted by several Israeli medical schools, he chose to study at the Technion in Haifa. My father was scheduled to leave Israel a week before my brother's final exams at the end of his first year in medical school, and we begged him to postpone the trip so my brother could complete the year. When he refused, my brother decided to skip the exams. Naturally, he was not allowed to return to school when he came back to Israel, so the trip essentially forced him to sacrifice his future. Soon after their arrival in Canada, my father was killed in a car accident. One morning, my brother called and told me, in a choked voice, that Dad had been killed. Friends helped us arrange to fly the body back to Israel. When I stood near the plane as they lowered the coffin from the cargo hold, I remembered the same scene when my family descended from the plane that brought them to Israel, not so many years ago. I identified my father and once again accompanied him to Haifa, this time to the cemetery.

This was the end of the story of my father's *aliyah*. My mother and sister had refused to go with him when he left Israel. My mother said she would never leave me—once had been enough. My brother returned with my father's body, and the whole family was reunited in Israel.

Chapter 16

After I finished my tour of duty at the Canal, I was sent to a tank commander's course, which passed without any incidents of note. Then I moved on to Officer Candidate School at Training Base 1, like everyone else in the operations branch of the Armored Corps. Something happened when I arrived at Training Base 1 that has wielded a strong influence over my entire life ever since. On one hand, it was a twist of fate, but it was also an instance of stupidity and obtuseness that I still find hard to accept. We were assigned to mixed platoons of tank commanders, gunners, combat engineers, and signal corpsmen. There were also cadets from the General Staff Commando Unit and the Naval Commando Unit. I did not understand why sailors had to go through an officers' course for land forces, and no one could explain the matter to me. Since then, things have changed and naval commandos now do their officers' training in a course run by the Navy. Training Base 1 gave me an extraordinary opportunity to get to know the IDF better, but the problem began when I first got there.

The cadets were assigned to squads. Although different names were used, these were squads in the military sense. Like every squad in the army, every one of us was issued a squad or platoon weapon in addition to his personal gun. The course instructors sent me to a unit where I received the platoon weapon—a 52 mm mortar, every cadet's dream. This was a weapon that never caused any problems, was easy to maintain—and was almost never used during the course. But I didn't want the mortar. I wasn't familiar with infantry weapons and wanted something more serious. I went to the instructor and asked, "Perhaps I could switch my mortar for something else? Give me a different weapon, whatever you want. Perhaps a MAG." This machine gun was the most difficult weapon in the course—it was used frequently and required extensive maintenance.

The instructor, a paratroop officer, responded angrily. "That's what was decided and that's what you'll receive."

I tried appealing to his logic. "Listen, I'm a tank commander. I don't know what this 'pipe' is. I've never used one. Please, give me another weapon."

It was not until much later that I found out that saying I was a tank commander was tantamount to giving the infantry instructor a slap in the face. The conflict and friction between the infantry instructors at Training Base 1 and the Armored Corps cadets, particularly the tank commanders, was well known. The infantry officers usually interpreted comments by tank commanders as mocking or belittling infantry combat. Indeed, we didn't think much of infantry fighting—but that wasn't relevant in this case. I returned to him and asked who would teach me how to use this "pipe," and when. His answer sealed my fate. The instructor responded, "There are cadets in your squad from the Engineers and the Signal Corps. Ask them, they know the mortar."

So I asked the combat engineers in my platoon (they had better infantry training than the others) to teach me how to maintain and shoot the mortar. They showed me how to take it apart and put it back together and explained the firing procedure. Everything seemed to be simple. But there was a small problem. You never fire a mortar during the entire course at Training Base 1, not until near the end. We had a final live-fire exercise about two and a half weeks before the end of the course. After that, there was only one topic left—combat in a built-up area, which is relatively easy. In this exercise, I was stationed as a mortar operator to lay down covering fire. I was supposed to fire while some of the troops were charging the enemy position, in accordance with the battle plan. I did what the guys had told me to do—shell loaded, trigger pulled, shell on its way. Because orders were to keep up continuous covering fire, I shot at a murderous pace. Suddenly, I felt sharp and excruciating pain, as though someone had stuck a knife in one ear and then the other. I dropped the mortar, grabbed my head, and pressed hard on my ears to relieve the unbearable pain.

The instructor, an infantry officer who was standing next to me, asked, "What happened?"

"My ears," I mumbled, grating my teeth to keep from losing consciousness. He took the mortar and started firing instead of me. After all, the drill had to go on and the covering fire had to continue.

I had fired more than a dozen shells in just over a minute. It turned out later that the problem was in the difference in the firing technique of tanks and infantry. In the IDF, a tank commander stands with half his body outside the turret. When the tank fires, he does not bend over the way infantry men do, but actually stands a little taller so he can see where the shell hit and feed a correction to the gunner. A tank commander practices raising his head with every shot, not lowering it the way you have to when you fire a mortar. The barrel of the tank gun is fairly long, and the trajectory of the shell is ahead of the tank. As a result, the shock wave goes around the tank and doesn't affect the crewmen's ears. Tank crews never suffer damage to their ears as long as they're inside the tank when it's firing. Most injuries to tank crewmen are from machine gun fire or mortar fire.

A mortar is a different story, though, particularly a small short-barrel like the one I had. When an infantryman fires a mortar, he keeps his head as close as possible to the ground. That is the firing technique that every infantry soldier learns, but that no one had taught me. For the engineering cadets who explained how to operate the mortar this was obvious; they couldn't imagine any other technique. Nor were they professional mortar instructors, and none of the Training Base staff had checked to make sure I had learned the firing technique properly. The officer's negligence, for which there can be no justification other than disregard for his role and rank, caused severe damage to my ears that has left me disabled for the rest of my life. I got off easy, but hundreds paid with their lives for that attitude so pervasive in the IDF in the pre-Yom Kippur War years, and thousands paid with physical injuries.

When I returned to the base, I went to see the doctor. Wordlessly, he sent me to the central clinic at Tel Hashomer, where they examined my ears, checked my hearing, gave me a slip of paper, and said, "Go back to the base."

The envelope was sealed, so I didn't know what it said. At the base, I reported to the doctor, a major. After he read the report he told me, "Both of your ears have been damaged—one severely, the other moderately. Your profile will temporarily be reduced to 36. Go to the quartermaster and hand in your gear. You're done with the course. You can't continue here with that profile and those injuries."

I was in shock. I protested that there were only two and a half weeks left until the end of the course. But the doctor cut me off. "These are the regulations." Burning with frustration and fury, I saluted him and left.

The doctor's office was in the staff wing of Training Base 1. Cadets were not allowed there without a summons from the base commander (which was extremely rare during the course), unless you were sent to wash the floors in that wing when you were on the cleaning detail. After thinking about it for a few seconds, I turned right instead of going to the barracks and headed for the office of the school commander. I went into the outer office and saluted his executive officer, a captain. She looked at me with surprise. "What are you doing here, cadet?!" Instead of answering the question, I asked if the school commander was in his office. To my surprise, she responded in the affirmative.

"Please tell him that cadet Yakov Kazakov would like to speak to him."

She was somewhat dazed by my rather impudent request. Cadets do not tell officers what to do, certainly not in Officer Candidate School (OCS). At OCS, a cadet does not just barge into the commander's office without permission or a summons, skirting the chain of command. And if he is granted an interview with the school commander, that can take a week or more to arrange. The captain asked if the commander had sent for me. I admitted that he hadn't, but insisted that she deliver my message. She went into the commander's office and came out even more befuddled. "Please go in," she mumbled. I thanked and saluted her and entered the inner office.

I saluted and stood at attention, waiting for the commander to acknowledge my presence. I had heard a lot about Col. Zvi Barzani (later Bar) from the elite paratroopers in the course who had served under him.

"Yasha, come here," he said. "Sit down. What's your problem?"

I told him that my ears had been damaged during the last live-fire exercise, that my profile had been reduced to 36, and that I had come straight from the doctor who had told me I had to drop out of the course because of my medical problems.

"So what do you want?" Barzani asked.

"There are just two and a half weeks left and only one field exercise—combat in a built-up area. That isn't critical for tank officers. I want permission to stay and finish the course."

He looked at me, and I looked straight back at him, as always. He sat there silently for several minutes. I could see that he was wavering. I felt an incredible tension, but kept looking at him. Despite the stress, I didn't move a muscle. Finally, in a very human voice that did not sound like an order at all, he answered. "Okay. Go back to the doctor. You can finish the course."

I could see a light smile playing on his lips. I stood up, saluted, turned around, and left. In the outer office, I saluted the executive officer again, this time with a smile. "Thank you!" I told her, and went back to the doctor.

He was astonished to see me. "Why did you come back?" I told him that I had been to see the school commander. Before I could go any further, the phone on his desk rang. The doctor lifted the receiver and I could tell, from his body language and tone of voice, that it was Barzani on the line. The doctor tried to argue, but to no avail. In the end he put the receiver back in its cradle, visibly annoyed.

"You are an idiot," he said angrily. "And your commander is an idiot! It's against regulations for him to do this. He isn't allowed to take responsibility for you! You will end up without ears. You'll go deaf. Don't you understand that you shouldn't even be exposed to the sound of a tank engine? You shouldn't be climbing into an APC! But the commander has assumed responsibility, so go back to your platoon. You are exempt from live-fire exercises. You can participate in all the dry-fire exercises. The moment they switch to live fire, you have to get out of the tank, retreat at least 200 meters, and cover your ears."

I thanked him, saluted, and returned to the platoon.

During my three and a half months at Training Base 1, I sometimes encountered idiotic rigidity and even negligence, alongside deviations from regulations and outright disregard of orders on the part of the instructors and commanders who were supposed to turn us into officers. The decision by the school commander made some amends for the stupidity that had led to my injury. I completed the officer's course, but I could never be a tank commander. After serving in a tank battalion and enduring the intensity of the tank commander's course, those of us from the Armored Corps felt that OCS at Training Base 1 was like being in summer camp. Tanks teach soldiers, and even more so commanders, that they have to be meticulous in following the rules and regulations. Tanks require total discipline and a much higher level of professionalism than is needed in the other ground forces.

Still, despite all my criticism and reservations, and the desire for better drills and training, the officer's course at Training Base 1 was worthwhile, interesting, even pleasant. We lived in conditions that we had never known in the Armored Corps. Tank crewmen in the field sleep on top of the tank, or under the tank, with no hot showers anywhere in the vicinity. By these standards, Training Base 1 was a luxury hotel where we could sleep indoors, in real beds, in concrete structures. OCS may have been less than what we had anticipated or wanted, but it nonetheless taught us many important things. Above all, Training Base 1 put the final touches on my integration into Israeli society.

In the last weeks of the officer's course, I began thinking about what I would do next. I didn't want to leave my new posting to chance when I reported to the Armored Corps headquarters with my medical profile. I had already learned something in the army—first of all, never trust the system to make the right decision. I phoned the deputy commander of the Armored Corps, Motke Tzipori. Once, when he called me in for an interview while I was in the Armor School, I saw the *Herald Tribune* on his desk. That an officer was reading one of the most serious newspapers in the world was evidence not only of his high intelligence but also of his wide horizons, which should be de rigueur for anyone who wears an officer's insignia and respects himself and the profession. Tzipori knew that I was in OCS. I told him that my ears had been damaged and I had received a temporary profile of 36, but that I would complete the course. I asked whether he thought I could be assigned to the advanced course for Armored Corps officers. His response was laconic: "With that profile, you can't even pass through the gates of the Armor School."

"Forget about tanks," he said.

"So what advanced course can I do?"

"There are advanced courses for the Adjutant Corps and the Quartermaster Corps."

I instinctively stated exactly what I thought of that idea: "Not an option. That's not why I enlisted in the IDF. I will not be a clerk in uniform."

Tzipori treated my extremely insolent response with unwarranted leniency and asked what I had in mind. I answered without hesitation, "The only course that leaves me in the combat branch, which is why I enlisted and abandoned my university studies, is the officer's course in intelligence."

"Okay," he said. "Let me look into it."

Two days before the end of OCS, I received a phone call from an officer in the personnel section of the Armored Corps. She told me that when we completed the course at Training Base 1, all of us would receive a weeklong furlough, after which all my friends would report to the Armor School and the Armored Corps officer's course. I would be sent to the course for intelligence officers instead. When I left Training Base 1, I would receive further explanations and my posting orders. I breathed a sigh of relief.

Two days later, after the closing review, we were released for our furloughs. Naturally, I was very emotional when I received my platoon commander's pin. It reminded me of how I felt when I breathed Israeli air for the first time or when I first put on my army uniform. Only two and a half years earlier I had still been in Moscow, at the height of my struggle to make *aliyah*, feeling all but hopeless, and today I was graduating from the OCS of the Israel Defense Forces. It was another amazing, albeit small victory in my constant battle with reality, my struggle to live my life the way I wanted, despite where I came from, despite all the military rules and regulations, against all the odds.

After my week's leave, I reported to Training Base 15, the School for Military Intelligence. All the other cadets were from the Intelligence Corps. I had seen all of them at Training Base 1 and they were all in the general course, except for one who was in the infantry course, Yon Feder, a member of the Egoz Commando Unit who had already served in the field as a second lieutenant. He had been posted to

Training Base 15 because he had been designated to serve as his unit's intelligence officer. There were also two guys from the General Staff Commando Unit with us in the Intelligence Corps track. All officers of the General Staff Commando Unit were sent to an advanced course in intelligence. I began to learn more about the Intelligence Corps, previously shrouded in mystery for me. I discovered that it was an interesting branch, but my view from the inside revealed that it's not all it's cracked up to be. I have always been sorry that I didn't go to the Armored Corps officers' course and couldn't return to the tanks. I had been given a low profile and labeled an invalid for the rest of my life, so I was not allowed to serve in a combat unit. Since that time I have never heard silence—I always have a metallic buzzing in my ears that never goes away.

The truth is that I had already deceived the IDF about my health. No one knew or ever found out, and it isn't recorded anywhere. When I was fourteen, still in Moscow, I was playing team handball (a cross between soccer and basketball) in the yard. When I straightened up to throw the ball, one of the other kids gave me a shove and "helped" me fall. When I got up, something was wrong with my right arm, but I didn't understand what had happened. About two hours later, I began feeling severe pain. I went to the doctor, who diagnosed a fracture. When they removed the cast a month later and examined me, the doctor said that the damage to my arm would never heal. The place where the bone had split, at the elbow, would never fuse, and my arm movement would always be limited.

When I went for my medical examination at the Soviet draft office, at age seventeen, I had forgotten all about it. One of the doctors who examined me got upset. "Why are you lying? Are you an idiot or something? Why didn't you tell us that you have an unhealed fracture in your arm?" I told him, honestly, that it had simply slipped my mind. The Soviet military doctor told me that with a fracture of that kind, I could not serve in a combat unit, but only in the rear echelons, in a job requiring no combat or physical strain. He inserted a notation to this effect in my file in the Soviet draft office. When I enlisted in the IDF, though, I "forgot" about the fracture again and somehow it was overlooked in my physical examination. I have no pangs of conscience about lying to the IDF about my broken arm. I met many soldiers and officers, particularly in the reserves, who deceived the army about health matters of varying severity, and all for a single goal: to remain combat soldiers. This is one of the things that make the Israeli army so superior.

To never surrender, no matter what, to never give up—I had internalized this principle on the streets of Moscow in the 1950s and 1960s. Nothing was worse than surrender. You always had to keep driving towards the goal. I didn't need to learn this in Israel, because I had already learned it in the Soviet Union. It was thanks to this that I got so far, including making it to the officers' school of the IDF Intelligence Corps.

The first thing that surprised me was the large number of female soldiers there. There were women everywhere in the IDF, of course, but you hardly ever saw them in field units and in the Armored Corps. Suddenly I saw a different army, one I had not known before. I realized that I was in a totally different place than I had been used to in the Armored Corps.

The intelligence officers' course is one of the most interesting courses in the IDF. You learn a lot, traveling all over the country and through every sort of terrain. You study with top teachers and learn the best thinking and planning strategies, which are quite different from that of other corps, where the focus of training courses is drilling. We had lots of navigation exercises which were very hard, to the point that even the guys from the General Staff Commando Unit had problems; sometimes even the instructors got lost and had trouble orienting themselves in the field. The instructors were on a high level, particularly as compared to Training Base 1. What stood out most was their intelligence, general culture, and professionalism. It was a refreshing change. Only in the intelligence officer's course did I begin to feel that I was truly an officer in terms of my abilities, knowledge, thinking, and performance.

There were also a few curious incidents during the intelligence officers' course. At the start, an NCO from field security came to run a security check on me. He started filling out a standard questionnaire and asked me what year I made *aliyah*.

"1969."

"You mean 1959."

"No, 1969."

He gave me a look and innocently asked me, "Wait a minute, how did they even let you pass through the gate of the base if you made *aliyah* in 1969?" The year was 1971, and he looked to be in utter disbelief.

Another interesting incident happened in the final exercise, in which our team had to evaluate what methods would be used by the Egyptian Army to cross the Canal in wartime. We identified several locations in Sinai that we believed to be likely sites for the Egyptians to land commando and paratrooper units and their Special Forces. I had an argument about this issue with the course commander. He told me that overall our team had done good work, but our assessment that the Egyptians would drop paratroopers in those places didn't mesh with standard combat doctrine. He said that according to the prevalent tactical doctrine, you don't drop paratroopers in a place where you won't be able to link up to them within 24 hours. The units land with only enough equipment and ammunition for one day, so they will be wiped out if the main force doesn't reach them within 24 hours. As usual, I did not hide my opinion and told him that I did not know what army the commander was talking about. But the armies I was familiar with, including the Arab armies, didn't care about whether they would be able to link up within 24 hours; they would drop the paratroopers anyway. The commander's response was that this simply wasn't done by armies anywhere in the world, and our script was thrown out of the exercise. Two years later, at the start of the Yom Kippur War, the Egyptians dispatched commando and paratrooper units with no concern for how long it would take for the main force to reach them and whether they would hold out or be overrun.

Something rather amusing happened at the end of the course. One day we were given an overnight leave. In the morning, we had to be back at the base, change into dress uniform, and participate in the graduation review, after which we would be allowed to wear our officer's insignia. In the morning, while we were changing into our dress uniforms, I was approached by a friend in the course who had just come back from Haifa.

"You won't believe it," he told me, and started giggling. "I was in Haifa, and one of my friends told me he heard that Yasha Kazakov had been exposed as a Soviet spy and arrested by the General Security Service."

My friend tried to refute his friend's scoop and told him that Yasha Kazakov was in an IDF intelligence officers' course with him, and was about to receive his second lieutenant's bar, to no avail.

"You don't know what you're talking about!" my friend's friend retorted. "I heard it from my buddy in the General Security Service, and it's true."

"So I see that the GSS released you?" my friend asked.

"What could I do? I convinced them to let me go for the final review so that I could be a spy with officer's insignia."

We both laughed. I continued to smile even when Maj. Gen. Aharon Yariv, the head of Military Intelligence, uncovered my insignia and added a few sentences in Russian. I answered in the same language and he gave me a warm smile and wished me well. I wondered whether he had any inkling that he was wishing success to a Soviet agent who had been released by the GSS only in order to receive his insignia. Many years passed before I learned that Yariv himself had approved my participation in the course, overruling the opinion of field security.

Chapter 17

After completing the advanced course for intelligence officers at Training Base 15, I reported to Armored Corps headquarters. Usually, everyone goes back to the unit and corps that sent him to OCS. I reported to the staff officer whose job was to find officers postings in the corps. He flipped through my documents and told me to go home and come back a few days later. When I returned, he told me that given my low profile, he could not assign me as an intelligence officer to an armored battalion, and because he didn't have an open slot for a staff intelligence officer, I was being posted to Armored Brigade 274 as a liaison officer. I didn't know what this meant and asked him what he was talking about.

"He's the adjutant in a reserve battalion who handles everything related to call-ups and keeping in touch with the members of the battalion."

I tried to argue. I had done a course for intelligence officers, not for manpower clerks. But the staff officer, a lieutenant colonel, ended the argument with the flat statement that this was an order. There would be no debate about it and I should report to Brigade 274.

So I reported to the brigade to serve as the liaison officer of one of the battalions. It was a brigade of captured Soviet-made tanks that the IDF had renovated and enhanced. We had replaced the cannon, the engine, and the communications systems. This wasn't particularly interesting to me though, because I wasn't allowed to have anything to do with tanks and their operation. When the brigade commander told me that I would soon be sent to a professional course for adjutant officers, I told myself that I would absolutely not spend the rest of my service dealing with manpower affairs. I couldn't understand the logic of sending a soldier to an officers' course in one field and then as soon as he graduated and was qualified, sending him to a completely different course which had no connection to the training he received in the first course. I couldn't understand what the problem was, but I had the sense that something was going on there. My profile had indeed been lowered, but the IDF knew this before I was sent to the intelligence officer's course, so it was probably not the reason. It was only a few years later that I found out the real reason, quite by accident.

When I transferred to a new unit, I was given my file to bring to the new unit. It included a letter from the Intelligence Corps HQ stating that the head of the Intelligence Branch had approved my being posted to the intelligence officer's course, with one condition. Field Security had stipulated that at the end of the course, I would not be assigned to the Intelligence Corps or to any position in the military intelligence system. Naturally, I hadn't known that at the time, but I sensed—and encountered much proof in later years—that IDF Field Security was not marked by outstanding professionalism or great brilliance and understanding. In my case, they could not swallow the fact that a boy who had made *aliyah* from the Soviet Union only two and a half years before could receive a high security clearance. They had no ability or willingness to consider my unusual biography. To make it easier for them to deal with immigrants, they simply kept extending the cooling-off period after the date of *aliyah*. The people in Field Security weren't capable of anything more sophisticated than this. They were not capable of understanding that it would not be logical for me to do such great damage to the Soviet Union just for the slight chance of worming my way into a classified position in Israel. Many years later, after I was already part of the system, I heard from General Security Service officers that their organization simply ignored IDF Field Security decisions about whether a person constituted a security risk on the grounds that the latter was not professional enough, and conducted its own investigation. I was not aware of the restriction in my file. And even if I had known, I probably couldn't have done anything about it.

But I refused to give up. I weighed the matter and came to a decision. I went to the Kirya, the Israeli Pentagon in Tel Aviv. In those days IDF bases, including the General Staff offices in the Kirya, were not exactly the last word in security. I entered without anyone stopping and checking me. True, I was in uniform—but IDF uniforms were easy to come by. I went up to the floor of the Chief of Staff's suite—but that wasn't where the man I was looking for had his office. I went down one floor and entered the office of the head of the Intelligence Branch. I went up to the executive officer and saluted. "This is a personal letter to the head of the Intelligence Branch. I would like him to receive it."

The officer's expression remained unchanged. "Leave it here," he said, and returned to his paperwork. I placed the envelope on his desk and left the office and the Kirya. In my letter I reminded the head of the Intelligence Branch that I had completed the intelligence officers' course and considered the failure to find me a posting in the Intelligence Corps to be improper and wasteful. I complained angrily that I was being assigned to a job for which I was not qualified and stated that I had no intention of becoming an adjutant officer.

A week passed and I received a summons from the deputy commander of the Armored Corps, Motke Tzipori. I went into his office, saluted, and stood at attention. Tzipori looked at me and I saw that he was trying to maintain a grave look on his face. But the corners of his eyes revealed a smile that expressed his true feelings. In a dry voice of feigned reproach he asked, "You've committed another breach of discipline?"

"What breach?" I asked with sincere innocence and astonishment.

"Did you try to contact the head of the Intelligence Branch?" he half-asked half-stated. "Yes," I confirmed.

"You bypassed the chain of command," he explained. "Not through your brigade commander. Not even through the head of the Armored Corps, but directly. You should be punished for this. Bypassing the chain of command is a very severe offence in the IDF."

"I admit my guilt," I said contritely.

With that, Tzipori changed his tone of voice completely. "The decision is that you will leave Brigade 274," he said, "You will be posted as an intelligence officer at Armored Corps HQ. But as punishment for bypassing the chain of command, the transfer will be delayed for a month. Dismissed."

I saluted and left the office. I couldn't thank him, because that was forbidden in an interview that was essentially a trial. I was elated and smiled to myself because I was on the way to becoming a professional intelligence officer, but also, and even more, because of my intense feeling of satisfaction. Once again I had been forced to go up against the system, in a situation that seemed to be a dead end—and once again I had triumphed and changed my fate, against the rules.

The commander of Brigade 274, Gidon Altschuler, was furious with me. How dare I leave his brigade, he stormed, which was the best in the IDF, and so on and so forth. I told him that I valued him and appreciated the brigade, but I did not want to be an adjutant officer. I had a different military profession and I would serve in the profession that I wanted and had qualified for.

During those two or three months that I was with the brigade, I got to know one of the most amazing people I ever met, a legend in his own time—like so many people in Israel. I had even heard about him back in the Soviet Union. One day, I saw a group of men, some in uniform and some in civilian dress, standing outside brigade headquarters. One of them looked at me closely.

"Are you Yasha?"

When I responded in the affirmative, he introduced himself. "I'm Arkady Timor."

I was in shock. I immediately remembered where I knew his voice from. It was a voice familiar to every Jew in the Soviet Union, that of the military commentator of the Voice of Israel in Russian. Arkady Timor (Salzman) was born in Bessarabia. He served as an armor officer throughout the Second World War and was the commander of the first Soviet tank battalion that entered Berlin. Late in the war, he passed through his home town, where he learned from the neighbors that his entire family, including his little sister, had been murdered by the Nazis. Timor later told me about the first two things he had done when he entered Berlin: He gave an order to set up a field kitchen in the street and hand out food to any hungry German who asked, and he organized a kindergarten for the abandoned German children who were wandering the streets. "That was my revenge against the Nazis—a Jewish revenge," he said with a sad and painful look. When I heard the story from him, and now as I write about it, I am deeply moved by this man, by his humanity and the nobility of his soul.

After the war, Timor completed the armored corps academy and married a woman from Poland. After he let slip a few incautious utterances about Judaism and the State of Israel, he was arrested, tried, convicted of anti-Soviet activity, and sentenced to a long term in a prison camp. After several years in the camp, he was released because of his outstanding service as an officer in the war and thanks to the intervention of his former commanders. Because his wife was a Polish citizen before the war, they received an exit visa to Poland, as part of the repatriation of Polish nationals, and from Poland they came to Israel.

But there was another fascinating chapter in his life that he didn't talk about. While he was stationed as a Red Army officer in Germany, he crossed the lines and made contact with members of the Mossad la'Aliyah Bet (which organized the clandestine immigration of Holocaust survivors to mandatory Palestine), including its head,

Shaul Avigur. At its request, he wrote up training manuals about the M1 Sherman tank, which was in service with the IDF during the War of Independence and afterwards. Timor had spent most of the Second World War fighting in Shermans (the United States provided thousands of them to the Soviet Union). Then he risked his life by smuggling training manuals to Israelis. Had the Soviets discovered his contacts with members of the Mossad la'Aliyah Bet, his fate would have been summary execution.

When Timor reached Israel, his knowledge of and experience in tanks and armored combat exceeded that of the entire IDF. But the IDF was afraid to enlist the officer who had fought four and half years against the best armor formations in the world, the soldiers of the Wehrmacht Panzer divisions. The State of Israel decided that he could not be trusted. On the other hand, they couldn't just pass up his knowledge and experience. So he became a civilian employee of the IDF, responsible for rebuilding and enhancing the Armored Corps. He pulled off a feat that neither the Germans nor the Soviets had managed during the Second World War. Even though both sides captured thousands of enemy tanks, they were not able to return them to service and put together an operational armored unit of captured tanks, despite the tremendous efforts they made throughout the war years. Timor was the only person in the world who succeeded at this task. Thanks to his professionalism and devotion, the team that he organized and supervised, and the engineering solutions he found, Soviet-made tanks taken as spoil from the Egyptian Army constituted a regular brigade in the IDF. During the Yom Kippur War, this brigade was sent to Sinai and took part in the fighting against the Egyptian forces. Later, a full division of captured Soviet-made tanks was established. In a word, Timor presented the IDF a present of an entire armored division!

Timor readied the tanks and armored personnel carriers for an operation in which the IDF landed forces on the west bank of the Gulf of Suez during the War of Attrition. The captured Soviet-made vehicles were landed on the Egyptian side of the Gulf, where they wrought havoc on the Egyptian rear. They destroyed facilities and a few tanks, and returned to Israel after causing incredible damage to Egyptian morale and bringing glory to the IDF. During that operation, an IDF tank ran over a jeep full of Egyptians. The IDF officers didn't know that one of the passengers in the jeep was a Soviet general, part of the Soviet military delegation sent to assist the Egyptian army.

But that isn't the story. The story is that when the tanks and APCs were rolling onto the LST on the bank of the canal, Timor boarded the vessel with all the soldiers and officers. A captain from Field Security held him back on the grounds that he had no authorization to embark on the LST and would have to stay there on the shore. Timor turned white. But he gathered all his courage and strength and held his peace. He was left there alone on the east bank of the Gulf of Suez, without food or water, under the burning sun. He became dehydrated, lost consciousness several times, and almost died before the force returned from the operation. To this day, I cannot understand the commanders in the field who allowed an idiot from Field Security to commit this abominable and criminal act. Even in the Red Army, during Stalin's reign of terror, officers were known to interfere with the mad asininities of Field Security personnel in similar situations. Here, commanders and officers, free-born Jews with no Diaspora complex, cowered like rabbits and avoided looking him in the eye out of shame! I cannot excuse this. Had I been a commander there, or even just on that beach, no Field Security officer would have dared to do what that captain did to Timor. But Timor was happy that the operation succeeded. He was ecstatic that the tanks that he fixed up ran like clockwork. He kept his pain to himself and swallowed the insult and never spoke about it. He had gone above and beyond the call of duty for his country and his people, without worrying about the compensation he received from the State, despite all the humiliation. All he wanted was to give to his country, because he simply did not know how to behave any differently. For me, the man, his morality and humility were the quintessence of a Jew and an Israeli.

Arkady Timor died a few years ago of cancer. Till his dying day he tried to give, to do something. He never received the recognition that he deserved. Nor was he honored with a military commission, even though he was far worthier of one than many who wore officer's insignia. To the end he remained a civilian employee of the IDF. His wife and invalid son are barely able to make ends meet from the modest pension paid to IDF civilian employees. He was recommended for the Israel Defense Prize, but others were deemed worthier, or perhaps had better connections than this humble and amazing man.

On the appointed day, I reported to Armored Corps HQ, where I did the rest of my compulsory service. I had already received a letter from the head of the Manpower Branch to the effect that on the basis of my vital statistics—age, year of *aliyah*, and family status—I was required to serve six months only. The IDF thanked me for completing the full term of compulsory service (I was only two months short of a three-year tour of duty) and would reclassify the last year of my conscript service as service in the regular army. Like all my friends, I had committed myself to an additional year in the regular army when I finished the officers' course. But now, in one fell swoop, I completed my conscript and regular service simultaneously, almost a year before the expected date. Instead of completing my service in April 1974, I was discharged from the IDF in June 1973.

Chapter 18

By the time I completed my military service, I was already married and had a son. I was now faced with the task of coping with civilian life, which I knew nothing about. During the year or so that I had been in Israel before joining the army, I lived a student life. Most of my time in Israel, from August 1970, I had spent in the army. I had been what is called a "lone soldier," eligible for special leniencies because until my parents arrived, I had had no home to go to on the weekends. There weren't many lone soldiers back then. I almost never spoke Russian, except when I went to my parents in Haifa. I even spoke Hebrew with my wife, although she too had made *aliyah* from the Soviet Union in June 1969. My knowledge of civilian life in Israel was therefore quite limited.

I found a job as a security officer with Arkia, the Israeli domestic airline. The whole field of airport and air transport security was still in its infancy then; airlines were only just starting to formulate a comprehensive approach to security. We were put through a security officers' course. Unlike today, there was no difference back then between a screener, a guard, or a security officer on the ground. One person did everything. This gave me the opportunity to study and work in a new and interesting field as it took shape. We worked at all of Israel's domestic airports: Sde Dov in Tel Aviv, Lod (now Ben-Gurion), Eilat, and Sharm e-Sheikh. I received a relatively good foundation, at least in terms of knowledge and comprehension of the topic. My life began to fall into a routine.

On Yom Kippur 1973 at one o'clock in the afternoon, I heard a knock on the door. I was living in Holon, just south of Tel Aviv. The neighbor from the apartment above us, whose family had made *aliyah* from Iraq the year before, was standing there in shock. She told me that she had just heard on an Arabic language broadcast from one of the neighboring countries that a war against Israel had begun. I ran to the radio and turned it on, not knowing what to expect because the Voice of Israel shuts down on Yom Kippur. Air raid sirens were going off and the announcer reported that we had been attacked by Syria and Egypt. Immediately afterwards, he started reading out the call-up slogans for various reserve units. I got dressed and told my wife, "I'm heading over to the Armored Corps base to find out what's going on."

Traffic had already begun to move on the streets and the Armored Corps base was bustling. I went up to friends in the office whom I knew from my service and asked them what was going on.

"Seems to be war. We're not sure," I was told. "We're calling up all the armored units." I told someone not to look for me, because I was going to Armored Corps headquarters, where I had served. The norm is that an officer is assigned to a reserve unit within six months after completing his conscript service, but half a year had not yet passed since my discharge and I hadn't been placed in a reserve unit.

I went home and put on my uniform. My wife managed to shove some food into me, because I hadn't eaten since the previous afternoon. I asked her to come with me. When we reached Julis, the Armored Corps HQ, I parked my car outside the base. I went inside to the intelligence unit where I had served until recently and walked over to the maps. At once I heard and saw that there was a war and that the situation was serious. I went outside, told my wife that it was probably a war. I would stay on the base and update her afterwards. We said goodbye and she drove back to Tel Aviv.

Thus began my first war in Israel. I was grateful that I had insisted on serving in the IDF and was already an officer. The commander of the Armored Corps, Maj. Gen. Avraham Adan ("Bren"), was also the commander of Division 162. The division was trying to get organized and was starting a hasty movement towards the northern sector of the southern (Suez Canal) front. The division intelligence officer told me to stay behind and serve as the liaison officer for divisional intelligence on the Southern Front. When I asked him to define exactly what that role entailed, he said they'd tell me later. In the tense and chaotic environment, many things were unclear, so his response sounded reasonable.

The division moved quickly. The next day, Sunday, the casualty reports began coming in. Sitting in the operations room, I went over the lists of the casualties—killed, wounded, and missing—and saw names I knew from my service. No one had an up-to-date and clear picture of what was happening on the front, and wild reports and rumors were circulating. I approached the staff officer and asked to be attached to a unit on the southern or northern front. He told me to wait—he would call me as soon as he had something to offer me. I was the only intelligence officer left on base and saw that I really had nothing to do. I summoned a driver and told him to take me down to the border with Sinai at the Sa'ad Junction the next morning, and then to return to base. I would find my way to the forces in Sinai by myself.

In the morning, I grabbed a gun and set off. The driver let me off at the Sa'ad Junction. I ran into the adjacent kibbutz for five minutes to see Arye Kroll, who worked for Nativ. When I was a soldier in a battalion in Sinai, my coat had been stolen while we were out in the field on maneuvers. When I came back, I reported the theft. Before we left for the tank officer's course, I was summoned to a court-martial for losing military equipment. I reported to the officer and explained that my coat had been stolen during a training exercise. To my surprise, he told me that I had to pay for it even if I wasn't guilty, because somebody had to compensate the country for lost equipment. The result was that I was left without a military coat: the quartermaster didn't issue me a replacement and I never asked for one.

So now I asked Arye Kroll to finagle a coat for me. I took it and began hitching rides to the Armored Corps base at Refidim (Bir Gafgafa), in central Sinai. When I arrived, I entered one of the offices where I bumped into some acquaintances. I asked them to assign me to a unit. They said that a tank would be returning from the repair facility in Tasa the next morning, and although there were many other candidates, they'd make sure I got it. I could take the tank with its crew and join one of the battalions. I plead guilty: I exploited my connections and this time it worked. I asked the adjutant to inform the staff officer back at Julis that I was joining such and such a unit. The adjutant complied, but the staff officer asked me to come to the phone myself. He insisted that I return immediately, because he was putting together an armored battalion for the Northern Front and I was to be assigned as its intelligence officer. That was an order.

I thanked my friends and told them about the change in plans. In the morning, I went to the airstrip where a Hercules transport plane had just landed with a load of ammunition. I told the pilot that I needed to return to the Armored Corps headquarters immediately. He told me to get onboard and I flew back to Lod, where I reported to the personnel officer. To my surprise, he said that I wasn't going anywhere but would be staying at headquarters. I asked him what about the battalion for the northern front, but it was clear from his response that the idea was just a sham and there was no such battalion. I restrained myself from punching him—after all, lieutenants don't hit lieutenant colonels. On my way out, I ran into Ehud Brog, my company commander in Battalion 79, who was by now a lieutenant colonel.

"What are you doing here?" I asked, "Aren't you off at Stanford University?" I had heard that after his stint as commander of the General Staff Commando unit, Ehud had gone to study for a master's in systems analysis in California.

"I'm putting together a battalion," he said. "And what are you doing here?"

"I'm looking for a battalion."

"So come with me," he suggested. "Help me put together a battalion, stick with me. I don't have an intelligence officer or an operations officer. You can be in my tank, if you still shoot like you used to."

I agreed, but I did have one request: that he not inform the personnel officer in my battalion, because I had already been recalled from Sinai once. Ehud played along and ordered his adjutant not to report me to the personnel officer.

To this day I have no idea why the personnel officer tried to prevent me from serving at the front. Perhaps he truly believed that there was something to the idea that I was a Soviet spy and mustn't be allowed near the front. Or maybe he didn't want me to be wounded or captured, given my name and the unfortunate impression it might make. I don't know, nor do I care.

My deal with Ehud was that I would serve as the battalion's intelligence and operations officer. Battalion 100 began as a mixed force, under the control of Southern Command. It consisted of two companies of tanks and one reinforcement company whose personnel was drawn from the mechanized infantry, the General Staff Commando unit, the Shaked Commando, plus a few more soldiers from special units. It was a battalion-level special force, originally designated the "Special Tasks Unit." Most of the officers and men had returned to Israel from abroad after the outbreak of the war. Most of them were veterans of the War of Attrition and had lots of experience.

We loaded up on ammunition at the Armored Corps school in Julis. We took all the vehicles they had there—tanks in operational condition, armored personnel carriers (APCs), a few jeeps and guns. We didn't have enough APCs because they had all been assigned to the mechanized infantry company. Ehud and I agreed that there would be no APC for intelligence or operations. Command would be concentrated entirely in his tank and I would work from there. The usual procedure is for the operations officer to be with the battalion commander during a battle if the commander is in a tank, while the intelligence officer stays in the intelligence APC. It is true that my proposal wasn't standard operating procedure, but it was the only feasible solution given the shortage of APCs and officers.

I loaded extra communications gear on the tank so that we could broadcast and receive on multiple channels. I also added another machine gun on the turret, tied on with ropes. It was a MAG, not an 0.3 left over from the Second World War like the other machine guns on the tanks. Ehud's friend, Maj. Yishai Yizhar, who had served in special units and participated in operations that are still classified to this day, became the fifth member of our crew. He would sit on the turret and operate the extra machine gun I had mounted there. I positioned myself where the loader-radioman sits. The operations office always takes the place of the loader-radioman, even though I enjoyed gunnery and was good at it. I tied three more crates onto the turret—two crates with ammunition belts for the MAG and another crate that I filled with hand grenades before every battle. We had a well-equipped tank.

We were transported to Sinai on tank carriers. I remember a conversation with an officer from the Shaked Commando, Capt. Itzik Rosenstreich. The whole way there, he asked me about tanks and said that after the war he wanted to be retrained for the Armored Corps, because he had gone as far as he could in the infantry. He also told me that the night before, he had found time to stop off at home. He had been married shortly before the war. Itzik Rosenstreich was killed ten days later in the battle of the Chinese Farm. I visited his family after the war. When I entered his home, I saw that his wife was pregnant. The next time I stopped by, she had already given birth to their son.

It wasn't clear how and in what formation the battalion would fight. We were under Southern Command and our orders kept changing, because headquarters had only a vague idea of what was going on. Southern Command had various plans for our battalion, some of which were extremely daring and almost delusional, probably because of the unit's personnel and the fact that the battalion commander came from the General Staff Commando Unit. For example, they considered having us take part in the attempt to break through to the besieged Metzach Fort or to participate in the amphibious landing, planned but never carried out, in Adabiya Bay, on the Egyptian side of the Gulf of Suez. As soon as they were ashore, the tanks were supposed to turn north and cut off the Egyptian Third Army, which would allow for a rapid passage of other units through the Deversoir (where the IDF actually did cross the Canal near the end of the war).

On October 13, our battalion was attached to Brigade 460, which fought as part of the 162nd Division under Maj. Gen. Eden. This was the Armor School brigade. Thus in the end, I reached the front as part of the division to which I was assigned on the first day of the war, but as a fighter and not as a staff officer. The soldiers who came from the General Staff Commando Unit left the battalion to join other units or fight on their own. Some were killed, included Capt. Amitai Nahmani, one of the top officers in the commando unit, who fell in the battle for the Fayid airport. I remember how he always had a smile on his face and an inquisitive look. The battalion was left with the ten APCs of the mechanized infantry company and two tank companies with a total of 27 tanks.

On the night of October 14, we took our place in the immense traffic jam along the Akavish Road, where the bulk of the IDF forces had been concentrated. That same day we received the order to cross the Canal, with details of the units involved. Ariel Sharon's 143rd Division would cross first, on October 15, and establish a bridgehead. Our division would cross the Canal right after it, on the bridges that would be thrown up, attack the Egyptian forces on the western bank, and move south towards Suez City in order to cut off the Egyptian Third Army. Sharon's division would move north and surround the Second Army. We followed its progress on the wireless and heard that the first units were on the other side. On October 16, however, we realized that the crossing was not going as fast as had been planned, so we continued our slow advance on the main road towards the Canal.

That night, we received an order to rescue a paratroop battalion that had run into trouble on the Tirtur Road. We were told it was Battalion 890 and given its approximate coordinates. At dawn, we moved towards the road and made radio contact with the paratroopers. It was hard to distinguish them and their positions from the Egyptians. Ehud asked them to shoot off a flare so we could locate them. It turned out that there were only a few dozen meters separating them from the Egyptians. The terrain was flat and almost all the paratroopers were in a place that was covered by Egyptian fire, in the killing zone. There were only a few small furrows in which some of the paratroopers were bunched together. At Ehud's order, tanks began targeting the Egyptian positions. We hit several of their tanks and the Egyptian fire on our paratroopers eased off. But this did not solve the main problem, which was getting the paratroopers out of there. Every paratrooper who raised his head and tried to move exposed himself to Egyptian fire, particularly from small arms and machine guns. Our tank held its fire because Ehud was focused on directing and coordinating the battle. After a while, he decided to charge the Egyptian positions and try to overrun them, which would release the paratroopers and put the road out of the range of Egyptian fire. After the order was issued over the wireless, all of the tanks, including ours, began the assault. The Egyptians fought stubbornly, even courageously. I remember one incident when a tank of ours was charging ahead and suddenly an Egyptian soldier jumped up, stood erect, and fired his Kalashnikov at us. When we got closer, he dove beneath the tracks and got up and continued shooting after we passed. We had to move back and forth twice and make a full circle in order to kill him.

During the fighting, my job was loader/radioman, which meant I had to operate the machine guns and load shells into the cannon. Yishai Yizhar was in the fifth seat, in the rear, his legs in the turret and almost his entire huge body outside the tank. He operated the second machine gun I had mounted on the turret. I heard the screams along with the firing—ours and the Egyptians'—and suddenly I felt something pressing on me from behind. I told Yishai he was making it harder for me to load the shells, but the pressure grew stronger until he was almost resting his full weight on me. I turned around and saw him crouching there, his face pale, with a narrow line of blood on the right side of his neck. Just as we had been taught, I put my finger in the wound and pressed to stop the flow of blood. Yishai gave me a bashful and apologetic look and moved his arms as if to say, "Sorry—what can I do?" His lips barely moved, and I couldn't hear or understand what he was saying. The blood stopped flowing and I thought I had been successful, but suddenly a torrent of blood gushed from his mouth and washed all over me. The bullet must have pierced an artery, and when I blocked the entry hole all the blood flowed through his mouth. Yishai kept looking at me and I saw how his eyes were glazing over as the life ebbed from his body. He remained conscious until the last seconds, as his face lost all color and turned to a white mask. Suddenly, the blood stopped and I realized his heart had given out. Almost the entire six liters of blood in the human body had poured out on me. My clothes remained soaked with Yishai's blood for several days. I didn't have a spare coverall and couldn't get a new one as long as the fighting continued without letup.

The battle went on. I shifted a bit to the side so that Yishai's body wouldn't be too much in the way. I put a new ammo belt in the other machine gun and told Ehud that Yishai was dead. Then I climbed up, stuck my body outside, nudged Yishai's body aside, and began firing the machine gun he had been operating only a few minutes earlier. The ammo belt he had started to shoot off wasn't even used up. Ehud kept firing the commander's machine gun without turning his head. He merely asked, without a pause in the shooting, "Are you sure?"

"He's dead," I said laconically.

Ehud kept firing. "We have to get him out of the tank." Even without turning around he must have perceived my astonishment at this. So he added in a quiet and matter-of-fact voice, as was his habit, "if he stays inside the tank, I won't be able to swivel the turret."

I realized he was right and asked the driver to bring the tank to a halt. A few minutes later, when there was a lull in the firing, he pulled up next to a group of paratroopers who were lying in an improvised trench. I looked at them and was overcome by anger and shame. The paratroopers were lying there, some of them wounded, with their cumbersome FNs—Belgian-made carbines that were known for misfiring and jamming frequently. The weapon was quite unsuited to the conditions in the Sinai desert. They had run out of ammunition. Some of them had no water left. They looked exhausted, all their physical and emotional strength gone. They scurried up on the tank, thinking we were going to take them with us. But Ehud gave an order, "No one is getting in this tank."

I relayed the message. "You're not getting in this tank. Help me remove our dead comrade." The paratroopers gave me a hand with Yishai's corpse, which we laid on the ground. The tank started moving again. I went back to the machine gun and we resumed our advance.

Now I understood why Ehud didn't allow the paratroopers in the tank. We overran the Egyptian positions, shooting at the infantrymen and crushing them under our treads. Suddenly we came under a hail of Sagger wire-guided anti-tank missiles from the left (north), from the direction of the Chinese Farm, a spot designated "Missouri" on our code maps. I saw the white ball of fire flying in our direction, making small circles in the air. I heard the characteristic whistle as it passed over our head and saw the missile strike the tank next to us. We began counting as the crew started jumping out: one, two, three—but no four. That was it. It meant that two crewmen were dead or severely wounded with almost no chance of survival, because the tank was burning and the ammunition inside was blowing up.

We kept moving and the battle continued. I suddenly saw a ball of fire flying with incredible speed towards our tank. Everything happened in a split second. Estimating the missile's trajectory, I concluded it would strike the front of our tank. I got ready for the impact. I grabbed hold of my Uzi and told myself I mustn't leave it behind in the tank. I made sure its strap was around me and automatically checked my canteen. I had seen cases when crewmen abandoned their tanks without a weapon or canteen. I knew there was almost no chance of surviving in the Sinai sun for more than a few hours without water, particularly if you were wounded. Nor did I want to find myself without a gun among Egyptian soldiers. But I didn't utter a sound. I didn't yell to Ehud that there was a missile coming up on our left, nor did I scream to the driver to stop. I must have been in a momentary daze. Suddenly the missile gained elevation, for some reason, passed over the driver's cabin but in front of the turret, and left only its screech and heat wave to remember it by. Only then did Ehud notice the missile. It was not the first that had been aimed at us, but it came the closest. We continued our advance.

After the battle, we removed the wires of at least a dozen Saggers which had become entangled with the body of the tank. The intense missile fire meant that we could not advance straight towards our target. We spread out along the length of the Tirtur Road, just over a mile away, and positioned ourselves so that our fire would cover the Egyptian positions and prevent them from massacring the paratroopers who were pinned down. In this battle, seven of our 21 tanks were hit by missiles, enemy tank fire, and RPGs. Most of the crews jumped out on their own or were pulled from their tanks, except for the three that were hit by missiles. Ehud decided to try to use the APCs of the mechanized infantry company to evacuate the paratroopers and began coordinating with the brigade for artillery cover. The commander of the mechanized infantry company had been killed early in the fighting. His deputy, Lieut. Gideon Dvoretsky, who had taken over, took the APC into the paratroopers' position under heavy Egyptian fire. Our tanks and the brigade artillery provided covering fire and a smoke screen. Time after time, Dvoretsky and the driver went in under fire, right under the Egyptians' noses, even in spots where only a few dozen yards separated between the paratroopers and the Egyptians. His APC picked up the paratroopers and the crewmen who escaped from the tanks that were hit, including the wounded. This near-suicide mission went on for over an hour, perhaps more. It is difficult to estimate time during a battle. Some things seem to go on forever, but in the end turn out to have taken only a few minutes, and vice versa. All the paratroopers were rescued. Some of those on the far side were extricated by the brigade's reconnaissance company. That was the end of the battle. If I remember correctly, we suffered 14 dead and more than 20 wounded. It was my first battle of the war and turned out to be the most difficult. Dvoretsky was awarded the Medal of Courage (the second-highest decoration in the IDF) for his exploits, but didn't live to receive it. He was killed a few days afterwards in the battle of the Fayid quarries on the west bank of the Canal.

After the war, I heard about the "paratroopers' heroic battle at the Chinese Farm." At first, I did not realize that this was the same battle we had been in. After all, we had fought on the Tirtur Road, and the "Chinese Farm" was the source of the missiles fired at us. It was years before I understood that the "paratroopers' heroic battle at the Chinese Farm" was the one we had fought in. I don't know what the people who referred to that pathetic skirmish as a "heroic battle" had in mind. I saw a battalion of paratroopers that foolishly got caught in a battle they weren't ready for, encountered an Egyptian force about which they knew nothing and which occupied entrenched positions, was backed by tanks, and fought with equipment far superior to their own. The battalion was chopped to bits by the much larger Egyptian force, which was well prepared, organized, and ready. The whole thing was a bloody mess, a battle to escape the trap, to be rescued, and to survive. The paratroopers hugged the ground, hoping to survive, almost out of ammunition, wounded, most of them without water. It was not a formal fighting unit under a unified command, but random groups and individual soldiers who tried to help each other, with little success. They did not stop or delay an Egyptian advance, because there never was one. The paratroopers, who had been sent out to reconnoiter and look for "tank hunters," were clueless, trapped by an organized Egyptian deployment.

"Tank hunters" is a term coined by the "staff heroes" of the IDF. There really were "tank hunters" during the Second World War. In 1973, various armies, notably those of the USSR, Egypt, and Syria, which followed Soviet military doctrine, had formal anti-tank units with effective tactics and well-trained soldiers. The IDF sent a paratroop battalion in search of legends from the Second World War. I don't know who decided to depict this command fiasco and military disgrace as a "heroic battle," or why. There isn't very much heroism in trying to get out alive and survive, though there may be some in rescuing others. Apparently—and I learned this during this war as well as in subsequent conflicts—the greater the failure, the more the system has to boast about the supposed heroism of the soldiers and glorify those who were killed, in order to avoid having to respond to the difficult question of "why did they die?" In this, the IDF is no different than other armies. Alongside instances of real heroism, the Soviets invented mythical heroes and valiant battles to raise morale and cover up their failures. In my opinion, "the paratroopers' heroic battle at the Chinese Farm" is an Israeli version of the Soviet method of propaganda and a way to cover up for incompetent commanders.

Later, I was no longer surprised by these and similar stories of "heroism." The ultimate example of the politicians' and IDF's cynical exploitation of heroism was the Second Lebanon War (2006), the greatest fiasco of all. This is not to say that there wasn't true heroism in Sinai. For example, there was Yair Tal, the son of Maj. Gen. Yisrael Tal. When we were still in courses together, he amazed us with his unparalleled dedication and honesty. In the war, although wounded, he took a tank whose chassis had been damaged and attached it to another one with a turret out of commission, and had the tank with the damaged turret tow the tank with the working turret from position to position. And, despite his injuries, he continued to direct the firefight with the Egyptians.

We kept on exchanging fire with the Egyptians until nightfall, but there was no movement by the forces on either side. After it grew dark, I suddenly saw the silhouettes of tanks of an unfamiliar model which were coming to relieve us. I identified them as M60s, acquired by the IDF only very shortly before the war, and operational only with Brigade 600. I heard a shout from one of them, "Yasha, how are you? Are you alive?"

I strained my eyes and recognized Zlotnik, my instructor in the tank commanders' course. I was happy that he too was alive; in wartime, you are constantly checking which of your friends is still alive and who isn't, every time you see them. This was one of many such encounters during the war. You run into somebody for a moment, and a short while later, you don't even know if he's still alive. I ran into Zlotnik after the war when he was serving as an NCO in the reserve battalion to which I was assigned. In the IDF, it was fairly common to leapfrog your one-time instructor and have him serve under you. It didn't affect our relationship. I always saw him as my instructor in the tank commander's course, even when I was an officer and he was still a sergeant.

We spent half the night getting organized and restocking with ammunition, and then began to move out towards the Canal. On the way, Ehud looked off to the left and burst out laughing. There was a roller bridge there, stuck in the sand. The IDF was supposed to cross the Canal on the roller bridge, but, as always happens in war, the device didn't make it to the Canal for 1001 different reasons. During the firefight with the Egyptians, when we were on the Tirtur Road, we saw the self-propelled rafts moving along a road parallel to us. We prayed that they would not be damaged. Every so often a missile would strike a vehicle moving along the road. Sometimes it was an APC, sometimes a truck, but the rafts made it through unscathed and reached the Canal.

I knew the area selected for the crossing from my tour of duty at the Canal, when my unit held the central sector. We were familiar with the entire sector, including the fort whose current code name was "Matzmed." Suddenly we saw the water, which was placid. For a few minutes, a heavy artillery bombardment brought everyone to a standstill. Then we drove onto the bridge of linked rafts and crossed the canal. Some crossed on individual rafts, because occasionally the bridge split apart. It was a strange feeling. All the tension of the day of battle had dissipated and there we were crossing the Canal—a few more minutes and our tracks would touch the Egyptian shore.

I had looked through binoculars at the Egyptian side of the Canal so many times. Suddenly, I recalled what had happened to me once while patrolling along the Canal in 1971. I was a gunner then. As we were moving a few yards from the Canal embankment, I suddenly felt the tank leap into the air and then fall back. I tensed my body and pressed against the inner wall of the turret to guard against breaking a limb. It turned out that we had rolled over a sandwich mine—three Soviet-made anti-tank mines tied together. The entire track, the torsion bars—everything was ripped off. The tank sank into the sand, but we all got away without a scratch. I climbed out of the tank and saw that one of the mines had not exploded. I bent over because I was curious to read the Russian labels. Two mines had been enough to damage the tank; had the third one exploded, we would probably have flipped over. Ours was the company commander's tank; he ordered me to take a machine gun and climb to the top of the ridge in case an Egyptian squad tried to reach us, although a ceasefire was in effect. I lay down on the ridge and looked across the Canal at the Egyptian officers and soldiers huddled together there, looking at us from their shore and waving at us. That was the first time I saw Egyptian soldiers and officers from a distance of less than a hundred yards. During the battle the day before, I had seen them differently.

When we touched down on the Egyptian side, I asked Ehud, "When were you last here?"

He thought a moment before answering, in his normal calm tone, "A few months ago, I think," as if he were talking about going to the movies. I knew that Ehud, as the commander of the General Staff Commando unit, was familiar with every strip of land in neighboring countries. Here the environment was pastoral. We began moving towards the Sweetwater Canal and prepared to park for the night. In the bivouac, everyone was told—and I repeated the order several times—to sleep under or inside the tanks. No one was to sleep on top of them. When I crawled under our tank and prepared to finally get a little sleep, shells began raining down on us. It was a volley of Katyushas, targeted square on our bivouac. I watched the shells falling one after another, like hail. In the morning, when I saw the marks left behind by the shells, I thanked God that He had protected us through the night under the tanks. In the next brigade, some of the soldiers had not obeyed the order and never woke up, or woke up because they were wounded.

We kept moving. The Egyptian forces were very thin. After we passed the Sweetwater Canal, we attacked an anti-aircraft missile base. Ehud gave the order to halt fire at the rockets. Instead, he ordered two or three tanks to damage the battery's antenna and command hut in order to paralyze it. But when we entered the base, one of the officers in the battalion gave in to his enthusiasm and fired at a SAM-2 missile anyway. The impact of the shell ignited the rocket engine and the missile began careening between the tanks, rising and falling, rising and falling. There is nothing you can do in such a situation except pray that the missile doesn't hit you. The missile flew over us, veered off in another direction, and eventually exploded somewhere without hitting anyone. Later Ehud gave the officer a good dressing-down.

Soon after we renewed our advance, Ehud surveyed the terrain with the binoculars. "Do you see that distant antenna?" he asked.

"Yes," I said.

"If we can knock it down," he said, "the entire anti-aircraft array will collapse." He requested permission from brigade HQ to shoot at the antenna. When authorization came, he instructed Moshe Sukenik (Ivri), the commander of Company B, to arrange the tanks on the slope, facing uphill, and to fire at a steep angle at a range of about four miles, which is generally too far for tanks. After a few shells and range adjustments, we saw the antenna begin to topple over. From that point on, the Egyptian anti-aircraft system in that sector was blind.

About an hour later, the Air Force showed up, and to our surprise we saw dozens of planes patrolling in the blue sky. We felt as though we were sitting in the theater, watching the planes circle overhead and some of them fall. We noticed that only Egyptian planes were falling. In the Yom Kippur War, all of the planning was futile: it was the Armored Corps on the ground that cleared the skies so the Air Force could operate. The Air Force was unable to neutralize the Egyptian anti-aircraft batteries on its own, because it was exhausted by all the strafing missions it had to conduct as a result of the high command's misreading of the situation on the ground.

One rather interesting event was associated with Moshe Dayan, then the Defense Minister. We heard that he had come to visit the front and was not far from us. Suddenly, we saw an Egyptian helicopter fly nearby and then we heard an explosion. The helicopter spun around and appeared right above us, flying very low and very slow. Two APCs that were standing next to our tank trained their machine guns on it, and I joined in with my MAG. It is an incredible feeling to see your volley with the tracers penetrate the fuselage of the helicopter—a feeling that tank gunners, who usually fire their cannon and aim at a distant target, rarely have. We saw the pilot and continued to fire until we riddled the helicopter and it landed a few dozen meters from us. At Ehud's order, our tank advanced a few meters and fired a shell that smashed the helicopter into smithereens. This helicopter had dropped canisters of napalm right next to where

Dayan was standing. Miraculously Dayan was not killed, although the Egyptian pilot had no idea whom he was attacking. A few minutes later, an Egyptian Sukhoi bomber flew low overhead and the scene was repeated. Four machine gun volleys, one of them from my MAG, pierced its fuselage. The plane began spinning out of control, before plummeting to the ground and exploding not far from us. Then, at a range of about 1,600 meters, another Egyptian helicopter landed and stayed on the ground for a few seconds. Ehud barked an order and our gunner, Galili, who was a friend of mine from our days in basic training, pulverized this helicopter with his first shell. The final score for that day, our armored battalion versus the Egyptian Air Force, was two helicopters and one Sukhoi bomber. Not bad!

We resumed our westward advance in the direction of Cairo. We began slowly and took up positions against the last outpost of the Egyptian Army between us and the capital. But then we received an order to veer off southwards towards the Geneifa Hills and the Fayid airport. Another unit replaced us. We were only sixty miles or so from Cairo.

On October 20, we were already holding the Geneifa Hills. We received an order to clean out the area around the Fayid quarries and the outskirts of the Fayid airport. After all the fighting, our battalion was left with only 12 of the 23 tanks it had started with. So we attacked the Fayid quarries that day with 12 tanks and the mechanized infantry. Despite the reports we had received that the Egyptians were running away, they fought a stubborn rearguard action. On the western bank of the Canal, the fighting was much easier than it had been on the eastern side. The Egyptians had no military order whatsoever. There were no large formations, only isolated units no larger than a battalion, with no artillery support or organized command or control. Nor did we encounter any anti-tank missiles or organized anti-tank units on the western bank. There were only squads with RPGs, so the armor felt much more secure. Nevertheless, the Egyptian infantry, commando units, and occasional tank put up the fiercest resistance they could. We suffered losses and had to fight for every mile we advanced.

During the battle in the Fayid quarries, Dvoretsky's mechanized infantry and APCs advanced on our left and descended to Guy Spring, where the ridge hid them from view. Suddenly we heard a horrible volley of machinegun fire. Hundreds of tracer bullets were flying from the direction of both the APC and the Egyptians, but we couldn't see what was going on. We advanced, because the Egyptian lines were broken. It was already evening by the time we established a new line and the battle ended. We kept trying to find out what had happened to Dvoretsky's APC, but no one knew. It didn't show up at the rendezvous and didn't respond to radio calls. The battalion moved into its overnight bivouac and sank into the routine of getting organized, restocking ammunition, servicing the guns and vehicles, and taking care of our personal needs. Suddenly, Ehud came up to me and asked for more hand grenades. I had mounted a full crate of grenades on the left side of the turret and refilled it every morning, because over the course of the day it would empty out as I hurled grenades at the enemy. I didn't understand why he needed grenades in the bivouac. "I'm going to look for the APC," Ehud told me quietly, as though anticipating my question. "And I'm going alone—no one is coming with me."

Many times since then, I have gone back and thought about this incident. Ehud set off to do something that was totally insane. A battalion commander was going off by himself at night, in search of an APC that might have been damaged? But I understood him. He had an unusually strong sense of responsibility for the lives of his men. He could not accept a situation in which their fate was unknown. That is how he understood his role as their commander. So, against all military logic, he decided to go look for them. His was a different kind of logic, the logic of a higher morality and of humanity at its best. To this day, I am still tremendously impressed by the morality that Ehud Barak demonstrated then. I will always admire him for his brave act in the Fayid quarries, which should serve as a model for every IDF officer and commander. I remember the darkness and watching his figure fade into the distance, with a radio set on his back. Suddenly, we received a message from the brigade's reconnaissance company to the effect that Dvoretsky's APC had been hit and destroyed and was at such and such a location. We called Ehud back immediately. He was very quiet and sad, just as he had been on the day that Yishai Yizhar, his good friend, was killed on the Tirtur Road. When the battle was over, Ehud took me aside and asked for full details of Yishai's death. He asked me several times if I remembered the exact place where we had left the body. The next day, after the IDF had established control there, he personally verified that Yishai's body had been found and evacuated to the rear. After the war, when I visited all the families of the fallen members of the battalion and gave them maps with the locations of the deaths of their loved ones, Ehud said, "I'll go to Yishai's family myself. I have to do it."

It was now October 22. We formed up at a short distance from the Bitter Lake, facing south towards the Suez City–Cairo road. Somewhat earlier, in one of the battles on the Geneifa Hills, I got a lesson in the effectiveness of the Air Force. We climbed one of the hills and were surprised to see a battery of Egyptian cannons—four of them, Soviet-made D-30s, I think, about two miles away—a regular battery deployed according to the book. Ehud ordered us to halt and wait. I asked why we didn't destroy the guns. After all, a tank squadron could do so in a few minutes. Ehud responded that, according to his orders, this was a job for the Air Force. I got down from the tank, which was on the far slope, and climbed to the top of the ridge with binoculars to wait for the Air Force to put on a show. Soon four Skyhawks appeared, swooped low over the Egyptian artillery, and missed. The foursome reappeared half an hour later, swooped down, and missed again. The Egyptians ran into their trenches every time, but when the sortie was over, they left the trenches and resumed firing. The Skyhawks attacked the battery several times over a period of almost

two hours and never did hit the target. In the end, a truck arrived
and the Egyptian soldiers clambered aboard and decamped, leaving
behind the unscathed battery, with stacks of shells neatly arranged
behind the cannons. That was when I understood that the Air Force
is wonderful—but not all the time and not in every situation. In this
instance, a few shells lobbed over there by two or three tanks would
have sufficed to complete the mission.

Another incident in the Geneifa Hills is engraved in my memory.
While we were advancing, I saw that the tank to our left was moving
up a hillock and taking a position at an angle that was totally against
the rules, with its belly facing the enemy. Sure enough, it was hit by
shells within a few seconds and began emitting a cloud of grey and
black smoke. We began counting the crewmen who jumped out and
ran away from it, apparently wounded: one soldier, two, three, four.
A few dozen yards from the tank, the medics spread out and began
treating them. The engine of the damaged tank was still running,
and the thought passed through my mind that it might be possible
to shut it down and tow the tank away. On second thought, I decided
that the idea was crazy—but then Ehud told me, "Go on, shut down
the engine." Without a word, I jumped from our tank. I asked Ehud
to hand me a fire extinguisher, because I wasn't sure whether the
extinguishers in the burning tank were functional. He passed me
one and I began running towards the tank. I prayed that the tank
would explode now, before I got to it, because that would be my
only chance to survive—but the tank didn't explode. I reached it
and went around the back. The whole time, the engine was running
and smoke kept rising from the turret. I decided to climb on from
the side. A tank crewman never climbs up the side of a tank, only
from the front. But the front was facing the Egyptians. I pressed
myself against the chassis and scurried up, expecting the explosion
any second. I pressed close to the tank so the Egyptians wouldn't
see me and straightened up slightly to look into turret. The flames
were licking at the ammunition and instruments and I felt a wave

of heat on my face. I stuck the extinguisher inside and aimed at the burning shells. As I did this, I glanced in the direction of the Egyptian positions. I saw an anti-tank position with one or two guns, and Egyptian soldiers standing there and looking at the tank. I couldn't understand why they didn't fire another shell. The standing orders are that whenever you fire at a tank or from a tank, you should fire again after the first hit to make sure you destroy the target.

In the meantime, I pushed my way inside the burning turret. I emptied my extinguisher onto the flames, and then the tank's own extinguisher, and the fire went out. For a moment, I had the thought that I might be able to operate the cannon manually even if the hydraulic system wasn't working. But I realized almost immediately that the tank was at a footing that made it impossible to lower the cannon far enough. The Egyptian guns were too low and the tank was too high. To move the damaged tank and shoot, as a one-man crew, was impossible. So I gave up the idea of destroying the anti-tank battery. It was also impossible to move to the driver's seat from the turret. I had no choice but to leave the turret and climb into the driver's seat from the front of the tank, in full view of the Egyptians. I rolled over the top of the tank and jumped into the driver's seat, worried that they might come to their senses and fire again. When I sat down in the driver's seat, I released the brake in a fraction of a second, put the tank in gear, and stepped on the gas pedal. The tank jerked backwards at a frightening speed. I tried to orient myself by memory, because I couldn't see where I was going and I knew that behind me there were tanks and medics treating the wounded. Somehow, I estimated how far I could pass and where I could go. I drove about twenty yards down from the top of the hill and brought the tank to a halt. I shut off the engine and left the tank with a sense of relief. I had done it this time. I don't think the risk was necessary, but an order is an order even if you don't agree with it. The whole incident lasted much less time than it takes to tell or write about it.

I went over to the wounded crewmen. We all knew each other from the tank commander's course and from the professional course. I turned to one of them and told him, "You're lucky you're wounded, because you deserve a beating!"

"Why?" he replied in astonishment.

"Didn't I transmit a message over the radio before the attack, repeating the order to roll down your sleeves?! Look at yourself—what have you done to your arms?"

The tank's hydraulic system had been hit and the oil inside caught fire immediately. His arms, which should have been covered by the sleeves of his coverall, were grey and scorched, with bits of skin dangling off. I wished him a speedy recovery and sped back to my tank.

Ehud smiled. "What was with that crazy driving backwards? You almost killed us all." I knew he was joking.

Thus ended another day of combat in the Geneifa Hills.

On October 22, we knew that a ceasefire was about to take effect. We spent half a day getting organized; in late afternoon, we were ordered to move out towards a large Egyptian base. We entered it around six pm, just when the ceasefire went into effect, and saw two Egyptian commandos standing by the fence. Ehud ordered us to hold our fire and turned to me: "Go tell them to get the hell out of here, there's a ceasefire."

I left my Uzi in the tank and walked towards the Egyptians without a weapon. They looked at me. I looked at them. The two officers were about my age, and we even had the same build. They stood about a yard from me, with their fingers on the trigger of their guns. It was the first time I had seen the enemy from up close. I told them in Hebrew to get out of there, and then switched to English. When I saw they understood English, I told them that there was a ceasefire and if they left we wouldn't shoot at them, because the fighting had ended. They smiled. Suddenly the officer who had ignited the missile on the anti-tank base showed up in his tank—for some reason he had been delayed in reaching the Egyptian base. Without waiting to find out what the situation was, he fired a volley from the machine gun in our direction. The Egyptians tensed. I looked into their eyes and out the corner of my eye at their fingers on the triggers of their Kalashnikovs. I was unarmed. But the tank didn't fire again. The Egyptians smiled, saluted, and turned to leave. I saluted them, breathed a sigh of relief, and returned to my tank.

The ceasefire went into effect at six o'clock on the evening of October 22, but beyond the announcement that the ceasefire had begun, we didn't see many changes. We set up our overnight bivouac. It was the first night that we had to deal with many prisoners, who were flowing in all the time. We processed them as quickly as possible and locked them in a stockade. Those who required medical care were sent to the battalion's medical aid station for treatment by our physicians and medical staff before being transferred to the POW stockade.

The next day, we stayed put until 2 pm. We then received an order to move south and cut off the Suez City–Cairo road, completing the encirclement of the Third Army. The brigade commander asked Ehud, who knew the area better than anyone else, to place his battalion at the head of the brigade and the division. We launched a classic armored charge: More than a hundred tanks sped forward at full throttle, while IDF planes flew low from time to time, en route to attacks just ahead of us. They dropped their bombs very close to our tanks, but fortunately none of them hit us. Egyptian formations— soldiers, trucks, tanks, and APCs—scattered in every direction. Our tanks dashed madly forward. Nothing can compare with the beauty and power of an armored division on the move. I was as excited and happy as I had been when I received my Soviet exit visa. I was proud that this was my army, my country's army, that we were winning this cursed war, and that I had played a part in that victory.

We advanced towards the Cairo–Suez road. Through my binoculars, I could make out cars driving along it. Some of them made it through safely; others did not. I thought of a book by Konstantin Simonov, *The Living and the Dead,* in which he described the 1941 Soviet retreat and the bridge that some of the soldiers managed to cross. The bridge,

Simonov wrote, divided the soldiers into the living and the dead. Those who crossed the bridge did not know that they were staying alive; and those which did not make it across may not have known it yet, but they were already dead. When I saw the cars fleeing from Suez City as we approached the highway, I could predict which would have time to escape us and which would not, and thought how their drivers and passengers still didn't know that the next few minutes would determine which of them would live and which would die.

We took up a position along the road, with Suez City just east of us, and the Canal a few kilometers away to our left. The highway leading west, towards Cairo, was empty. Prewar intelligence surveys had made me quite familiar with the Egyptian Army and its defensive formations. I knew that only one brigade-size armored force, the Armored Corps School on the outskirts of Cairo, stood between us and the city, and that it had yet to take part in the fighting. Only this armored brigade separated three IDF divisions and the Egyptian capital. In military terms, it would not have been a problem for an armored division to cover this distance in a few hours and go on the attack. But our orders were to move south and cut off Suez City, and within two hours we took up positions three kilometers southwest of the town, thereby completing the encirclement of the Third Army. Two hours later, after dark, Arye Keren's brigade passed by with all its lights on, racing down the road towards Adabiya Bay. We didn't know what was going on with the Egyptian Second Army, but in our sector, at least, the mission we been assigned on October 14 had been carried out.

That night, we ran into the problem of hundreds of Egyptian POWs, most of them soldiers with a few officers mixed in, primarily from administrative and support units. Almost all the combat troops were on the eastern side of the canal. We were not equipped to deal with so many prisoners, so we told them they were free to go in the direction of Cairo, but they refused. After we disarmed them, we concentrated them on the side and told them to sit down, eat, and go to sleep. The night was cold. We gave them blankets and food. In the morning, I was stunned at what I saw. A sea of khaki—the color of Egyptian uniforms—engulfed the tanks and the APCs. There were at least as many Egyptian soldiers there as we had in our battalion, and at first sight it seemed like a utopian idyll: Egyptian POWs and the crews of the Israeli APCs and tanks were making breakfast together, opening tinned rations and lighting fires. Our shared breakfast was almost like a picnic. The Egyptians even volunteered to hand out the food and wash the dishes.

Ehud came back from brigade HQ. "We're going into the city," he announced.

"What idiot gave that order?" was my instinctive and blunt reply.

"It's an order. We're going in."

Our battalion led the assault. We left our prisoners in our staging area, with K rations and blankets, and told them that whoever wanted to could start walking towards Cairo. When we came back that night, after a day of fighting, all the Egyptians were sitting there waiting for us. They were even ready to help service our tanks and APCs and join in preparing supper. It took some time for us to get rid of them and transfer them to those whose job was to handle POWs. That first day and night outside Suez City were truly surreal.

Before we entered the town, I was overcome by fear to an extent I had never felt throughout the war. I was never afraid during battles. When you are carrying out your mission, you are focused and work like a machine. Even when I saw death in front of my eyes, I stayed calm. The fear came at night, after the tanks were parked, after we turned off the engines. When all the organizational details of the battalion had been completed, after we finished all of our tasks, complied with our orders and serviced our vehicles and weapons, and we had a few hours to rest or sleep—that's when the fear came on suddenly. That's when you recall the day you just went through, those moments when you felt death so close and smelled its chilly odor, the faces of your friends who perished, your last meeting with them a few hours or minutes before they died; or, what was more common with tanks, when you heard the reports and the codenames on the radio and remember the living comrades you had seen and spoken with only a few minutes or hours or months before. That's when the fear overpowers you and won't let go.

The fear terrorizes you again in the morning. You wake up, and your first thought is whether this is the last day of your life: Will you be among the living or the wounded by nightfall? Will you have at least one more morning? Instinctively, you look at your arms and legs, and you can't help wondering whether they will still be with you at the end of the day. The fear and tension remain, at least among tank crewmen, until the order comes—"Engines on!"—and the fear evaporates within a moment. Once you hear the order "Move out," you feel how this metal monster moves and shudders, and you are part of the war machine. You think, you function as you've been drilled to do throughout your military service. There is no fear, but there is also no mercy. Only anger, sometimes rage. When you see a friend killed, you are seized by an animal-like fury and desire for revenge. That's how I felt after Yishai died in my arms. I fell upon the machine gun and emptied three or four belts, without feeling anything. A MAG shoots much better than an 0.3, and when I saw Egyptian soldiers falling, mowed down by my volleys, I didn't feel anything except for anger and primitive lust for revenge.

During the battles on the eastern bank of the Canal, when we discovered the intensity of the anti-tank fire and heard the Saggers flying over our heads, what we felt wasn't fear but a sort of mechanical, technical response—tension, awareness of the danger. But on the western side of the Canal, there was no serious resistance, no missiles or substantial anti-tank fire. The main danger came from RPGs, mainly in the agricultural buffer zone where there was dense vegetation. We tried to keep our distance from it or send paratroopers or infantry to sweep the area before we moved in. The RPGs had a maximum range of 220 to 330 yards, so the sense of danger was nowhere near that on the eastern bank. But when we went into Suez City, all the tension and fear I had felt in the battle on the Tirtur Road returned.

A long, snakelike line of tanks crawled slowly down a narrow street in the town. There were buildings on the left side and the long fence of a refinery to the right. We were on edge. When we asked brigade intelligence what Egyptian forces were in the city, they answered that they weren't really sure. They thought there were only a few stragglers from units that had disintegrated, perhaps a few commandos, but they didn't expect we would encounter any organized and serious resistance. We advanced slowly to the central square. Along the way, there were one- and two-story buildings on one side of the street, and half-empty lots and a factory on the other side. This was still reasonable. As we moved, we aimed our cannons and machine guns at the buildings, moving from window to window and from entrance to entrance. After the square, though, we were on narrow streets with buildings that rose to five, six, or seven stories. For tanks, that was a suicide mission, because there was no way that we could protect ourselves. You can't point the cannon or machine guns at a steep enough angle, so attackers on the upper stories have a free hand against you. We received an order to stop in the square. We saw almost no Egyptians. Only here and there at the far end of the street did we glimpse a figure moving quickly and disappearing. We could have cut the tension with a knife.

When we halted in the square, Nachum Zaken's battalion, part of the next brigade, passed by and entered a narrow street lined with five-story buildings on both sides. Soon we heard machine gun fire and grenade explosions, and screams and shouts over the radio. As we were tuned to the same frequency as Zaken's battalion, we heard the orders and the reports of casualties. After things quieted down somewhat, we moved our tank down the street and reached Zaken's. He was pale, in shock, totally drained. He looked at Ehud and me with a pained and stunned expression. Zaken had been the deputy commander of Battalion 79 when Ehud was a company commander and I was taking the squad/platoon/company commander course. In a voice choked with tears he said, "What have they done to me?! I've lost all my tank commanders. They threw grenades and shot from above. Almost everyone who was standing in a turret was killed."

Later that day, Zaken's battalion withdrew from the street and we saw paratroopers entering the town. At the end of the day, we received an order to pull out of the city and bivouac outside it. We took the same route we had used coming in that morning. We were tense, tired, and glad to be alive. I couldn't understand the sense of our operation that day—we had penetrated the city, fired a few rounds here and there, and left, and tomorrow we would have to do it all over again, if the order came. Why? What for?

Sure enough, the same story was repeated the next day. We advanced to the city square once again. But this time, the assault force that passed us was made up of paratroopers rather than tanks. I remember half-tracks with the paratroopers passing by us, paratroopers waving to us and disappearing into the narrow streets of Suez. After half an hour, I heard horrifying bursts of firing and frequent explosions, but couldn't see anything because the fighting was on streets far away from us. All of a sudden everything fell silent—blood-curdling silence. The half-tracks appeared, dashing madly back. When they passed us, we were dumbfounded. They all looked the same—a horrible sight. A driver or someone sitting in the driver's seat, and behind him a sea of blood, body parts, living soldiers, dead soldiers, wounded soldiers. It had been a massacre. The half-tracks were open on top, and the Egyptians had simply tossed grenades into them, where they exploded among the soldiers, while snipers posted on the top floor of the buildings picked them off with their Kalashnikovs or machine guns. More than 70 soldiers were killed in the Battle of Suez. I don't know what the point was of entering the town after it was encircled. We never gained control of Suez City. We did not advance, at least not in our sector, beyond the square we had reached on the first day. When the ceasefire went into effect, it turned out that the city was swarming with Egyptian commandos. We saw them. Just a few yards from our tank, I saw dozens of officers and hundreds of Egyptian soldiers, every one of them armed with a Kalashnikov, against our overmatched Uzis and carbines.

After the second day of the fighting in Suez City, we bivouacked inside the town. We found a spot next to the stadium that was protected on all sides. Even so, we were afraid to sleep, because the Egyptian commandos were all around us. They had no problem sneaking up on the tanks in the darkness, because unlike us, they were properly equipped with night-vision equipment. We were dreadfully short of binoculars and didn't even dream of night-vision equipment. The next day we went back to our position at the square. I remember there were Egyptian anti-tank squads with RPGs about twenty yards away, in the entrances of buildings. Our tank held its ground and aimed its cannon at the entrance, just in case. When an Egyptian soldier took a position and pointed an RPG at our tank, Ehud gave the order to fire. For the first time, I saw what happens to a man when he is hit by a tank shell. We were very close, and the result was visible in all its gruesome horror.

As soon as the ceasefire went into effect, Ehud asked me to go to the refinery and treat the Egyptian civilians who had taken refuge there during the fighting. I found around 100 panic-stricken people— men, women, and a few children—sitting there. I picked out a few who had a look of authority and asked them to help me organize the people for evacuation. Accompanied by two of our soldiers, I led them to the checkpoint in the square where we had been spending so much time. Egyptian commando officers were standing on the far side. I called one of them over and told him in English, "These are your people. We are passing them over to your side. Take them." The Egyptian started to argue, but I told him that the issue was not up for discussion. I gave our soldiers an order to move and told the civilians, "Go through. From now on your soldiers will take care of you." I did not see joy among the Egyptians, neither the soldiers nor the civilians. They all looked tired and drained. Most of the civilians looked apathetic and resigned to their fate, mixed with a fear of soldiers, both Israeli and Egyptian. Looking at these civilians, I felt ashamed and even angry at myself. Human beings, civilians, terrified to death, afraid to raise their eyes. Women and girls trembling. The thought of my mother, wife, and sister in this situation drove me crazy. My entire being revolted that I was carrying a weapon and leading them through their own city, their lives dependent on me. I didn't want to be there. I have never spoken about this with anyone, but I will never forget that dreadful feeling.

That was how the war ended for me, on Oct. 25, three days after the ceasefire—a ceasefire that none of our commanders and political leaders had intended to observe until the goals they thought so important had been achieved, so important that the lives of dozens of soldiers could be sacrificed. After the war, when I visited the parents of the soldiers in our battalion who fell in Suez City, I could not find the words to explain why their loved ones had fallen after the ceasefire.

The next morning I decided to shave. I hadn't shaved throughout the war—I don't know why. Now I shaved and took a makeshift shower with cold water from a jerrycan. I washed off all the dirt and sweat that had caked on during the days of the battle. I placed the coveralls I had worn the whole time, along with the lieutenant's bars pinned to them, with my things. I put on a clean set of coveralls with fresh insignia, which I took out of my bag. The dirty coveralls were stained all over with brown—the clotted blood of Yishai Yizhar, who died in my arms. For the first two days, soldiers who saw me had been taken aback, because they thought it was my blood. I took the insignia stained with Yishai's blood home as a memento. The war wounds scarred over and could never be washed away; the emotions stirred in me by the war have not dimmed with time. They are still with me. As the years pass, they grow even deeper.

Chapter 19

Just when we started taking showers and getting dressed, a half-track with multiple antennas suddenly appeared. I identified them as telephone antennas. The half-track halted alongside us and the soldiers inside announced that they had been given an order to let us make a phone call to our loved ones. In the 1970s, of course, there were no cell phones; in Israel, there weren't even landlines in every home. Because it was 7:30 in the morning, I decided to wait until nine and catch my wife Idit at work; we didn't have a phone in our apartment. At 9:05 I went to the phone and dialed her office. When she answered, I said "Good morning." There was silence on the other end of the line. Then, after a few seconds, she asked in a trembling voice where I was calling from. I said in Russian that I was far away, by the Red Sea. She asked, in a voice full of fear, hope, and concern, "Are you hurt?" "No," I said.

But Idit was not convinced. "Why can I hear you so well? Are you in a hospital nearby?"

I tried to persuade her that everything was fine, that I was not wounded and that I was with my unit, which was stationed very far away. She didn't really believe me, but at least it was clear to her that I was alive.

Idit and everyone left behind at home were fighting a war of their own, one we soldiers at the front were unaware of, the fight to protect our children and ourselves from the realities of the situation. My wife, a young woman, the only daughter of a Jewish family from Czernowitz, who had made *aliyah* in the summer of 1969, could never have imagined what an oddball she was marrying and what experiences and problems awaited her in her life with the guy who had run into her at the Technion. When we talked about marriage, I told her that if she married me, I would promise her two things: That she would have a much more difficult life with me than anything she possibly could imagine, but that it would also be more interesting and fascinating than she could imagine. She followed me blindly, putting her full trust in me. She did not expect difficulties of this kind. In fact, no one really expected them. But she behaved like a real woman of valor, particularly during the war.

A few minutes before we began to move out towards Sinai, at the beginning of the war, I called her and told her that everything was fine and that she could call Armored Corps headquarters, the place where she had dropped me off. If I was busy, there might be times when she couldn't reach me, but she could leave a message with the secretaries. I gave her the phone number of the operations office at the Armored Corps HQ. Then I called the secretaries and asked them to tell my wife, if she called, that I was nearby and too busy to return her call, but that everything was fine. I asked them not to tell her that I had gone down to Sinai. This worked for three days. On the third day, the young secretary with whom I had spoken didn't cover the receiver with her hand, and my wife overheard her asking one of her coworkers, "It's Yasha's wife again—what should I tell her? Is he even alive? Where is he?" When she heard this, my wife realized that everything she had been told in the past few days were just soothing words. She hung up and never phoned again.

Rumors were spreading throughout the country, as usual, and she heard them too. There were reports that I had been captured—some said by the Egyptians and some said by the Syrians. But she kept these tales to herself and did her best to live with the thought that her husband was a prisoner of war. She worked her connections and called Lily, Ariel Sharon's wife. We were acquaintances—they came to our wedding and we had been at their home several times. Idit asked Lily to ask Ariel where I was or what was going on with me. A day later, Lily called back and told her that I was on the Southern Front, not in Arik's division but in Bren's, and that as of yesterday I was alive and well. This was both a calming and scary way to put it. One of my wife's friends at work told her that her boyfriend, who had been wounded, had said he had seen me. My wife asked where the boyfriend was hospitalized and was told he was in the military section of Ichilov Hospital in Tel Aviv. Idit went there, but they wouldn't let her in. So she went to the Defense Ministry where she worked, switched clothes with one of the female soldiers, and walked into Ichilov as a soldier. She found the wounded boyfriend who told her that he had bumped into me at such and such a place the week before, just when the fighting had started and my battalion went into action. That was the last time that he had seen me.

From then on, she knew nothing of my fate until my phone call from Suez, aside from the fact that I was on the front lines. That same afternoon, we were told that soldiers could receive twenty-four hour furloughs, with preference given to those who were married and had children. Because I fit that definition, I was among the first to leave. I made my way to Fayid, where the airfield was back in operation. It was very chaotic there, and with great difficulty I managed to board the last Hercules of the day. We flew low over the Bitter Lake for fear of anti-aircraft missiles. We climbed steeply when we were above Sinai and the plane landed in Lod half an hour later. I hitchhiked to the Defense Ministry complex in central Tel Aviv and got there as soon as I could. The guards knew me because I had often come to visit my wife, but they told me to leave my gun behind. I was carrying an Uzi and a pistol I had taken from one of the captives. It was a nice pistol, an Egyptian-made Helwan. I refused to leave my weapons there and decided to wait for my wife at the gate. I saw her from a distance walking out the door of the Defense Ministry building with a security officer. The security officer wasn't sure who had come to see her, because all he had been told was that an officer with a gun had arrived. He was worried there might be bad news and wanted to be nearby if that was the case. When he saw me, he breathed a sigh of relief, waved goodbye, and walked off.

From Tel Aviv we traveled to the ulpan in Haifa to see my parents. I also had time to see my brother and sister, who were going through difficulties of their own. My mother recalled the terrible war she had endured back in Russia. She remembered her brother, the tank crewman, who had been critically wounded and whom she had been able to visit in the military hospital before his death. My father, too, had memories of World War II. He thought about how he had bumped into his father then, quite by accident, two soldiers traveling on two different trains. It was the last time he saw his father, who was killed a few months later.

When I returned to my battalion, it was no longer in Suez City. The night I left for my furlough the battalion was ordered to redeploy on the eastern bank of the Canal and take up a position opposite the Egyptian Third Army, in case of a decision to annihilate it.

Right after the war, Ehud asked me if the battle on Tirtur Road was fresh in my memory. "Yes," I said. From the battalion commander's tank, you have a good view of the battlefield, and when you are right next to him you have a much better understanding of what's going on. Almost a third of our tanks were knocked out in that battle, and many of the officers who fought in it were killed or wounded before the war was over.

"Some fellows came from the Morgue and Identification Unit," he said. "They want to locate the bodies of crewmen and try to identify them. Go find our damaged tanks and help them."

I wasn't prepared for what I was in for. I went back to the battlefield, which looked very different than before. I realized that everything looks different from a tank in combat, nothing like what you see when riding in a jeep. I walked among the damaged tanks and identified the three that were ours—we had managed to evacuate all the others under fire. But there was a problem we had not expected. I had to remember every tank and its number. The tanks were burned and one had even blown up. The identifying numbers painted on them had been consumed in the flames. When I saw the exploded tank, I remembered the burning tank I had jumped into and put out the fire. "Look what you escaped," I told myself. "You were lucky."

I really was lucky. After the war, I decided that I was living on borrowed time. Every day, every minute, every year that I was alive was a gift that I had received. I decided that I should approach life in a different way and express my thanks that I was still alive. And when my life would come to an end, I wanted to have time to say a thank you that I had been privileged to live longer than my friends.

When we got to our tanks, I had one of the worst experiences of my life. I slipped into a burned-out tank and saw several charred objects. I remember that one was a yellow lump that looked like a shapeless piece of modeling clay. When I moved it, the soldier from the Morgue Unit gave me a strange look.

"Be careful," he said, "that's a human being you're holding in your hand."

All that was left of a man who had been burned up in the tank was a yellow mass that looked rather like a frozen lump of clay and weighed only two or three pounds. He asked me if I remembered who sat in this seat in the tank. The problem was that our battalion had been pieced together after the fighting began, made up of a motley group of soldiers and officers, most of whom had flown back from abroad at the start of the war and were assigned to crews at the last minute. Because no exact records were kept of who sat where in which tank or of changes in crews, it was an excruciating task to identify these yellow lumps we found in the burned-out tank, lumps that had once been soldiers. I did my best to remember the number of the tank, who the tank commander was, which of the crewmen I could remember. But this feeling that I was scraping my friends off the charred wall of the tank deck did not leave me. I never got over it and it has shaped my feelings about war ever since.

We left the tanks with plastic bags containing body parts, with notes giving details I'd written regarding the location of the tank and where the body parts had been found. In some of the tanks, we had found dog tags, fragments of dog tags, or some other signs that may have been connected with the men who had fought and died in these tanks. On the way back to the jeep, I suddenly noticed that barbed wire had been strung around the area, with triangular signs hanging from it reading, "Warning! Minefield." I smiled wanly. I had already run over anti-tank mines, and death had passed me by on this very spot.

The war was a difficult time for me, but I was in for an even more difficult period afterwards. I came up with the idea of giving every bereaved family a map indicating the place where their son or husband had fallen, a short description of the circumstances of his death, and a dedication by the battalion. I went to see every family that had lost a loved one, except for Yishai Yizhar's, as Ehud had requested, and these visits were much harder to bear than anything I had experienced in combat.

The most difficult visit of all, which left me scarred for the rest of my life, was to the parents of the battalion doctor, Dr. Oded Ben-Dror. I didn't know him and had seen him for only a brief moment while the battalion was getting organized. In the first battle on the Tirtur Road, he was killed by an Egyptian shell while treating the wounded. Two medics who were working with him were also killed. I went to see his parents, who lived in a small apartment in Ramat Gan or Givatayim. I found two people who seemed very old and quiet. There were photos of Oded on the lowboy in the living room. We sat down and talked. The parents, who were originally from Poland, were Holocaust survivors. They survived Auschwitz and met after the war in the Jewish State, their new country. They emerged from the inferno of Europe battered, broken, and destroyed, and began a new life and family in their new country. A son was born to them, their only child. He had completed his medical training before the war and started work as a pediatrician at Tel Hashomer Hospital. A doctor for a son—every Jewish mother's dream, but now he was gone. After the Holocaust, cruel fate had given them a respite of almost thirty years, until it returned to deal its final blow, leaving their life devoid of any meaning or goal. I stared at these two people with their dimmed look, all their vitality drained from them. They had no one and nothing to live for, no hope, only the immense pain that never left them for a moment.

In their presence, I felt what I felt in every home I visited—mortification that I was alive. Parents always wanted to hear every detail about how their son was killed, how he behaved in his last moments. I told them what they wanted to hear, and, I must confess, not always the whole truth. I couldn't tell parents that their son had been killed by a stray IDF shell—a not-unknown occurrence. I almost always said that death had come quickly and that their son had conducted himself heroically, like a soldier. I don't know whether they believed me or not, but my words seemed to ease their pain. In their sad looks, I detected a question that hung heavily in the air, even if they were not aware of it and would never utter it: "Why he and not you? How could it be that in the same battle, one dies and another lives?" I have no answer, only an abiding sense of guilt for being alive.

Chapter 20

I emerged from the war a changed man. That war has never left me. I remember almost every battle, every action. While still in the army and later after I joined Nativ, I kept going back, time and again, to analyze what had happened. Every time I did so on the basis of new information and new experiences. This happened with particular intensity when I was studying at the National Security College, again during the first Lebanon War, and even more so the Second Lebanon War, the most wretched and botched of all Israel's armed conflicts.

When I looked back at the war and how it was conducted, I reached several unpleasant conclusions. I am used to confronting difficult conclusions, however unpalatable, and not running away from them. There is nothing worse than self-delusion, which is a recipe for failure; the truth begins when a person refuses to deceive himself. I resolved that I would never lie and have held firm to this decision my entire life. When I think about the Yom Kippur War, I ask myself whether it was necessary. Could it have been prevented? Were the 2,800 deaths necessary? The Agranat Commission didn't address this question; the Israeli public did not give it a deep enough look. Preventing war is not the Israeli public's strong point. We have never prevented any unnecessary war. Even though we have ostensibly had our fill of fighting and have supposedly learned the lessons of the past, we have never managed to avert all the unnecessary wars, one after another. Except for the War for Independence, every other Israeli war could have been avoided. The public has been dragged along like sheep, accompanied by hysterical cries in support of the war, without understanding, or even making an effort to understand what was happening. And when the fiasco and the bereavement wake us up, we finally begin to understand something. That's when the shock and astonishment take hold and paralyze us, leaving us apathetic.

The outcome of the Yom Kippur War brought us to a political situation we could have achieved without the war. The worst is that the problems that brought about the Yom Kippur War, with all of its failures and consequences, were not specific to a particular politician, but to the system as a whole—on both the political and military sides. I remember the campaign posters that were being displayed right before the war, like "Our situation has never been better" and "You can trust us." Our national leaders echoed the statement that our situation was stable and we could maintain the status quo for years to come. If we measure the Israeli position before the war against the peace treaty with Egypt signed only six years afterwards, the pain and anger merely increase. At the time, I didn't yet see the matter with such clarity. I hoped that had there been a different government, the outcome would have been better. It was only the peace treaty with Egypt and the (first) Lebanon War that brought me to my senses and gave me a deeper perspective on the problem.

Worse still is that compounding the failure of the political echelon, the military system failed as well, despite the incomplete victory on the battlefield. The war did not reveal anything new that the IDF and Military Intelligence had not known about the Egyptian and Syrian armies. But the General Staff, the Intelligence Corps, and the IDF as a whole did not understand the information they possessed. The IDF did not use this information to prepare its organization, tactics, and strategy. The primary failure of the Intelligence Corps was not towards the entire IDF, but towards itself. Military Intelligence is not authorized to make the final assessment about the likelihood of war.

It is the political leader or commander who receives the assessments supplied by the Intelligence Corps and draws operative conclusions based on those assessments. The Egyptian Army did not know for certain that it was going to war until the order was passed down to it. Only one person knew—the president of Egypt—and even he was not positive when he gave the order to attack. Sadat's vacillation could easily have ended with a decision to shelve the order to cross the Canal. The Egyptian General Staff did not want a war; the Egyptian armed forces were aware that they were weaker than the IDF.

Prime Minister Golda Meir believed that the IDF would keep its promises, and the IDF disappointed. Neither the Air Force nor the ground forces nor the Southern and Northern commands kept their promises. Everybody laid the blame on the Intelligence Corps. But if the Intelligence Corps had issued an alert that war would break out on October 6, would it have made any difference? Would we have prevented the Egyptians from crossing the Canal? Would more reinforcements have been sent up to the Golan Heights before the fighting broke out? After all, the General Staff was sure that the regular IDF units, at the balance of forces it had set, was capable of holding the Egyptian and Syrian armies at the 1967 lines for at least 48 hours.

Ehud Barak once told me that before the war, the General Staff had debated whether to set up a new armored division or a Phantom squadron. The decision was for the warplanes. But one squadron more or less had no impact on the Yom Kippur War. By contrast, if the IDF had had another armored division, everything would have looked completely different, on both the Northern and Southern fronts. That was the effect of the General Staff's judgment about which forces Israel needed. It is sad and worrisome that more than thirty years later, the IDF continues to give exaggerated preference to the Air Force, repeating the same mistake and forcing us all to pay the price.

The IDF had a full order of battle in Sinai which was deployed according to plan, but it did not hold up. The order of battle on the Golan Heights at least matched the plan. Shortly before the war, Moshe Dayan decided to overrule other opinions and dispatch the 7th Brigade to the Golan. But despite the reinforcements and the heroic resistance by IDF soldiers, there was no Israeli military force left between the Syrian tanks and the Jezreel Valley after the first day of fighting. Thus, the Intelligence Corps was not to blame that Syria captured almost the entire Golan Heights, including the division headquarters. The blame rests on the high command, which failed in its assessment of the capabilities of both the enemy and our own forces, even at the most basic level of a reasonable balance of forces. The forces deployed against the Egyptian and Syrian armies were too small to prevent them from crossing the Canal and capturing the Golan Heights.

The significance of the wide-open spaces of Sinai is the protection this depth affords Israel. As Moshe Dayan put it, "There are no Kibbutz Deganyas in Sinai." So why did the IDF contest every foot in Sinai as if it was defending Deganya or Tel Aviv? The main benefit of the Sinai Peninsula—the strategic depth, the room to maneuver and absorb an attack—was not fully exploited in this war. Instead of maneuvering forces and taking advantage of the domains where we were superior to the Egyptians, we insisted on stubborn defense of every foot in the Canal region. The defense plans that were drawn up were unprofessional. Not only that, despite all the self-sacrifice and valor of our soldiers, their implementation was pathetic and miserable. The IDF demonstrated no strategic capability, only a lack of professionalism even at the tactical level. All the talk about an existential danger to the State of Israel was baseless. The Egyptian Army was quite incapable of crossing Sinai and posing any threat to the country. The Egyptian Army had neither the military nor logistical capabilities to do so. It could not have defeated the IDF divisions. It had no air cover beyond a narrow strip along the Canal.

It had insufficient stores of fuel and ammunition and no logistical capacity to advance units that far. Had the Egyptian Army entered the wide spaces of Sinai, it would have found itself in a killing field from which it would not have escaped. Several days passed before the Egyptian armored divisions crossed to the east bank of the Canal. I remember that we kept waiting for Fourth Armored Division to do so. Had it stayed on the western side of the Canal, we would not have been able to cross the Canal successfully.

During the night of October 6, Division 162 was hurriedly dispatched to the northern sector of the Canal. But "there are no Deganyas in Sinai." Why wasn't the division sent to the Golan Heights? The real danger to the country was in the north, and the main effort was against Syria. To stop the Syrian Army, the IDF had to transfer a division from the Jordanian border, gambling and taking the risk that the Jordanian Army would not get involved. Had Jordan decided to attack, it would not have found any opposing Israeli forces. We exposed ourselves on this front while focusing our efforts against the Egyptians and checking the Syrian advance with our last available units. We invested in Sinai, where there was no real danger other than to our military prestige.

Even before the war, like most officers, I watched the Egyptian drills with envy: their soldiers took only sixty minutes to assemble a bridge on which tanks could cross the Canal. That is precisely what they did when the war began, and that was how they operated throughout the war, just as in their exercises. The entire IDF was aware of them, watched them and did nothing. By contrast, we needed more than two days to build a single bridge to cross the Canal, even under light fire! It was on this poor bridge, which escaped destruction purely by a miracle, that the IDF crossing depended. Only thanks to the unprofessionalism and poor coordination of the Egyptian command were the bridgehead and the bridge itself not wiped out. The Egyptian artillery could have done so easily, with no need for infantry. Without this single bridge, the situation of the forces that had crossed the

Canal would have been catastrophic. Tanks are not worth much without fuel and ammunition. Had the Egyptians interdicted our fuel and ammunition supply for a single day, the tank unit would have turned into a horde of steel monsters, unable to move or fight. They could have been captured with bare hands. But luck was on our side—much more luck than intelligent planning, in my view. When it came to issuing orders and seeing the overall picture of the battlefield, the Egyptian generals turned out to be lousy commanders, in contrast to their relatively fine and courageous soldiers, and that is why they failed on the Southern Front.

We won the battle, trapping the Third Army and bringing it to the brink of destruction, but it was Sadat who won the war, because its result coincided with his goals, not ours. We were unable to prevent the Egyptians from crossing the Canal, as we thought we could. The IDF failed to keep its promises to its government, in contrast to the Egyptian Army. We knew everything about the Egyptian Army—its composition, armaments, equipment, combat doctrine, training programs and war plans—and the same applies to the Syrians. Before the war, after an incident on the northern border, I visited the technical branch of the Intelligence Corps, where they showed me a captured Sagger anti-tank missile. I held the missile and the suitcase it comes in. I saw user manuals in Russian and in translation. In the Intelligence Corps, they knew exactly how to operate the missiles, the scope of their capabilities, and the best tactics for using them. They even test-fired a few captured missiles. When I saw the Saggers flying over our tanks in the war, I remembered that I had held one in my hands a few months earlier. The IDF knew about them but never planned, trained, or made preparations for the Arab armies' use of the missiles and other effective anti-tank weapons. Nor did it prepare for the real war, despite all the exercises, including the large maneuvers conducted only a few months before the war.

The following incident illustrates the failure to comprehend what was going on, particularly on the Egyptian front, and the overall caliber of the command echelons. As part of the Israeli counterattack on October 8, our forces were issued what amounted to a half-order, half-guideline to try to capture one of the Egyptian bridges and transfer some of our forces to the western side of the Canal.

How could any senior commander, a professional military man, demonstrate such folly? In the Second World War, it was sometimes possible to capture a bridge and send forces across it. But there were no rigid bridges over the Suez Canal that could be used. The bridges erected by the Egyptian soldiers were intended for their vehicles and equipment. The Soviet-made tanks employed by the Egyptians weighed 40 tons, whereas IDF tanks exceeded 50 tons. Would any sane person try to drive an Israeli tank over an Egyptian bridge? Even if several tanks did make it across, by great good fortune or miracle, sooner or later the bridge would be damaged or break apart. The Egyptian combat engineers, well equipped and well trained, often fixed damaged bridges in a matter of minutes, but the IDF could not. What would have happened to those using the bridges? We had no way to service or repair the Egyptian bridges. Cut off from their supply lines, unable to withdraw, any forces that made it to the other side of the Canal would have been destroyed or captured. When I first heard this plan, I could not believe my ears; I was sure that no professional officer would have issued such an order. Over the years, though, I have heard about it from various people, and unfortunately have no choice but to believe this sad and disgraceful story.

But more than anything, I was shocked by the contempt for soldiers' lives and the abandonment of the personnel manning the forts along the Canal. What was the point? After all, it was obvious that the forts were not intended to keep the Egyptians from crossing the Canal. And the penetration into Suez City—what was the purpose? Why did more than 70 of our soldiers perish there? To conquer another building and another? Did the occupation of Suez have the slightest influence on Israel's political situation? Did it change the pace of our withdrawal from Sinai or affect the peace treaty with the Egyptians? No.

There is a dangerous detachment between political thinking and military thinking, and the battlefield lends itself only too well to the satisfaction of generals' ambitions. We launched an attack after the ceasefire had gone into effect, because the IDF was pressed to "improve its positions." In other words, even after the war, it was the IDF that actually set the goals. We have not learned that the goal of every war is solely political. We were not wise enough to refrain from sacrificing soldiers' lives in order to glorify or defend the honor of the leader or of some general. We didn't learn this lesson in the Yom Kippur War or in the First Lebanon War, and certainly not in the Second Lebanon War.

To mollify the army and the public, the IDF decided to promote every officer who had been in combat. Regardless of their performance, no matter how they executed their mission, they all received a promotion in a grotesque and stupid festival. We are talking of no more than three weeks of war. Only a few individuals were in combat throughout the entire period; most were in battle for only a few days, some for a week, and some for two weeks. A week or two of fighting—no more than a battle or half a battle by the standards of the Second World War—won people promotions and ranks that were, save for a few exceptional cases, not justified by their knowledge or experience. But a failed war is always accompanied by wholesale promotions and a festival of medals and heroic tales—some true but most fabricated and overblown, intended to raise the nation's morale and divert attention from what actually took place during the war. Whether the stories of bravery were real or imaginary didn't really matter.

The Yom Kippur War reminded me of the German attack on the Soviet Union on June 22, 1941. I was raised on the myths of that surprise attack, after which the Red Army withdrew all the way to Moscow and Stalingrad and the war went on for years. Without the surprise attack, the whole war would have looked different. In the case of the Soviet Union, people blamed Stalin, who had supposedly ignored the intelligence warnings. In the Soviet Union's near-collapse

IDF → Intel Corps

in 1941, the Intelligence Corps was blamed for everything and served as a scapegoat to cover up the Red Army's lack of preparedness for war and the high command's gross ineptitude. Similarly, the IDF tried to obfuscate its lack of preparedness in the Yom Kippur War in almost every respect—equipment, assembling the forces, tactics, and strategy—by shifting the blame onto the Intelligence Corps. It was not the Intelligence Corps that failed the IDF. The IDF and its unprofessional commanders failed themselves.

In both these cases, there was a big lie and an attempt to whitewash the situation and foist the blame on others. The colossal failure of the Soviet Union at the beginning of the war was the fault of the Red Army high command. Its incompetent, unsuitable, and unprofessional generals produced the military fiasco of the early months of the war. The Red Army simply collapsed like a house of cards and did not fulfill its promises to the political echelon. The shock of a surprise attack fades after the first week or two, in the worst case. The Intelligence Corps did fail in the Yom Kippur War, but that wasn't the problem. The information and assessments it made available should have been sufficient for the IDF to plan and prepare for a war. Hoping that intelligence would provide a timely warning of H-hour and basing all the defense plans on that expectation was so simplistic and primitive as to be amateurish. There is no way to predict a surprise attack, and no professional intelligence system would ever promise to do so. Military intelligence is not an oracle or a fortune teller, despite the beliefs of most of the dilettantes among the politicians and generals who lack a basic professional culture for understanding and working with the intelligence apparatus. The Israeli Intelligence Corps supplied more than enough information about the Egyptian and Syrian combat doctrine and tactics. But the IDF high command never treated this issue with the seriousness and professionalism it deserved.

My gloomy conclusions about the war also relate to combat intelligence. I discovered that the working methods and doctrines we had studied in the course for intelligence officers were almost never employed in wartime. There was no set of orders that resembled anything like what we had learned in the course. Something similar cropped up here and there in the IDF's standard battlefield procedures. But what worked in the classroom and on maneuvers simply wasn't effective in a real war. Every attempt to get an overall picture of the situation from the brigade intelligence officers led nowhere. It turned out that they didn't have a global view of the situation, at least not at the operational level. Almost everything we knew came from our own observations and troops. So we knew very little about the enemy forces facing us, about their vehicles and weapons. I'm not sure that battalion commanders knew what they wanted and what they could receive from their battalion intelligence officers during the war, or even afterwards. The Intelligence Corps is a support unit. Commanders who do not know how to use the information that they receive from intelligence, to serve them when making decisions, render the intelligence useless. In the IDF, the culture of using intelligence is on a very low level and, at the battalion level, it hardly exists at all. To this day, no one knows, and except in certain situations, no one can explain what a battalion intelligence officer is supposed to do and how that impacts the battlefield for an armored battalion, the most important fighting force. I don't know what goes on in infantry, artillery, or engineering battalions.

My commander, Ehud Barak, was one of the best, with exceptional experience and fighting ability in special operations. So were his comrades and subordinates from the General Staff Commando Unit, who were in the battalion with us. I couldn't understand why they didn't make better use of their abilities. Why did Yishai Yizhar have to look for an opportunity to fight? Why did Amitai Nahmani have to die as a scout in the attack on the Fayid airport? Why did Ehud Barak have to serve as commander of an armored battalion? Almost no special operations were carried out during the war, so most of those who were trained as commandos fought as regular soldiers and officers. Every officers' course at Training Base 1, including ours, simulated raids on anti-aircraft missile batteries. When we were on the western side of the Canal, I wondered why we weren't launching raids on them. It was an utterly stupid waste of the extraordinary capabilities of the IDF special units and their soldiers and officers. I saw this as the embodiment not only of the IDF command's confusion and disorganization, but also as a severe lack of preparedness and an abysmal level of military planning and thinking.

It was only after I returned home that I was exposed to what was called "the War of the Generals." During my leave, I was astonished that everyone was talking about Arik Sharon and his division, which had crossed the Canal and won the war. Everyone who fought on the Southern Front knew that the crossing had not been the individual initiative of any one divisional commander. Sharon's division was selected to cross into "Africa" not because of him, but because its location and abilities were better suited to the plans for and conditions of the operation. Bren's division, or some other unit, could just as well have been designated to be the spearhead, and another division could have been selected to move through it and go into combat on the other side, towards Suez City.

I loved Ariel Sharon and always thought that he was one of the most talented commanders in the IDF, but mine was no blind admiration. I knew that had the high command listened to him and tried to cross the Canal when he wanted to, the force would have been decimated. We had no way to get across the water and no way to hold a bridgehead on the other side until the bridges were in place. The cynical use of a fawning journalist and dissemination of rumors that did not fit with the true situation grated on my ears. The War of the Generals revealed an ugly phenomenon that was only just beginning to emerge then, but which has become a broader trend in the IDF and Israeli society over the years. It threatens our very ability to survive and manage the problems that plague us: running away from responsibility, a disgraceful, shameful shirking of duty, accompanied by telling lies and blaming others.

I didn't have the courage to analyze the destructive tendencies revealed during the war and try to understand them deeper—perhaps out of fear that my mythological belief in the IDF, the country, and its values might be undermined. I was still too new in Israel and too unsure to reach such trying conclusions. It was only years later that I came to understand the dangerous implications of the phenomenon.

Against our expectations, the war changed the face of the Middle East and of the State of Israel. After the war, I was kept on active duty until May 1974. I think that I may have been one of the very last reservists to be released. I did 273 days in uniform. The reason they gave me was prosaic: Because you're a reserve officer, we can hold you here as long as we want. But we have to release officers in the regular army when their contracts are up. So my friends who were in the regular army, who had contracts running to April 1974, were released, while I, a reserve officer, was not. During that time, I kept thinking that I had been in Israel for five years, of which I had spent more than three and a half in the army. The war had essentially completed my process of absorption. Although I knew next to nothing about civilian life, my emotions, thoughts, and to some degree even my way of thinking had grown to resemble those of my friends who were born here or had lived here much longer than me. An important layer had been added to the foundation of my personality, which had been formed in the Soviet Union and steeled in my struggle for *aliyah* and afterwards: the IDF and the Yom Kippur War. For me, like so many others, the war sobered me up from an almost fanatic idealization of the State, its leadership, and its army.

But what worried me most of all was that my young son, who had been so attached to me, didn't recognize me when I returned from the war, and was frightened and cried when I held him in my arms.

Chapter 21

In the period after the war, nothing really important happened in my life. In advance of the Knesset elections in 1977, Moshe Dayan weighed leaving the Alignment and setting up an independent list. He contacted me through a mutual acquaintance and proposed that I join his slate. When I asked about the ideological basis of the list, the answer was that the goal was to prevent the return of the Territories. On every other issue, he would give me a free vote. My response was that I was in sympathy with the idea of kicking out the Alignment, because of its corruption. My position on Judea, Samaria, and Gaza should not worry him; any differences we might have there would probably be rooted in the fact that my position was more extreme. We came to an agreement in principle and decided that we would discuss the details after Dayan made a final decision about the independent list. In the event, Dayan did not have the courage to leave the Alignment—which did not really surprise me. Thus ended the only real attempt to involve me in politics.

I don't know what would have happened had Dayan gone through with the idea. I assume that he would have won several seats; I would have been elected to the Knesset along with him and my life might have turned out very differently. Looking back, I'm somewhat embarrassed that I was willing to join him. My ethical and moral standards have become sharper and more extreme since then; today I would not even consider linking up with one of the individuals most responsible for the Yom Kippur War and its outcome. Back then, however, Dayan still had not totally lost the aura of the hero of the Six Day War and remained the hope of many. Since then, my ideas and perspective on the State of Israel, including its place in the region and policies, have changed and grown more sophisticated, and the ethical standards I demand of its leadership have become more stringent.

In the 1977 election campaign, I was involved in a public effort to pressure the government to change its policy with regard to Soviet Jewry. We demanded a more vigorous and more aggressive stand towards the Soviet Union and greater support for *aliyah* activists and refuseniks. By that time, I already knew all the political bigwigs in Israel. We received the strongest support from the opposition parties, including members of the State List established by Ben-Gurion in 1969, and the Liberal Party, but also from parties within the coalition, including the Independent Liberals and the National Religious Party. The most solid support, as we thought then, came from Menachem Begin's Herut Movement. In his speeches, Begin incorporated a demand for a new policy towards Soviet Jews and their struggle. I felt at home in the Herut Movement but didn't join it. I was still loyal to the principle that partisan politics should be kept out of the campaign for *aliyah*, because the struggle had to be apolitical. Moreover, despite my ideological sympathy with Herut, not everything that took place in that movement was to my liking.

I remember one instance related to Meir Kahane that sounded alarm bells for me. The first time that Kahane was arrested in Israel was for one of his provocative demonstrations. I thought that Prisoners of Zion and *aliyah* activists should not be blasé about his arrest, just as he had never been indifferent to our struggle, and tried to initiate a petition in his support. This was support for Meir Kahane the person, not for his ideas. I tried to get *aliyah* activists who happened to be in Israel then to sign the petition and was surprised by the response of some members of Herut. For instance, one of its most prominent members told me that we did indeed have a moral obligation to Meir Kahane and that she and her colleagues supported the petition—but the party would "frown upon it." I recoiled at this statement. It was not the last time I encountered this line of thought, which was characteristic of the Soviet system, with its commissars who insisted on the supremacy of the party over independent thinking. These people had merely replaced the red flag with the blue-and-white banner and Soviet demagoguery with Zionist demagoguery; and some of them put a *kippa* (skullcap) on their heads.

I had a similar reaction to the blind and fanatical worship of Menachem Begin. I knew the man well and esteemed him; I visited his home often and knew his family. He was very intelligent, very well educated, and had excellent analytical and rhetorical capabilities, but I was bothered by his slips into the outdated demagoguery of the 1930s. I also noticed his almost obsessive hypersensitivity to his status. He did not tolerate opposition or differences of opinion, particularly within his party and among his close associates. He expected total veneration and obedience from the members and particularly from the senior ranks. Extremely able alumni of the Revisionist Movement who stuck to their independent opinions were pushed out.

A prominent example was Benzion Netanyahu, Binyamin Netanyahu's father. Jabotinsky's one-time secretary, he was shunted aside and rejected not only by the national and government apparatus, but also by the party that had supposedly been established on the basis of the Revisionist Movement and claimed to be its heir. Only Menachem Begin was allowed the title of Jabotinsky's closest follower and successor, as the Herut Party replaced the Revisionist ideology with blind obedience to the commander of the Irgun. This was unacceptable to me and did not increase my desire to join the party. I was happy when Yitzhak Shamir and Geula Cohen joined Herut and were elected to the Knesset in late 1973—especially Geula, whom I saw as the very embodiment of loyalty to the land, the people, and the state, with the extraordinary devotion, passion, and temperament that she brought not only to the issue of Soviet Jewry, but to everything she said and did. Their arrival achieved a sort of reconciliation, though never complete, between the pre-state rivals, the Irgun and Lehi. When Shamir later became chairman of the Likud and prime minister, he was upset by the attitude of former Irgun members, who had some reservations about serving one of Lehi's former leaders. I personally witnessed the anxiety this caused him.

In advance of the 1977 elections, I agreed to appear in several television spots for the Likud. But I was willing to speak about one topic only: Soviet Jewry and support for its struggle. On other topics, I said, I have no relative advantage and leave them to those who are better qualified to express an opinion. When Yochanan Bader spoke about the economy, people took it much more seriously than when Yasha Kazakov spoke about the economy. But with regard to Soviet Jewry, my words had greater weight. I called on the public to vote for the Likud in both Hebrew and Russian—only the Likud could transform Israeli policy and adopt an approach that would bring in hundreds of thousands of *olim* (immigrants).

The Likud won the election and Menachem Begin formed a government, after almost three decades in the opposition. The Likud triumphed because it was seen as a viable alternative to a regime that was rotten, failing, and corrupt, and that most people were disgusted with. On the morning after the election, I raced my car through the streets of Tel Aviv and Ramat Gan, just for the fun of it. I had a sense that a new era was dawning, that everything in the country would be different now. All the injustices, all the problems, all the failures would be rectified, and the country would finally find itself on the right path. Justice had finally won out. Those who advocated a fairer, more efficient, and more Jewish society, with less government control, would lead the State of Israel to a better future.

Right after the elections, I attended a meeting of the Herut Central Committee at the party headquarters, Jabotinsky House, although I was not a member of Herut and certainly not of the central committee.

I wanted to hear the discussion about the new government's policy and direction. Begin put the candidates for ministerial posts to a vote, one by one. When they reached the fifth and last slot available to Herut, which should have been filled, according to his position on the Knesset list, by Moshe Arens, Begin asked to say a few words. What he said astonished me and left a bad taste in my mouth. I was not the only one who was taken by surprise. Begin began by praising Arens—which was fishy. Then he said, to almost everyone's surprise, "I am asking the movement to approve David Levy as a minister." A stunned silence settled on the room. Begin did not explain his request. He simply said, "Trust me. I promise that the next person in line for a portfolio is Moshe Arens." In terms of his talents, abilities, rank in the movement, and suitability for a ministerial position, there was no comparison between the two men. But the leader said his piece and everyone jumped to obey, even while gritting their teeth. Begin's considerations were guided by electoral politics rather than suitability for the role. And so I learned another lesson in Israeli politics and internal party "democracy." The familiar reek of the Soviet Communist Party assailed my nose once again.

A short while later, I asked for a meeting with Begin. It was held in late August 1977; Yehuda Avner, the Prime Minister's advisor on Diaspora Affairs was also in attendance. I didn't yet know what this member of the Prime Minister's staff did. Over time, I discovered that his main function is to write speeches in good English for the Prime Minister, especially for appearances before Jewish and non-Jewish audiences abroad.

After the usual exchange of pleasantries, Begin asked me, "What do you have to say?"

"During the election campaign," I replied, "you declared that the Israeli government's policy towards the struggle of Soviet Jewry has to change. We supported you, among other reasons, because of this. Now that you are Prime Minister, please start changing the policy. But you cannot revise the policy unless you replace the people who set and are implementing the policies that all of us reject. If you don't replace the senior echelons, particularly Nehemiah Levanon, the head of the Liaison Bureau (Nativ's public name), there won't be a change in policy."

Begin looked at me with curiosity and remained silent for several moments. Finally, after a quiet sigh, he replied in a serious and somewhat pathetic voice. "I have a proposal for you. I think that in light of your experience and knowledge, you should come work in that organization."

As the Israeli comedy team The Gashashim would say, the head rose to my blood. But I recovered and told him, with all the politeness I could muster (but not without a measure of anger), "I didn't come to ask you for a job. That's not what I want and it's not why I came here. I'm talking to you about a change in national policy, not about myself."

But Begin responded in a fatherly way, "I am the Prime Minister and I think that you can make a contribution there. With everything you've done and all your experience, you cannot say no when the Prime Minister asks you."

I was in shock. I had not expected this development. I had been prepared for an argument with him and had come armed with examples of new measures that should be taken—but not for what I heard. I had no good reason to reject the proposal and really couldn't refuse. Nonetheless, I somehow found the strength to put him off. "Thank you very much. Perhaps you are right. I'll weigh your offer and give you an answer within a week." It was insolent of me to answer the Prime Minister' generous proposal this way, but that was my response. It was clear to both of us that I couldn't say "No" and that my answer would be in the affirmative. Right after the meeting, my wife and I took a vacation abroad—our first ever. When I returned, I called Yehiel Kadishai, Begin's bureau chief and his loyal aide for many years. "Please tell the Prime Minister that my response is affirmative."

That was the last meeting I ever initiated with Menachem Begin. From the moment I joined Nativ, I never set foot in Jabotinsky House, although I had previously been a frequent visitor there. I thought, with a naïveté uncommon in Israel, that it was not appropriate to mix political views, preferences, and connections with work in a government office, particularly in the intelligence community. Afterwards, I discovered that on the evening after the meeting, Yehuda Avner called Nehemiah Levanon and gave him details of my conversation with Begin. Panic broke out in Nativ. Begin's "spy"—that fellow Yasha Kazakov—was about to join the organization.

Levanon invited me in for an interview. He received me warmly. Until then, we had always had normal relations. He told me he had received instructions from Menachem Begin and that he would be happy to have me join the organization. He wanted to know what kind of work interested me and whether there were jobs I was unwilling to take on. I told him that I had three conditions: "The first condition is that I do not want to work in the West or with the West. I don't like working with Jews in the West and don't have a very high opinion of them. I don't know the West and it doesn't attract or interest me. The second condition is that I want to work as closely as possible with Soviet Jewry, whom I know and who really do interest me. The third condition is that I will not work with Zvi Netzer."

Years earlier, Zvi Netzer had issued instructions to slander me by telling Jewish organizations in the United States that I was a Soviet spy. Levanon did not look surprised by what I said about Netzer, but was clearly not expecting my refusal to work in the West. He wound up the meeting by stating, "I understand about Zvi. I'll get back to you. But in the meantime, get a start on your security clearance."

It was supposed to take six months to get a security clearance. I remember what I was told by one of General Security Service agents who conducted it: "Be patient. We are interrogating you and asking many difficult questions. But it is possible that we will be working together in the future, so keep that in mind and understand our position." He was right. In the years that followed, we often collaborated and helped each other. I relied on the GSS agents and learned a lot from them. Some of them are my friends to this day. Some of them also became my subordinates later on, when they were seconded from the GSS to Nativ.

Levanon invited me for another meeting and told me that they intended to send me to Vienna, because the organization was receiving no information about what was happening in the Soviet Union from those people who reached Vienna but did not continue to Israel. We could debrief those who came here and get an up-to-date status report about both the Jews and the Soviet Union, but the increasingly large group of those went elsewhere after getting out simply vanished from our radar, and they wanted me to fill in the gaps. I told him that the job interested me. I also asked him for a commitment that if I kept working for the organization for a year, I would be taken on as a regular employee at Nativ, not just as the prime minister's "envoy." I was aware of the political intrigues in bureaucratic organizations. I knew that because I had been brought in through political pressure, the minute the government changed they could tell me, "Thank you very much. But you can go home now." Until I joined, Nativ was composed one hundred percent of Mapai supporters, with a preference for those who had been members of the Gordonia youth movement. My arrival was an earthquake and the first step towards the depoliticization of Nativ. It was also the first step in the integration of *aliyah* activists into its ranks.

As part of my preparations for the job, I was authorized to read various documents and perused many reports and assessments. Several points drew my attention. I was also shocked by the sloppy style and structure of the reports, particularly when compared to what I had learned to write in the IDF and what I had expected. The reports and investigations sounded like confused short stories, with no summaries, no basic structure or format. From time to time, I did uncover professional reports, but those were written by the members of the General Security Service or were copies of reports by the GSS and other agencies.

Finally, my security clearance came through. I scheduled my arrival for May 1, which immediately raised eyebrows in the still socialist-bastion of Nativ: "You want to work on May 1, of all days?!"

Chapter 22

On May 1, 1978, I landed in Vienna with my wife and son. In accordance with the arrangement between Nativ and the Foreign Ministry, I traveled on a diplomatic passport, which soon turned out to have been an unwise decision. An employee of one of the airlines looked at the passport and smiled. "No one but spies travel on diplomatic passports." But I didn't care; in any case, the "mistake" was corrected later.

In advance of my assignment abroad, I was asked to take a Hebrew surname. They told me that when I returned to Israel I could decide whether to keep it or go back to my original name. I chose "Kedmi." I was not particularly aware that one meaning of *kedem* is "the east" and that Kedmi was a common name among Oriental Jews (those of Asian and North African origin). My choice was based on my desire to maintain the first letter of my last name. I also wanted the name to have a meaning suited to my personality. When I enlisted in the IDF, I decided that I must always be moving forward (*kadimah*), at the front-most (*kidmi*) line. I never wanted to see the back of another Israeli soldier or officer in front of me, but only the face and eyes of the enemy. My ambition was that if there was a war or battle, I would be in the first wave of the attack and look the enemy face to face. So I selected the name Kedmi and we got used to it. When I returned from my posting, I felt comfortable with it and decided to keep it. It wasn't that the name Kazakov bothered me. I had many reasons to be proud of it and it was perfectly respectable, but I also felt that it had become too well known. Everywhere and every time people encountered that name, they would always ask questions, maybe express admiration and even adulation, and that bothered me a little. After I adopted the name Kedmi, I found that it evoked no response, particularly in Israel. It felt comfortable to be treated like an ordinary citizen.

So on May 1, 1978, my life as Yasha Kazakov came to an end, and the Yakov Kedmi chapter began—which was, of course, based upon and a sequel to the adventures of Yasha Kazakov.

My job in Vienna was to gather information from people who had just left the Soviet Union but were not continuing on to Israel. This was Nativ's attempt to expand its knowledge about what was going on in the Soviet Union and among the Jews there, to gain a better understanding of their situation, aspirations, and desires, and to learn the reasons for the increase in the number of dropouts from the *aliyah* track.

The dropout phenomenon began in 1971. A certain American Jewish philanthropist contacted Nativ and reported that a family of distant relatives was about to leave the Soviet Union. Like all *olim*, they were supposed to arrive in Vienna and then continue to Israel. But the philanthropist asked for a favor—please help his family come directly to the United States, without having to go through Israel.

In those years, there were two American Jewish organizations active in Vienna—HIAS and the Joint Distribution Committee (JDC). HIAS, an American Jewish organization, was established in the late nineteenth century to help Jews immigrate to the United States and integrate there. The JDC, founded in the early twentieth century, was a Jewish organization that assisted Jews in distress, particularly in Eastern Europe. Both HIAS and the JDC had maintained offices in Vienna since the end of the Second World War. Their last major campaign had followed the Soviet invasion of Czechoslovakia and the mass departure of Jews from Poland, after the Polish Communist leader Gomulka denounced them as Zionists and supporters of Israel. The Polish Jews made *aliyah* through Vienna. That city was also the way station for Jews from Czechoslovakia and Poland who preferred to go to the US or Western Europe; the HIAS and JDC offices in Vienna helped them with the formalities. After the end of the Polish and Czechoslovakian *aliyah*, the organizations decided to close their offices in Vienna, which had nothing left to do.

Two weeks before their closure, Nativ asked the Jewish Agency representatives in Vienna to deal with the philanthropist's request. They, in turn, referred his relatives to HIAS and the JDC as soon as they reached town. The arrival of this one family from the Soviet Union led the two organizations to put off closing their offices, because they expected other Jews to follow. Indeed, shortly after the first family was processed for immigration to the US, another family that had come to Vienna learned of this and asked for similar assistance. Without much thought, it too was referred to the American organizations.

The rest is history. More and more families discovered that there was an alternative to Israel and announced upon arrival in Vienna that they wanted to immigrate to the US. Later, other families asked to go to Australia and Canada. The Austrians were astounded by this phenomenon: These people were coming to Vienna on an *aliyah* visa, en route to Israel, and a change in their destination was a violation of the transit visa they had been issued. But the Austrians, who had become hypersensitive to Jewish issues ever since the Second World War, did not want to tangle with the Jews and the Israelis and thus decided (legitimately, from their perspective) not to get involved. The prevalent view in Nativ was that there was no cause for concern and that Jews should be allowed to go where they wanted. No assessment was made of the reasons for the new phenomenon or of its impact on *aliyah* in the future. Thus, the dropout phenomenon emerged from a failure to take the matter seriously and a misunderstanding of its motives, until it reached proportions that almost put an end to *aliyah* from the Soviet Union.

By 1977, Israel had realized the danger of the phenomenon and begun attempting to put an end to it, but not until after a long debate on the right course of action. A group of Soviet-born members of Herut resolved that the dropouts should be left in peace and no attempt made to end the phenomenon. They justified their position by citing freedom of choice. Menachem Begin was convinced. Around the same time, Prime Minister Yitzchak Rabin informed Begin of his intention to ask American Jewry and the US administration to suspend all assistance to Jews who left the Soviet Union with visas for Israel but continued to the US instead. His considerations were ethical and pertinent. The Jews were going to the US because they had been granted refugee status, a result of the pressure exerted by American Jewish organizations in the early 1970s to permit Jewish immigration beyond the normal immigration quotas.

The Israeli government, for its part, worked to get the US to recognize the Soviet Jews leaving for Israel as refugees. The reason for this was financial. If the Jews from the Soviet Union were defined as refugees, Israel could receive tens of millions of dollars a year from the US government to help with their absorption. As a result, refugee status was conferred on all Soviet Jews with an *aliyah* visa. But if they were refugees, they could also enter the US under that rubric. Rabin had decided to combat this phenomenon and ask that these Jews be denied refugee status on the grounds that Jews who waived their right to make *aliyah* to Israel, their original destination, could not be considered refugees. Their decision to go to the US turned them into immigrants instead.

The Israeli establishment was not willing to give up the refugee status granted the Soviet emigrants, for fear of losing American aid. The millions of dollars they brought in were important. Money was more important than anything else, even if it meant that fewer Jews made *aliyah*. The irony was that the funds that the American Jewish organizations allocated to the dropouts came from a special campaign whose avowed purpose was to raise funds for the State of Israel. The Israeli establishment hesitated to lock horns with the fundraisers about supporting dropouts with money intended for Israel. When he contacted Begin, Rabin hoped to win his backing for his position, on the assumption that a nationalistic Zionist party would support it, or at least that the Knesset opposition would not attack his government for its action. Begin turned down the request on the grounds that the decision would be made after the coming election and he would not yet make any commitments. When I arrived in Vienna in 1978, the dropout phenomenon was still in its infancy—some 20% of all Jews who left the Soviet Union dropped out. Israel had not yet found a way to deal with the phenomenon and probably did not understand its true reasons and significance.

Nativ worked in full coordination with the JDC and HIAS personnel in Vienna. The usual procedure was that the dropouts would first speak with a Jewish Agency representative, who tried to persuade them to change their minds. The Agency and the American organizations did this in order to save face. After "the persuasive interview" failed to persuade them, the emigrants were referred to the JDC and HIAS to continue the immigration process. We agreed with the JDC that I would have a chance to talk with people before their meeting with the Jewish Agency representative. My job had nothing to do with information and propaganda. I concentrated on the effort to gather the background that interested me—information about the Jews' situation, problems, aspirations, the authorities' treatment of them, and the reasons for all of these. We were afraid that the dropouts would not cooperate or answer my questions, but it turned out that their willingness to talk far exceeded our desire and needs. Apparently one of the dominant traits of *Homo sovieticus* was talking to the authorities. In Italy, for example, where the dropouts spent around six months while waiting for the bureaucratic process to be concluded, the line outside the office of the American intelligence services representative was always the longest. The emigrants came of their own initiative to tell what they knew or thought they knew, and particularly to spill the dirt about others on the basis of solid knowledge, rumors, or imagination run wild.

In short order, I amassed quality information, which I began to analyze and summarize for myself. At first I first did this to become knowledgeable and focus the questions and conversation more effectively. Before I was posted abroad, I asked Yosef Meller, the head of my department, whether I should summarize my findings from time to time and submit reports to headquarters in Israel. He replied that this would not be necessary—Nativ did not engage in summaries and analysis. I should forward only the transcripts of the conversations. When preparing for my assignment, I hoped to receive some sort of guidance about conducting the interviews and reporting on them. But I was told that there was no system and everyone did what he wanted. In my month of preparation, as I read thousands of reports and debriefings of *olim*, an unpleasant picture emerged. Drawing on the report-writing procedure I had learned in the IDF and in military intelligence, I formulated a uniform and more professional style of writing reports. When I began submitting reports in this format, my superiors raised an eyebrow and asked me what it was all about. I responded that I believed this to be the right way to compose reports. They did not argue with me. As the situation in the Soviet Union became clearer, I decided that I had no right to keep my conclusions to myself and should put them in writing and forward them to my superiors.

In late 1978, after some six months in Vienna, I worked hard to prepare my first situation assessment. I analyzed the phenomena of *aliyah* and dropping out, the Jews' motivations, and the expected volume of emigration from the Soviet Union. I reached several surprising conclusions. First of all, the Soviet authorities had evidently decided to allow almost everyone to emigrate who applied on the basis of an invitation to Israel, whatever the degree of kinship to the person who sent the invitation. The exceptions were in cases related to refusals on the grounds of security, or failure to fulfill obligations to one's family or to the State. This change in attitude had generated a rapid increase in the stream of applications and the anticipated number of emigrants. My analysis of the reasons people gave for emigrating led me to conclusions that angered many and continue to anger others today, but I still believe they are true and the evidence backs me up.

In my opinion, Jews were leaving the Soviet Union for three reasons: dissatisfaction with their personal situation, particularly financial and social; their assessment that they would be better off in the West, whether in Israel or some other country—and the responses of *olim* to Israel and of immigrants to other countries reinforced this opinion; and finally, the possibility and ease of the transition—that is, of leaving the Soviet Union. Because the first two reasons were constant and common to most of the Soviet *intelligentsia*, including the Jews, only the third reason—the ease or difficulty of emigration—determined its scope. When there were more and easier opportunities, the number of emigrants would rise. As long as the situation in the Soviet Union remained unchanged or worsened and the impression of the situation in the West, including Israel, and the prospects for absorption there were rosier than the situation in the Soviet Union, the desire to get out would increase as a function of the availability of emigration opportunities.

After a thorough and serious investigation of the nationalistic argument and of the Jews' sensitivity to anti-Semitism in the Soviet Union and elsewhere, I concluded that it was not anti-Semitism but the three factors that I noted that were behind the decision to emigrate. Jews in an anti-Semitic country want to leave not because of anti-Semitism, but because of what they see as much more serious reasons. The scale of anti-Semitic manifestations in the Soviet Union was not severe or threatening enough to spur emigration. The presence or absence of anti-Semitism is not a major factor in the emigrants' choice of destination, because it was not the main reason for their decision to leave. Their Jewishness was essentially the only (and the most effective) means for them to get out of the Soviet Union; expressing their religion was not their goal. It was only a small minority, really just a handful, for whom living as Jews was the focal point and goal of their lives.

With regard to the dropouts, I wrote that Jews, like other nationalities, would choose what they deemed the best among the options available. Soviet Jews would always prefer the non-Israeli options—the US, Canada, Australia, even Germany—to Israel. These were large, multinational countries, offering much greater possibilities and prospects, and, most importantly, they were not in a state of war. Other problems were trivial for them in comparison to their situation in the Soviet Union. Israel—a small country in the Middle East, not very well developed and not very European, with a tense security situation—would always lose in competition with the US or another Western country. I also noted that if these Soviet Jews had a better option than America, they would prefer it; were Switzerland, France, or Great Britain to open their gates to Jews, Soviet Jews would hasten there in preference to the US. But because this opportunity was not available to them, they made do with what there was, and the US struck them as being better than Israel. The stories of anti-Semitism, racial problems, and so forth in the US, whether true or spurious propaganda, did not scare the Jews or deter them from settling there.

I concluded that the percentage of dropouts would increase among emigrants from all Soviet cities; the rate of the increase was a function of when the Jews joined the pool of emigrants in significant numbers. My assessment was that the process of deciding to emigrate lasted between a year and eighteen months, and that the environment in which it took place as well as the considerations that entered into that decision were important. Those who left the Soviet Union in 1978 had begun weighing the emigration option in 1976. Their decision reflected their situation and assessment then, when most of the emigrants were going to Israel. Over time, though, the proportion of *olim* among all emigrants would decline. Those who began thinking about emigration in 1978 and would be able to leave within a year found themselves among increasing numbers of dropouts, particularly in cities like Kiev and Minsk, where emigration had only recently begun. I asserted that within a short time, a majority of the emigrants from those cities would be going to the US or other countries, not to Israel. We would soon arrive at a situation where an overwhelming majority of the emigrants from the Soviet Union—more than 90%—would prefer Western countries over Israel. Only a handful would make *aliyah*—for family, ideological, religious, or medical reasons. I also wrote that no means of persuasion or information campaigns would change the mind of the Jews leaving the Soviet Union, because their decision derived from their worldview, which was itself shaped by the conditions in which they lived and the Soviet reality. The only thing that could alter the situation was a development that thwarted their ability to immigrate to other countries—the denial of refugee status and consequent suspension of financial assistance.

Later, in many conversations with senior officials of Nativ and the Jewish Agency, Israeli leaders, Americans, and Jewish organizations, I tried to explain my assessment and found myself embroiled in many arguments. I also dealt with another question: If the Jews were deprived of the US option, would they prefer to go to Israel or would they stay in the Soviet Union? This was the "hypothesis" of a few "experts" on Soviet Jewry. I claimed that the Jews would prefer to make *aliyah* and not stay in the Soviet Union, even if they could not immigrate to the US. The *olim* in Israel, especially with the absorption system as it was run back then, were far better off than they would have been had they stayed in the Soviet Union. It should not be forgotten that we were talking about several tens of thousands of immigrants a year, in the best of cases. In the end, Begin made the categorical decision not to try to prevent people from dropping out. With regard to his reasons, people told me what he revealed in private conversations: he needed the support of American Jewry in the struggle for the Land of Israel, Judea and Samaria, and was not willing to risk this campaign by creating a crisis in relations over the dropout problem. In the meantime, my assessment of the scope of emigration and the number of *olim* and dropouts was reflected in the number of people who reached Vienna.

In the absence of any willingness or programs to seriously address the dropout phenomenon, various actors wanted to show that they were doing their part to combat it. After a lot of verbiage and proclamations, the Jewish Agency floated the idea of sending a team of six or seven emissaries to Vienna for a short period—no more than two months—where they would try to persuade the dropouts to make *aliyah*. A member of the Likud Central Committee, a leading activist in Riga in the 1960s who had made *aliyah* in late 1968, was appointed to head the project. She was very active in Herut and essentially coordinated among its active members who had come from the Soviet Union. She was also the moving spirit of the resistance to diplomatic action to combat the dropout phenomenon.

The dropouts stayed in Vienna for about a week before continuing to Italy. It was necessary to exploit this window to persuade them to change their mind. With the same goal in mind, a few permanent emissaries were posted to Italy, where the waiting period was between six months and a year. This activity had minimal success; only a few families changed their mind. Although this was important, it was not enough to affect the scope of the phenomenon. These were people who had been hesitating because of family or other considerations. Some also saw it as a chance to stay on in Vienna and have a good time for a few days—if they originally declared their intention to go to the US and then supposedly changed their minds at the end of the week and expressed a desire to make *aliyah*. After the terrorist attack on a train full of *olim* in 1973, all Soviet Jewish emigrants were housed in a closed compound outside Vienna, guarded by Austrian security personnel, to protect them against terrorists. This was not an attempt to prevent them from dropping out, because they were not prevented from leaving if they said they didn't want to make *aliyah*. Only security was involved.

During that time, another phenomenon, albeit illegal, developed: immigration to Germany. Jews would stay in Vienna for a while, supposedly in anticipation of immigration to the US or Canada, waiting to be transferred to Italy, where the American authorities conducted their investigations and processed immigrants. While still in Vienna, though, these people found a way to contact smugglers, some of them Jewish and some Austrian or German, who would get the Jews across the border to Germany by car, train, or other conveyance. I caught on to this system fairly quickly. I knew who the smugglers were and how they worked, their methods and their timetables. In my conversations with the Austrians and Germans, who were also aware of this, they told me, "We will not initiate anything. But if we receive a request from you, we will block this channel within 24 hours. Sneaking across the border is illegal, and those who engage in it are criminals, not human rights activists. But unless the Israelis ask us, we will not mess with the Jews."

On one of his visits to Vienna, I proposed to Nehemiah Levanon, the head of Nativ, that he obtain advance permission from the government to act to end this embarrassment of Jews' sneaking into Germany. On his next trip to Vienna, Levanon told me that he had spoken with Begin, whose his response had been, "What? We should hand over Jews to the German police? Never!"

This was such a typical line for Menachem Begin. So we did not hand the infiltrators over to the German or Austrian police. Between 1978 and 1981, some 20,000 Soviet Jews crossed illegally into Germany, some from Austria and a few from Italy. We increased the Jewish population of Germany while showing contempt for everything that could be said about the memory of the Holocaust. By not intervening, we simply helped Jews, the children of those who were killed by the Nazis or fell in the war against them, to enter Germany illegally and enjoy slightly better conditions than they would have had in the US or Israel. The phenomenon of Jews' fleeing *to* Germany in such a humiliating way disgusted me; I was ashamed that we, the State of Israel, were abetting this deed by sitting on our hands and doing nothing.

In the meantime, the flow of information led me to a somewhat worrisome conclusion. All the testimonies I heard, which I then cross-checked and verified, left the impression that the Soviet authorities were taken aback by the increasing number of Jews applying to emigrate. The removal of so many of the obstacles against leaving in 1976–1978 generated intense pressure on the emigration offices; they were hard-pressed to cope with the tidal wave of applications, particularly because their staffs were not beefed up nor were their procedures streamlined. The information I collected and fairly simple calculations pointed to an increasing gap between the number of people applying to emigrate and the Soviets' technical ability to keep up with the flood. The waiting period between submitting documents to the emigration offices and receiving a reply now stretched to six months or more. This produced a cottage industry of bribery and brokers who could help people jump the queue. Given the authorities' failure to address the problem in any way, I concluded that they were about to take steps to limit emigration and limit the issuance of exit visas. I focused on attempting to extract hints to gainsay or confirm this conclusion and learn what kind of change they had in mind.

Shortly thereafter, various reports about the new system emerged from multiple sources. In the future, it seemed, emigration would be permitted only in the context of "family reunification," strictly speaking. Only people who had first-degree relatives abroad—siblings, parents, or children—would be allowed to submit requests to emigrate. However, I gauged that anyone who had managed to apply under the old terms would be allowed to leave, because the Soviet authorities were not interested in increasing the numbers of refuseniks. They had already learned that refuseniks quickly aggregated into militant pressure groups, which they found difficult to deal with in light of the international support for Israel and the Jewish organizations. A refusal to accept documents on the grounds of the lack of a close family relationship would be much more effective in decreasing the number of emigrants without increasing the numbers of refuseniks. In my opinion, the Soviets were aware that the requests were only sent by real Israeli citizens, so that the tens of thousands of dropouts could not send invitations to their relatives. I believed that the authorities, for their own reasons, had no intention of allowing Jews to emigrate on the basis of invitations from family members in the West. I also managed, more or less, to predict the date when the new policy would be imposed in the main urban centers.

In early 1979, I wrote a summary assessment in which I provided details of the new system and the dates for its introduction in various cities. On this basis, I estimated the number of emigrants from each city and an overall total for the coming year. For example, if memory serves, I judged that Odessa would be the first city where the system would be applied, as of April 1, 1979. I added that it would be several months, perhaps even half a year, before the new system had an impact on the number of emigrants from a city. Until then, the scale of emigration from each locality would coincide with the rate at which applications were submitted before the change went into effect. Fairly simple calculations, therefore, showed that the number of emigrants would rise rapidly until September-October 1979, after which there would be a steep decline to only a few thousand in 1980, as opposed to the 50,000 of 1979.

When Nehemiah Levanon came to Vienna, he told me that he was surprised by my report and that every agency in Israel and the US, including the State Department and the CIA, disagreed with my assessment and rejected it outright. Nonetheless, I stuck to my predictions. On April 1, I asked émigrés from Odessa who were staying in Vienna to call their acquaintances back home. They reported back that earlier that day the emigration offices had officially announced that from now on, only invitations from first-degree relatives would be accepted. The events developed exactly as I had written in the report, and afterwards you could put a check mark by every city in which the new system was implemented and its results. I had not been mistaken in my predictions for the major cities, and as far as I was concerned, the argument was over.

Although the claim that my report was wrong continued to be heard for another six months because the numbers of emigrants continued to increase, by the fall of 1979 everyone had realized that the situation had changed. And when the numbers plummeted in 1980, the "experts" proposed the explanation that the Soviets had cut back on emigration in response to the Western reaction to their invasion of Afghanistan. I was amused by this. Even today, some still hold to the "Afghanistan story." The Soviet decision to invade Afghanistan and the invasion itself took place in December 1979, a year after the decision to modify the emigration arrangements in late 1978, and almost a year after I warned about it in my report. On another of his visits to Vienna, Levanon told me that he was strutting around the US like a peacock—the Americans were amazed that the Israelis had known what none of them had been able to discover in advance. He said that we had won a great deal of credit for this. This made a big impression on me. From my conversations and contacts with the Americans and others, I had a low opinion of their ability to comprehend what was happening in the Soviet Union, particularly with regard to the Jews.

I was concerned by the Soviets' ability to find a solution and by the near-closure of the gates. Despite my report, it became clear that no one had made preparations for dealing with the new situation; even after it took effect, neither the Jewish organizations nor the State of Israel, including Nativ, took any steps to cope with the Soviet measures. Neither the refuseniks nor the activists who came to Israel responded in any serious way, and the Soviet authorities managed, almost without resistance, to limit Jewish emigration to several thousand per year. The campaign for Soviet Jewry was reduced to the suffering of the prisoners of Zion and refuseniks, while the overall emigration issue all but vanished from the agenda.

My prediction of the proportion of dropouts, too, proved accurate. In a few cities such as Kiev, Odessa, and Minsk, it reached 90%. Starting in 1980–1981, the total number of emigrants plunged, as did the number of *olim*. In 1979, around 51,000 people left the Soviet Union, of whom about 17,000 came to Israel. From then on, until 1990, the proportion of *olim* among the emigrants decreased. Throughout the 1980s, there were very few emigrants—no more than 1,200 a year towards the end of that decade. The vast majority dropped out, even though they had first-degree relatives in Israel and had received their exit visas on the basis of this close kinship.

Representatives of the Jewish Agency tried to stir their conscience. "You know that if you don't come to Israel," they moralized, "your relatives who want to leave will not be able to do so because it's only possible to send them an invitation from Israel. By going to the US or Canada, you are denying the rest of your family—your parents, your siblings, even your children—any chance of getting out of the Soviet Union. How dare you do this?"

Only a few were influenced by this sermon and made *aliyah*. Most of them, with or without shame, pursued their original plans and abandoned their kin still in the Soviet Union. I frequently saw how the lies and hypocrisy of Soviet society had warped the value systems of those who grew up there. After nine years in Israel, I was often shocked by their abject behavior and disregard for all principles of human ethics.

There were painful incidents of cynicism. The Jewish Agency dispatched many people to talk to the emigrants and influence their destination. Some of these speakers, of course, were politically or personally close to their bosses, but there were also many fine people among them. One was Sophia Tartakovsky, who had been a professor of French literature at the University of Leningrad. Her husband, one of the leading neurosurgeons in the world, was later elected as Israel's representative to and chairman of the World Federation of Neurosurgical Societies. When she was sent to speak to Soviet Jewish emigrants who had decided against *aliyah*, Sophia Tartakovsky was shaken by one particular experience. As usual, she spoke to a group of dropouts in one of the hotels where they were housed. During her lecture, she noticed a young man looking at her intently. She said she felt that he wanted to ask her something. At the end of the lecture, the young man came up and asked to speak with her privately. He told her that he had a problem and was sure that only the State of Israel could help him. Filled with pride, Sophia Tartakovsky told him that the country would certainly find a way to help. What she heard thereafter dumbfounded her for months and made it difficult for her to converse with dropouts. The young man shamelessly informed her that on his way to Vienna he had stopped over for a few days at the Soviet border point in Chop (Ukraine) and had contracted an STD while there. He hoped that the State of Israel could cure him before he went on to the US.

One way or another, tens of thousands of Soviet emigrants crossed my path during my two years in Vienna, and I interviewed many of them. The knowledge and experience I accumulated proved to be of great assistance, then and now, in understanding the Jewish problem in the Soviet Union. I met refuseniks, "*aliyah* activists" who employed ideological arguments to justify why they weren't making *aliyah* despite all their Zionist pronouncements back in the Soviet Union and the support they received from the State of Israel during the period of their refusal. I understood their reasons, even if I didn't agree with them. Some of them were embarrassed but continued to the US, while others weren't discomfited in the slightest. It was particularly difficult for me, and I was forced to curb my natural feelings. I had fought to be allowed to make *aliyah*—and now I had to watch these people destroy the great undertaking with their own hands. I felt and saw the accelerating threat to the entire *aliyah* enterprise. Nonetheless, I overcame those sentiments and did not let them affect my assessments of the situation or my relations with these people. I felt that individuals have the right to decide their fate, but we didn't have to help them if it meant breaking laws and rules and damaging our own national interest.

I was offended by the hypocrisy and materialism of the American Jewish organizations. Due to the fact that they channeled the American government funds to help the immigrants, the dropouts were a source of jobs and money they did not want to miss out on. The utter hypocrisy of all their declarations about respect for free choice and individual freedom were shown up when it became the turn of the Jews from Ethiopia. Not one of the American organizations that set up camps for Ethiopian Jews and encouraged their *aliyah* proposed that they, too, deserved the same freedom of choice as Soviet Jewry. Maybe the Ethiopian Jews wanted to move to Los Angeles, San Francisco, New York, or Miami, like the Jews of Kiev or St. Petersburg. I often heard non-Jewish Americans, government officials who visited Vienna, say that they were willing to deny refugee status to Jews who left the Soviet Union with an exit visa for Israel, but they wanted to ensure that the American Jewish organizations would not accuse them of anti-Semitism and subject them to a wave of political and other pressures. The American officials were not willing to sacrifice their futures to put an end to the dropout phenomenon, even though they saw this as the correct solution.

Around 1980, "the wise men of Chelm"—the Jewish Agency, the State of Israel (including Nativ), and the American organizations—came up with a new system: a special transit camp in Italy. The Jews would stay there a week, during which they would be exposed to intensive Israeli propaganda, without the presence of representatives of American Jewish organizations. If they persisted in their disinterest in *aliyah* afterwards, they would be transferred to the care of the American Jewish organizations for continued processing of their immigration to the US. When I was asked for my opinion of this idea, I said it was a cheap and unnecessary attempt to pretend that some token effort was being made. A Jew who had already reached Italy, where he could smell the fragrance of Rome, freedom, and the Miami he yearned for, would simply spend another week on the beach in conditions he had never dreamed of, and this would just make it easier for him to weather the Israeli propaganda, whatever its quality. Having dealt with propaganda their entire lives, they were in fact immune to it. Soviet citizens who catch the slightest whiff of propaganda immediately disconnect and ignore it; it was doubtful that any of them would change their minds. I also expressed my opinion that this was work for naught, a waste of money and a charade.

But this "solution" gave the entire Israeli and Jewish establishment that dealt with Soviet emigrants a pretext to declare, "We are doing everything we can to fight the dropout phenomenon." So it was decided to implement the idea and a search began for a transit camp location near Naples. Nativ sent me to take part in the search. I discovered that in Italy, you have to collaborate with the local mafia in order to rent a place and operate it. In the end, nothing came of it, though not for lack of involvement with the Neapolitan mafia.

After two years in Vienna, I was called back to Israel. Nativ, which had decided to reorganize and introduce a computerized system, wanted me to focus on work at headquarters while making use of the experience I had gained in Vienna. Without many regrets we packed up and returned home. When we arrived in Israel, I realized that I had grown accustomed to the name Kedmi. My wife and son had also gotten used to it, while my daughter, who was born in Vienna, didn't know another name. So it was not Yasha Kazakov who returned to Israel from Vienna, but Yakov Kedmi. An unknown man, an employee of Nativ, the Liaison Bureau in the Prime Minister's Office.

Chapter 23

For years, I conducted a serious study of Nativ, its essence and its goals. I tried to crystallize the organization's philosophy in my mind. When I was named its director, I assigned someone to investigate and document its history. I believe that I know the history of the organization and the reasons for its establishment and its existence better than any person alive today.

Prime Minister David Ben-Gurion decided to establish Nativ in December 1951, on the recommendation of Reuven Shiloah and Shaike Dan. Shiloah was the head of the Mossad, which he had in practice founded, while Dan, a natural phenomenon even on the Israeli scene, was one of the young men of the Yishuv who volunteered for the British MI-9 intelligence unit. Its members were parachuted into Nazi-occupied countries to work alongside the Jews. Shaike Dan was dropped in Romania. (Hannah Szenes, another member of that unit, was parachuted into Hungary.) After the war, Dan was involved in purchasing arms and bringing *olim* from Eastern Europe. Shiloah and Dan proposed to Ben-Gurion the establishment of a special agency to serve as a liaison to the Jews beyond the Iron Curtain. In the order that established Nativ, Ben-Gurion wrote that he accepted their proposal and had decided to set up such an agency. He emphasized that this agency must be part of the "espionage community," and that is how Nativ was designed.

"Nativ" is a relatively late name for the organization. At first it was called "Mellet," and then "Bilu." Initially its activities focused on forging links with Jews in the countries of the Soviet bloc, and first and foremost on helping extricate those who could get out. Various and sundry methods were devised to carry out this mission. In its infancy, the organization managed to smuggle out some forty Jews. This was considered a heroic and crazy period of time, fraught with dangers. Jews were rescued one by one, at risk to their own lives and those of their rescuers—it was likely that anyone caught would be executed.

Above all, though, the daring and devotion of the State of Israel merits praise. A country that had just been born, surrounded by a hostile Arab world, with meager resources and a very insecure existence, decided to risk a serious confrontation with the biggest, strongest, and most threatening power in the world. The tiny and vulnerable state set up an agency to operate a secret war with the Soviet Union and its satellites in Eastern Europe, with their terrifying regimes, to rescue even a few dozen Jews. I dare say that the current Israeli leadership would not do anything of this nature, if only because of considerations of cost versus benefit. The best operatives of the intelligence community during that period, who had to help ensure the survival and security of the state, were assigned to the rescue of their brothers and sisters behind the Iron Curtain. Their amateurism and the mistakes they made are trivial in comparison to that historic and strategic decision, one of the most important of that time. I would rank it right after Ben-Gurion's decision, against all odds and all opinions, to declare the state.

Soon after the founding of Nativ, Reuven Shiloah was injured in a traffic accident and replaced as head of the Mossad by Isser Harel. When I spoke with Harel about this (he was past eighty at the time), he remembered every detail of what had happened in Nativ. He told me how he was forced to devote his entire first day as head of the Mossad to Nativ. Nativ was planning to launch some complex operation against one of the Soviet missions in Europe and he had to look over and approve the scheme. In the end, he rejected the operation, and rightly so, to judge by what I know about the matter. In 1953, Shaike Dan sponsored the appointment of Shaul Avigur, the former head of the Mossad la'Aliyah Bet (the pre-state clandestine immigration agency), to head Nativ. Avigur (Meirov) had lived in seclusion on his kibbutz since the end of the War of Independence, broken by the death of his son Gur in that war. Nonetheless, he did not refuse the request that he return to service as head of Nativ, within the Mossad. By then, however, Ben-Gurion had left the premiership for the first time and been succeeded by Moshe Sharett. Avigur was married to Sharett's sister, and Isser Harel, not wanting to stick his neck into the political and family briar patch, told Avigur that he should report directly to the Prime Minister. In addition, Avigur enjoyed a special status in Israel and had a close and unique relationship with Ben-Gurion, which created certain problems for Harel. Thus, for reasons that were quite extraneous to the main issue and largely personal, Nativ, though still officially part of the Mossad, became an independent agency directly subordinate to the Prime Minister.

Avigur's political connections and personal status were transmitted to the organization when he headed it. Shaike Dan's special position also strengthened Nativ far beyond its formal position. But it was not until 1971 that then-Mossad chief Zvi Zamir granted the head of Nativ permission to confer directly with the Knesset Foreign Affairs and Defense Committee for approval of its budget. Zamir wrote that he was willing for Nativ to manage all matters related to its budget, including its approval and the deliberations with the Finance Ministry. Ever since birth, Nativ has been at loggerheads with the Foreign Ministry. The senior echelons of the latter have always claimed that Nativ interfered with its diplomatic efforts, obstructed proper relations with both the Soviet Union and the West, and stuck its nose into diplomatic affairs. There were only short interludes without conflict with the Foreign Ministry—when Golda Meir, who was close to Shaike Dan, served as Foreign Minister, and later during Moshe Dayan's tenure.

Nativ placed the Jewish interest—rescuing Jews and helping them make *aliyah*—above and beyond any political considerations. Almost everyone in the Foreign Ministry thought differently. The Jews and the focus on Jews bothered them; some saw it as an inappropriate occupation for professional diplomats. I ran into these people especially in the 1990s. Some of them even saw Nativ's work as beneath the dignity of the State. Their position, albeit unstated, was that we, the State of Israel, are different from the Jews—we are above "those Jewish considerations." As a result, Foreign Ministry personnel always had reservations about Nativ's work, whether consciously or subconsciously. Until the mid-1990s, however, Israeli prime ministers saw the Jews and relations with the Jews, along with efforts to rescue Jews and help them make *aliyah*, as the supreme Jewish and national value. The backing they gave the Nativ organization essentially defined the country's priorities, even though this was not always defined in formal texts. But then, formality was never the strong side of the State of Israel during its first three decades.

This is what Nativ was like when I entered it as a rank-and-file employee at its headquarters. I was appointed deputy director of the department that dealt with the Soviet Union. Shortly after I took up this position, the agency was audited by an attorney named Arye Marinsky, at Begin's request. Years later, I read his report and laughed. The audit had come in response to complaints against Nativ by Herut insiders. Begin sent Marinsky, one of his confidants and an old-line Revisionist, to review Nativ's work for "ideological purity." The focus of Marinsky's inquiry was whether Nativ employees really gave true and devoted attention to the Jewish issue: Were they committed to it or did they have extraneous ideological or political considerations? Of course, this did not include giving jobs to their cronies, which was standard practice in Israel back then, even more so than today. It was not a professional investigation of the sort I would have expected from a representative of the Prime Minister. Marinsky rightly noted the extraordinary devotion of Nativ personnel, their loyalty to the country and to national values, and their commitment to saving and helping Jews. He cited their integrity, which was undoubted and was always prominent at Nativ. But he missed everything else. He didn't investigate the deficiencies—and there were deficiencies, as there are in every organization—some of them objective, organizational, or professional, and some subjective. He was not the right person for a review of this kind. Marinsky submitted the report to Begin, who was very pleased with it. The document reminded me of the reports by Soviet party commissars, who wrote exclusively about ideological purity and devotion to the principles of Leninism, Communism, and any other reigning "-ism."

I have already recounted my meeting with Menachem Begin, which led to my being drafted into Nativ. As I said, I never met with him again. Nevertheless, there are two things that I will always remember and will never forgive him for—and I feel I am justified. The first is his failure to make even the slightest change to Israel's policy on Soviet Jewry. All his bombastic words, all his fiery speeches about "our struggling brothers" and the need for the Government to change its tune—they were all revealed as empty verbiage, nothing but election propaganda with no substance or goal. From the moment he came to power, he was busy "making history."

The second thing, which left a deep wound within me that has yet to heal, is the peace treaty with Egypt. No one who voted for Begin in 1977 could have imagined that the first thing he would do was to conclude a peace treaty with Egypt and withdraw from Sinai. It was not for this that his voters brought him to power, but it seems that Begin's unwavering belief in his greatness and historical destiny allowed him to dismiss what his voters wanted. Despite his polished manner in public, he didn't care a bit for the opinions and desires of his voters and of his fellow members of Herut. Their job was only to worship him and carry out his orders. As long as you supported him, he would shower you with respect and honor. I remember the humiliating and scornful tone he used with Haim Landau, one of his closest and most loyal supporters, only because Landau had dared to express doubts about the treaty with Egypt. Begin marshaled his finest rhetoric and seasoned it with harsh and insulting phrases to put down Landau, who had been a commander in the Irgun and was a senior member of Herut, for the sin of daring to express his own opinion and doubting the leader's words.

When Begin launched the negotiations with Egypt, which entailed giving back all of Sinai, I felt betrayed. I felt that the man was simply lying to me. Moreover, I was disgusted by the behavior of the members of Herut. After all, were somebody other than Menachem Begin— or, heaven forbid, a different party—to make even a fraction of the concessions that Begin did, he would have been ripped to shreds. But when the leader spoke, everyone stood at attention and saluted. You do not argue with the leader; you worship and obey him. With its blind loyalty and obedience to authority, Israel in the late 1970s reminded me of the country where I was born. I had left a country with an ideological and personal dictatorship and could not condone a similar phenomenon in my new country. But because I served in a closed and professional agency that had to stay outside politics, I had no outlet for my anger and indignation.

I remember Geula Cohen's concern and anxiety when we met after Sadat announced his coming trip to Jerusalem. "Yasha," she said, "I am worried by the thought of what we will pay for this visit." Geula's instincts did not betray her that time—though she too could never have dreamt that the price would be all of Sinai, to the last grain of sand.

Today, more than 30 years later, I totally support the peace treaty with Egypt and regret my opposition to it then. But I cannot forgive Begin's behavior, his scorn for the principles of political and democratic fairness as I understand them. My arguments in support of the peace treaty with Egypt today are different from those that Begin used to justify his step. What seems even more ridiculous today is the section of the treaty that deals with autonomy for Judea, Samaria, and Gaza and leaves it to the residents to decide within five years whether they want to be citizens of Israel and have the territories annexed to it. If that article had been implemented … heaven help us! But history has no "what if's."

When I returned from Vienna and took up my post at the Soviet Union Department in Nativ headquarters, I was surprised to learn that there was no organized staff work in the organization. There were no topic-focused discussions and certainly no integrated ones. A few senior officials did hold occasional meetings, but these were informal conversations rather than formal deliberations. The flow and exchange of information were also very "strange." Sometimes you got the impression that everyone was keeping information to himself, as though it was his own private property.

It was Yosef Meller, a Jew from Riga who had been convicted of Zionist activity and sent to a Soviet prison camp, who established the Soviet Union Department. In the mid-1950s, when he was released after Stalin's death, he managed to make *aliyah* by way of Poland. He was a vigorous but modest man, with boundless devotion to the issue of Soviet Jewry. Meller initiated and organized a detailed list of every Soviet Jew on whom Nativ had information. Arye Kroll, a kibbutznik from Sa'ad and an alumnus of the Bnei Akiva youth movement, developed a system to dispatch citizens of Western countries on missions to make contact with Jews in the Soviet Union. But Kroll did not have access to Meller's database, which was kept in the Soviet Jewry Department under the latter's control. When Meller was in a good mood, he would tell his secretary, rather offhandedly, "Give Arye a few addresses before his trip." When he was not in the right mood, he would refuse Kroll's request for addresses. There was a sort of disconnect between "Bar," the Nativ section that dealt with activities in Western countries on behalf of Soviet Jewry, and Nativ itself. Any coordination between the two was incidental.

There was a turnover of personnel at Nativ during my first year back from Vienna. Some of the veteran staff retired, including Yosef Meller. As was common then, they continued to work in the agency part-time, with a different status, and enjoyed both a pension and a salary. It was not until a few years later that the Finance Ministry demanded we put an end to this procedure. In effect, though, the old hands' retirement left the Soviet Union Department under my direction. Nehemiah Levanon continued as director of Nativ; we had a correct working relationship based on mutual trust at the professional level, despite occasional disagreements. My general approach was different from that of Levanon's and others at Nativ, but I did not yet have enough experience to formulate it at a professional level and format. I argued, but I didn't fight.

Chapter 24

Except for my period in Vienna, I continued to serve in the IDF reserves over the years. Battalion 100 in which I had fought had been converted into a regular battalion and I did my reserve duty as an intelligence officer in a different armored unit. I was lucky—my commander was Amnon Marton, an outstanding human being, extraordinary in his personal and intellectual integrity, and one of the best battalion commanders in the Armored Corps. He was later promoted to command the brigade. Marton was a left-wing kibbutznik, a member of Mapam, so we had obvious ideological disagreements. People laughed at how we loved each other and got along so well, and he would smile and tell them, "You'd be surprised how much we have in common. When it comes to values, both national and ethical, we have no disagreements."

I learned a lot from Amnon—about thinking in general and about military thinking in particular, including organization and planning. My experience in the war and service in the reserves did wonders to develop my thinking, my understanding, and my professional ability as an officer; later, my military insights continued to develop in other fields as well, and in different circumstances.

The first thing Amnon asked me to do when I joined the battalion was to gather all the officers and try to explain to them what had been happening in its battles during the war. Amnon had also been a battalion commander then, but he was wounded in his battalion's attack on the "Missouri" sector of the "Chinese farm." This was after our battalion had already crossed the Canal. Amnon told me that he felt that some of the officers in the battalion lacked confidence in their ability to win a battle. I spoke with the officers and studied what they had gone through in combat. Because I also knew the picture on the Egyptian side, I reached conclusions fairly quickly. I invited all the armor officers from the battalion to a meeting and asked them to explain what they saw as the problem—the reasons for our inability to attack and fight successfully. They told me that when they had launched the attack, they were inundated by heavy cannon fire and volleys of missiles; the battalion was nearly destroyed within a matter of minutes. I asked each of them to tell all of us what he had seen on the battlefield. After everyone had spoken, I explained to them that in every brigade that was ordered to attack, two battalions charged forward and one stayed behind to provide covering fire. In their case, the second battalion got stuck in a minefield and could not advance, so their battalion carried out the attack alone. The maneuver was carried out in the usual way—two companies in front and the third behind. This meant that out of the entire brigade, only two companies lacking their full strength charged the Egyptian compound—fifteen tanks, with another seven on the second line. I asked them if they knew anything about the target of the attack and the forces facing them. They had no idea, even a year after the war. I asked them to tell me what kinds of fire were directed at them and to point out its sources on the map. After they answered, I used their replies to explain that they had been attacking the artillery and anti-tank concentrations of an entire Egyptian division—an impossible imbalance of forces, and almost totally without artillery cover from our side. So the problem was not the combat abilities of our tanks as opposed to Egypt, but that they were sent into a battle that was hopeless. "It was suicide," I said emphatically. "It was unprofessional to send you out like that, from both the operational and intelligence perspectives."

We began to teach them new tactics that had been devised for fighting on a battlefield saturated by incoming missiles, and the correct use of coordinated cover, artillery, mortars, and various types of smoke screens, as well as how tanks could screen themselves. We emphasized and drilled the importance of correct movement, covering fire, and occupying positions. We proved that it was possible to reduce the losses from missiles to almost zero if we fought correctly against the Syrian and Egyptian armies. What was sad was that the principles that we began to formulate had been thought up and implemented by both the Wehrmacht and the Red Army in the late 1930s.

But when we launched the Second Lebanon War, I saw that it had all been forgotten. When I saw direct hits on Merkava tanks, from below and from behind, I told myself that the IDF had forgotten everything we had known 30 years earlier—the ABCs of armored warfare. In my time, we were proud that IDF tank crews shot more live shells in practice than those of any other army in the world and that IDF tank drivers had more experience and better skills than anyone else. But the tank crewmen of the Second Lebanon War went into battle with a total of four hours of driving practice, with crews that had not seen the inside of a tank for years, and with officers who had no idea what an armored battle is, because they had never learned or had long since forgotten—division commanders who had no clue what a tank is and how it works. I felt deep embarrassment and pain that such things could happen in my army in the early twenty-first century.

Chapter 25

In June 1982, the IDF's best-planned conflict—the Lebanon War (24 years later, it became known as the "First Lebanon War")—began. I received a call-up notice. Our battalion was part of a General Staff division and our plans changed every few days. We had nothing to do in Lebanon, where six divisions were already operating—certainly more than enough. Once, we got an order to move to the Lebanese front and deploy as a reserve, so we began to load the tank-carriers. After all the tanks were loaded, our orders were changed and we had to prepare for redeployment to the Golan Heights and an attack against Syria. From our orders and preparations, as well as all the changes, we could more or less understand the situation. In addition, I occasionally received updates from division intelligence.

I remember that after one order we received, we studied a mountainous road we were supposed to take in order to reach the Lebanese town of Jezzine in the central sector. According to the intelligence reports we received, a Syrian tank battalion was stationed there.

"What will we do with the Syrians?" I asked, because our orders made no mention of them. The answer to my question surprised me, but it reflected the confusion of the high command and its lack of understanding of the situation. I was told that we were to "fire in the direction of the Syrian positions, but not at their forces. As soon as we shoot a few rounds, the Syrians will turn tail and leave the road open for us."

"And if they don't, do we attack them?" I asked innocently.

I received the impatient response, "Of course they'll fold! Don't attack them directly. And in general, there is no reason to waste time with unnecessary questions."

These orders were cancelled, but later I looked into what actually happened in Jezzine. It turns out that the Syrians fired back and we found ourselves in a battle with them.

For about a week we were kept on the tank-carriers, until they finally sent our battalion home on the grounds that they had sufficient forces in the field and did not want to waste us. We were told to wait and they would call us back if they decided to advance on Damascus. Thus my second war in Israel came and went. I did not particularly regret that I had not taken part in it. Although I was pretty much in agreement with its goals at the time, the war did not excite me.

The conduct of the first Lebanon War and its results sowed the seeds for the Second Lebanon War—and all this just so Yasser Arafat and his people would decamp from Beirut to Tunis? We paid much too high a price for a war that had been planned for over a year and was launched at a time of our choosing. There was no real connection between the war and the terrorist attack on the Israeli ambassador in London. Ambassador Shlomo Argov was targeted by Naef Hawatmeh's organization, whose headquarters were in Baghdad, not in Lebanon. As a veteran of the Yom Kippur War, I was sorry to see that nine years later, our army was much larger but much less professional. Overall, despite its vast superiority, the IDF did not manage to carry out any of its missions, neither with regard to the Syrians nor the terrorists, within the timetable set. Most disappointing for me was the behavior, or more accurately, the dysfunctional behavior, of Prime Minister Menachem Begin. Aside from his public statements, which were pompous and demagogical, he was barely felt. This was most definitely a war that belonged to Defense Minister Ariel Sharon, who launched it and ran it in his typical way, for better and for worse. Even without the tragedy of Sabra and Shatila, we could not have been proud of this war, of how the IDF fought, how decisions were made, and the disgraceful way the war was conducted by the political and even more so the military echelons. I was again disappointed by the fact that the IDF deployed its special units in a very limited way, far below their capabilities and ignoring their purpose.

The phenomenon of shirking responsibility infected almost all those involved in the war, from the Prime Minister and the political leadership to nearly the entire IDF command network. The tragedy and embarrassment of the Second Lebanon War were a natural sequel to this fiasco.

Chapter 26

When I was released from the reserves, I went back to Nativ. After my appointment as head of the Soviet Union Department in 1982, I got into things more deeply and found a startling picture that I had never imagined possible in a country like ours. From the list of authorized positions and the human resources chart in the department, which included job definitions and grades, it became clear to me that there was no resemblance between the actual allocation of employees and their jobs and the formal human resources chart, because the job definitions had been set many years earlier and no longer coincided with the real situation. I also found out that employees did not know what authorized positions they held, what employment grades applied to their jobs, or even the exact nature of their jobs. From time to time, an employee would receive a promotion without any clue of the reason: Had he served the defined stint in his job and grade, or did his boss, the head of the department, want to reward him? Employees were transferred from job to job without even knowing about it or with no good reason, just to free up some authorized slot or for a promotion. I decided to introduce a different approach.

In an attempt to establish a correspondence between jobs and job definitions and the people who filled them I began interviewing everyone in the department. This gained me an immediate protest by the Human Resources officer: Where on earth did I get the idea of telling employees what positions they were filling and how their jobs were defined?! There was no precedent for this; I was undermining the work relationship. I ignored him and continued to redefine jobs, with the approval of the Civil Service Commissioner. I called in every member of the staff, explained their description, the applicable employment grades, and their possibilities for promotion. Some of them were astounded to learn that the only way they could reach a higher grade was to change jobs, something they could not do because of the nature of the work or their unsuitability. It was difficult to explain to people why they could not keep receiving promotions as they were used to. I could not transfer employees from job to job just to allow them a higher grade, as my predecessors had done, unless the job was linked to the employee's post, abilities, and skills.

I was rather disturbed by the fact that the workers in a government office had the feeling that they were completely dependent on their supervisor's will. I was particularly surprised that these arrangements were instituted, in breach of all laws, by people who said they were socialists. The agency's director and some of its senior officials were kibbutzniks who claimed to be concerned with workers' rights. In the meantime, Nehemiah Levanon had decided to quit for personal reasons. I don't know whether his reasons had anything to do with the fact that he now had to work under Menachem Begin, who was not exactly his favorite person. I never talked politics with anybody in the organization because I thought it was inappropriate to do so, and people there didn't discuss political matters with me because of their suspicion that I represented a different political force. Levanon's appointment to head Nativ in 1969 had marked the start of a new era for the organization and its work—more open, more flexible, more effective. During his years at the helm, and in large part thanks to his efforts, the State of Israel and world Jewry turned Nativ into a vast apparatus to assist Soviet Jewry in their struggle. Without Levanon, it is doubtful we would have achieved all of this. I think it would have been possible to do much more and do it much better; but in those years Israel could not have placed anyone better in that position.

We were informed that the agency was getting a new director, Prof. Yehuda Lapidot. I didn't know who he was and had never heard his name before. Later I discovered that he had been a commander in the Irgun, using the nom de guerre "Nimrod." He had been the deputy commander of the operation in Deir Yassin and was fairly close to Begin. He was a member of Herut but not politically active. Until his appointment as director of Nativ, Lapidot was a professor of biochemistry at the Hebrew University. It was not clear what qualities this biochemistry professor had that suited him to run the agency—he had never been involved in anything remotely like Nativ's modus operandi and hadn't the foggiest idea about the Soviet Union or Eastern Europe. By contrast, the political nexus was crystal clear. It was said that when Begin was elected prime minister, Yehuda Lapidot came and asked for some government job. As the story goes, and I don't know if it's true, he was hoping for appointment as an ambassador, perhaps in South Africa. But that was when Nehemiah Levanon decided to retire, and Begin decided to appoint this fine man, who had suffered so acutely under the Mapai regime because of the fallout from Deir Yassin, which Mapai exploited against the veterans of the Irgun and Lehi.

Lapidot came to Nativ in late 1981. Changes were felt immediately in the nature and quality of our work, in work relations, and especially in the attitude to the issue of Soviet Jews and their struggle for *aliyah*. To put it mildly, he was not suited for the job. His approach caused serious grumbling among most of those who dealt with *aliyah* and the *aliyah* campaign. It wasn't a matter of politics, even though many of the old guard saw his job performance as typical of the quality of the people in Begin's camp. Members of Herut and the Likud, too, expressed a strongly negative assessment of his work, and did not keep this criticism to themselves. In short order, I saw the changes and the damage he did to the organization, its image, and the issue in general. The damage went beyond the lack of a calculated or guided policy to the deterioration of the professional and even ethical considerations on which the work was based, almost to the point of their destruction.

A delegation from the Organization of Prisoners of Zion, most of them old-line Revisionists, met with Begin to discuss Lapidot's performance at Nativ. Its head, Avraham Shtukarevich, who had been a member of Beitar back in Lithuania, had been close to Begin for many years. According to the reports I heard about the meeting, Begin listened to what they had to say, but concluded by saying that he could not do anything that would hurt "Nimrod." On more than one occasion, various people close to Begin had tried to persuade him of Lapidot's unsuitability for the job. Begin was not happy about their pressure and usually simply did not respond. I also considered requesting a meeting with him, but dropped the idea when I realized that it wouldn't help. I often wondered why Begin appointed Yehuda Lapidot to head Nativ, and my conclusions were quite appalling. I saw the appointment as a logical continuation of Begin's path when he totally failed to modify Israel's policy towards the struggle for *aliyah* after his election as prime minister. Nonetheless, I wondered how it was possible to treat the matter so offhandedly as to place at its head a man with no ability to handle or connect to one of the most complex and important issues facing the country. Was political comradeship holier than all other considerations?! Later, when the IDF launched the Lebanon War, everything fell into place in my understanding of Begin. If a prime minister could show such a devil-may-care attitude and lack of seriousness about a matter as fateful as going to war—how could I complain about his choice to head Nativ?

After Begin resigned, long after he had effectively stopped functioning, Yitzhak Shamir took over as prime minister. I asked for a meeting with him. Over the years, I had met with Shamir frequently; he had supported the *aliyah* campaign from the very beginning and his interest and involvement in the topic never flagged. I reviewed the situation for him and expressed my negative assessment of Lapidot's work. I backed up my claims, cited proof from various sources, and warned him that if the situation continued, there was liable to be serious damage to the *aliyah* issue and to the Jewish People as a whole. To my surprise, Shamir agreed with me. He said he was aware of the situation because he had heard similar things from all directions. Nonetheless, he asked me to be patient because he was not totally free to deal with Lapidot. Shamir was a Lehi man, while Lapidot had belonged to the Irgun. If the historical rivalry between the two organizations were not enough, Shamir also had to maneuver between the camps in the Likud, those of David Levy and Ariel Sharon. I told him that I understood his situation and would try to do my job, but as prime minister he could not ignore the problem. Later on, we continued to meet to discuss this topic.

Lapidot once called me in and asked about a certain employee: did I know that she was a member of Peace Now? I told him that I didn't know anything about that; it was certainly possible but it didn't interest me.

"Don't you think that her opinions will influence the way she does her job?" he asked.

I replied that I saw no connection between the positions of Peace Now and the struggle or our activity with Soviet Jewry. I also said that the General Security Service had never listed Peace Now, unlike other organizations, as an organization whose members or supporters posed a security risk.

"Strange," he responded with surprise, and that was the end of our conversation.

In both the Mossad and the General Security Service, I had encountered people whose opinions were different from and even antithetical to mine and very close to those of Peace Now. Their political opinions made them no less professional. One of the things that disgusted me even in back in the Soviet Union was discrimination against people on account of their opinions.

One fine day, Lapidot summoned me to his office. Arye Kroll, one of his most loyal henchmen, who enjoyed a free hand to do whatever he wanted, was also sitting there. Lapidot told me that he had heard that I was meeting with the Prime Minister and discussing various matters, including himself and his job performance. When I confirmed this, he asked me what I had told the Prime Minister and what Shamir had told me. I responded that I was not in the habit of talking about my conversations with the Prime Minister and certainly not about their content. He could ask the Prime Minister himself. If the Prime Minister deemed it appropriate, he would tell him what we had spoken about and would also explain why he was willing to meet me even though this amounted to bypassing the chain of command. I added that even though I would not tell him the topics of my conversation with the Prime Minister, I was willing to tell him my opinion of himself and his work if he wanted to hear it.

"Please," he said.

I told him that, without going into detail, his work had done serious damage to *aliyah*, to the support for the struggle, and to Nativ itself. I told him he should be sent home from Nativ, and the sooner the better, because every additional day that he was in the job caused the country more harm. Lapidot stared at me with no expression and asked how, if this was my opinion of him, we could continue to work together. I answered, rather insolently, that I would continue to do my job, and that I didn't know what he did, nor was it important as long as he didn't interfere with my work.

He replied that in his opinion we could no longer work together and I should get out of his office.

My answer was brutal and angry "You came here looking for a cushy job. For me, this is an issue I have devoted my entire life to. Of the two of us, you are the one who should leave the office—not me."

Lapidot continued the conversation and asked whether I had met with Shaike Dan. From the minute Lapidot came to Nativ, Shaike Dan had never set foot there. Nativ was the apple of his eye; he had founded it, built it, and breathed life into it, and was devoted to it till his last day.

"Of course," I replied.

Lapidot continued his interrogation. "What do you talk about?"

I told him that I spoke with Dan about whatever we felt like—we were friends and had a lot to talk about. But Lapidot blistered me with his suspicion that I was discussing Nativ matters with Dan, in violation of the law, providing him with classified information he was not privileged to know.

I told Lapidot, almost with scorn, that I didn't know any classified topics that Nativ addressed which its founder could not know about. But if he had a problem with this, he could refer the matter to the competent parties.

In a last attempt to impose his authority on me he said, "I forbid you to meet with Shaike Dan and talk with him."

I kept my cool. "You can't forbid me to meet with Shaike and my other friends and telling them what I think." I made it plain that I would continue to meet Dan, both as a former member of Nativ and as a friend, and that I had the right to consult with him about professional questions in light of his experience and knowledge. With this, our surrealistic conversation came to an end.

Lapidot summoned me again about a week later and asked me my opinion about Rafi Pizov. Pizov, a Jew from Riga, was a very talented fellow. Like many other *aliyah* activists, he had been interrogated by the KGB. In 1972, he made *aliyah* with his parents, enlisted in the police, and then transferred to the IDF. He was already a major when I "intercepted" him and persuaded him to leave the army and join Nativ. Pizov began working in Nativ a few weeks before my conversation with Lapidot. In light of his skills, his knowledge, and his experience in the Soviet Union and the IDF, I asked him to take charge of the reports and of processing the information that had accumulated in the department. This domain had been neglected in the past and I thought we needed to formalize it and handle it in a professional manner. You cannot make decisions without knowing or understanding what is going on in the field, and my experience in Vienna had strengthened my opinion.

Lapidot told me that Pizov had already been working for a month and a half and that, in his opinion, he was unfit for the job. As director of Nativ, he had decided to fire him. I did not tell Lapidot what I thought were the real reasons for this step. I understood that because he could not get at me he wanted to hurt somebody who was close to me. He didn't care that Pizov was a new immigrant who had recently got married, started a family, and left the regular army to come to Nativ. Lapidot wanted to throw him out merely because I had recruited him and he was working with me.

I answered him in an angry and threatening tone: "I work with Rafi and I am his supervisor. Only I have the ability to assess his suitability or unsuitability for the job—and in my opinion he is suited for it. You have no way of knowing if he is good or not. You don't work with him, you don't read his materials, you have never spoken with him even once. I won't let you fire him."

He was taken aback by my response. Nevertheless, two days later, Pizov came to me, pale, trembling, in shock. He had received a letter from the head of Nativ informing him that he would be terminated in thirty days.

Rafi Pizov was a fine young man. Even though he had been an officer in the IDF, he never learned how to deal with this kind of pressure. I frequently encountered officers like that, including many with a combat background. Most of the staff officers I knew had different talents, but courage and endurance were not their strong points.

"Don't worry," I told Pizov, "I'll take care of it."

I called the Prime Minister's office and asked to speak with Shamir. I told him what had happened and asked him to intervene. His answer was short and to the point: "Okay, I'll take care of it." And Yehuda Lapidot received an order from the Prime Minister to leave Pizov alone.

But Lapidot's desire to continue abusing the young man and perhaps me through him got the better of him. He wrote another letter, informing Pizov that his dismissal was deferred for a month. Again Pizov came to me in shock. I told him to relax and that the issue would be taken care of. At the end of the month, I contacted the Prime Minister's office again and the same thing happened. Shamir again called Lapidot, who in turn wrote another letter that the termination was postponed for another month. This was a form of Chinese water torture. I maintained my own composure but took pity on Pizov, whose nerves were shot.

"Keep working," I told him. "I won't let them throw you out."

The harassment went on for a long time and even continued after Shimon Peres became prime minister. I went to him, and following Shamir's lead, he too ordered that Pizov stay on. In the end, Pizov remained at Nativ until he retired early in the new century. Even today, that petty and low-down way of running things leaves a bad taste in my mouth. Without my stubborn resistance, they would have thrown the man to the dogs without reason or justification.

Although he was prime minister, Shamir did not dare to remove Lapidot. He merely instructed that I was "off limits" for him and forbade him to take any steps against me. Lapidot, for his part, ordered me to be left out of the loop of incoming information and reports. This produced a virtually total detachment between the head of Nativ and the head of its Soviet Jewry Department. Naturally, he couldn't deprive me of access to material whose source was my own department. I also continued to meet with and debrief *olim*, particularly the activists among them. Arye Kroll grudgingly continued to send me reports submitted by the Western "tourists" operated by his department, if only because it was necessary to update the large amount of information and data in those reports, which could be done only by the Soviet Jewry Department. These materials were enough to allow me to assess what was actually taking place on the ground.

There were a few other nasty tricks, like revoking my entry permit to Ben-Gurion Airport, which was granted to every other department head. I needed the permit so I could debrief or converse with *olim*, particularly the activists among them, as soon as they landed—but I overcame this obstacle. There was also the time that Kroll asked a member of my department for a sample of my handwriting. When she complied, he said he needed a sample in Russian. Her response was that I did not write in Russian, only in Hebrew, and she had never seen anything I had written in Russian. She was telling the truth; I indeed wrote only in Hebrew. It seems that Kroll, in cahoots with Lapidot, wanted to send a sample of my handwriting to a graphologist working for them, so that he could get a professional opinion that I was unsuitable for my job and for Nativ. I knew nothing of this at the time. It was only some years later that the woman worked up the nerve to tell me the story.

As mentioned, I also spoke with Prime Minister Peres about Lapidot's malfeasance. After Shamir's term I had an abundance of new examples that Lapidot provided. Not only did Peres order him to stop sending Rafi Pizov the monthly deferred-dismissal letter, he eventually mustered the courage to sack Lapidot. On his last day at the organization, I went out to the gate and watched from the side as he left for good. When he passed me, I did not tell him goodbye or say anything else. I looked at him with a half-smile and remembered what I had told him in our charged conversation several years earlier: "Of the two of us, you're the one who will be leaving—not me." He got into his car and I never saw him again. Almost four years passed from the day he entered Nativ until his departure—some of that overlapping with his predecessor and successors. He was in full control for three years, more or less, from the end of Begin's term to about a year after Shimon Peres became prime minister.

Many years later, he called and asked to consult with me about some question and receive information from the office. By then it was the late 1990s and I was the director of Nativ. We met, spoke cordially, and I fulfilled his request without asking any questions. At the end of the meeting, I wished him good luck. I did not feel anything towards him. In my view, his was a very sad case from a human perspective and it's too bad that he and all of us were involved in it. Because of an unwise decision by Begin, who hadn't the slightest idea of how to manage systems, Lapidot found himself in a place where he did not belong. Had Begin appointed him ambassador to South Africa or some similar position, he would probably have been much more successful. He was really the wrong man in the wrong place at the wrong time, and running into someone like me certainly didn't make things easier for him (and not only for him). It only exacerbated the problem.

Chapter 27

At some point during the two years I was embroiled with Lapidot, Arye Kroll called me in to talk. Our relationship went back a long way and was complicated.

"What are you doing?" he asked me. "Who are you fighting against? Do you know what kind of backing he has in the party? Who are you? What are you? Who will support you? You're alone. You are fighting a hopeless war!"

I smiled. "Arye," I said quietly, "I've been fighting hopeless wars all my life. I'm used to it. I'll win this time, too."

That conversation is the source of this book's title: "Hopeless Wars"—wars in which there is no chance of victory, which I have fought alone, with my back against the wall, with no hope for help or support from anyone—persisting until I emerge victorious.

During Yehuda Lapidot's time at Nativ, the quality of the staff work declined from the standard that prevailed under Nehemiah Levanon. Though I had my criticisms and disagreements with both Levanon's actions and political line, he had vast experience, knowledge, and understanding of the topic. He didn't receive the position through the spoils system. He devoted his life to the issue of Soviet Jewry. Deprived of his knowledge, understanding, and dedication, Nativ started going downhill. Almost all the veteran agents who had experience with the Soviet Jewry issue left the organization (most of them retired).

Outside the Soviet Jewry Department I headed, there was no one left at Nativ with the background or capacity to understand and assess events in the Soviet Union. Few members of the staff were fluent in Russian. The disconnection between the senior echelons and my department made it impossible for them to make the right decisions about Soviet Jewry and its situation. Nativ's work became limited to organizing and participating in international conferences and meetings "on behalf of Soviet Jewry." Its status as the leading and most serious actor in the matter plummeted. As a consequence, so did that of the State of Israel.

Kroll had established a fabulous and extensive mechanism to dispatch "tourists" from all over the world to meet with Jews in the Soviet Union. But other than the idea itself and the dedication displayed by Kroll and these "tourists," the system was dogged by a lack of professionalism and a flawed approach. Kroll joined Nativ in the early 1970s, but he lacked the tools needed to understand the dynamic and complex processes taking place in the Soviet Union and their implications for Soviet Jewry. And this wasn't just because he didn't know Russian. In fact, it is impossible to work effectively, forging contacts and overseeing the activities of hundreds of people in a hostile foreign country—a country thousands of kilometers away and with one of the finest security services in the world—if you do not engage in analysis and assessment of both the individuals and groups involved, with their characteristics, problems, dynamics, and ties, if you do not sketch out an overall picture, define objectives and work plans, draw conclusions, and scrutinize and evaluate your work. Kroll, who did not know Russian (nor did anyone around him), tried to run the entire system on his own. As a result, the support provided by his department reached only a comparatively small number of activists who were inundated with visitors, while most of the activists and refuseniks never met any of his "tourists." Kroll called this "building up the man." I kept hearing him say that he was going to "build up" some activist or other, without having tried to understand or properly assess the man, his abilities, and his weaknesses. The main consideration was whether the person was loyal to Kroll and refrained from contacts with other non-establishment Jewish organizations. The concentration of the means and contacts in just a few hands corrupted some activists and warped the relations among them. This, of course, greatly diminished the efficacy of Jewish activities in many senses.

The fact that a majority of these "tourists" were affiliated with the religious Bnei Akiva youth movement distorted the message that was being transmitted and received. What is more, it made it much easier for the Soviet security services to identify Kroll's agents in advance of their arrival in the Soviet Union. When I first started reading the reports they submitted, I identified too many tell-tale signs of their true identities in their personal data, itinerary, and travel requests. For example, a vegetarian meal on the plane: In the 1970s, it was patently obvious that two young "tourists" on the same flight who requested vegetarian meals did so because they kept kosher. Afraid of losing total control of the issue, Kroll, with Lapidot's support, rejected every attempt to base the project on professional work. In fact, the general situation and Israeli and Jewish policy were too complex and thorny a problem to be dealt with using the simplistic and primitive approach they had developed and grown accustomed to over the years. This led to many fiascos.

The Soviets' decision in late 1978 to reduce emigration to a minimum succeeded beyond their expectations. Over the course of 1979, every relevant office in the Soviet Union began processing exit documents only in response to invitations for family reunification submitted by first-degree relatives. The rapid increase in the number of emigrants was because those who had left earlier sent invitations to all their relatives left behind. But the accelerating dropout rate meant that a majority of those still in the Soviet Union could not apply to leave, because their relatives who had not gone to Israel could not send them invitations. As a result, the number of people applying to emigrate declined sharply. The number of those receiving exit visas decreased, with no equivalent increase in the number of refuseniks, which actually grew smaller.

I learned that most of the refusals to grant exit visas were justified by Soviet security rules (and those of other countries as well). I became fairly knowledgeable not only about the standard Soviet hierarchy of security clearances, but also about the grounds for each level and the associated cooling-off period. I often checked my evaluation against concrete instances, and the correlation was usually very close. There were certainly outliers and exploitation of the problem of security clearance in both directions, but the guidelines were clear and were generally followed, with only rare instances in which the pressure of the political echelons caused refuseniks to receive exit visas over the objections of the professionals. One of the best-known cases was that of Vladimir Slepak, a key *aliyah* activist who had to wait seventeen years for an exit visa. Under the rules, Slepak, who helped plan the strategic anti-missile defense system around Moscow, should not have been allowed to leave the country even then. Some refuseniks were quite unaware that they had been exposed to classified materials. I investigated hundreds of such cases and quickly discovered the grounds for the refusal, even when those affected had no idea what the issue was. Only professionals could assess the true value of the classified and sensitive information that "escaped" with the émigrés. The Soviets never had an inkling of the damage done to their security by the information the émigrés carried with them. A person is an almost inexhaustible store of information, though for the most part he is unaware of its scope or true value and will often pass it on to a professional interrogator with no idea of what he has revealed.

In any case, refusal was not a tool for restricting emigration in the 1970s and 1980s. The number of new refuseniks declined, while, with few exceptions, the veteran refuseniks, including those whose security classification had expired, could not leave if they did not have an invitation from a first-degree relative in Israel. The struggle in the West came to focus on Prisoners of Zion and refuseniks. The more general campaign was forgotten, aside from the slogan "Let my people go"—whose meaning had long since been forgotten, if it had ever even been relevant. I had actually begun my journey and struggle because of this worldview, so I felt the full severity of the problem. Nativ and the State of Israel, and American Jews even more so (for their own non-Zionists reasons), did not demand unfettered *aliyah* to Israel. They preferred to emphasize freedom of religion and culture and the principle of family reunification. Moreover, after the emergence of the dropout phenomenon, it was ridiculous to speak about *aliyah* when the vast majority of those who left the Soviet Union did not go to Israel. Thus, the dropouts effectively pulled the rug out from under the demand that the Soviets allow *aliyah*. It was easy to demonstrate with a picture of some Prisoner of Zion and go home with a clean conscience, but hardly anyone was still concerned about the restrictions on *aliyah* and emigration.

In various discussions and in response to the pressure exerted on them, the Soviet authorities were willing to talk about refuseniks and Prisoners of Zion. The Vanik-Jackson Amendment, in force since 1975, could no longer be brandished as a threat. It should have been employed as a deterrent—like nuclear weapons, which are only threatening as long as they aren't used. Nativ in the post-Levanon era was totally unaware of the real problem. After the Lebanon War, the Israeli leadership was immersed in confrontations associated with the Occupied Territories, and even more so in struggles for power. No one in the government had the leisure to consider the problem of Soviet *aliyah*. They thought it was enough to show up at a reception for some former Prisoner of Zion or refusenik in Lod, or at an international conference on behalf of Soviet Jewry. Without the dropout phenomenon, the number of émigrés who made *aliyah* would have been several times greater, even under the new regulations, and the momentum of *aliyah* would have continued. The dropouts vanquished *aliyah* and helped the Soviet Union put an almost total end to emigration and *aliyah*. Only the collapse of the Soviet Union could have revived *aliyah*—and that is indeed what happened. Until then, we were losing the decisive battle of those years, though we did not realize it and were not particularly concerned by the matter. This was the situation as I saw it at the end of Lapidot's tenure, when David Bartov took up the reins of Nativ in 1986.

I have written about my first meeting with David Bartov in Moscow in 1967, during my second break-in to the Israel Embassy. Bartov was sent to Moscow in 1964 to head the Nativ unit there. He was a very gentle man, averse to quarrels and disputes, and always tried to reach a compromise. Perhaps his training as a lawyer contributed to this. Many *olim* came to know his hospitable family and had been guests in their home. I, too, visited them many times after I made *aliyah* and received a warm and friendly welcome. Although I was delighted by Bartov's appointment to head Nativ, I knew that, despite his fine qualities and exceptional attitude towards *aliyah*, he was not a manager. He did not have the experience or skills for the job. He tried to stay on good terms with everyone and never get into an argument—and that was impossible. I had a very good working relationship with him throughout his tenure at Nativ. Arye Kroll, who had been responsible for sending foreigners to the Soviet Union, left after Bartov arrived and the entire field was transferred to my purview. Now everything associated with the Soviet Union was concentrated in one unit—mine. Bartov did not always agree with me, but in the end he always preferred for things to get done rather than to argue about them.

As a result of Bartov's appointment, Shaike Dan returned to the picture as well. One of the ideas that gained momentum around this time was the establishment of an *aliyah* route by way of Romania, in addition to the emigration channel through Vienna. This meant we had to persuade the Romanian authorities to again issue transit visas to Jews en route to Israel. Until the suspension of *aliyah* in 1967, after the Six Day War and the severing of diplomatic relations between Israel and the Soviet Union, there had been a short period when Jews, particularly those from Moldova, made *aliyah* through Romania. This idea was floated by Yehoshua Pratt, then the director of Bar (the Nativ department that sought to influence public opinion in the West). The underlying logic was that Romania, a Communist state under the dictatorship of Ceausescu, would not allow Jews to change their destination after they reached Romania. Shaike Dan used his connections with the JDC and the Americans to obtain the promise of an American loan of $100 million, and Romania gave permission for Jews to come through Bucharest. There had always been a Nativ unit in Bucharest, meant to deal with *aliyah* from Romania. Now, its staff quickly and efficiently established a way station for Soviet Jews.

But why should *olim* go through Bucharest rather than Vienna? I proposed that those who came through Romania be refunded the cost of their train ticket out of the Soviet Union in dollars and at the official ruble-dollar exchange rate. The Jewish Agency agreed. Generally speaking, *olim* had a problem getting their possessions out. A family of four had to pay between 1,500 and 2,000 rubles for their passage to Romania. After *aliyah*, they received a refund of $1,800 to $2,600, which was a respectable sum for families that were forced to leave most of their property behind and prohibited from taking out their money. As a result, the Romanian route became increasingly popular and most *olim* came through Bucharest. Most of those who went through Vienna were planning to go on to other countries. Nevertheless, the volume of emigration continued to diminish, reaching a low point of only 1,200 émigrés in all of 1988, including a few hundred *olim*.

Nativ had a special relationship with the Israeli postal censor, going back to the 1950s, which facilitated its acquisition of information about Soviet Jewry. At Nativ's request, the censor provided copies of all personal correspondence with the Soviet Union. The idea was to allow Nativ to collect and update the names of Soviet Jews, the addresses and vital statistics of their relatives in Israel, and the nature of their contacts. The content of the letters was an inexhaustible source of information about the situation of the Jews and the situation in the Soviet Union, even though the letter-writers were aware and leery of the Soviet censor.

When Yosef Meller retired and I succeeded him as head of the Soviet Union Department, I inherited his authorization to intercept the mail of all Israeli citizens. The censor's office decided whether to send us only the main points of the letter or the entire text. A letter that we received, whether in summary or verbatim, was held back until we reached a final decision about it. I had the power to order that a letter be "lost" or proceed to its destination. Several women in our department read and processed the letters forwarded by the censor, while the final decision about their fate was reserved to me. At some point, I enlisted the censor in the effort to put an end to the sending of forged invitations to Soviet Jews. The Soviet authorities would accept family-reunification applications only against an invitation, which was supposed to come from a close relative in Israel, accompanied by a Foreign Ministry document in which the State of Israel undertook to provide the invitees named in the request with an entry visa to Israel after they received a Soviet exit visa. The signatures of the inviters and the official seals had to be validated by a notary public and by the Foreign Ministry. Nativ had the Attorney General's permission to affix the Foreign Ministry's rubber stamp. Dropouts could not send invitations to their loved ones to join them in Israel, since they had not made *aliyah*. And, as mentioned, the Soviets instituted a new policy that only an invitation from a first-degree relative was acceptable as grounds for *aliyah*. They required that the invitation arrive in an envelope sent from Israel with an Israeli postmark. So some clever Jews, including a few notaries, went into the business of creating and sending forged invitations from Israel.

From time to time, groups of "good" Jews in Israel organized to forge and dispatch invitations—for a fee, of course. Genuine invitations could be made and sent only through Nativ. Our concern was that the Soviet authorities would suddenly announce that all the family-reunification invitations from Israel were fictitious and that on some bureaucratic pretext, the entire system of sending invitations from Israel would collapse, including those to people who did have relatives in the country. At our request, the censor helped us locate all the forged invitations and hunt down their authors in Israel and the United States. We referred these cases to the antifraud unit of the Israel Police and to the State Prosecutor. Consequently, several people were tried for forging official state documents, notarizations, and Foreign Ministry forms. Naturally we obtained a court order banning publication of all these incidents. In this way, we soon put an end to the phenomenon of forged invitations.

We also used the censor to intercept the correspondence between refuseniks and their relatives or friends to extract more information about them and their situation. This also taught us how letter-writers—both recent and long-term *olim*—described conditions in Israel and supplemented our knowledge about the Soviet Union and the Jews.

In the late 1980s, after consulting with Bartov, I informed the censor that we could dispense with his services; Nativ's interception of correspondence with the Soviet Union came to an end. I do not apologize for our recourse to the censor. It was necessary in those days and in keeping with the rules instituted by the state.

Towards the end of that decade, we had to issue tens of thousands of invitations each month. The more invitations we sent out to Soviet Jews, the more requests we received for new invitations. As more Jews received invitations and submitted applications to emigrate, the pressure on the Soviet authorities increased. The scale of emigration reflected, among other things, the number of applications filed. It was clear to us that we would not be able to keep up with the accelerating pace by sticking to our old and mostly manual working methods. We had to modify the format of the invitations, and fast. I drafted a proposal for these changes and asked the Justice Ministry to approve it. The Justice Ministry was forthcoming almost immediately. In essence, we devised a new format that reduced the huge number of forms required for each invitation and eliminated the need for notarization. Most importantly, the person in whose name the invitation was sent no longer had to sign it. We had already instituted a computerized database to store all the information about Jews, previously recorded in a manual filing system. In the late 1970s, Yosef Meller had the foresight to computerize the Soviet Union Department; the system was set up under the supervision and professional guidance of a different organization.

When I returned from Vienna, the computer system and its development became one of my new responsibilities. I soon reached an agreement with the other agency that it would henceforth serve as a purely professional consultant, while we managed the system ourselves. But we needed several dozen workers to input the data in order to operate the computers—and that is where we ran into a brick wall. The State of Israel did not want to fund more positions to the tune of a few hundred thousand dollars a year, forcing us to seek financial resources outside the State budget. Until the 1960s, Nativ, like the other intelligence agencies, was not funded through the State budget. Formally speaking, staffers of Nativ and these other agencies were not even employees of the State. It was only after the Six Day War that the State began to partially bankroll these agencies, including Nativ, supplementing the funds from outside sources. Half of Nativ's budget was underwritten by the Jewish Agency, while the other half came from government funds. In the mid-1980s, Finance Minister Yitzchak Moda'i decided that the State would cover Nativ's entire budget. But our budget barely sufficed to keep the organization afloat—office upkeep and salaries, but no more. There was never funding for our operations, which depended on nongovernmental sources. Left with no choice, once again, we found outside solutions to cover the cost of computerized data entry.

Chapter 28

One of the best methods developed by Arye Kroll took advantage of the Moscow book fair, held every other year. Kroll always put together and prepared the Israeli delegation, composed of top people in the literary world, and made sure they took a lot of materials with them to distribute to Jews and activists. By 1987, I was already responsible for all Nativ activities in the Soviet Union, including this domain, so I called for a revision of all our plans in anticipation of the book fair to be held that autumn. I instituted a new principle: We would do everything possible, to the very limit of the Soviets' rules, and then push further—as far as their tolerance could be stretched. The method was to go ahead with our plans—and, if the Soviets resisted, to dig in our heels and pressure them until we achieved our goal, even if only in part. The idea was to try to get away with things the Soviets had never permitted before. In my briefings to the delegates before they left, I told them to be more aggressive and demonstrative. For example, I asked whether it was true that in past years the observant among them had been told to hide their skullcaps and wear hats. When they admitted this was the case, I prohibited them from doing so this year. I instructed every observant man to openly exhibit his Israeli identity by blatantly wearing a skullcap. I told them not to be afraid of any provocation by the Soviet authorities. They were surprised, but did as I said.

We wanted to bring in new equipment to the book fair for the first time, such as computers, a video system, and a movie projector. I commissioned a Russian-language promotional film about Israel, essentially a propaganda movie. Most of the people around me were hesitant. "Why on Earth would we ask the Soviets to screen movies at a *book* fair?"

"They won't ask any questions—they will understand. We can always find some formal excuse if need be."

And that's how it went. My instructions were that the movie depict modern Israel—no deserts, no kibbutzim, and certainly no cowsheds, because no one in the Soviet Union wanted their children to end up on a collective farm. They produced a fine propaganda film that deeply moved the tens of thousands of Jews who watched, day after day. We set up large screens around the pavilion and ran the films nonstop while the pavilion was open. Both the variety and number of books were unprecedented. The Soviets objected to our handing out maps because the Israeli borders marked on them were not those of the partition lines. But I instructed Robert Singer, the head of the delegation, to stand firm and not give in. In the end, the Soviets capitulated half an hour before the exhibition opened and the maps were brought to the pavilion.

As mentioned, the delegation was headed by Robert Singer—his first assignment after joining Nativ. He was an outstanding young man, with excellent organizational skills and a font of ingenuity, Singer had made *aliyah* from Czernowitz as a child in the 1970s. He graduated high school in Israel at age 15, and by 21 completed his university studies and was drafted into the IDF. The brilliant fellows in Field Security insisted that he could serve only in the Education Corps (where he proved to be a great success), and not in intelligence, as he had hoped. He was 32, a lieutenant colonel in Southern Command, when I picked him out and persuaded him to join Nativ. I wanted him to build up, operate and manage our entire public relations apparatus for Soviet Jewry. I saw the PR system as the most important element of our activities for the Jews. Its content and form had to shake them up and induce them to make *aliyah*, naturally while also showing them what they wanted to see. I believed that Singer had all the qualities necessary to give this new and complex topic a strong push. I am happy to say that he fulfilled and even exceeded my expectations. He built a vast system, the best PR apparatus the State of Israel had ever seen, and within a short period of time had flooded the entire Soviet Union with information.

"Operation Book Fair" in Moscow was a difficult baptism of fire, and Singer withstood it admirably. He supervised the delegation, saw to the preparation of materials, and we achieved our goals. It was no accident that we came to call it the "Six Day Fair." Thousands of Jews crowded into the pavilion, took our materials with tearful looks, and saw pictures of Israel for the first time ever. It was an experience that opened many eyes and produced a tidal wave of *aliyah* applications. All the material and equipment we brought to Moscow, including the computers, we passed on to activists—as at prior fairs, but this time in much greater quantity. Every day, during and after the fair's opening hours, the members of the delegation would leave the pavilion with overstuffed suitcases and bags and vanish into the big city, where they met with Jews and gave them tons of material and equipment. Within hours, everything had been distributed and was on its way to every corner of the Soviet Union, just as we had planned. We had done the same thing at previous fairs, but this time we felt we could be more daring and the Soviets would give in, because of their growing vulnerability. We pushed the limits shamelessly—and got away with it.

Meanwhile, the coalition rotation agreement took effect: Yitzhak Shamir returned to the Prime Minister's office and Shimon Peres replaced him as Foreign Minister. I had first met Peres when I made *aliyah* in 1969 and I thought highly of him. Still, several things bothered me, such as the fact that he had never served in the IDF. During his term as Foreign Minister, he made crucial contributions to Soviet *aliyah*, although he wasn't aware of this and did not understand the full implications of his decisions. An excellent team coalesced around Peres in those years. For my money, no group of young Israel civil servants has ever matched the talents, work ethic, and creativity of his "boys"—Yossi Beilin, Nimrod Novick, Amnon Neubach, Uri Savir, and Boaz Applebaum. They came up with fantastic ideas and they managed to take advantage of Peres' good qualities, while blurring and even hiding some of his negative aspects.

Under Peres, there were joint political deliberations involving Foreign Ministry personnel and the intelligence community, with input from academics as well. We were included in the sessions that had to do with the Soviet Union. The intention was to shed light on the problems in Israel's relationship with the Soviet Union, to assess the situation from various angles, and to crystallize principles to guide policy. These discussions were usually run by Beilin and Novick. In one of these meetings, Peres said something that essentially changed Israeli policy vis-à-vis the Soviet Union and produced astounding results. He was the first Israeli policymaker to state officially that Jews and *aliyah* were Israel's main interest in its dealings with the Soviet Union. I saw astonishment and displeasure on the faces of the Foreign Ministry staffers and of some of the academics and intelligence community representatives. But none dared openly oppose the Foreign Minister's edict, not even those who disagreed with him. Instead, Foreign Ministry officials, aside from the righteous few among them, never made any serious effort, to put it gently, to implement the policy promulgated by their boss.

I formed a special relationship with Peres and his advisors. It was very important to them to receive an up-to-date and credible picture of the situation. It was clear that Nativ, which always kept its finger on the pulse of developments in the Soviet Union and conducted many inquiries, and which had worked there for many years and amassed extensive knowledge and experience, had an excellent ability to assess the situation in that country. Other agencies did not have their own independent sources of information and had to rely on foreign sources and assessments. Nor did they have the infrastructure of professionals needed to handle the issue of the Soviet Union. Even the IDF, the Mossad and especially the Foreign Ministry, who dealt the most with the issue, lacked Russian speakers and had other responsibilities as well that got in the way of dealing with *aliyah*. We were the only ones with professional continuity and accumulated knowledge and experience, with an organization that went back to 1951.

When I was given responsibility within Nativ for everything related to the Soviet Union, I began to recruit and promote an increasing number of recent young immigrants from the Soviet Union who had the requisite professional knowledge and experience. I hired several persons, like Rafi Pizov and Hanan Ahituv, who had been *aliyah* activists in the Soviet Union and understood the situation there. They had an organizational and professional culture quite different from what had been the rule in Nativ until then. In this way, I assembled a diverse and highly professional staff who worked like a finely-tuned machine. They managed to get the most out of one another's relative advantages and neutralize their weaknesses, all in the service of a single goal—helping the Jews in the Soviet Union.

We created a system for information exchanges and regular updates with Peres' people at the Foreign Ministry. The career foreign service officers' sensitivity about Nativ led to a number of absurdities. Before every secret or public meeting between Soviet representatives and Peres' entourage or Peres himself, I would send assessments and recommendations as to topics I thought we should raise at the meeting directly to his office, bypassing the normal Foreign Ministry channels. After these meetings, I received a written report of their substance and I sent back my assessment of the meeting itself and its results—again directly to his office without the knowledge of the Foreign Ministry. It is too bad that we were forced to work like this, but it turned out for everyone's benefit and allowed us to make a major contribution to improved relations with the Soviet Union.

In the summer of 1987, after a series of secret meetings between Nimrod Novick and Soviet representatives, a Soviet diplomatic mission was dispatched to the Finnish Embassy in Tel Aviv to deal with the extensive Soviet real-estate holdings in Israel. (In the absence of diplomatic relations, Finland represented Soviet interests in Israel, while the Dutch represented us in Moscow.) That fall, during one of our sessions at the Foreign Ministry, I proposed that at the next meeting with the Soviets, we ask to be allowed to station Israeli diplomats in the Dutch Embassy. The then-director of the Eastern Europe Department of the Foreign Ministry responded to my idea with a barrage of screams: "What on Earth? What are you babbling about? What justification can we offer for such a request? It's not realistic. What do we need it for? What do you want to do there?"

Almost all the other participants had similar, if more tempered reactions to my proposal. The Foreign Ministry reaction did not surprise me. In earlier discussions about relations with Hungary, both the Foreign Ministry and the intelligence community rejected the idea of opening an Israeli interests section in Budapest on the grounds that a mission with a status below embassy or at least consulate level would be demeaning to Israel. Peres, who was running the discussion, asked to hear Nativ's position. I told him that Nativ favored opening a diplomatic office in Budapest because we needed to be in contact with the Jews there and wanted to be able to station our people to work among them. Peres decided to open the Interests Section so that Nativ could do so, ruling that the Jewish issue took precedence over all other considerations.

In one of the discussions about opening an Israeli Interests Section in Moscow, Yossi Beilin, who was presiding, asked how I proposed to justify our request. "The same way the Soviets did," I replied. This earned me a sarcastic remark from a Foreign Ministry representative who asserted that we had no property in the Soviet Union.

"Of course we do," I countered: our embassy building, whose condition we could ask to check. In addition, we could investigate the treatment of Israeli citizens in the Soviet Union, just as the Soviets were looking into our treatment of their citizens here.

At this point, one Foreign Ministry officially really outdid himself and sneered at me: "You mean the Jews over there with the bogus Israeli citizenship you gave them?"

I gave him a withering look and did not respond. "We will ask to verify and examine the nature of the consular processes and consular work for those emigrating to Israel," I said.

Beilin asked how long we should ask for the delegation to stay in Moscow.

"Reciprocity, of course. The Soviets asked us to allow a three-month mission and we'll do the same, and after that we'll keep getting extensions. As long as their delegation is in Israel, our delegation will be in the Soviet Union."

Beilin summed up the discussion by asking me to submit my proposal in writing, along with the supporting arguments. When I got back to the office, I gathered the staff. We drafted the document according to the parameters I had presented and I sent it to Beilin by courier. Afterwards, I reported on the matter to David Bartov and told him that we had to start preparations for the dispatch of a delegation to the Soviet Union. The truth is that for several months already, we had been doing staff work to crystallize the organizational and operational basis for a Nativ office in the Soviet Union. I informed the relevant persons that we were starting to come up with ideas for working in Moscow as part of a mission under the auspices of the Dutch Embassy, so if they had any suggestions, comments, or questions, now was the time to raise them. They were surprised, but treated the issue with seriousness and professionalism. A few days later, Beilin sent me a copy of the note to the Soviets requesting that we be allowed to send to a delegation to Moscow. I was glad to see that the formulation pretty much matched my recommendation. Soon thereafter, the Soviets announced that in principle, they were willing for us to send a mission to work out of the Dutch Embassy.

For me, this was more than just a validation of my political vision and analyses. The real joy was that we would be returning to activity in the field. Although we were hopeful, we still didn't know what huge changes this would bring.

Now we started talking about the composition of the delegation. The Foreign Ministry decided that it would comprise two ministry staffers, one security man, and one representative of Nativ. I opposed this idea and Bartov supported my position. In the letter he sent to the Foreign Ministry (with a copy to the Prime Minister), we asked for at least two Nativ representatives, and the Prime Minister and Foreign Minister accepted our position. But Bartov and I outsmarted them by assigning Gershon Gorev, who had worked for Nativ in the Israel Embassy in Moscow in the 1960s, as the second Nativ man. At the time, Gorev was posted to the Nativ office in Vienna. We decided that his wife, who was also a veteran Nativ operative, would accompany him to Moscow. After all, there was no prohibition on sending along spouses. The Foreign Ministry tried to argue, but soon gave up the fight. We knew there wouldn't be any problems with the Soviets, only with our own Foreign Ministry. The result was that we had three Nativ staffers in the delegation, and the Soviets didn't object.

Because of the Foreign Ministry's flawed work procedures, the selection of their representatives dragged on for months. On two or three occasions, the Soviets asked for the list of the delegation members to approve them and issue visas. And then some scoundrel at the Foreign Ministry leaked to the Israeli media that "the delay in the dispatch of the delegation to Moscow is because it also includes Yasha Kazakov, a former dissident, and the Soviet authorities see this as a provocation and hostile move." Not only did they want to shift the blame for the delay to others, but more than anything they wanted to prevent me from going to Moscow as part of the delegation. Unable to override the decision by the Foreign Minister and the Prime Minister that I be included in the delegation, they hoped that the Soviets would seize on the leak and make some objection about me.

But their ignorance and lack of understanding of how the Soviets think backfired on them. It was clear to me that the Soviets would not dare check everyone under a magnifying glass and would not say what members of our delegation they liked and didn't like. In fact, they never mentioned my name at all, and the entire delay stemmed from our own Foreign Ministry which spent months struggling to find candidates for the delegation.

In late spring, after a few months' delay, the Foreign Ministry finalized the composition of the mission. Its head was the ministry's Meron Gordon, who at the time represented Israel in the Vatican. Gordon had made *aliyah* from the Soviet Union as a child. He was talented, very intelligent, and deeply involved in Russian culture. By Foreign Ministry standards, he was well-versed in Soviet affairs. He was certainly a good choice—the right man in the right place. He made a major contribution and would probably have done even more if not for his sudden death a few years later. The second Foreign Ministry staffer came from the Israel Embassy in the Netherlands and was essentially intended to lubricate our relations with the Dutch. After all, the delegation was officially part of the Dutch Embassy.

There were several meetings at the Foreign Ministry in advance of our departure. One was devoted to the issue of security. The director of the Foreign Ministry's security unit wanted the delegation to adhere to the rules followed by Israeli diplomats in Western Europe, especially by hiding all identifying signs that we were Israelis and taking precautions against terrorist attacks. I was familiar with all the rules, as were all the others who had experience working as Israeli diplomats abroad, and I objected strenuously. I was amazed that he failed to consider what country we were going to and the situation there. I tried to explain to the "experts" that all of us, along with our accommodations and motor vehicles, would probably be subject to round-the-clock surveillance, and this would also be our best possible protection against terrorists. As for hiding all signs of Israeli identity, I said that we should behave in the exact opposite manner—we should make our Israeli identity known in every possible way, with flags and Hebrew stickers on our cars and bags and with Israeli symbols on our clothes. The security man who was delivering the briefing almost fainted when he heard me; the matter was referred to Foreign Minister Peres to adjudicate. I presented my position to Peres, who accepted it completely. And that is what we did in Moscow. All of us wore an Israeli-flag pin on our clothes. The Foreign Ministry officials objected that it was not proper to attach the flag to our clothes, nor was it acceptable for diplomats to broadcast their national affiliation. I ignored their comments, even when I paid a visit to the Soviet Foreign Ministry. It was only after President Bush stuck an American-flag pin on his lapel that Israeli officials and senior figures, especially in the Foreign Ministry, began emulating the "boss."

Around this time, the Israeli government made an unfortunate decision that had a disastrous effect on thousands of immigrant physicians—refusing to recognize the diplomas of those who had completed their medical studies in Eastern Europe. There was no professional or legitimate justification for this. Thousands of doctors made *aliyah* from Romania, Poland, and the Soviet Union, and their professional level was in no way inferior to the Israeli standard. Bartov and I tried to persuade the relevant authorities that the restriction would hurt *olim*, but no one wanted to listen to us. After all, *aliyah* was negligible—and the real reason for the decision was the increasing number of Arabs who went to Eastern Europe to study medicine. The government was simply looking for a way to exclude them from the Israeli medical system. The excuse was deceitful and foolish and harmed thousands of *olim*. The lesson I learned was that discrimination condoned by society will sooner or later hurt others and not just the original targets, and in the end will become a norm.

Chapter 29

In late July 1988, we finally left for the Hague. We stayed there for a few days while holding meetings with officials of the Dutch Foreign Ministry. The Dutch were somewhat disconcerted. On one hand, they were formally responsible for us; on the other hand, they wanted to maintain their status, outlook, and working methods vis-à-vis Soviet Jewry. In our conversations, I said little and tried not to stand out. I remember that we received passports. I saw a Soviet diplomatic visa affixed to my Israeli diplomatic passport for the first time. I remembered what I had been told when I received my exit visa: "You will never enter the Soviet Union again." And here I was, returning there as an Israeli diplomat to help my people make *aliyah*.

My feelings on the flight to Moscow were complex. In addition to my natural and understandable excitement, I was filled with a familiar sensation—the tension after the tanks receive the order, "Start engines," and you start moving forward and the battle is about to begin. You have studied your enemy and feel you know him. You feel a burst of adrenaline in anticipation of coming face to face with him and are all fired up to launch the attack. I was very curious to see the Jews. I had met most of the activists who had reached Israel and now I was eager to work with them, shoulder to shoulder, and give them the help I had needed and not received during my fight to make *aliyah* just nineteen years earlier.

The plane landed. When the door opened, the first thing I caught was the stare of the Soviet Border Patrol guard. In a flash, everything came back to me, as though I had never left the Soviet Union. On the way to the hotel, I couldn't take my eyes off the streets we were passing through, familiar even after the passage of nineteen years. For the first few days, I had the feeling that I had passed through a time tunnel and gone back twenty years. I was a different person now, but the people still looked, spoke, and answered just as they had two decades before. When I looked at the Jews and listened to them, I felt that I was looking at the person I would have been had I not left nineteen years earlier. I was shaken—not because they weren't fine people or because they were inferior to me, but because I saw what they had missed out on and what I had gained by living in Israel, in terms of my personal development, my way of thinking—everything. I was pained that they lacked this and was happy to have been spared their fate. This was my encounter with the Soviet Union on July 31, 1988, when I took up my post in Moscow and began a new chapter in my career.

The first thing we had to do in Moscow was to learn the environment and get acquainted with the people and the staff of the Dutch Embassy. The day after our arrival, when I rode in a car with the rest of the delegation to the Israeli Embassy building, I realized that I knew the way, even thought I had never driven in Moscow. The authorities knew we were coming—checking the building was part of our assignment. The building was shuttered and vacant. With pent-up excitement, I approached the locked gate. A police officer jumped to attention, saluted, and asked how he could help. The caretaker, a Soviet official who watched the building and kept the courtyard clean, came out. He greeted us, turned his key in the lock, and opened the gates for us.

Overwhelmed by emotion, I entered the courtyard that was so familiar to me. I walked up to the flagpole, where I remembered the Israeli flag waving proudly, and from there to the door, now locked, through which I had first entered the Embassy. Minute by minute the long-distant scenes came back to me. Everything was so far away, almost imaginary, but also so close, as though it had been only yesterday. Within seconds, the young man who broke into the Israeli Embassy morphed into a man who walked in as if he owned the place. It is impossible to describe my feelings and impossible to forget them.

Afterwards, I drove to the apartment block from which I had left for Israel, nineteen years earlier. I looked at the windows of our apartment and walked around the courtyard, where everything was so familiar and yet so foreign. I looked at the children running and playing and saw myself at their age. It was as though nothing had changed and soon I would finish my game and climb the stairs to my home. Only the trees had grown much taller. Old women with headscarves were sitting on the benches, just as they had back then, but I didn't know any of them. And, just like then, they fastened a curious and suspicious look at the foreigner who was walking around the yard as if moonstruck, and was clearly not Soviet. I remembered the lesson we had all been taught in school—report to the police about every foreigner and every car with a diplomatic license plate that we saw in the neighborhood.

I went to the school I had attended. I didn't enter the building but only turned into the yard. I suddenly saw tall trees and was gripped with excitement. "My trees!" These were the trees that we had planted in the schoolyard. I had planted these trees in the earth of Moscow, the capital of Russia, and their roots, like mine, were planted deep in its soil. Whatever the nature of the regime, no person or government could destroy that connection.

In keeping with standard practice, the Soviet authorities provided the delegation with a chauffeur, who was also supposed to keep our cars in shape. This young fellow's movements, behavior, posture, and gait left no doubt as to what kind of school he had attended and where he really belonged. He didn't spend much time maintaining the vehicles. He clearly had more important things to do, even though our cars were in a horrible state of disrepair. One evening, when we were sitting in our hotel room, I observed out loud, "If I find that car in the same condition one more morning, I'll throw out this driver—and I don't care what his rank is." Then I added, "If they want their people to follow us around, let them work, too. We simply will not put up with this kind of negligence."

My colleagues looked at me in amazement, but I merely said, "Wait and see what happens tomorrow morning." Sure enough, the next morning the young man was waiting for me by the Embassy door. He said that he had checked the car, found a few problems with it and fixed what he could, but he wanted permission to take it to a garage. Then "the car will be in tiptop shape." And the same with the second car, he said, and I didn't have to worry—the cars would be fixed up and clean. I could barely keep from laughing. Once again, it was plain that in the Soviet Union it paid to talk to the walls.

We quickly developed good relations with the Dutch. After two days, I told Meron Gordon that I wanted to modify the arrangements. I asked him to inform the Dutch that they would continue to issue visas—given their status and ours, the law allowed only the Dutch to sign visas—but henceforth only we would deal with people who came on Israel-related matters. We would receive and check their documents and interview the people. We would prepare the visas and the stamp; all the Dutch official had to do was add his signature. Gordon thought for a bit and then agreed. We went to the Dutch ambassador with our idea and he was perfectly amenable. From that time on, everyone who came to the Embassy on Israel-related matters had nothing to do with the Soviet receptionists or Dutch officials and saw only Israelis. That more or less meant the Nativ staff—in those days, the Nativ operatives were the only members of the delegation who spoke Russian. I thought it was very important that this work be executed only by Israelis. A few months later, the second Foreign Ministry staffer on the delegation was replaced by someone from the consular division, who handled tourist visas and visits.

Aside from those receiving exit visas—the *olim*—the Embassy also dealt with many Arab students at Soviet universities, Israeli citizens and residents of the territories. On our first day of work, I sat at the reception desk. A young Arab man came up to me, a student, and I noticed on his lapel the symbol of a Palestinian terrorist organization—I believe it was the Popular Front. He addressed me in broken Russian. I replied in Hebrew, in a sweet voice accompanied by a smile, and asked whether his friends, too, wore the symbol of the Popular Front, or only him. The boy grew pale, stood there stunned and immobile for a few minutes, and then mumbled something about obtaining some required paper. According to his documents, he was a resident of the territories, not an Israeli Arab. After that, we didn't see Arab students from the territories wearing the emblem of a terrorist organization. Evidently, the Israelis' arrival at the Dutch Embassy had become common knowledge in very short order.

One of the Dutch diplomats asked us for permission to speak with applicants from time to time. It was common for people who were afraid they would not be able to take their personal documents out with them to give them to a Dutch official to be sent in the diplomatic pouch. Nativ headquarters in Israel would receive the documents and pass them on to their owners or dispatch them to their new country of residence. The Dutch took advantage of this to interview people and harvested important information from their conversations. After all, contact with local citizens, even those who were about to leave the country, could enrich the diplomats' knowledge and understanding in all fields. This was important for the Dutch, so we agreed they could talk with whomever they wished. Moreover, the diplomat in question spoke good Russian, which he had learned at the NATO language school during his army service in the Netherlands.

From the very first moment, I set myself a rule and stuck to it: I would not accept anything that went beyond the domain of personal documents—no scientific inventions, no work materials, no sketches. We would not entangle either the Jews or Israel in thorny situations.

The first encounter with the refuseniks and activists was moving. We were not the first Israelis they had met. After all, Arye Kroll's vast army of "tourists" included some with dual citizenship, and an increasing number of Israeli visitors had recently come to Moscow. Israelis also came as part of international delegations to the Soviet Union. We always included people whom we had briefed in such delegations and asked to carry out assignments for us.

This had been Nativ's standard operating procedure from the outset, in the days of the first Israeli cargo ships that brought crates of oranges to the Soviet Union. There were always Nativ agents on board as part of the crew, or authentic crewmen who had been enlisted to the cause. It was rare for an Israeli delegation in the Soviet Union not to include our people or persons acting on our behalf. This was true of the delegation to the Youth Festival and most others, including athletes and scientists. This time, however, Soviet Jews met Nativ personnel of a different stripe, who employed different work methods. We were much more aggressive and more inventive, with a much better understanding of them and the conditions in which they lived. The Jews certainly found out quickly who I was, and this made our contacts and relationship easier. In my opinion, they had a much better feeling about their ability to communicate with me.

The Soviet Jews began to find their footing, building and expanding an infrastructure for Jewish activity, but now along with our close involvement and guidance. At the same time, they were also developing contacts with local non-Jewish elements—public, government, and others. One day when we went to meet with Jews, one of the activists told me that somebody there had come from the provinces with an old Torah scroll that wanted to have taken to Israel. It was too dangerous for the man to go back home with it. To leave the Torah scroll in the apartment was no less hazardous; in the event of a sudden or deliberate search, the owner would find himself in prison. Afraid of wiretapping and eavesdropping, we conducted the conversation on slips of paper. The Soviet surveillance team that always stuck close to us had taken up positions outside, as usual, and I didn't see any suspicious movements. I put the Torah scroll into the bag in which we had brought books and pamphlets to give the activists. We wound up the meeting quickly and I left with a member of the delegation who had come with me and walked to our car. There was an iron rule that, except in the hotel and the Embassy, no Nativ member was ever left alone; there was always somebody else from the delegation with him. If no other Nativ agent was available, we were accompanied by a Foreign Ministry staffer or security man. This time, my partner was a security man. We had known each other for many years. On the way, I told him that we were going to the Embassy and that he shouldn't say a word or ask any questions until we got inside. When I pulled out of my parking space, I verified that we were being followed and continued on my usual route towards the hotel. When we reached the turn into the hotel, I floored the gas pedal and raced through the streets of Moscow at over 60 miles an hour. I saw in the mirror that our tail didn't understand what exactly had happened, and by the time they caught on I was already far away. They sped up too, but I reached the street of the Embassy within a few minutes. When I pulled up in front, the policeman on duty opened the gate for us. I saw that our pursuers had stopped at the corner. I took the bag, entered our office, and locked the Torah scroll in the closet. With a feeling of relief and joy, I left the Embassy and drove back to the hotel, with our shadows trailing us as usual. I knew that I had broken the rules, but I simply could not bring myself, neither for my own conscience nor as a representative of the State of Israel, to abandon a Torah scroll. To do so would render our work as representatives of the Jewish state meaningless. I have never regretted that escapade.

On our first night in Moscow, I called my wife from the hotel and told her, half laughing, that I would never suffer from loneliness in the Soviet Union. Our "friends" would not leave me alone. And so it was. Usually, the close surveillance consisted of three teams in three cars—two right on top of us and the third hanging behind, ready to speed up as developments might warrant. There were probably other vehicles as well at a greater distance. Once when we were on our way to a meeting with Jews and being tagged by the usual shadows, I didn't know exactly where the meeting place was. Moscow is a vast city and I was not familiar with every neighborhood, especially not those established after I made *aliyah*. I stopped the car and asked a pedestrian where such and such street was. When we started off again, I saw in the mirror that one of the shadow cars had stopped by my informant. Two men sprang out, pushed him against the fence, and began interrogating him and writing down his replies. I saw the stunned man take something from his pocket, probably his papers. I understood the principle. Now, after every turn as I continued driving, I would stop for a minute and ask somebody a stupid question. The scenario repeated itself. Finding themselves in a pickle, our tails called for reinforcements to keep up with me. After about twenty minutes and a few more stops, I stopped teasing them. As a matter of principle, I never tried to elude them without good cause. After all, they were just doing their job. If there wasn't any important reason, why should I hassle them?

So I was used to being tailed and didn't really think about it. We also knew that the surveillance concentrated on Nativ and GSS agents. After a month, the surveillance became closer and more overt, even threatening, with the focus on me. The usual members of the surveillance squad had been replaced and the new people were almost glued to me. When I entered the elevator in a building, one of them always got in with me. They were never more than two yards away. When I walked, I trod on their shadows. At first I didn't understand why they were tracking me so tightly. After all, it didn't make sense to intimidate or pressure me. In the end, though, I thought I caught on. Around that time, a Soviet intelligence agent in Jerusalem, who worked under the cover of the Russian ecclesiastical mission, went missing with his family. I learned about his case on my visits to Israel. As far as the Soviets were concerned, he had disappeared and they still had no clue what he was doing or where he was. I interpreted the "special attention" I was receiving from the Soviet security services as groundwork for the possibility that they would have to haggle with the Israeli services about their vanished colleague. That was the only logical explanation I could come up with. It was an uncomfortable situation to be in. I couldn't speak about it with anybody, not even the delegation's security officer. According to later reports, the defector relocated to a third country. But the close surveillance on me continued until I was about to leave for home.

The day I was supposed to go back to Israel, I was standing on the stairs outside the hotel waiting for the colleague who was supposed to take me to the airport. There on my left, only a yard away, was one of my shadows. I said aloud, without turning to look at him, "That's it! In another hour and a half I'll be resting on the plane, and then I'll be home."

The man could not resist. "We're also going to go rest. Your running around has been killing us."

"What are you complaining about? Don't you guys switch off twice a day? See how many there are of you—and there's only one of me."

The man sighed and agreed, "True. You do have a hard job. But we have a hard job too. But never mind—another two hours and we'll get to rest. Have a nice vacation."

A real idyll! They followed me to passport control and stayed in the airport until my plane took off. When the plane took off, I breathed a sigh of relief. All the tension of the last few weeks dissipated in a moment. I immediately fell asleep and slept until we landed in Vienna. Upon my return to Moscow a week later, the surveillance was renewed, but in the standard format with the usual squad. While I was gone, the Soviets had found out what had happened to their man. I saw the members of the special team only once more, by accident, racing in their car after some other "suspicious character."

Naturally, I reported the extra attention to the GSS. Later, David Bartov told me that the GSS had told the Prime Minister that the closer watch was because I had smuggled out a Torah scroll. We laughed about the forced explanation. The tradition of trying to represent things in a more convenient manner and foist off the blame on someone else was still alive and well. But I couldn't understand how they could submit a false report to the Prime Minister.

I instructed our people to pay absolutely no attention to our shadows. Don't try to evade them, don't try to outsmart them, don't try to contact them. We have nothing to hide. If they want to know who we are meeting, by all means.

The surveillance frequently produced amusing incidents. When we worked in Moscow, we were supposed to fly to Vienna once a week, because that was the last stop for secure and classified mail. We used the Dutch for our diplomatic correspondence, but it was out of the question to transmit classified documents through their offices. This meant we could not receive the documents in Moscow, nor did we have any way of ensuring their security once there. So every week, someone went off to the Israeli Embassy in Vienna for 48 hours to open, send, and read mail, and to write and send out reports for other members of the delegation. Classified items had to be memorized; unclassified materials were brought back to Moscow.

Once, I brought some documents back from Vienna that I didn't want to read at the Embassy. The material wasn't particularly sensitive, but it was interesting. I drove to a large public square near Moscow University. I sat down on a bench in the center of the plaza, so my field of vision extended for several hundred yards and no one could approach without my noticing. As I read, I noticed my trackers' car opposite me, at the edge of the plaza. When I finished reading the documents, I began pacing out of habit. I like to walk while thinking. As I did a circuit of the plaza, I came close to the car and saw that a young man and woman were sitting inside and making out. Out of the corner of my eye, I saw the woman push the man away as soon as I passed the car. Let's have a little fun, I told myself. I walked twenty yards, turned around, and walked back. The moment they saw that I was coming their way, they were forced to go back to kissing. I walked slowly on purpose and saw that the fellow was enjoying himself. For the next half hour or so, I roamed aimlessly around the car. I think the man was very grateful to me, but the woman must have been ready to tear me to pieces. What people won't do for their country, I thought to myself. You chose this work—so work. After all, it's not every day and everybody that can enjoy their job.

Once, when I was on my way to meet some Jews, I noticed KGB men who were not part of "my" unit standing on the street corners nearby. I understood that two different sections of the KGB were about to run into each other. The Jews fell under the purview of the Fifth Directorate, which dealt with subversive activity, while our shadows came from the Second Directorate, which was responsible for counter-espionage and monitoring foreign diplomats. I deliberately turned in their direction. When I went past them, the Fifth Directorate agents stared at me, looked at one another and seemed confused—and then my "escorts" from the Second Directorate showed up behind me. The encounter between the two teams was interesting. They conferred, clarified their relations and jobs, and split up the assignment. I stood by the entrance to the house and kept my eye on them until they each took up their position. I went up to the meeting place while the two teams stayed downstairs, waiting for their respective "clients."

On one of my returns to Moscow from Vienna, the delegation's security officer came to pick me up at the airport. He asked me why I had flown on the Soviet airline Aeroflot—wasn't that against the rules? I acknowledged that I knew about the prohibition, which was based on the fact that we were forbidden from entering Soviet territory, and Aeroflot planes are Soviet territory. But we were on Soviet territory all the time, so what difference would two more hours make? The rule wasn't relevant for us; we certainly couldn't use foreign airlines on domestic flights inside the Soviet Union. I added that if he could make another argument, such as flight safety or poor maintenance of the aircraft, I would understand him. The security officer thought over what I had said. He decided that it made sense and said he'd ask the higher-ups at the GSS to allow those posted in Moscow to leave the country on Aeroflot planes, if there were no other flights. After about two weeks, he came to me with a sad, abashed look on his face. "I put in the request but the answer is negative: you cannot deviate from the rules."

But such thick-headedness was not limited to the GSS. The Mossad, too, demonstrated an equally winning form of obduracy. A few years later, representatives of the Mossad and the Russian Foreign Intelligence Service, the SVR, were stationed in each other's countries. When the head of the SVR came to Israel, someone from the Mossad office in Moscow came with him. The Russian stayed in the Sheraton Hotel in Tel Aviv, across the street from the Russian Embassy. When the Mossad man from Moscow came in the morning to take him and his staff to a meeting, the Russian said he needed to go into the Embassy for a few minutes, and the Israeli went inside with him. At the end of the visit, the agent was summoned for a dressing-down by the head of the Mossad security unit, because he had violated the rules for intelligence community employees and entered the Russian Embassy without prior permission from his superiors.

"What was the problem?" asked our man in Moscow.

He was told that the Embassy is Russian territory and Israeli intelligence officers are not authorized to visit it without advance permission from Mossad security. The stunned agent reminded his interlocutor that he was posted to Russia and lived on Russian territory all the time. It didn't help; he received an official reprimand for this breach of security.

Chapter 30

One Friday in December of 1988, I was working as usual in my Tel Aviv office when I received a phone call that there had been an apparently criminal incident in the northern Caucasus region of the Soviet Union. The attackers had commandeered a plane and ordered it to fly to Israel—it wasn't clear whether they had taken hostages. I immediately left with another Nativ staffer and headed for Ben-Gurion Airport. We arrived to find the team that had assembled to deal with the matter. The room was full of many soldiers, police, and GSS men. Ehud Barak, who was coordinating the operation, was standing at the head of the table. When I entered, he turned to me with no unnecessary preliminaries. "Yasha, you will be joining Prof. Ariel Merari on the team to negotiate with the hijackers."

I had heard a lot about Merari. He was an eminent psychologist, highly respected outside of Israel as well, and often put in charge of negotiations with terrorists. Barak introduced me to those who did not know me by saying, "Yasha knows the Russians better than anyone."

Merari and I put our heads together and planned how to conduct the conversation with the hijackers. According to the information we had received from the Soviets, the hostages were no longer on the plane; only the crew and the hijackers remained. For me, for Nativ, and for the State of Israel, it was important to verify that the hijackers had no connection with Jews. Despite the years that had passed, the attempted hijacking by Jews that had led to the infamous Leningrad trial was still fresh in our memories. So we had to make sure Jews who wanted to make *aliyah* were not involved. If there was no doubt that the incident was purely criminal, the decision about how to deal with the matter was the province of the political echelons.

As the plane drew closer, Merari, several other people, and I headed for the control tower. We found that Defense Minister Yitzhak Rabin, Barak (then deputy chief of staff), and Maj. Gen. Amnon Lipkin-Shahak, the head of Military Intelligence, were already there. Radio contact was made with the plane and the flight controller raised the pilot, who spoke in broken English. We did not communicate with the hijackers while the plane was in the air. The pilot received instructions for his descent.

"If the hijackers aren't Jews," decided Rabin, "and the whole thing is criminal, the criminals and the plane will have to be returned to the Soviets."

We left the control tower, entered a car, and drove to where the plane was parked. "Go aboard, Yasha," Lipkin-Shahak told us, "and find out who these people are."

As I was walking towards the plane, two GSS operatives suddenly sprang up out of nowhere—Ben-Ami and Shraga. The latter had been in Moscow with us and I knew him very well. The plane door opened to reveal a man with a Kalashnikov. He jumped to the ground and came up to us. With a suspicious look, and without taking his hand off the weapon, he addressed us in Russian with a heavy Caucasian accent. "Where are we?"

"You're in Israel," we told him.

"So why are you speaking Russian?" he asked us, his suspicion not mollified in the slightest.

I took out my driver's license and showed it to him. "You see? I said. "This is written in Hebrew—that's the language of the Jews. And here, in the corner, there's a Star of David, the symbol of the Jews. This is my ID card, an Israeli ID card. There's nothing like this in Russia."

The documents persuaded him. A smile suddenly appeared on his face and he turned the Kalashnikov away from me.

It quickly became clear that this was a criminal affair. Ben-Ami left and I was left only with Shraga, who asked me to put my gun away. A few people with guns in their hands, including a woman, were crowded by the open door of the plane. The man said something in an unfamiliar language and a bag was thrown down from the door. He ran towards it and started to open it. Shraga grew tense—after all, we didn't know what was in the bag. It proved to be full of money— banknotes in wrappers—dollars, pounds, marks, and various other currencies that were hard to identify in the dark.

"I've got more than two million dollars here," the man announced. "I'm offering half of it to the State of Israel, and we'll keep the other half. Give us a plane and we'll continue to another country."

We told all the rest to disembark. It was a transport plane; a ladder was lowered from the door and all the hijackers climbed down. To begin with, we asked them to put down their weapons—pistols and sawed-off carbines—and they complied. The hijackers seemed to be drugged or drunk; a strong stench of alcohol and drugs wafted from them. We explained that we would drive them to Tel Aviv, and after a few formalities, they would be taken to a hotel. Shraga had completed his mission and left, having determined that the case did not fall into the purview of the GSS. I explained to the hijackers that, as a matter of procedure, they would first have to be interviewed by the Israel Police—but everything would be okay and they would soon be allowed to continue on their way.

Suddenly, the woman in the group signaled that she wanted to speak with me. I took her aside. She told me that she was the wife of one of the hijackers, but they had forced her to come with them and she was not involved in the hijacking. I calmed her down and told her that I would pass on that she was not involved. In the meantime, the police arrived. After the hijackers were seated in the police van, I went over to Rabin's car and reported to him. Rabin asked to meet the hijackers. We proceeded to the police van, and Barak and Lipkin-Shahak joined us. I was the only one who could communicate with the hijackers. Rabin, Barak, and Lipkin-Shahak asked a few questions; I translated the questions and their responses. Rabin said quietly that they should be sent back to the Soviet Union. Then all the generals and the minister left, and the police drove off with the hijackers and the money.

I stayed near the plane. When the crew got off, I spoke with them and tried to soothe their jitters. I told them that the hijackers were on their way to jail and everything would be fine. Suddenly, everybody began to stream towards the plane—soldiers, officers, brigadier generals, policemen all raced to board the aircraft. The pilot grew tense and asked me to stop them: under international law, the plane was Soviet territory and Israel did not have diplomatic relations with the Soviet Union at the time. I was forced to get involved. First, I got everyone off the ladder into the plane and then ordered them all to pull back. I marked out a line and said that no one could go beyond it. In the meantime, Air Force personnel from the military section of the airport arrived and set up a cordon around the plane. Then everyone, including the flight crew, was driven to the base headquarters.

In the officers' club, we found the head of the Soviet Interest section in the Finnish Embassy in Tel Aviv, Grigory Martirosov, the base commander, and two representatives of the Foreign Ministry. One of them was Deputy Director General Yeshayahu Anug, who had been assigned to deal with the diplomatic side of the crisis. He was one of the best Foreign Service officers Israel had, among the few I knew who addressed every issue with the appropriate seriousness and understanding. We had been on excellent terms even before the incident. In the officers' club, I was again the only Israeli who knew Russian. I introduced myself to Martirosov. He certainly knew my name, just as I knew his.

The immediate and urgent need was to move the plane off the runway. The airbase commander, a pilot with the rank of colonel, the Soviet pilot and copilot, the head of the Soviet delegation in Israel, and I, a member of the Israeli delegation in Moscow, went to the plane. We climbed aboard, and following the base commander's directions, the Soviet pilot taxied the plane through the Israeli military airport. After about ten minutes we reached the parking lot and disembarked. The pilot locked the plane and Air Force men were assigned to guard it. The plane's journey through the Israeli airbase was a surrealistic sight that moved us all. The most emotional was the base commander: an Israeli pilot, a colonel, suddenly finding himself on a Soviet plane with Soviet pilots, traveling on the taxiways of his base! After a consultation at base headquarters, it was decided that the crew would spend the night in a hotel and the decision about what to do with them would be made the next day.

Martirosov asked if Israel would extradite the hijackers and if the plane could take off with them in the morning. I replied that it was clear to us that we were dealing with criminals and he should not anticipate any reservations on our part with regard to their extradition, after the legal and diplomatic niceties, of which I was sure he was aware. But, I told him, he was apparently unaware of how problematic it would be to let the plane take off with the criminals aboard. I explained to him that it was impossible to fly the criminals, even if they were shackled, because a transport plane has only its flight crew, which is not trained to deal with dangerous prisoners. What would they do if the criminals went on a rampage on board? Martirosov asked what I suggested. I told him that the best and most convenient solution, from all angles, would be for them to send members of their antiterrorism unit to accompany the criminals on the plane. It would be much more difficult for us to assign some of our people to go with them to Moscow or to an intermediate destination.

Martirosov was somewhat astonished by my suggestion. "You will let them land?!"

I told him that there would be no problem and we would agree to let them come if they decided to do it this way. In the meantime, everyone began to disperse. The Air Force provided the Soviet crew with a bus, and Anug asked me to accompany the crew to the hotel that the Soviet mission had reserved for them on the Tel Aviv beachfront. I returned home after handing them over to the Soviet diplomats there.

The next day—late Saturday morning, Anug phoned and told me that the Soviets had sent a plane with a special squad to deal with the hijackers. He asked me to go to Ben-Gurion airport to talk to them and continue to manage the affair. When I got to the airport, I headed straight for the runway where the plane was about to touch down. I had a very strange feeling as I watched the craft land and taxi at Ben-Gurion airport. After all, in 1988 Israel, this was an extraordinary event. I stood at the bottom of the ramp as a short, stocky man with an athletic build sprang down the steps. He looked very tense and kept scanning his surroundings with his eyes. His handshake was cold and firm. I introduced myself by my first and last names. He also introduced himself: Sergey Goncharov. We clarified some technical issues such as the number of people who had arrived, and then I asked him to collect their documents so I could take them to Passport Control. After the documents were stamped, I brought them back to the plane. Most of the newly-arrived squad were young and had an athletic appearance and build, except for two who were somewhat older. One was the head of the group, General Zaitsev, the commander of the Alpha antiterrorism unit from which the team was drawn. I later found out that Sergey Goncharov was the deputy commander of the unit.

We took a minibus to the Air Force base, where Anug was waiting for us in the officers' club along with another Foreign Ministry representative and members of the Soviet mission. We began to discuss the problem. Essentially, we agreed in principle that the hijackers would be handed over that very night to the Soviets and the two planes would take off for Moscow. Goncharov and I focused on the technical details; the diplomats from the Foreign Ministry dealt with the formalities and the wording of the agreement with the Soviets. There were a number of issues on which Martirosov had to get permission and new instructions from his superiors in Moscow, so he asked to be taken to the delegation offices in Tel Aviv. Because of the need for an immediate response, it was decided that several members of the delegation would go there. I accompanied them on the Air Force bus to their office on a small street off a plaza in central Tel Aviv. Many journalists had already begun to gather outside.

One of the newcomers was a man whose name I was surprised to see when I inspected the passports. He was a KGB official who had previously come to Israel to investigate the issue of the Soviet agent who had defected. It stood to reason that he was from the department that dealt with the KGB's espionage activities in Israel. Before I ordered the doors of the bus to be opened, I went up to him and addressed him in the Russian fashion, by his first name and patronymic. He knew who I was. I told him that I didn't think he would like to see his photograph in the newspaper the next day.

"No, no!" he responded, almost in a panic.

In that case, I told him, he should do exactly as I said and stick close to me. When the doors of the bus were opened, I told everyone they could get off, and the Soviet diplomats led everyone to the building. I stayed on the bus with the KGB man for a few more minutes until the journalists had dispersed. Then I told him to come with me, and walked towards an apartment that the Soviets were using. One of the photographers recognized me and turned his camera away. Journalists and photographers knew me and that it was forbidden to photograph me and that I did not look favorably upon such attempts. In those days, at least, they still respected the ban. After about an hour, when all the telephone issues had been settled, we returned to the Air Force base.

In the meanwhile, Soviet foreign minister Eduard Shevardnadze announced that same day that permission had been granted for the Israeli diplomatic mission in Moscow to move into the Israel Embassy building, empty since 1967, and work from there. It was clear that this was a gesture to encourage and motivate Israel to extradite the criminals and return the plane. I was particularly gratified and pleased by his statement.

That evening was the first night of Hanukkah. "Yasha," the airbase commander said, "it's Hanukkah. What are we going to do?"

I told him that we would light the candles and conduct the normal ritual. I invited the company to gather around the table, which was set for a festive meal with a Hanukkah menorah and traditional donuts. In Russian, I explained to the Soviets that tonight Jews all around the world were celebrating the holiday called Hanukkah. I told them about its meaning and the custom of lighting candles. A sergeant stationed on the base lit the candles and all the Israelis sang "Maoz Tzur." The members of the KGB's Alpha unit and its commander, General Zaitsev, along with Martirosov, the head of the Soviet diplomatic mission, stood at rigid attention, their mouths agape, stunned by the half-religious, half-national ritual of the imperialist Israeli army that they were taking part in. For the first time in their lives, they were present at a religious ritual—and in the military, of all places! When we went to eat, the Soviets asked me if we really were on a military base. I replied with a smile that this was military food. They were used to the Soviet military chow of those years, which is hard to describe to a Westerner.

In the meanwhile, an unexpected problem had cropped up. Under Israeli law, no one could be extradited to a country where he might face the death penalty. But under Soviet law, airplane hijacking was a capital offense, and all the more so in light of what had preceded this incident. So the State of Israel asked the Soviet Union for a commitment that they would not be executed. Zaitsev could not give such a commitment, because he was a KGB man from the antiterrorism unit, not a representative of the political echelons. Martirosov, who was authorized to make commitments on behalf of his government, tried to call his superiors in Moscow for instructions.

Suddenly, a police brigadier entered the officers' club and approached me. He told me that a report was circulating that a group of citizens and lawyers had organized and were going to ask a judge to issue a restraining order against extradition of the hijackers, on the grounds that the case might be a political and human rights issue, not a criminal one. This was absurd: Here was a gang that had seized a school bus full of children and used it to get to the airport. At the airport, they had received a plane and released the children after obtaining cash and a promise to be allowed to take off. And now Israel would refuse to extradite these people—criminals, airplane hijackers, and child kidnappers—on the grounds that the group might be human rights activists, and especially against the background of Arab terrorism and hijacking? That was the last thing we needed.

I went up to Anug, Martirosov, and Zaitsev, who were trying to find a way to overcome the need for a commitment by the Soviet government, and told them, "You have five minutes to decide. If no decision is reached within five minutes, you are liable to be held responsible when a judge issues a restraining order and the people are not extradited." I told them about the report that had reached me and about the pending court hearing. They were stunned and somewhat bewildered.

Martirosov was in greater shock than the others, as it was he who bore responsibility for negotiations on behalf of the Soviet Union. He again tried to call Moscow but was unable to get through.

"You'd better make a decision," I told him, "If you don't, your superiors will hold you to blame for the failure to extradite the hijackers."

Martirosov withdrew to a corner of the officers' club to ponder the matter. After a minute or two he came back. "I have made a decision. I am making a commitment in the name of the Soviet Union that the hijackers will not be executed."

This was an extraordinary thing for a Soviet functionary to do. He had made a political decision without authorization from his superiors. Afterwards, the Soviet government gave him a high-ranking decoration for making a decision in critical conditions of uncertainty; General Zaitsev was recognized as a Hero of the Soviet Union for his conduct during the hijacking, including the release of the children. Without delay, I went over to Sergey Goncharov and told him that we had received permission for takeoff and he should order his people into action. He and I had already agreed on the arrangements for dividing the hijackers and Alpha crews between the two planes and taking custody of them from the Israel Police. Police vans with the hijackers inside were already parked at the airport, waiting for the order to turn them over to the Soviets.

We went out to the TU-154 plane that had brought the Alpha unit and was now parked on the Ben-Gurion runway. I assumed that the Alpha operatives would not be interested in having their faces in newspapers around the world. Moreover, the photographers were certainly eager to photograph Israeli policemen handing over the prisoners to the Soviets, and none of us was interested in pictures like that. I asked the police to keep the journalists away and they promised to do so. Even so, when we arrived at the plane, the tarmac was swarming with journalists. I told the police to form a circle and herded all the Alpha men inside. I told them to stand with their backs to the photographers and to block the sight of the actual transfer of the prisoners with their bodies.

And that's how it went. Everyone was photographed from behind, leading prisoner after prisoner up the ramp onto the plane. I boarded after them, accompanied by a police representative, Chief Inspector Lev Kaplan, whom I knew from a previous joint operation with the Israel Police. Kaplan, who had made *aliyah* from Lithuania in the 1970s, had also been a police officer in the Soviet Union. In the Israel Police, he was a member of the International and Serious Crimes Unit. Some three years after this incident, he served as a Nativ representative in one of the Soviet successor states, and, still later, as the Israel Police representative in Ukraine. Kaplan was holding the sack full of money that the hijackers had brought.

Now we encountered another dilemma. According to standard procedure, the two sides have to count the money—two million dollars in assorted currencies, banknote by banknote. It was a nightmare. The problem was solved by General Zaitsev, who decided it wasn't necessary to count the money. "We trust that no one took any of it," he said with a smile.

I moved down the aisle to bid goodbye to the Alpha operatives one by one, along with Zaitsev and the KGB man, who were to fly on that plane. I also passed by Yashkianz, the handcuffed hijacker and the head of the gang, who had been the first to get off the plane. He gave me a look seething with hatred and angrily spit out, "Israel, huh? This is how you welcome your guests? Really!"

The Alpha men sitting on either side of him "clarified" to him in no uncertain terms that he would be well advised to shut his mouth. He immediately fell silent and did not complete his sentence.

I got off the plane with Sergey Goncharov and we drove to the second plane, the IL-77 in which the hijackers had arrived. It was parked on the apron in the military section of the airport. There was no one around but the base security guards. Here we encountered a small problem in getting the prisoners on the plane. The ladder was narrow and only one person could climb up at a time. So the policemen hoisted each prisoner separately and the Alpha agents jerked them by their handcuffs into the plane.

I entered the plane to say goodbye. Suddenly, Sergey Goncharov had a disturbing thought. "Yasha, what are we going to do with the handcuffs? Don't they need to be handcuffed the entire flight? How are we going to return them?"

"You have a KGB museum," I told him. "Give them to the museum as a present from Israel." After the collapse of the Soviet Union, when the museum was opened to the public for a short period, I read an article with a picture of handcuffs, said to be those worn by the hijackers. It said that the incident had been handled jointly by Israel and the Soviet Union and that the handcuffs were a gift from the Israeli Mossad to the Soviet Union. I smiled to myself.

Goncharov, who upon arrival that same morning had been cold, tense, and stony-faced, bid me a warm farewell. I later met him many times in Russia. Our relationship turned into a cordial friendship that we maintain to this day.

Later, I discovered that my relationship with the KGB museum was more complex and had a longer history. I once sat with generals and senior officers of the intelligence apparatus in one of the countries that emerged from the ashes of the Soviet Union. "How long do you think I've known Yasha?" asked the highest-ranking among them. And without waiting for a response, he told how back in the 1970s, in his fourth year at the KGB academy, the cadets received permission to visit the KGB museum. He said that one corner of the museum was devoted to the career of Yasha Kazakov. That was his first encounter with my story and picture. I didn't bother to verify whether the story was true, but it sounded nice.

The affair of the plane hijacking had many positive ramifications. The Soviet Foreign Ministry went out of its way to motivate Israel to extradite the criminals. Foreign Minister Shevardnadze promised that if the criminals were extradited, we would be allowed to return to our Embassy building in Moscow. This pledge was more than a public hint that Israel was regaining an independent diplomatic status in the Soviet Union, even if, officially, we continued to operate under the patronage of the Dutch Embassy. Shortly thereafter, it was agreed that the two countries' missions would be upgraded to consular delegations and no longer be merely interest sections within the Dutch or Finnish Embassies. Our collaboration during the hijacking broke a taboo and shattered many prejudices that were widespread in the Soviet bureaucracy. And whereas the voices in support of improving relations with Israel had previously been weak, suddenly everyone saw that Israel and the Soviet Union had cooperated and that Israel had behaved with grace and efficiency, and much more rapidly than several countries with which the Soviet Union had diplomatic relations. Underlying the political triumph was the decision in principle by the Prime Minister and Defense Minister and the outstanding performance by the Israel Foreign Ministry. The handling of the affair constituted unambiguous evidence that the two countries could have mutual interests. Thus, the official ice was broken and the process of re-establishing diplomatic relations began and gained momentum.

When I went to Moscow a week later, the Soviets told me with a half-smile that they had seen pictures of Shraga and me in the newspapers and on television. From their faces and hints it was clear that they didn't exactly classify this operation as part of the usual work of two diplomats serving in Moscow. Aside from a smile, I did not respond to the comments.

But I drew a few operational conclusions about how we did things in Israel. For some reason, no mechanism existed for dealing with an incident like this and no one had been assigned responsibility for the overall management of the affair. The IDF was involved only against the possibility that we were dealing with terrorists who had to be subdued. Many years later, I heard worrisome things from one of the main personages involved in the affair (not Ehud Barak) about the military command structure. A few very senior officers had advised Defense Minister Rabin to shoot down the plane. They thought it was a Soviet provocation, insisted they were right, and believed that Soviet commandos were going to leap out of the plane and seize control of Ben-Gurion Airport. Rabin sent them packing.

I was shocked by the creative stupidity and irresponsibility of the officers who made the suggestion. They had learned nothing from the tragedy of the Libyan passenger plane that was shot down over Sinai in 1973. The pilot of the hijacked plane told me that it was only by miracle that a disaster had been averted. A tanker had been parked on the runway to stop the plane, but no one had taken into account the minimum landing distance of a Soviet IL-76 transport plane. The pilot had slammed on the brakes and brought the plane to a halt just a few yards short of the tanker. The IDF vanished from the scene once it was clear that this was a criminal case and not a security matter. The police dealt only with the criminals. The Foreign Ministry dealt only with the political aspects. In other words, there was no overall responsibility and the whole affair was managed in a haphazard manner. But somehow everything worked out in the end, as is so often the case in Israel.

Chapter 31

In the wake of the hijacking incident, we were allowed to return to the Israeli Embassy building. One of the things I was curious to see there was whether the tunnel had been blocked off. The story of the tunnel was famous. In 1964, the Israel Embassy took up residence in new premises in Moscow. Shortly after the diplomats moved in, David Bartov, who was then the number-two official in the Embassy and the head of the Nativ bureau, discovered a tunnel under the ambassador's office which led to a nearby building. The tunnel had a low ceiling, so people could not stand at full height inside. I knew all the details of the story from Nativ documents and from Bartov himself. One fine day, after the Soviets realized that the tunnel had been found, they invaded the Embassy, claiming that a water main had burst. The invaders were violent and showed utter disregard for the Israeli employees' attempts to stop them. The Soviet "workmen" poured concrete into the tunnel and sealed it off. Clearly the tunnel had been intended for Soviet security forces to infiltrate the Israeli Embassy. Through diplomatic channels, the Israeli ambassador was warned that were the matter of the tunnel made public, the Soviet authorities would vent their wrath on the Jews and restrict *aliyah*. This was the main reason that Israel had buried the story for years. We assumed that during the years that the Embassy was empty, occupied only by Soviet watchmen, the Soviets would have taken advantage of the situation to plant whatever devices they wished.

After we returned to the Embassy building, we could receive Jews—tourists and the increasing number of *olim*—in a more dignified manner. Of course, there was also the satisfaction of the symbolism and of this broad hint that diplomatic relations between the two countries would soon be restored. Because the Dutch continued to countersign every document and visa issued by the Israeli diplomatic mission in the Soviet Union, we set aside a room in the building for a representative of the Dutch Embassy.

In December 1988, soon after the plane hijacking, a massive earthquake struck Armenia, wreaking immense havoc. Tens of thousands were buried alive under the ruins. Israel quickly organized a military humanitarian delegation, which included the IDF Rescue Unit and several physicians, to help rescue wounded people from the rubble and treat them. The evening before the delegation flew out, Bartov called and informed me that the Prime Minister had decided that I should accompany the delegation. I took my IDF uniform and diplomatic passport and left for the airport. There I met the head of the Soviet mission in Israel, Martirosov. Together we began organizing matters and loading equipment onto the Israeli transport planes.

The loading process went on for three hours. Just when the passengers were about to board, Martirosov came up to me, and trying to avoid my gaze, said that he had just received instructions from Moscow that holders of Israeli diplomatic passports could not accompany the delegation. He immediately added that the order wasn't directed at me personally, but was a general directive. I didn't argue. I waited for all the planes to take off and went back home. I understood that there were still those in the Soviet Union who were doing everything in their power to frustrate a rapprochement between the two countries. They did not want an Israeli rescue delegation to have any political coloration whatsoever.

But Soviet disasters and Israel's involvement in them did not end there. In June 1989, a natural gas pipeline exploded in the Ural Mountains, resulting in hundreds of deaths and many more victims being badly burned. Aryeh Levin, the head of the Israeli delegation in Moscow, informed me that a contingent of IDF physicians was being sent from Israel to treat the wounded. As I was visiting Moscow at the time, Levin asked me to meet the delegation and watch over the members until they could be sent on to the destination of the victims—evidently in the Urals. He gave me the number of their Cyprus Airways flight and its estimated arrival time. He did not yet have a list of the delegation members.

Upon reaching the airport, I quickly persuaded a Soviet Border Patrol major to process the delegation quickly. His only question was how we would locate the people if we didn't know their names. I asked him to send two soldiers with me and have them take aside the travelers I pointed out. The officer, surprised, asked how I would recognize them. I told him not to worry. When the passengers entered the terminal, I pointed out those to be taken aside; we had assembled the entire delegation within minutes. The Soviet officer was astounded. I went up to the new arrivals, introduced myself, and asked for their passports. Then we went off to the VIP lounge to wait while their passports were inspected and processed. Incidentally, the Cyprus Airways flight had originated in Tripoli, Libya, and continued to Moscow after an intermediate stop in Larnaca where the Israelis boarded. Most of the passengers were Libyan.

Suddenly, the head of the delegation turned to me. "Aren't you Yasha?"

I responded in the affirmative.

He smiled. "You don't recognize me? I'm Shuki, your battalion doctor during the war."

After our battalion doctor was killed in the first battle, Shuki Shemer replaced him. And now here he was, over fifteen years later, reporting to Moscow in the capacity of the IDF's deputy chief medical officer. We hugged.

The members of the delegation were excited to be in Moscow. After a few minutes, I asked if they had brought uniforms; they had. I told them that they had five minutes to change into them. They looked at me in disbelief: Was that allowed? What would the Soviets say? I said that they were representing the IDF, and like any representative of a country's armed forces, they should wear their uniforms. As for the Soviet response, I told them to leave it to me. Within five minutes, a unit of IDF soldiers stood in the lounge in dress uniforms. One of them was a medical corps lieutenant colonel—a woman who had begun her service in the paratroops and was now in paratrooper uniform with paratroopers' wings. That was how we left the airport and went to the hotel. When Aryeh Levin saw us in uniform, he almost fainted. I reassured him that they would wear their uniforms only in their free time and wear civilian clothing in the hospital when they worked. At the last minute, the Soviet authorities, apparently traumatized by the thought of allowing Israeli soldiers into Siberia, decided that the delegation would stay in Moscow and work in the local hospitals that were treating victims of the explosion.

I stayed with the delegation for a few days. We went to a number of hospitals and helped the doctors there. Our team distributed equipment and drugs they had brought with them and helped out in various treatments and operations. In those days, Israeli physicians were among the best in the world at treating burn victims. They had mastered innovative methods that were not yet known in Russia. The Israelis were impressed with the competency of the Soviet doctors, particularly considering their wretched and outmoded equipment and drugs.

One incident occurred that was sad and irritating, but most of all, I felt, a disgrace to our status as representatives of the Western world. In one hospital, Soviet doctors showed us ointments sent by the United States in response to the disaster. Our doctors found themselves in a quandary when they realized the tubes dated from the Vietnam War and that the ointment had been banned from use in the United States several years earlier. I told them that they were duty-bound to inform the Soviet doctors, because medical ethics were more important than the vain honor of some American who had messed up. But the Soviet physician who was treating the wounded just sighed and said, "We don't have any other ointments. Better we should use what the Americans sent than nothing at all. This way, we might at least be able to help some of our patients."

We arranged for Shemer to meet the commanders of the Soviet Medical Corps. One doctor in our delegation, a major, had made *aliyah* from Leningrad and was a graduate of its Medical Institute. I exploited the delegation's presence for meetings with Jews, too; we arranged a meeting in the Moscow synagogue, and thousands of excited Jews crowded in. It goes without saying that the arrival of a group of IDF officers in uniform caused a huge commotion in the synagogue.

We also used this time to hold conferences with the medical staff in several hospitals. Dozens of doctors showed up, most of them Jews. For many, this meeting was the start of their road to Israel.

The delegation's visit to Red Square and the Kremlin was an emotional experience. It was simply amazing to see IDF soldiers in uniform walking around the Kremlin. At the entrance to the compound, the soldier who inspected those entering asked me what army the visitors were from. Were they from Cuba? His jaw dropped when he heard that they were from the IDF.

The truth of the matter, however, was that the Soviet leadership was not happy about the delegation. Although they did not keep us out, they tried to restrict our activity to a minimum and prevent any public acknowledgement that assistance had been provided by Israel—and by the IDF Medical Corps, no less.

Chapter 32

During these years, Nativ was establishing a presence all over the Soviet Union and making contact with all the relevant groups—Soviet bureaucrats, the Jews, and non-Jews. We created an effective system that was far superior to the other Israeli agencies. It enabled us to accurately analyze topics related to Jews and national problems. We avoided and categorically prohibited our employees from giving even the slightest impression, even inadvertently, that we had any interest in security or military information. That was none of our business and was outside our purview. The vast amount and high quality of the information we gathered enabled us to formulate precise, correct assessments of the situation in the Soviet Union on every topic, and especially what concerned the Jews. Thus I was able to make an educated guess as to the number of *olim* we could expect in 1990 and thereafter.

In 1989, the number of Jews who left the Soviet Union—*olim* and particularly dropouts—increased from month to month. In 1988, we realized that the Soviets had begun requiring *aliyah* applicants to have an invitation from a first-degree relative. In years past, the authorities occasionally used emigration to Israel as a way to get rid of "undesirables," even those who had nothing to do with Israel or Jews. In 1989, though, the use of this stratagem reached massive proportions. For example, more and more exit visas were given to

Pentecostals, a Christian sect that has no connection to Jews or Israel. Some 13,000 Pentecostals left the Soviet Union in 1989, increasing the number of those emigrating on visas to Israel to a record 89,000.

I quickly saw that if the trend continued, the number of émigrés would reach 50,000 a year and would soon approach 100,000. I was worried by the fact that a majority of the emigrants, including the Pentecostals, were going to the United States, where the authorities would find themselves dealing with numbers far beyond what they were willing to absorb. In part this was a matter of money. The Jews who left the Soviet Union with visas for Israel were defined as refugees, which entitled them, unlike other immigrants, to a subsidy from the federal budget. The American administration was willing to change the rules for Soviet Jews and place them on equal footing with other immigrants, and had been doing so for some years. More than one American official had told me this; but the administration was afraid that the Jewish establishment in the United States would denounce such a change as anti-Semitism. The Jewish establishment and organizations had a vested interest in Jewish immigration because of the vast sums it brought into their coffers, notably from the federal government but also from the United Jewish Appeal. By this time, though, the number of Soviet Jews immigrating to the United States had surpassed what the federal budget could support. And without government assistance, the Jewish organizations would be unable to fund the newcomers' absorption. I was skeptical about the American government's ability to further increase the quota. The new chairman of the Jewish Agency, Simcha Dinitz, supported the idea of setting aside up to 75% of the UJA funds for the dropouts, but that was woefully short.

In July 1989, I wrote a situation report in which I estimated that there would be at least 100,000 emigrants from the Soviet Union in 1990. This meant that if the American government changed its policy on admitting Soviet Jews and decided to allow only direct immigration, all those who received exit visas to Israel—roughly

100,000 people—would be making *aliyah* in 1990. I asked the research department to summarize the data on the more than 100,000 Jews who had left the Soviet Union for Israel and other countries since 1979 and to prepare a demographic and professional profile of the expected wave. The calculations were based on the mandatory questionnaires for emigrants I had instituted when I took up my post in Vienna in 1978. Later, in Moscow, I introduced similar forms, which included personal data on the applicants.

Aryeh Levin, the head of the Israeli mission, asked whether I had received permission from the Foreign Ministry legal department to introduce those forms. I responded that these were Nativ documents and beyond the control of the Foreign Ministry. Our analysis produced an exact profile of the anticipated *aliyah:* how many university students, how many schoolchildren and in what grades, how many welfare cases, how many in poor health. The analysis also classified the number of men and women who were expected to arrive by occupation (about 100 categories) and by ten-year age coordinates for an influx of 100,000 persons. We noted that if the number of *olim* exceeded 100,000, as predicted, these figures could be ramped up proportionally. I added this as an appendix to the situation report. I am proud to say that the discrepancies between our occupational predictions and the actual figure proved to be negligible—no more than a few percent.

I asked for meetings with Prime Minister Shamir and Finance Minister Peres. Peres met me first, and I gave him the report and explained its implications. I recommended that he draft a budget in anticipation of 100,000 *olim* the following year, and that he make it modular to allow for a larger number. I promised that during the new few months we would be able to provide a more precise figure. About two months later, if I remember correctly, I submitted another report, which anticipated 150,000 *olim*, and towards the end of the year I submitted our final assessment—as many as 200,000 *olim* in 1990. The actual figure that year turned out to be 184,000.

Two or three days afterwards, I met with Prime Minister Shamir. He listened attentively and asked why I had written the report. "The *olim* will come and we will absorb them, just as we did in the past," he said. I was surprised by his nonchalance and patiently explained that it would be impossible to handle the numbers we were predicting without advance preparation. The country had the capacity to absorb up to 100,000 *olim* in the first year through conventional methods. But for more than 100,000, we needed to make special preparations.

"And what will be with the *olim* if we cannot absorb them?" Shamir asked pensively.

Looking him straight in the eye, I retorted with my typical cheek and bluntness. "I don't think you're phrasing the question properly. If you can't absorb them, you'll be thrown out of office."

"That bad?" Shamir responded with surprise.

"Yes. That bad."

Despite my report, the Finance Ministry drew up a budget to cover only 40,000 *olim*. The bureaucrats there did not believe my assessment. I never really expected them to believe it, but in a functional system they would have drawn up contingency plans for this option as well. When the *olim* began coming en masse, everyone panicked and the mad race began.

In light of the changes that were taking place in the Soviet Union in early 1989, I decided to revisit the idea of direct flights. I set up a meeting with the CEO of El Al, Rafi Har-Lev, hoping to get a picture of the national airline's situation and find out what he knew and what had been done so far. Har-Lev explained the situation to me and emphasized El Al's desire and willingness to introduce direct flights in any way that might coincide with the best interests of the State of Israel. He also noted that he had held several meetings with Aleksei Chistyakov, the head of the Soviet Interest Section in the Finnish Embassy in Israel. It was clear that the idea was going nowhere because of opposition by elements in the Soviet political system.

In the summer of 1989, I had a brainstorm: setting up flights between the Soviet Union and Israel through another country that was friendlier to us, Hungary. To probe the idea, I met with a representative of the Hungarian airline Malev in Moscow and suggested that it fly *olim* through Budapest. Malev would introduce special flights for *olim*, leaving from Moscow and stopping over in Budapest before proceeding immediately to Israel. I told him that eventually they might not even have to land and could just change the flight number in the air instead, and then fly straight to Tel Aviv. In this way we would have a direct flight without making the arrangement formal. The financial accounting with El Al, which did not fly to the Soviet Union at that time, would be a purely technical issue.

When the Malev representative asked why we didn't want to land in Budapest, I cited the many security-related problems and complications involved in having the passengers disembark and re-embark. This was true, but my real concern was to ensure there would be no dropouts in Budapest, unlike the situation in Vienna. The idea was to provide a solution to the predicted dramatic increase in the number of people leaving the Soviet Union. The Hungarian was intrigued by the proposal and attracted by the financial aspect. I knew that if it came off, the deal would make a major contribution to Hungary's foreign currency income. We agreed that he would transmit the proposal to the Malev management and the Hungarian authorities. We met a few more times over the next months, because although the airline was very interested in the deal, the Hungarian government was hard put to find the political formula that would make it possible. We agreed to wait for the political approval.

And then I decided that the situation was ripe for me to meet with executives of Aeroflot, the Soviet national carrier. At my request, a meeting was set for me with the CEO. But on the morning of our appointment, Aeroflot notified me that the meeting had been cancelled. An inquiry determined that company management had received instructions from the Soviet Foreign Ministry not to meet with me. I insisted that they find out which official in the Foreign Ministry had issued the order. It turned out that this was our old friend Chistyakov, now back in the Soviet Union and the head of the Israel/Palestine desk in the Foreign Ministry. Chistyakov was an old-school Soviet Orientalist with an extremist ideology and intense hostility towards Israel. He never tried to hide his pro-Palestinian bias and enmity towards us. I immediately asked to be put in touch with Chistyakov and asked whether he was the one who had banned my meeting at Aeroflot. He said yes. When I asked him why, he said that such a meeting was incompatible with our delegation's mandate. Seething with anger, I told him in a slow and menacing voice that our mandate was exactly the same as that of their delegation in Israel. I added that nobody in Israel had ever barred him from meeting any Israeli, including the CEO of El Al. I demanded to know by what right he was imposing restrictions on us that we had not imposed on them.

It was plain from his voice that he was at a loss; he had not expected my tone of voice and choice of words. The Soviets were accustomed to being inflexible and aggressive, but he did not expect that attitude from an Israeli representative. Not knowing what to say, he simply repeated, "It's outside of your mandate."

I had assumed that this would happen and continued, speaking even more slowly. "Listen carefully, Mr. Chistyakov, and remember this for the rest of your life: We will place the same restrictions on your people in Israel that you place upon us here. If you don't let us move around, not a single person from your delegation in Israel will leave the Finnish Embassy building and you will talk only with the Finnish. If that's what you want, keep playing your games."

He almost choked, utterly astonished by my manner. When he recovered, he asked whether I was speaking only for myself or stating an official position.

I replied, with wry emphasis. "You need to learn that we do not employ your methods. We didn't call a Party meeting or hold a political consultation with the secretary of our Party branch. Nonetheless, you can trust me when I say that relations between our countries will be only on the basis of full reciprocity. Your restrictions on us will become our restrictions on you in Israel." And with that, the conversation was over.

Not long afterwards, Aryeh Levin received an urgent summons to the Soviet Foreign Ministry. He returned from the meeting stunned and invited me for a walk to discuss the problem.

"What have you done? How did you talk to him?" he asked. "They called me in and complained that you had spoken in very undiplomatic language and threatened Chistyakov."

I explained the background to my conversation with Chistyakov and emphasized that we must not allow the Soviets to place restrictions on our delegation while theirs enjoy full freedom of action in Israel. Levin began going on about how I was fouling the air and that this was likely to throw a wrench into the relations between the two countries.

"Relax," I told him. "This is the only language they understand. An eye for an eye. Complete reciprocity. We cannot relent on even the tiniest detail." I added that I would settle accounts with Chistyakov one day. After two hours of walking around in the frosty streets of Moscow, Levin was reassured and we put the matter behind us.

The CEO of Aeroflot certainly didn't want to mess with the Soviet Foreign Ministry. But as fate would have it, an El Al delegation landed unexpectedly in Moscow, in tandem with representatives of Malev, for talks with Aeroflot. It turned out that Malev had decided to try to make headway on the idea of flights from Moscow to Israel via Budapest. Har-Lev had given me advance notice of the visit by the two delegations. "If you can," he told me, "come help us in the negotiations. We'd be glad to have you with us."

I decided to try my luck again; after all, the Soviet Foreign Ministry couldn't prevent me from being part of an Israeli delegation. I sat in on the meetings with the Hungarians and the Soviets. At lunch, I sat next to Har-Lev and the CEO of Aeroflot. I spent two and a half hours explaining to the latter that we foresaw a huge increase in the number of *olim* to Israel and that we were interested in establishing direct flights. I presented my calculations of how much Aeroflot stood to gain in foreign currency revenue if it decided to cooperate with El Al and fly *olim* directly to Israel. He was excited by the idea, but couldn't shake his worries about the political echelons. I reassured him with a promise that we would look into the matter. Would he be willing to start negotiations on direct flights if the Soviet Foreign Minister announced that this would not cause political problems? "Right away," he responded.

When I was next in Israel, I approached David Bartov, who was about to visit the US, and asked if he could find a way to slip in a question about direct flights between the Soviet Union and Israel to Foreign Minister Shevardnadze, who would also be there. I don't know if it was a result of my request or just a coincidence, but when a reporter did raise the matter at a press conference, Shevardnadze replied, "That is not a political question. It is a commercial matter and the government of the Soviet Union will not get involved."

Shevardnadze's comment was published in a Soviet newspaper. I called the CEO of Aeroflot. "You see? The issue has been settled."

"That's good enough for us," he responded gladly. "Let's begin negotiations."

Aeroflot wasted no time in inviting Har-Lev to Moscow. When he arrived with his staff, he included me in the negotiating team. The talks with Aeroflot on running direct flights between the Soviet Union and Israel together with El Al were conducted efficiently and progressed rapidly. The sticking point was the price. The Soviets were asking for a hefty $700 a ticket, and their insistence produced a deadlock. We asked for a recess in talks. I flew to Israel and reported to Shamir that, aside for the dispute over the price, everything was settled.

Shamir was angry, and rightly so. "Why didn't you agree to the price?" he scolded me. "This is not a question of money. Go right back and agree on any price the Russians ask—the main thing is to have direct flights."

I felt truly foolish. I was of the same opinion but had not dared make a decision about the exorbitant price on my own. I was actually glad that Shamir had rebuked me and was proud of my Prime Minister. I informed Rafi Har-Lev of the Prime Minister's instructions and we returned to Moscow.

The agreement was signed within a few days. It was decided that the two airlines would inaugurate charter flights on January 1, 1990. Our only concern was security. Representatives of El Al prepared for obstinate negotiations on the subject of armed guards. To their surprise, the Soviets agreed immediately. Moreover, they took it for granted that the guards would stand with their Uzis visible. Now it was the Soviets' turn to be surprised when we told them that the security men would keep their weapons concealed. They promised to give all the help and collaboration we needed and even offered us use of their shooting ranges.

Representatives of the Jewish Agency were eager to take part in the negotiations and pressured us to obtain entry visas for them. The Soviets were adamant in their refusal. "What in the world?" they demanded. "The negotiations are between the airlines. Why should a nongovernmental organization we know nothing about participate in the negotiations and why should we give entry visas to its staff?"

Zvi Barak, the head of the Jewish Agency Finance Department, asked to be allowed to come to Moscow, but the Soviets refused to issue him a visa. Although we tried to have the contract include a mention of the Jewish Agency as the source of the funds, the Soviets refused point blank. "Don't you dare," they told us. "The Jewish Agency is an organization that deals with immigration, and the political echelons will not tolerate any reference to it. We don't want to hear anything about the Jewish Agency. Forget about the Jewish Agency. The agreement is between El Al and Aeroflot and that's that."

On January 1, 1990, the Habima Theater was slated to begin a run in Moscow. It was decided that the El Al plane that brought the actors to Moscow would return to Israel with *olim* aboard. The next direct flight, which had already been set, would be operated by Aeroflot. In late December, I flew back from Israel to Moscow on the El Al flight with the Habima actors. Any other time, I would probably have been excited by the fact that Habima, which had been founded in Moscow, was finally returning there. But there was a much stronger and deeper reason for my excitement and apprehension this time. When the plane landed, I went out into the passenger terminal as if moonstruck, just to look at the line on the arrivals board of the Moscow international airport with the words "El Al" and its flight number. It was an amazing feeling. Once again, I had accomplished something that just a few weeks or months earlier had seemed impossible. The crazy dream of direct flights between the Soviet Union and Israel had come true before my eyes. I spent only a few minutes in the passenger lounge before returning to the plane. The whole way back to Israel, I could not calm down. After the plane took off, I walked down the aisle and looked at the passengers' faces. The people were drained, indifferent to the implications of this flight, and the children were half asleep. I wondered whether they realized that in just a few hours, they would land in the State of Israel direct from Moscow.

Meanwhile, back in Israel there was a great tumult. Everyone who was anyone wanted to come to Ben-Gurion Airport to be present for the arrival of the first direct flight from the Soviet Union. David Bartov showed discretion. He urged all the bigwigs to keep quiet about the event, not to publicize it, not to make a celebration or come to the airport. The Minister of Absorption and other senior officials heeded his arguments and went back home, even though they were already on the way to the airport. There were no leaks and certainly no publication of the direct flight and the agreement we had signed.

When the plane landed and I disembarked, I encountered Rafi Har-Lev. He looked at me with tears in his eyes, hugged me, and said, overcome with immense feeling, "I always wondered what the messiah would look like, but I never imagined he would look like you!"

Har-Lev was exaggerating, of course, but his remark merely expressed every Israeli's yearning for mass *aliyah* from the Soviet Union. It bears noting that by that point, the dropout phenomenon had ended and all those who left the Soviet Union were coming only to Israel—and in growing numbers. Har-Lev's devotion to the cause was understandable, as was the excitement that gripped him when he saw the Jews landing in Israel. He was a retired general in the Israel Air Force, a pilot who had fought in all the country's wars, and he was flying them to Israel! This was the Israel that I loved, that enthused me and made me stronger, that Har-Lev embodied.

But our excitement was soon dampened. In a speech a few days after the flight, Yitzhak Shamir announced that we were on the verge of a great wave of *aliyah* and that "a large *aliyah* needs a large country. We need many Jews to settle in Judea and Samaria."

His remarked angered not only the Arabs, but also the Soviets. As a result, Foreign Minister Shevardnadze nixed further direct flights between Israel and the Soviet Union and the agreement was frozen until further notice. The second plane, which was Aeroflot's, was already prepared to leave, but because of the ban on flying to Tel Aviv it landed in Larnaca, Cyprus. That night, I flew in a two-seater plane to Cyprus with a satchel full of cash, and paid the Cypriots to fly the *olim* on to Israel. With no particular problems, we transferred them to the Cypriot plane as soon as they reached Larnaca, and I returned to Israel with the *olim* on that same small plane. This was the ignominious end to the almost-successful campaign for direct flights—all because of an incautious remark at the wrong time. A year passed before direct flights resumed, in different forms and under different conditions. By then, they no longer had the same meaning or the same impact.

Chapter 33

In Moscow, in September 1989, Aryeh Levin told me that the American Embassy had notified him of a briefing on the topic of immigration, with the participation of representatives of various foreign missions, including ours. He wanted me to attend. A senior embassy official informed us that Washington had decided to transfer management of the process of Soviet emigration to Moscow. This meant that anyone who wished to immigrate to the United States would now have to submit their applications to the embassy in Moscow; the embassies in Rome and Vienna would no longer accept or process immigration requests. He added that for a transition period of a few months to a year, emigrants in Italy who had already filed their applications would continue to be processed.

I went back and reported to Aryeh Levin and then went off to ponder the matter. The new decision verified my basic assessment, which I had submitted a few months beforehand. I was very angry that we had not received any report about the new policy, neither from headquarters in Israel nor from our representatives in the United States. It turned out that no one in Israel knew anything about the decision until after it had been made. I recalled a discussion in our office in late spring 1989, attended by the Nativ representatives in the United States and Western Europe. When I asked about the likelihood that the American authorities would transfer the processing of

Soviet emigrants to Moscow, and whether we could do anything to encourage them to do so, they all laughed. According to those who dealt with the Jews in the United States and Western Europe, America would never agree to do that, for a thousand different reasons. When I insisted that the reason would be financial—that the United States could not cover expenses for such a large wave of emigration, while the Jewish organizations did not have sufficient resources—they dismissed my assessment out of hand.

I realized immediately that we had been given a one-time opportunity to put an end to the drop-out phenomenon. But it was also clear to me from their narrow and schematic approach that the Americans did not understand the complexity of the problem. They did not consider what would happen to Jews who reached Vienna and wanted to immigrate to the United States. If they were not allowed to continue their journey, Vienna would soon be flooded with thousands of indigent Jewish families. The American government, the Jewish establishment, and the Austrian authorities would not be able to withstand the pressure and Soviet Jewish immigration to the United States would be resumed. I was convinced that unless we prevented Jews from reaching Vienna, the United States would not be able to keep Jews from abandoning their road to Israel and requesting American immigration visas in Vienna and Italy. I decided to try to implement the method I had formulated much earlier, when I was looking for ways to eliminate the dropout problem.

This method was based on my understanding of the psychology of Soviet Jewish emigrants and the ingrained patterns of Soviet citizens in general. The principle was that those who received a Soviet exit visa to Israel would not receive their Israeli *aliyah* visa, without which they could neither leave the Soviet Union nor enter any other country unless they presented their airline ticket to Budapest or Bucharest. The way stations for *olim* we had established in Budapest and Bucharest ran like clockwork, and the arrangements there made it impossible for them to drop out or reach any destination other than Israel. With that idea in mind, I immediately flew to Israel. Zvi Magen, a Nativ staffer, was all in a panic when he greeted me at the airport. As he saw the matter, the newly-opened option for Soviet Jews to emigrate to the United States was a catastrophe. Jews would fly there directly—even those who were planning to come to Israel. I asked if they had already issued a report with this assessment. When he said no, I ordered the assessment to be shelved. I explained that the situation was exactly the opposite of what he thought. This was, in fact, our golden opportunity to stamp out the dropout phenomenon once and for all. Magen didn't quite understand how that could be, but had to obey my order.

The next day, I went with David Bartov to see Prime Minister Shamir and presented my idea in general terms. Shamir surprised me with his response. He was one of the very few people whose heart was wholly with the *olim* and *aliyah*. He hated the dropout phenomenon and was always terrified by it. Unlike Begin, Shamir had openly denounced the dropout phenomenon to American Jewish leaders and tried to force them to stop supporting it. But he was too late; the response of American Jewish organizations was highly negative. All the same, he consistently continued to raise the issue. But Shamir was a man full of contradictions; sometimes, he was given to excessive caution. This was one of those times.

"You may institute the new policy of conditioning a visa on presentation of an airline ticket if you wish," he told me, "but first coordinate details with the Dutch and get their permission."

"All right," I said. But inside, I was boiling and felt that everything was falling apart. I didn't throw up my hands, though, and decided on the spot that I would do what I knew was best. I would not let this opportunity pass and would not repeat the historical mistake that had opened the way for the dropouts. When we left the Prime Minister's office, I told Bartov, "I'm not going to ask the Dutch for permission. I'm simply going to tell them."

"Do what you think is right," Bartov replied.

I think that this was one of David Bartov's great moments on this issue. I doubt whether anyone else in his place would have made that decision after he had heard the Prime Minister's explicit directive. I'm not convinced that Shamir really understood my scheme, and am even less certain that he agreed with me that we could eliminate the dropout problem in this way.

Back in Moscow, I met with the Dutch ambassador. "I have just returned from Israel, where I had an interview with the Prime Minister," I told him. "In light of the changes in the process of immigration to the United States, we are introducing a new operating method." I explained to him only the principle of issuing the Israeli visa "at the end of the day" after presentation of a flight ticket. It was implicit in my words that the Prime Minister was aware of what I was saying. I didn't ask him for the ambassador's agreement and emphasized that I was simply informing him, in accordance with the agreement that required us to update the Netherlands about our work arrangements.

I gave the same explanation to Aryeh Levin. Levin did not involve himself with *aliyah*. Whenever he asked questions about our work arrangements, we told him in no uncertain terms that he and the Foreign Ministry were not to interfere in our work and our methods, but we would update him about everything. I met with the Austrian consul in Moscow and explained to him that as of such and such date, the Israeli mission would be implementing certain modifications in the *aliyah* visa procedures, in line with our new policy and the changes the United States had introduced. I did not go into great detail and asked that no one be issued an entry visa to Austria without showing an *aliyah* visa to Israel, as required by international law. I added that I was sure the Austrians were not interested in having masses of homeless people roaming the streets of Vienna, given the new American procedure, and that it would be better if the Jews didn't reach Vienna at all. My thinking was simple: We would issue the *aliyah* visas after 5 pm, when the embassies were already closed. Because their tickets were for planes taking off that same night, people would not be able to go the Austrian Embassy and receive entry visas after they left our embassy. I decided that those who received their Soviet exit visa before a certain date could go to Vienna and continue on to the United States, but those who received visas after that date would be subject to the new arrangement.

The tension mounted as the effective date of the new procedure approached. On the last night, I left my hotel and pondered the matter as I walked down the street. I doubt whether anyone but me was aware of the significance of the next day—that we were on the threshold of an extremely dramatic and critical event in the saga of Soviet Jewish emigration. We were about to deliver every Jew leaving the country with an exit visa directly to Israel, putting an end to the disgraceful dropout phenomenon, which was born in sin and folly. Starting tomorrow, I would have the opportunity to halt it in one fell swoop. I knew that if I succeeded, this policy would change the face of *aliyah*, and even more so, of the State of Israel and its future. Once again, I felt the loneliness of having almost no one who shared my idea and vision and was as devoted to carrying it out as I was. Before I left the Embassy building, I sat with my coworkers, the handful of Nativ staffers in Moscow, on whom the future of *aliyah* was hanging. I explained again what awaited us the next day and repeated my briefing one last time. They grasped the idea and the momentousness of the occasion, but they did not see the dropout phenomenon as I did. Unlike them, I had fought for *aliyah* and had seen in Vienna how the dropout phenomenon was destroying it.

The following morning, we assembled in the Embassy. As the start of office hours at 9:00 o'clock drew near, I went outside as usual. I looked at the faces and expressions of the people standing there, waiting for the embassy doors to open and for us to begin processing applications. I told myself, "They don't know and aren't aware of it yet, but destiny has already divided them into those who will still make it to the United States, to New York and Los Angeles, and those who will have to make *aliyah* and settle in Kiryat Malachi or Tel Aviv, despite their plans."

At 9:00, people were admitted to the embassy courtyard and gathered to hear instructions. There were more than 500 people assembled there. I picked up a megaphone and took a step forward. Utter silence. I again surveyed the hundreds of pairs of eyes, and saw faces that were full of curiosity and free of worry. Just a minute more, and for some, the words I was about to say would change their plans. The process I had initiated and was about to implement would drastically alter the individual destinies of hundreds of thousands of people. Such moments, when a person is aware that a historical turning point for his people is about to unfold before his eyes, that he himself is controlling it and influencing the course of Israeli history, are rare.

The thought that I had determined their fates did not trouble me. I was resolved to make a supreme effort to direct everyone to Israel. I was calm but tense, just like before going into battle. I was at peace with myself then, and remain so today, about this step I took on behalf of the country. But when it comes to the fate of all those people, I am less certain today and sometimes even feel regret. Did I cross the boundary of what is permitted for one individual to influence the fate of hundreds of thousands of people in such an extreme manner? I do not have a clear answer to this difficult question. Although it is quite possible that I would do the same thing again today, I no longer have the same confidence that what I did was truly the best for those people. For the good of the country? Undoubtedly! For the good of the people? I'm not certain.

In my characteristic manner, speaking clearly, slowly, in a quiet and confident voice that suppresses the listeners' inclination towards disobedience and desire to argue or resist, I explained the new arrangement. In the same tone, I asked if they had any questions. There were only a few, which were asked with great hesitation, and no arguments. I gave short and precise answers. The people listened and said nothing. I saw it in their eyes that they understood the overall implications, that they were in shock and still unable to digest what I had said, but were unwilling or incapable of resisting. There was total silence. I turned around and told our staff to start processing the applicants.

Earlier that morning, I had told our staff that if we could hold on for one day, we would be 70% successful, and if we held on for two or three days, we would have total success: We would put an end to the dropout phenomenon and everyone would make *aliyah*. What happened, in fact, was exactly as I had planned and predicted. The applicants followed our instructions to the letter and in silence, with no resistance whatsoever. There were no attempts at evasion or arguments. The herd instinct, the psychological pressure, Soviet education, the inborn obedience and compliance with orders that were issued in the proper form and tone, Soviet citizens' lack of desire or inability to struggle or resist, unless they were sure they were authorized to do so and had a chance of succeeding—all these worked in our favor, just as I had predicted. The main point in my explanation was to give people the sense that the matter was closed and that they had no choice or opportunity, if they tried, to reach any country other than Israel. The truth was that if they had wanted to leave, they could receive a passport with our visa at 5 pm, go to the Austrian Embassy that next morning and receive an Austrian transit visa, throw out their plane ticket to Budapest, and take the train to Vienna. We couldn't prevent this. There were a thousand and one ways to circumvent our new arrangement. Only one thing was missing: the boldness and capacity to deviate from what had been dictated to them, to step out of the herd, to stray even one step left or right.

Within a few days, the new arrangement became routine and it was clear to everyone that "America is closed off. Everyone is going to Israel." People in our Foreign Ministry asked me if this was ethical. Aryeh Levin, too, said that it wasn't right to coerce people this way. "Everyone will reach Israel," I retorted. "You people should focus on your business and not interfere." They dropped the issue.

The Jewish Agency tried to influence the immigration routes and asked me whether we could let the people go by train. My answer was firm: absolutely not. Once upon a time, in a moment of inattention, we had created the dropout phenomenon and had lost hundreds of thousands of *olim*. I would not let this happen again and I would not be responsible for bringing it about, directly or indirectly. There was only one route, only one way: direct flights through Budapest or Bucharest, and to Israel alone. Or people could apply to immigrate to the United States. All those who had supported or encouraged the dropout phenomenon were proven wrong. They had claimed that were the path to the United States blocked, the Jews would stay in the Soviet Union and not make *aliyah*. My answer was always that the Jews wanted first and foremost to get out and would go anywhere, including Israel, if they had no choice. If the choice was between Israel and Moscow, they would always prefer Israel. If they were given the opportunity to immigrate to Zurich, Geneva, or Paris, they would prefer them over New York. But if the choice was between Krasnoyarsk or Petah Tikva, they would choose Petah Tikva. It was clear to anyone who saw the Soviet Union then, with the empty shelves in its stores, the collapse of its economic and social system and its rampant crime, pervasive confusion, instability and insecurity, that these people would be willing to escape and go anywhere that would take them, because the country they were living in was falling apart at the seams.

The time was ripe to turn the people in the direction we preferred. Had we missed that golden opportunity, it would not have come again. There would have been a mass exodus of Jews from the Soviet Union, but only a handful would have come to Israel.

Chapter 34

The *olim* began to arrive in Israel in growing numbers. All our assessments were realized with amazing precision. As usual in such situations, everyone who had got in the way or, at best, stood on the sidelines, tried to jump on the bandwagon. Among the first was Simcha Dinitz, the chairman of the Jewish Agency. In negotiations with the American Jewish organizations a few months earlier, he had not even raised the idea of putting an end to the dropout phenomenon. In fact, he had agreed to a much greater allocation of United Jewish Appeal funds to support the dropouts in the United States and requested only that some share be left for the Jewish Agency. Never mind the fact that as the Israeli ambassador in Washington in the 1970s, he had been among the most vocal opponents of Nativ's efforts to win passage of the Vanik-Jackson Amendment (which imposed trade sanctions on the Soviet Union if it did not allow free emigration). Not one of those who trumpeted the Zionist victory, as manifested in the mass *aliyah* from the Soviet Union, had done anything in the United States, pressuring or at least urging American organizations to drop their opposition to a cut in the Federal government's support for the dropouts. The American administration provided this support out of domestic political considerations.

We knew the truth: no one but us could have even conceived of this option and possibility, let alone carry it out. Moreover, none of them had the foggiest idea of what had been done, how, by whom, and towards what goal. Had we not succeeded, the dropout phenomenon would have continued and the million Jews who came to Israel afterwards would not have made *aliyah*. What worried me then and troubles me even more today is that such a momentous decision was made by one person, with no orderly discussion, without recognizing that the system was incapable of making a decision with such fateful consequences for the Jewish state and the Jewish people.

With the dropout option essentially eliminated, the number of *olim* skyrocketed. People in Israel finally understood the situation. A committee of directors general of government ministries was established to deal with the operational aspects of the mass *aliyah* and find immediate solutions for the problems spawned by its dimensions. Deputy Finance Minister Yossi Beilin chaired the committee. The committee's work was quite effective, considering the constraints imposed by the convoluted government bureaucracy, but its reach was limited. I was a member of the committee.

At one of its meetings, I proposed that every *oleh* family receive a rent subsidy, whether or not another family of *olim* was living in the same apartment. At first, the other members of the committee did not understand my logic. I explained that in the Soviet Union, people were used to sharing an apartment with their parents. If every family received its own subsidy, parents and children would rent one apartment, thereby cutting their costs and expenses. And were the same model applied to mortgages, it would make it much easier for *olim* to purchase apartments. Beilin got the committee to approve my proposal, which solved part of the housing problem. Something else that made life much easier for *olim* was the decision, made somewhat earlier during Yakov Tsur's tenure as Absorption Minister, to institute an "absorption basket." All the diverse benefits that *olim* had previously enjoyed were replaced by a lump sum, which *olim* could utilize as they saw fit.

Ariel Sharon, who became Housing Minister in mid-1990, called me in several times to consult about ways to improve the *aliyah* absorption process. I suggested that he establish a ministerial committee on absorption to replace the committee of directors general, and explained what powers it should have. Sharon adopted my proposal and appointed himself to head the new committee. One important aspect of my proposal was not implemented: they did not give the committee budgetary authority or control of the entire absorption budget. Sharon also consulted with me about "the caravan program," which was later sharply, though sometimes unfairly, criticized. I'm not referring to the management of the competitive bidding process, a topic we never discussed. What I have in mind, for example, is the opposition of many localities to the placement of such portable structures on their land for fear of "decreasing quality of life" and lowering real estate values.

The original idea was that families would spend no more than twelve months in a caravan until a more permanent housing solution was available. No one had planned for them to live there for years. As a result, the units purchased were not designed for a long usable life. But the plans for conventional construction and the forecasts of the ability of *olim* to purchase an apartment were too optimistic. So instead of living there with the promise they would get out after twelve months, many *olim* were forced to stay in caravans for several years and deal with all the implications thereof. The logical solution would have been to transfer title to the plots on which the caravans stood to the tenants and provide them with funds to build a home. That might have solved the caravan problem. But because the subsequent handling was flawed, the problem remains unresolved to this day.

In anticipation of the opportunity to eliminate the dropout phenomenon and increase *aliyah*, Nativ revamped its organization throughout the Soviet Union. The system in Budapest and Bucharest was functioning beautifully. Those who came to the Embassy in Moscow could register for flights at the same time as they received their *aliyah* visa. The Embassy took care of everything, including their flights and the transfer of their belongings to Israel. It was a closed system that worked smoothly and was managed effectively at very low cost.

Our relations with the Jewish Agency constitute a separate chapter, sad and irritating, in the annals of Israel's involvement with Soviet Jewry in the 1990s. The Jewish Agency had always collaborated with Nativ before Simcha Dinitz became its chairman. Dinitz had political aspirations, but when his career reached a dead-end, he was elected head of the Jewish Agency in 1988 as a last hurrah (often the fate of unsuccessful Israeli politicians). I suppose he hoped that Soviet *aliyah* would be a launch pad for restarting his career.

From the day he entered his new job, the change in how the Jewish Agency was run became palpable. Dinitz started pressuring us to transfer some of Nativ's responsibilities to the Agency. One of his first demands was that we include Agency staffers in the Nativ office in Moscow. I worked with David Bartov to formulate our response: "Recommend people to us. If they are suitable, we will be delighted to include them in the delegation." But Dinitz's intention was different: He wanted these people to report to him—to the Jewish Agency, not to Nativ. We made it clear that this was out of the question. These were two different systems—one was part of the Israeli government, the other an international NGO—and while they could cooperate, there was no way to merge them. My view is that Dinitz was cynically and brutally trying to exploit the fact that half of Nativ's budget came from the Jewish Agency.

The Jewish Agency partially funded the budgets of some other government agencies, but it did not demand professional and operational control in return, as it did with us. This fell outside of its mandate. The executive agencies did the work, not those funding them. Our refusal led to foul-ups and incidents with Jewish Agency personnel in Vienna, a phenomenon that we had not previously experienced. The person responsible for the mess was the head of the Jewish Agency Finance Department, Zvi Barak. In the past, no one even knew the name of the head of the Finance Department, but Zvi Barak managed to impose his authority throughout the Jewish Agency and had everyone, including the most senior executives, shaking in their boots. He essentially ran not only the Finance Department, but also the entire Jewish Agency, in tandem with Dinitz and often by using him. Each worked to achieve his own goals.

Barak was guilty of the vilest deed I have ever encountered in the Israeli bureaucracy: He froze the transfer of funds to Nativ for the entire fiscal year. It was only a few days before the end of the fiscal year that he informed Nativ's stunned controller, who had previously served as the controller of a very important government agency known for its outstanding ethics, that he had transferred the money to Nativ. This effectively made it impossible to spend the money, because any funds that were not utilized by the end of the fiscal year had to be returned to the Agency. Bartov informed Finance Minister Yitzchak Moda'i of this ploy and made it clear that this was unacceptable. Moda'i was a man who knew how to make decisions. In response to the Jewish Agency's contemptible behavior, he announced that Nativ would henceforth be fully funded from the State budget, and he would collect the Jewish Agency's share in a different way. Barak and Dinitz tore out their hair. They ran to Bartov and Moda'i and begged them to restore the previous situation, promising that the failure to transfer funds would not be repeated. They didn't want to lose their leverage over Nativ. But we would not give in. As a result, we finally won financial independence from the Jewish Agency. Nativ has been fully funded by the Finance Ministry ever since.

After Foreign Minister Shevardnadze put an end to the direct flights from Moscow, the *olim* continued to leave the Soviet Union via Budapest and Bucharest, with no problems. One day, the Jewish Agency asked me to join in negotiations with additional airlines with whom it wanted to arrange flights for *olim* through other countries.

Although I couldn't fathom why the Jewish Agency suddenly wanted us to be involved in all the negotiations and arrangements, it was decided that I would accept the invitation. This was my introduction to the Jewish Agency's bureaucracy and work methods. Until then, I had been familiar only with the procedures and rules that applied to Nativ civil servants. During my service in Vienna, I got to know the Agency emissaries and workers there but was never exposed to the organizational culture. Now I flew to Vienna, a city I knew well, with the Jewish Agency delegation. Their bureaucracy arranged my accommodations in a luxury hotel. Nativ staff members had visited Vienna frequently, but we never stayed in hotels anywhere near that league.

The Jewish Agency's efforts to conclude an agreement with some other airline did not produce any real breakthrough. We visited almost every Eastern European country, as well as Finland, looking for another transit station. None of us at Nativ could understand why additional transit stations were needed. We never received a logical explanation, and Bucharest and Budapest were certainly managing to handle the pressure. Although successful, the attempt to open a route through Poland was completely unnecessary, because the number of *olim* using that route was negligible. The Jewish Agency apparently felt it was important to make an agreement with another airline and set up another way station, which, of course, would require them to staff and fund additional offices. But I am certain that it was quite superfluous, justified neither by the number of *olim* nor the reliability and security of their travel routes.

Just then, to our astonishment, the Hungarians decided to back out of our agreement, and a Hungarian Jew who lived in Canada simultaneously appeared out of nowhere and proposed that we fly the *olim* on an airline he would set up for that purpose. When I looked into his proposal, it turned out that the prices were higher than those that Malev had been charging. Nonetheless, the Jewish Agency was willing to sign a contract with him, and "for some reason," the Hungarians—the airline and aviation security—were not opposed. But the agreement was never signed, and the *olim* continued to fly through Budapest on Malev, which retracted all its new demands once it became clear that we would not sign the contract with the private company.

I have already mentioned how scandalized I was by the behavior of the Jewish Agency officials and emissaries. After our talks with representatives from Eastern Europe at the end of our first day in Vienna, the entire delegation went out to dinner at one of the most magnificent restaurants in the city. I had never eaten in a restaurant of that class, and as far as I know, neither had any other Nativ employee. It was a meal fit for a king. I almost choked when they ordered four different wines, a different kind for each course. When the bill arrived at the end of the meal, the Jewish Agency representative in Vienna pulled out his Jewish Agency credit card and paid it.

"What's going on here?" I asked in astonishment.

"That's how we do things in the Jewish Agency," they replied. And indeed, all the subsequent meals were similarly extravagant, with choice wines and delicacies. In Nativ, like every other civil service agency, it was emphatically forbidden to draw on the organization's budget to pay for hospitality for Nativ staff and employees of other government departments and Israeli public organizations, including the Jewish Agency. But the Jewish Agency lived on a different planet. Agency personnel were used to receiving a lavish per diem when abroad and being hosted on the tab of the local Jewish Agency representative; and for them, the Jewish people's money was cheap. When I returned to Israel and reported my expenses to the controller of Nativ, I followed his instructions and reconciled accounts with the organization.

Apparently Zvi Barak knew about this. At one of our meetings, he turned to me of his own initiative and explained that from time immemorial and long before his tenure, the Jewish Agency had followed its own rules and its senior officials were granted generous budgets and expense accounts that enabled them to stay in luxury hotels, pay for shopping sprees in boutiques, and much more, with all tabs picked up by the Agency. I remembered this remark, as well as the Lucullan feasts and all the other small manifestations of self-indulgence that I witnessed, when I read the verdict in the first trial of Simcha Dinitz. The judge explained his acquittal, in part, on the grounds that as someone whose entire being and thoughts were dedicated to the affairs of the Jewish people and its problems, Dinitz simply had not paid attention to the fact that he had charged tens of thousands of dollars of personal items and services to his Jewish Agency credit card. I smiled to myself and wondered whether it was the burdens of the Jewish people or the pleasures of the dining table that had distracted Simcha Dinitz from the proper mode of conduct and caused him to charge his extravagant tastes to the Jewish Agency.

Many years later I had my opportunity for a "payback" from the Agency. In the mid-1990s, one of the endless committees on the topic of Nativ and the Jewish Agency decided that a delegation headed by Zvi Alderoti, the director general of the Prime Minister's Office, would visit several sites in the former Soviet Union. The delegation would consist of a number of Agency personnel and myself, as head of Nativ, which was responsible for organizing the trip. At the first dinner, I clued Alderoti in about the Agency's peculiar "grace after meals." "Do me a favor," I told him. "Let's not say anything at the beginning of the meal. But when it's over, a Nativ representative will announce that everyone is paying his own tab. Watch the faces of the Jewish Agency people then!"

Alderoti was glad to play along. When the waiters took our orders, the Jewish Agency staff, as usual, chose the local delicacies. I had already told the Nativ staff to eat whatever they wanted and to pay no attention to what the others ordered until the end of the meal. After receiving the check, the Nativ organizer read off the amounts and announced that every diner would pay his own share. As we had agreed, Alderoti took out his wallet first. You might have thought that a bomb had exploded in the restaurant. All the "suffering of the Jewish people" was reflected in the Agency people's mournful eyes. The expressions on their faces revealed their astonishment and pain as they took out their per diem money and paid up. After that evening, no matter where we were, our Agency colleagues almost always discovered that they had to spend mealtimes in urgent discussions of Agency matters with their local representatives and couldn't sit down to eat with us. I decided that I didn't care that they were going off by themselves so they could have their local office pay for their meals. Alderoti was also delighted with the arrangement.

This was my small revenge on the "guardians of the funds of the Jewish people." It was particularly gratifying because whenever we got into arguments, Zvi Barak roared, without blinking an eye, that the donors demanded that the Jewish Agency monitor all outlays, and this is why it had to operate in the former Soviet Union. Over the decades, Nativ utilized tens of millions of dollars of donations for various purposes, like other organizations in Israel, and donors never questioned our credibility. Nativ paid for the Jews' *aliyah* with money contributed by the Jewish people. The donors always trusted us and relied on our integrity. It was only in the period of Zvi Barak and Simcha Dinitz that the Jewish people, who supplied the money, suddenly began to doubt us and ostensibly to demand that "only people like Zvi Barak and the heads of the Jewish Agency work in the field among the Jews."

Chapter 35

In the summer of 1990, I began studies at the National Security College (NSC). Bartov, my boss at Nativ, suggested that I take a leave to attend the college, and I am eternally grateful to him for that. I was already deputy director of Nativ and the situation was reasonable; I could be confident that the system I was responsible for would function even without my daily presence and involvement. Most of the objectives I had set for myself had been achieved: *Aliyah* had started to take off again and was on the rise, the dropout phenomenon had been eliminated, and the support mechanisms in the Soviet Union were working properly. Although Israel and the Soviet Union still did not have diplomatic relations, that was clearly only a matter of time. Even under the current situation, Nativ could still operate effectively.

The National Security College was an old-new institution. It had been the brainchild of Chief of Staff Chaim Laskov and opened in 1963. Laskov saw the college as an Israeli version of the British Imperial Defense College (IDC) and intended it to prepare senior IDF officers to deal with strategic problems. In 1966, at a time of budget cuts required by a difficult economic situation, the college was closed by Levi Eshkol, who served as both Prime Minister and Defense Minister at the time.

As part of the process of drawing lessons from the Yom Kippur War, Chief of Staff Mordechai Gur suggested re-opening the college.

The supporting position papers and discussions asserted that the IDF sorely lacked an institution to train its officers beyond the tactical level (the role of the Command and Staff College). When the officers had to work at the operations or strategic level, they were completely unprepared and therefore totally out of their league. It was also noted that IDF officers of those years were deficient in their capacity for analysis or even understanding at the political and military level. Moreover, senior commanders entered their posts with no background of basic facts and did not meet the standards for generals in a modern army. The college was reopened in 1976 as an institution for the study of military, political, and defense strategy.

The studies at the college were an extraordinary experience. I came out quite a different person, possessing the theoretical and conceptual ability to think and understand, to cope with extremely complex political and military issues and problems of all kinds. I had a much better understanding of how to manage, control, and monitor government systems, and most importantly, an ability to integrate these systems. The college also honed my critical faculties, openness, and skepticism. Many things that happened to me later can be attributed to my studies and the skills that I acquired there. My research for some of the papers that I wrote while attending the college continues to serve me to this day. This is especially true of the topic of intelligence and surprise attacks, and my thesis regarding political leaders and the use of intelligence. My fellow students were a fantastic bunch. We were essentially the elite of our age group. Most of us already had a rich and successful professional, and sometimes operational, record. The very interaction—the students' joint thinking and work—was one of the most important elements of the learning process. Most of us were serious students: when we graduated, we were ready to storm the highest executive and command positions in the military, security, and government agencies that had sent us to the college.

Our class was exceptional. More than 60% of us eventually attained the rank of brigadier or major general, or their equivalents in the prison service, police, and intelligence community. Had it not been for the death of Nehemia Tamari, OC Central Command, in a tragic helicopter accident, we would probably have also had a Chief of Staff in our class. As it was, we produced two IDF regional commanders and three corps commanders. The greatest failing of the Security College, and really also of the IDF and the whole country, was that the college was not considered to be a necessary stop for viable candidates for senior positions in the military and security establishment. The State of Israel has paid and still pays a very high and unnecessary price for this—and will continue to do so if the situation does not change. Many graduates of the college were not used effectively by the agencies that sent them there, or by the country. This attitude also meant that unsuitable candidates were sent to the college, because the system saw no imperative need to make use of them after they graduated. The consequence was that the broad goals that underlay the establishment and reopening of the college were not achieved, or if they were, only in part and by chance. Their studies in the college had an impact on the graduates and their personal abilities, but the college has never really influenced the quality of command and management, neither in the IDF nor in the other agencies that send their people there.

The college taught us how to run a country and how to make political decisions, however complex and convoluted. But after we graduated and I had a more profound encounter with the situation in the political and security decision-making echelons in Israel, I was shocked to discover that that there wasn't the slightest hint of what we had learned in the actual management of the country. In any case, this isn't the place to go into further detail about my time at the NSC. I mention this stage in my life only because it had a major impact on my personality.

About a month after I completed my studies at the college, I was invited for a talk by a department head in the GSS—an outstanding professional, one of the best men I knew in that agency. In our conversation, I noticed that he was somewhat uncomfortable. His awkwardness dissipated only after he confessed, turning his glance away from me, that he had a problem.

"I have to subject you to a security grilling. It doesn't matter what I think about this; I'm required to do so. We received a sort of complaint or question from IDF Field Security, originating in the National Security College. Somebody there noticed that you asked too many questions and made too many lists. Forgive me, but I have to ask you: Why did you ask so many questions and why did you make so many lists?"

At this point he couldn't hold back any longer and burst out laughing. So did I. In an apologetic tone, he said that he had to write down my response and report back to the "wise men" of Field Security. I do know which of the teachers filed the complaint, but that doesn't really matter. I went to the National Security College to learn, and I don't know how to learn without asking questions. I ask questions to better understand the material, and I make lists so that I won't forget it and can delve more deeply into it later. But some "genius" suspected me of passing copies on to Russian Intelligence or Argentinean Intelligence. And thus my studies at the National Security College came to an end.

I also had several moving experiences during my studies. The commander of the NSC, who had accepted me, was Maj. Gen. Yaakov Lapidot. He had been the commander of Armor Battalion 79, to which I was posted after I completed the Armor School. During the Yom Kippur War, he had been the commander of the battalion that was posted right next to us. We fought side by side, so I often heard him on the wireless and spoke with him. While I was at the college, Yossi Ben-Hanan became their new commander, a colorful and legendary figure and an amazing human being. We developed a fantastic relationship and stayed in touch after I graduated from the college. I received my diploma from Chief of Staff Ehud Barak; my friendship with him, including serving and fighting at his side, was one of my most formative and compelling experiences in Israel. But I was particularly touched when Prime Minister Shamir shook my hand, as he did every graduate's. I had met and gotten to know him right after my *aliyah*. For me, after everything I had been through, attending the National Security College of the State of Israel, graduating from it, and receiving my diploma from these people was a truly moving experience.

When I completed my year-long studies at the NSC, I returned to my office, even though I had never really been absent all those months. I had checked in almost every day, reading reports to keep on top of developments and issuing orders of some sort from time to time. I didn't interfere too much, but I kept my finger on Nativ's pulse.

Chapter 36

After I graduated the National Security College in August 1991, I had to cope with a problem that emerged during the year I was officially out of the office. Nativ director David Bartov and Zvi Magen, who had been filling in for me, decided that Nativ would no longer issue tourist visas—something it had been doing since the establishment of relations between the Soviet Union and Israel in the 1950s. Issuing tourist visas was very important for Nativ, because most of the tourists were Jews, and contact with them was the organization's raison d'être. Maximizing contacts with Jews was the foundation for all our work and kept us informed of the current situation, with regard to both government policy and the Jews—what they were thinking, what they wanted, what they knew, and the potential to influence them. I saw this unnecessary concession as a severe blow to Nativ's operational and information-gathering capabilities; but it was a done deal and could not be reversed. Another problematic decision taken by Bartov and Magen was that Soviet Jews who came to Israel as tourists and then wanted to change their status to *olim* would be handled by the Jewish Agency. I vehemently opposed this move. I contacted the Interior Ministry, which was also dissatisfied with the new arrangement, and managed to nullify the decision and turn back the wheel in short order. In other words, the organization that issued *aliyah* visas in the Soviet Union itself would determine applicants' eligibility for *aliyah* status. There was no logic in splitting the two processes between the Jewish Agency and Nativ.

These and other less critical decisions were the product of a crisis in faith within Nativ and certain conceptions I did not share. I remember one Nativ employee whom I hired after he had served a number of years as an officer in the IDF. He had been an *aliyah* activist in Vilna, and for him, Nativ was not just another job. He came up for tenure in 1988. In a chance meeting in the hallway, the fellow told Bartov (whom he had known since the 1960s) that he was waiting to receive tenure. To his astonishment, the director replied, "Why do you want to strike roots in this organization? One way or another it will be shut down in a year or two. So you've got nothing to do here."

Indeed, the idea of disbanding Nativ had been floated by the Budget Unit in the Finance Ministry, with the argument that "there aren't any more *olim*, so what's the point of the organization?" In fact, the Finance Ministry had proposed closing Nativ even when there had been significant numbers of *olim*, with the exact opposite argument: "What do we need it for? After all, masses of *olim*, even too many, are coming anyway." In other words, they simply wanted to shut down Nativ and were looking for excuses suitable to the situation. But what would have happened to *aliyah* had the Finance Ministry succeeded in its plan in 1988?!

I had a clear vision of what Nativ needed to do and how it should function in the dynamic Soviet situation. I could not see how gradually conceding spheres of our activity would be of any benefit to the Jewish state. Under intense pressure from the Jewish Agency, Bartov had agreed that Nativ would withdraw from Hungary and Romania and transfer its offices there to the Agency. I was quite unhappy with the decision, particularly in light of the use of the way stations that we had set up and were operating there. The transfer to the Jewish Agency was supposed to be implemented in stages, and only after many years, but Bartov had already given in and gotten the Prime Minister to agree as well. To their great dismay, the Nativ emissaries in Budapest and Bucharest were transferred to the Jewish Agency. On the other hand, they told us how astonished they were at the lavish budgets suddenly at their disposal. It wasn't money for their personal use, but to be invested in their work.

By late 1991, deprived of the way stations in Budapest and Bucharest, Nativ was operating only in the Soviet Union. Bartov's justification for this course of events was his hope that capitulation to the Jewish Agency in Eastern Europe would satisfy its hunger for a while and allow us to work in the Soviet Union in peace. Dinitz asked Bartov to lend me to the Agency so that I could coordinate its work with Soviet Jews. Bartov did not ask whether I was willing to do so and told Dinitz "no" without waiting for my reply.

We began to get the feeling that the Jewish Agency was running an independent shop in the Soviet Union, ignoring the fact that it had no authority to operate there, and lacked the organizational capacity, understanding, or knowledge required. Its activity was totally out of bounds. The Agency was not entitled to operate independently in foreign countries, certainly not in the Soviet Union, without coordination with the Israeli authorities—at least not until Dinitz took over.

The situation in the Soviet Union was very tense and dangerous before the attempted coup in Moscow in August 1991. Nativ was the only organization that alerted those who needed to be warned of the possibility that reactionary elements would deploy the military and security services in an attempt to seize power. That summer, the Jewish Agency organized camps for teenagers in the Baltic republics. When the coup began, Nativ picked up reports from the news media about the movements of Red Army paratroop and armor units in those regions, and the orders they were given. I immediately contacted Prime Minister Shamir, who confirmed Nativ's decision to close down or severely reduce all Israeli activity in the field should the situation deteriorate. I called the Jewish Agency and asked them to shut the camps in the danger zone immediately, in light of the possibility of imminent military operations there. That was the last thing we and the Jews needed—for Jewish summer camps, with Israeli counselors, to find themselves in the midst of a civil war that was liable to break out at any moment, and all the more so against the background of activities by ultra-nationalist and anti-Semitic elements. The Jewish Agency turned me down flat. "We will not abandon the Jews or capitulate to the situation," Dinitz pompously declared, and noted the tradition of Hanna Szenes. I saw his invocation of Szenes in these circumstances, which I believe demonstrated a gross lack of responsibility and endangerment of the lives of Jewish children, as an affront to her memory.

Chapter 37

In August 1991, the attempted coup in Moscow led to the Soviet Union collapsing within a matter of months. The process was all-encompassing, involving a loss of control across the board, extending to the financial, social, and even criminal arenas. Boris Yeltsin's victory in the Russian power struggle inspired hopes and dissipated concerns among Jews. As a result, some of the Jews who had been planning to leave reconsidered their emigration, postponing or even canceling it. The new hopes slowed the pace of *aliyah*, which had been determined by the deteriorating situation. Had the coup succeeded, even partially, the *aliyah* rate would have increased and even surpassed the previous year's record of 184,000 *olim*. Nativ was given the job of getting ready to handle this mass *aliyah*, including flights and ground transportation. Our small staff in the Soviet Union performed the task with the assistance of locals, both Jews and non-Jews.

In the meanwhile, there was increased pressure placed upon the various agencies, and in particular on Prime Minister Shamir, to introduce a new division of labor between Nativ and the Jewish Agency, even though the latter, as mentioned, was not supposed to work in the Soviet Union. But the pressure was successful and it was decided that management of the flights for *olim* would be transferred to the Jewish Agency, because it provided the funds. But the heads of the Jewish Agency weren't satisfied with this and exerted further pressure until a committee was formed to define the respective responsibilities of the Agency and Nativ. The committee chair was Michael Dekel, a veteran of the Irgun, a confidant of Yitzchak Shamir, and the deputy defense minister at the time. The other members were David Bartov and the director general of the Jewish Agency, Maj. Gen. (res.) Moshe Nativ. The committee decided that overall responsibility for Soviet Jewry was the province of the Israeli government—i.e., Nativ. It also decided that the division of labor between the Jewish Agency and Nativ would remain as is, with Nativ retaining all its current responsibilities. The Agency did not accept the committee's decision and continued its offensive against us.

During the years of Bartov's service as head of Nativ, the organization changed and became much more dynamic, wielding operational, analytical, and assessment skills it had not previously possessed. There is no doubt that Nativ as it was in the early 1980s would not have been ready for or capable of carrying out the tasks it was charged with in the late 1980s and early 1990s. It would have continued to deteriorate and would not have achieved its ultimate position, nor would it have had the ability to influence and define processes, neither in relations between Israel and the Soviet Union nor within the Soviet Union itself. It certainly would not have been able to carry out or even understand and plan the critical steps that determined the fate of *aliyah*. Bartov, as director of Nativ, deserves high praise for his work on this topic and for giving me the opportunity to be part of it all.

Before I took my leave of absence to attend the National Security College, Bartov told me that he would retire when I came back. This was logical, given his age (he was past 67) and other factors. But this didn't keep him from taking his time about quitting. In late 1991, he told me that he wanted to spend two years running the Nativ organization in the Soviet Union after he left the director's office. I saw this as a positive step. Bartov had experience from his work in the Soviet Union before the Six Day War and had gained even more in his many years at Nativ. He also had good relationships with important figures in both Israel and the Soviet Union. Although he did not particularly excel as an administrator and manager, I did not anticipate any problems, given the support he would receive from the headquarters staff, the people in the field, and our well-oiled system. Moreover, it was clear to me that we would have to broaden our activity to include all the new countries that had been born from the ruins of the Soviet Union.

On May 1, 1992, I assumed office as director of Nativ, twenty-three years after my *aliyah* and fourteen years after I began working in the organization. There was a certain symbolism in the fact that the head of the Nativ delegation in Moscow in 1967, when I first forced my way into the Israel Embassy, was the person who passed me the baton as head of Nativ. I felt it was also symbolic, not just for me, that the prime minister who appointed me to my new post was Yitzchak Shamir, one of the most vigorous and prominent supporters of a change in Israeli policy on the campaign for Soviet *aliyah*.

The first thing I decided to do after taking over the reins was to reorganize Nativ. The organization had already been improved in various ways at my initiative, but we still had to reorganize and redeploy in anticipation of the new conditions and our new activities. Starting in the early 1980s, I had formulated a cogent outlook on the organization, its goals, and its work methods. I had long ago reached the conclusion that Jews decided to leave the Soviet Union mainly because of the harsh situation in that country and their lack of faith in their future there. We could not influence that, but I knew we could count on the continuing deterioration of the Soviet Union in all areas.

I saw our role as developing the ability to take advantage of the emerging situation and translate the Jews' frustrations and aspirations into *aliyah*. We had to cope with the might of a superpower. The Jewish question fell into the purview of the most senior political echelons there and constituted one of the important elements of its internal and foreign policy, and often ours as well. Daily responsibility for dealing with the issue was in the hands of the Soviet secret police—the huge and fearsome KGB. We had to understand and correctly assess Soviet policy with regards to Jews, and, more importantly, possible changes in it. We also had to study Soviet Jewry, inspire them with national sentiments, and steer them towards *aliyah*. On the basis of all this, we had to draft political and operational recommendations for the Prime Minister and carry them out as he authorized.

Only a professional organization with suitable capabilities could handle this vast task, particularly because the State of Israel had no agency that focused on the Soviet Union itself. The Mossad had nothing to do with the country and did not operate there, so it had no independent capacity to assess events there in general, and certainly not with regards to the Jews. IDF intelligence was quite ignorant about the Soviets, except for military topics related to the Soviet presence in the Middle East. The GSS had the most professional understanding of the Soviets, but it was focused on thwarting Soviet espionage activities against Israel. The Foreign Ministry had no ability whatsoever to analyze and assess the Soviet Union. Because we could not rely on any Israeli agency, certainly not with regard to the domestic situation in the Soviet Union and the Jewish issue, we had to develop independent capabilities within Nativ. I had already managed to make some of the necessary changes. Now, as director, I could begin bringing Nativ's growth to completion, to give it an optimal ability to carry out its tasks.

Nativ already had a new staff, which I had previously recruited. Most of them were young, recent immigrants from the Soviet Union; some had been officers in the IDF. We also hired people who had been activists in the Soviet Union at some level or other. The combination of *olim* who were IDF veterans with *aliyah* activists produced an excellent, healthy, and functional system in Nativ. We forged an outstanding organization that leveraged and fully utilized the staff's strengths and reduced their deficiencies to a minimum. The balance between *olim* and native Israelis was another important factor.

When I recruited staff, I again encountered the unprofessionalism and negligence of IDF field security. A year after my appointment as head of Nativ, I hired my fellow-student at the National Security College, Zavik Bona. Bona, a native Israeli, had been a colonel in the paratroopers. An excellent staff officer, he was appointed head of the operations department of the General Staff after graduating from the NSC. I continued to have an excellent working relationship with him in his new position and we cooperated on several matters. I was amazed when, a few days before he was to begin his job at Nativ, I received a phone call from the GSS insisting that he could not join the agency until they completed investigations for a security clearance. I told the guy on the line that I was taking Bona from the Operations Department of the General Staff, where he had been exposed to almost all the darkest secrets of the Israeli military.

"True," the GSS man said. "But we're not responsible for the IDF. Field Security is. We don't accept their decisions and don't trust them professionally, so we start our investigation of military men from scratch. Moreover, Field Security's last investigation of Bona was when he was drafted in 1971. It was done at a relatively low level of classification, and he hasn't been vetted again since."

In other words, Bona had served two decades in the IDF, including his studies at the National Security College and his time as head of the Operations Branch in the General Staff, without the required security clearance! I had become blasé about negligence and unprofessionalism in the IDF—but this was too much.

Chapter 38

After the collapse of the Soviet Union, we had to open offices in the countries that rose from its ashes. I went to the head of the Finance Ministry Budget Division, David Brodet, and presented our new work plan. He listened to my explanation, read the plan, and approved the budget increase in full! That was quite extraordinary in Israel back then, and would be even more so today. But we were fortunate to be working with Finance Ministry officials who were outstanding professionals, including Amnon Neubach, Eli Yones, and Brodet. They displayed a nonpartisan attitude and understanding that were rare in the ministry. It was only thanks to them that we were able to translate Nativ's professional and operational needs into success on the ground.

I also implemented several new internal procedures. First of all, I decided that we would have an annual work plan. We drew one up and I forwarded it to Prime Minister Yitzhak Rabin for his review and approval. After he had signed off on it, I submitted it to the Intelligence Services subcommittee of the Knesset Foreign Affairs and Defense Committee, which oversaw our activities. The budget was derived from the work plan, a new arrangement for Nativ. From then on, whenever there were attempts to force serious budget cuts upon us, I confronted the Prime Minister with the dilemma: which part of the approved work plan did he want us to drop, with all of its implications? I explained the operational meaning of any budget cuts the Finance Ministry wanted to impose upon us, but shifted the decision and responsibility for canceling activities to the Prime Minister. I also implemented a decision-making procedure based on integrated discussions; all of our deliberations were recorded and transcribed. At my instruction, all the tapes were stored in the Nativ archives, so that during post-mortem discussions we could be cognizant of the goals and considerations that underlay the original decision. At first, the staff members were surprised, but over time they got used to having all the discussions recorded and everything written down, so that nothing could be done under the table or behind people's backs.

We also devised an excellent training system. All Nativ employees, including headquarters staff, were trained specifically for their jobs. We drew on other agencies throughout this process, and they responded to our requests with pleasure and professionalism, thereby enhancing the competence of Nativ personnel. I appointed an excellent man to run the training system, Yizhar Harden. He had made *aliyah* as a child from Poland, but had lived in the Soviet Union until he was ten years old. In the IDF, he rose to lieutenant colonel. Before he came to Nativ, Harden did excellent work and accomplished extraordinary feats, some of which will remain classified for many years to come. Despite his many talents, he wanted to work exclusively in training at Nativ, and he indeed built an outstanding system. He died at his desk of heart failure. The emissaries he trained had no previous knowledge of Nativ or similar agencies, but they left his department as professionals. I also introduced a professional screening apparatus, including psychometric and other tests, so that we could weed out unsuitable applicants in the early stages of the recruitment process.

Nativ's activities in the 1990s were based on precise assessments of possible scenarios and the dynamic of the changes in the Soviet Union throughout and particularly in the late 1980s. I based these assessments on analysis of the information to which we had access, mainly from our own sources but from others as well. According to the information we had in the early 1980s, the senior echelons of the KGB, Yuri Andropov and his coworkers, had reached a fairly distressing conclusion about the situation in their country. With all its problems and flaws, the KGB was an organization with strong professional capabilities when it came to assessing the domestic situation in the Soviet Union—unlike the rest of the government bureaucracy. It was one of the few Soviet agencies (perhaps the only one) that knew how to collect information about developments in the Soviet Union and the outside world, and draw the correct conclusions. Of course these conclusions did not always receive Communist Party (i.e., government) approval.

Andropov's conclusion in the early 1980s, before he became General Secretary of the Soviet Communist Party, was that in the absence of social, government, and economic changes, by the end of the century the country would no longer be able to compete with the United States for superpower status. And what was worse, its very existence was in danger. In other words, without the necessary changes, the country and regime were likely to collapse and disappear altogether. History has proved the validity of this professional assessment. But Andropov was a very sick man and did not have time to institute any real changes. There are many things that can be said about him, but one thing is certain: he was different from the other members of the Politburo.

Andropov was a loyal Communist, but he was intelligent and more thoughtful than most of his colleagues. His personality was strongly influenced by his tenure as ambassador in Budapest during the Hungarian Revolution in 1956. He was shocked and traumatized by what he saw: The revolutionaries dragged Hungarian Communists to the gate of the Soviet Embassy, skinned them alive and then hanged them head down until they died in agony. Similar atrocities took place day after day before the horrified eyes of Andropov and most of the embassy staff. Many of the revolutionaries had previously served in the regime of Adm. Miklós Horthy, the fascist dictator who was Hitler's ally. The Hungarians fought with the savagery typical of civil wars. About a week after the revolution began, the Red Army invaded Hungary and put down the revolution with great brutality, because the Soviets could not accept Hungary's desertion to the Western camp and the loss of Communist control there.

Hungary and the other countries of Eastern Europe were not under Russian occupation, but their Communist rulers relied on Soviet bayonets. For Andropov, the Budapest trauma was personal—his wife suffered a nervous breakdown at the sight of the atrocities and was never the same. The trauma plagued Andropov for the rest of his life and was the main reason he pushed so strongly for the invasion of Czechoslovakia in 1968. Friends who served in the Soviet military and participated in the invasion that year told me about the operation, so I had a fairly good picture of what happened in Czechoslovakia. Crushing the "Prague Spring" was certainly one of the greatest mistakes of the Soviet regime, whose blind adherence to ideology, even then, left it incapable of properly assessing or adapting to the changes and events in the world and their significance. The strain of the Hungarian Revolution drove Andropov to support the decision to invade Afghanistan as well. The Soviet Union's intervention in that country and conduct of the war were a series of fiascos in decision-making, political assessments, goal-setting, strategy, and tactics from beginning to end, at both the military and political levels. It was a replay of the disastrous war against Japan in 1904–1905 or the First World War, which toppled the Czarist regime. For the second time in Russian history, a failed war launched by a weak government resulted in the country's collapse and disintegration. Both the invasion of Czechoslovakia and the war in Afghanistan clearly displayed the cracks and failures in the administrative echelons, which proved unable to deal with complex political problems and find the correct solutions.

It was Andropov who selected Mikhail Gorbachev as his heir, and this proved to be one of his greatest mistakes. (Although the dinosaurs of the Central Committee ignored his choice and named Konstantin Chernenko to succeed him, Chernenko died after little more than a year in office and was succeeded by Gorbachev.) He saw Gorbachev as a Communist of the new generation—thoughtful, vigorous, open, intelligent, and down to earth. Andropov failed to see that Gorbachev had no leadership and decision-making abilities. Gorbachev was a weak man; when under pressure, he would fold and lose any shred of ability to function. He was also incapable of understanding the complex realities of his country.

I had the opportunity to meet Gorbachev after his fall from power. I sat with him for about two hours and left with a distressing impression. I wondered how the country and its controlling elite could have degenerated so far as to entrust power to a man like this, to allow him to run the empire (and run it into the ground). Gorbachev spent 95 percent of our talk telling me how great he was, how much his people loved him, and how he would win a majority in the next election, because he was the only one who could save Russia and the only one the people believed in. This is the man who was placed at the head of the country in 1985 and proceeded to make every possible mistake. His inability to make decisions at critical moments caused the country to collapse. The Soviet Union did not collapse because of deliberate planning or because someone wanted it to. All sorts of experts have offered retrospective explanations of things they hadn't understood before, during, or after they happened, but they completely misread the situation in the Soviet Union. Those who talk about a protest movement and a people that toppled the Communist regime in their drive for freedom and democracy simply do not understand what country they are talking about. The regime collapsed because of its internal decline and gradual degeneration and because the people who headed the country were incapable, at both the personal and organizational levels, of making and implementing the right decisions. The only figure in Russian history to whom Gorbachev can be compared is Kerensky. The weakness and incompetence of Kerensky and his government brought about the collapse of the Russian Empire and the Bolsheviks' rise to power in 1917. Gorbachev was responsible for the collapse of the Soviet Empire. In both cases, the real problem was that Russia didn't find better people to lead it.

Gorbachev hadn't the foggiest idea of the implications of his actions. He still doesn't understand them today. He became the darling of the West, decorated with awards and showered with love. For what? For destroying the country he was supposed to protect and defend? I think that anyone who looks at the Soviet Union in an objective manner cannot be happy about what went on in that country. But Russia and the other Soviet successor states, with their people, paid and are still paying a horrible price for its breakdown—a process that was uncontrolled, brutal, barbaric, and cruel. The bloodshed and the destruction of an entire generation could have been prevented. Let there be no misunderstandings, I am not sorry that the Soviet Union collapsed. I am trying to analyze it in an objective and professional manner, devoid of emotion, whether pro-Russian or anti-Russian. China, too, stood on the brink of collapse, but its regime found a way to introduce reforms and help the country recover without losing power, and, more importantly, without losing control of the situation. In economic terms, China's situation was far worse than that of the Soviet Union. China's economic and technological infrastructure was much more fragile, but the Chinese succeeded where the Soviet leadership failed. China is far from a democracy by Western standards and will remain so for many years, perhaps forever. But it is developing at dizzying speed and forging its own way, rather than kowtowing to outside dictates, and without the ghastly tragedy that befell the former Soviet Union in the accursed decade of the 1990s.

The disintegration of the Soviet Union in late 1991 was not a process planned by the Party or by any political force. Four Communist politicians, dyed-in-the-wool Bolsheviks, who had absolutely no interest in democracy, decided to break up the Soviet Union for reasons associated with their own ambitions and ethnic group. Boris Yeltsin started everything rolling because he wanted to get rid of Gorbachev. His personal enmity and calculations turned into an obsession; he knew that he had to eliminate Gorbachev if he wanted to reach the top, but did not anticipate that in so doing, he would bring about the collapse of the Empire.

The other three were the satraps of three Soviet republics—Ukraine, Belarus, and Kazakhstan—Community Party apparatchiks who wanted to stay in power. The despotic regimes, in the tradition of Soviet Bolshevism, survived in the new countries, under the veneer of nationalism (and sometimes ultra-nationalism). Gorbachev could have nipped the process in the bud and prevented the collapse of the Soviet Union, but he was psychologically unprepared to fight. A Soviet apparatchik, a Party hack with no leadership abilities or basic understanding of loyalty to the country and his position, he capitulated in a matter of seconds: he signed off on the dismantling of the Soviet Union, cried a little, and went to sleep.

By late 1991, it was clear to us at Nativ that the Soviet Union was in the throes of an internal crisis of the worst possible kind. The straw that broke the camel's back was the failed coup in August. But even without the coup, the regime's decline and the general breakdown of the Soviet Union would have accelerated. Moreover, the Soviet leadership had failed to produce someone who could make the right decisions and protect the country at a critical moment in its history. The Prime Minister, one of the heads of the coup, spent three days in a drunken stupor and had barely any clue of what was going on. I spoke about this with Vladimir Kryuchkov, one of the leaders of the coup and the then-head of the KGB. He had been posted in Budapest in 1956 and was fairly close to Andropov.

"From what I saw and I knew," I told him, "soldiers from your special units were posted at critical locations. How could you fail?" The matter interested me because I wanted a better understanding of the ability of the Soviet or post-Soviet system to function. His response surprised me. They were afraid of bloodshed. They thought it would be enough to intimidate people and threaten them and that there would be no need to open fire.

I received indirect confirmation of this from Sergey Goncharov, the deputy commander of the Alpha anti-terrorism unit, whom I first met in Israel during the Caucasus plane hijacking. We stayed in touch after that. When we met in Moscow after the coup, he told me that he had received instructions then to prepare to take over the "White House," Yeltsin's headquarters. He did some preliminary reconnoitering and his men took up positions around the building, where Yeltsin was holed up. According to Goncharov, Alpha could have implemented the assault plan it had drawn up, seized the White House within twenty minutes, and arrested everyone there. When I asked about their casualty forecast, he said that they did not expect to have any casualties, barring an unforeseen slipup. The defenders, in their assessment, were liable to suffer some 200 killed. In response to my question of why the assault was never carried out, he responded bluntly: "The order was never given. It's as simple as that." At the critical moment, when the critical decision had to be made, there was nobody to make it.

Chapter 39

The economic and social collapse of the Soviet Union and the ensuing loss of personal security provided fertile ground for increased *aliyah*. The Soviet regime, already incapable of ruling and running the country, had also lost the ability to hold on to its citizens. Starting in 1989, an increasing number of Jews received exit visas; and the more who received exit visas, the more that applied to leave. The elimination of the dropout option in 1990 did not affect the overall trend of increased emigration. More and more people reached the conclusion that the Soviet Union held no promise for their future, or for that of their children. If there was a chance to leave, it should be seized quickly. It hardly mattered whether they went to Israel or elsewhere. This was the main reason for the steady and rapid rise in the number of those who applied to emigrate. Had the coup succeeded and Yeltsin not come to power, the number of emigrants might have been even larger—perhaps surpassing 200,000. But Yeltsin gave people new hope. He saw the energetic young people around him, heard the talk of reform, and witnessed the abolition of the Soviet regime and the collapse of the Communist Party's hegemony, which symbolized for them everything that was wrong with their country. Some of them abandoned the mad dash to leave Russia, and the pace at which people queued up to make *aliyah* decreased and would probably continue to do so. *Aliyah* did decline, but it remained high, especially from the provinces, in part because years would pass before the situation in the former Soviet Union stabilized. It was very important for us to take advantage of the momentum now and make it as easy as possible for Jews to reach Israel. Our system worked well and we managed to overcome all the logistical and other obstacles.

Immediately after my appointment as director of Nativ in 1992, I started working to create a new infrastructure and planning methods to take advantage of the new situation in Russia and the other Soviet successor states. The Soviet system's weaknesses and collapse catalyzed several new ideas for us. One of them, which we had first instituted at the Moscow Book Fair in 1989, was to set up a permanent center in Moscow. The 1989 fair was very successful, although it could not hold a candle to the "Six Day" fair in 1987 in terms of its effect. This time, however, after the fair closed we left behind much of the equipment we had brought to Moscow. We got the authorities to agree to a permanent Israeli book exhibition in Moscow and the Soviet Union, based on the equipment from the book fair. In my mind, the idea was brewing of transforming the permanent Israeli exhibit into an Israeli cultural center. It would be affiliated with the Israeli Embassy and serve as a platform for our activities wherever the exhibit traveled.

This format was standard diplomatic practice. Many countries operate cultural centers—Soviet cultural centers in Soviet embassies, the British Council, the Institut Français, the German Goethe-Institut, the Italian Società Dante Alighieri, and the Spanish Instituto Cervantes. The diplomatic status was intended to ensure the security and stability that allowed the programs to be run legally without causing problems among the local population. We at Nativ were interested in the Jews, of course, but I thought that the non-Jewish population would also find the Israel Center interesting, out of intellectual curiosity so as to learn about Israel as a country or a civilization. I saw the center as a platform for every Israeli agency, including the Foreign Ministry, to conduct activities of various sorts.

As usual, it was our Foreign Ministry that opposed the idea. Every Nativ initiative or program that would allow us to expand our activities was rejected by the Foreign Ministry's functionaries, but their opposition to the cultural centers was particularly energetic. The Jewish Agency, as it was wont to do at that time, also expressed opposition, but it did not have standing on the issue and its position was irrelevant. In the end, the decision was made by the new Prime Minister, Yitzhak Rabin. Rabin was very excited by my proposal. He said it was an excellent idea and forced the Israeli bureaucracy, including the Foreign Ministry, to adopt and implement it. This was the first basic idea we began implementing to take advantage of the new situation that had emerged. In Russia, there were no laws regulating the activities of other countries' cultural centers. We quickly identified the offices that would have to draw up such laws and encouraged them to rely on us to draft certain articles so that they complied with international treaties. For us it was important to "help" them draft and enact laws in a way that allowed the centers to pursue our goals. The laws related to all foreign cultural centers and referred to the agreements to be signed between the foreign ministries of the two countries, to regulate their centers' activities in the other country on a mutual basis. In other words, Russia would have the right to conduct similar activities in Israel, if and when it desired.

The second important area I thought could be developed was education. The collapse of the Soviet Union and its routine led to the virtual disintegration of the school system in Russia and the other new countries. I came up with the idea of establishing a system of Israeli schools in the countries of the former Soviet Union, in collaboration with the Education Ministry. We presented our work as part of the cooperation between the Israeli Education Ministry and its counterpart in Russia, Ukraine, and so on, part of the effort to establish schools for ethnic minorities, particularly the Jews. The local authorities had no experience in this realm, and I saw cooperation with them as an essential condition. I wanted to create a legal basis for our activities so as to avoid problems for us and for the Jews among whom we would work. An agreement between the Israeli Education Ministry and the local education ministries would enable us to open joint schools. Jewish students would study subjects relevant to Israel and Judaism, including Hebrew, Israeli culture, Israeli geography, Israeli history, Jewish history, and so forth, following the Israeli curriculum and taught by Israeli teachers, who would be sent out by our Education Ministry. All this would be a supplement to the local curriculum, which would be taught by local teachers. The way I saw it, a Jewish child forced to grow up and attend school outside the State of Israel must receive the same education and the same national consciousness as my children and other Israeli children. Every Jewish child should share the same national value system—our future as a people depends on it.

This is why we wanted to use the standard Israeli curriculum. Moreover, I took into account the fact that many of the children in these schools would make *aliyah* sooner or later, and their absorption would be smoother and more efficient if there were not too great a difference between what they studied at school in their home countries and what they would study in Israel. This perspective was utterly incompatible with the Jewish Agency's notion of community schools, which follow the local curriculum and have nothing to do with the Israeli Education Ministry. The Agency raised a loud protest and accused Nativ and the Ministry of Education of invading its territory. Its fear was that a system supervised by the Education Ministry would replace the system of community schools it operated throughout the world. But the Jewish Agency and its programs, whether in the Soviet Union or elsewhere, did not concern us. I attributed supreme importance to setting up the very best education system possible for Jews in the former Soviet Union.

I had already submitted my idea to Zevulun Hammer, the Minister of Education in Shamir's government. I had met him and Yehuda Ben-Meir when they were still the "Young Turks" of the National

Religious Party and were among the first Israeli politicians to support us at the start of the campaign to break the Israeli establishment's conspiracy of silence in the early 1970s. Since then, we enjoyed both mutual esteem and a warm personal relationship. I met with Hammer in the Knesset and sketched out the plan for a school system and my ideas about education. I proposed that the Education Ministry assume responsibility for Jewish education in the Soviet Union. Hammer was excited by the idea and thus the system was born. It worked extremely well until it was abandoned and trampled upon by Ariel Sharon's government and Education Minister Limor Livnat, who tossed it to the Jewish Agency.

I saw the Israeli school system as the basis for my plan. It would serve as the foundation for a system of Sunday schools. My starting assumption was that we could not establish schools for all the Jews, let alone ensure that all Jews would send their children to entirely Israeli schools. But I thought that those children who did not attend "Israeli" schools, for whatever reasons, could at least study one day a week with the teachers and curriculum of the regular "Israeli schools." We decided to bolster the faculties with Israeli youth counselors. We would be able to bring the Israeli education system to almost every Jewish child who wanted it, in the full or partial version. There would be several times as many Sunday schools as regular schools, covering almost every city in the former Soviet Union.

The third level of the educational approach I had crystallized was the Na'aleh program, in which children could make *aliyah* before or without their parents. The program, as I envisioned it, rested on the idea that fifteen to eighteen—the high school years in Israel—is the critical age for the consolidation of one's worldview. I thought it was important to bring as many Jewish children as possible from the former Soviet Union to attend high school in Israel. In those days, the Israeli education system was much better than the Soviet or post-Soviet education system, which had simply collapsed. I consulted with psychologists, who stated their opinion that it would not be a good idea to take children under fifteen out of their family circle, because most children would not be able to endure the emotional strain of separation from their families and their natural environment. Instead, we came up with the plan of bringing older teens to study in high school after a psychological examination indicated that they could cope with the challenge of separation. The program was supposed to operate under the education agreements between the Israeli Education Ministry and its counterparts in the former Soviet republics. I planned to include sections about student exchange programs between Israel and the FSU. Under international law, these students could not be registered as *olim*, because minors could not be granted emigration visas of their own, even with the agreement of both parents. I decided, therefore, that no efforts would be made to change their status while on the program. I assumed and argued that a Jewish child who was educated in an Israeli high school and Israeli society would not want to leave Israel and would choose to link his or her destiny to the country forever. I never imagined that Israel and its education system would degenerate to their present abysmal state.

The Jewish Agency was the main opponent of the Na'aleh program, disseminating vile slurs to the relevant agencies and the media. The Agency protested that Nativ was trying to develop an anti-Zionist program for tourists. Things reached a peak when, during a discussion of education programs with Shimon Sheves, the director general of the Prime Minister's Office, the chairman of the Jewish Agency Executive blurted out that "Na'aleh is Yasha's program to bring Jews to settlements in Judea and Samaria!" Sheves smiled sheepishly at the base level of the accusation and signaled me to pay no attention. To our good fortune, Prime Minister Rabin was enthusiastic about the Na'aleh proposal and instructed us to launch it.

The program exceeded our expectations, though it could have gone further. I insisted that the teens coming to Israel on the programs be able to pass the Israeli matriculation exams. In the Soviet Union, almost no Jewish child finished high school without a matriculation certificate, and it was rare for a Jew not to go on to higher education. I said that we would not admit anyone if we had doubts about their ability to obtain an Israeli matriculation certificate, because being left without one would ruin their lives and was simply inconceivable for a Soviet Jewish family. We devised tests to check the teens' maturity and ability to withstand the pressure of their studies and adjustment to life on their own. We also examined their scholastic aptitude and learning abilities. We again encountered libels and media leaks by the Jewish Agency, which claimed that we were trying to select the smartest children and build an elitist program. But our caution proved itself. The Na'aleh administration and staff were truly outstanding and did fine work. The first pilot was a great success. After the children were tested by psychologists and admitted to schools, it turned out that, by Israeli criteria, thirty percent of them were "gifted."

We made sure that the children would be sent to schools that matched their academic level. We ruled out schools that were inferior scholastically, because the Na'aleh teens had a strong background and abilities. They were not coming to Israel to go down a level, but to go up in all senses of the word—to make *aliyah* and to go up in the development of their personal skills.

After I took up my position as Nativ director in 1992, I focused on setting up and expanding Nativ's infrastructure in the field. Robert Singer, who headed the unit that handled educational work and the operation of the Israeli cultural centers in the FSU, made sure new material was constantly being created and that activities kept expanding. A system of Hebrew-language courses was established, based on the Israeli ulpan model of intensive instruction. I again preferred to work in collaboration with another government agency— the Ministry of Absorption. The reason was simple and, in my view, critical. In Israel, Hebrew classes for *olim* were supervised by the Absorption Ministry, which ran dozens of *ulpanim* (intensive Hebrew language courses) all over the country. I thought it only logical for the same system to run pre-*aliyah* Hebrew studies. This would create continuity in the learning process: *Olim* could complete half of the language course before they made *aliyah*, and after their arrival in Israel, pick up where they had left off with the same syllabus,

When I spoke with officials in the Absorption Ministry, including the minister, I explained why I thought that absorption should begin with a year of pre-*aliyah* preparation, including occupational training. We organized courses with the Ministry of Labor for professional/ vocational retraining so that *olim* could slip smoothly back into the program after they arrived in Israel. By then, they would already have completed a significant portion of the course and learned the demands of their occupation in Israel. This saved time and made their occupational absorption easier. We also organized seminars for Jewish scientists from all over the former Soviet Union. At these conferences, they met scholars and representatives of Israeli research institutions and had the opportunity to get to know and understand the parameters of their scientific fields in Israel and what the Israeli academic system had to offer them. They could also develop professional relations and plan out their *aliyah* in an effective manner. Most of them were ready and willing to make *aliyah*, given the calamitous state of the scientific research system in the former Soviet Union. Israel had an opportunity to take in the cream of the scientific crop of a world scientific power, in numbers that no Western country could have dreamed of. Had we taken full advantage of the opportunity to absorb these scientists, Israel would be much stronger and more advanced today. But thanks to the narrow-mindedness of our bureaucracy and the bean-counters in the Finance Ministry, the opportunity was wasted.

Robert Singer managed and developed these programs in an extraordinary fashion, thanks to his contacts in both the former Soviet Union and Israel. Working relations were excellent, more Israeli agencies and institutions collaborated with us, and an increasing number of Jews in the former Soviet Union were exposed to Israel and got involved with it. Of course, this was a thorn in the side of the senior executives of the Jewish Agency. Its representatives tried to have government ministries barred from working among the Jews. The Agency saw its activities among the Jews as its "birthright" and was concerned that other government agencies would try to emulate our success working abroad, thereby threatening its survival. What justification would this bureaucratic monster's chairman have to beg for hundreds of millions of dollars to maintain the organization and its apparatchiks? For the big shots of the Jewish Agency, the main thing was to survive and raise money to ensure its survival; the welfare of Jews and *aliyah* were of lesser account. The Jewish Agency waged constant battles with Nativ, using both fair and mostly unfair means. It didn't interfere with our work, but we were forced to devote more attention to asinine debates and explanations.

The heart of my plan was to broaden our coverage of the field and get Nativ staffers into the Israeli embassies and diplomatic missions in the former Soviet republics, sometimes entering those countries even before an Israeli embassy opened. The Foreign Ministry moved with dreadful sloth. By the time it started moving, by the time it screened candidates, we'd lost all patience (never mind that after all the screening, those candidates turned out to be of disgracefully low caliber and completely unsuited for the job). Some of the Foreign Service officers who were sent out were amazing professionals, but that was quite by chance. We reached every place before them and had already made contacts, begun work, and rented the offices that later served the diplomats in the early months after their arrival. We gladly placed the contacts we had made at their disposal. We introduced them to all the local organizations and helped them with everything. In exchange, they generally treated our emissaries in a humiliating and belittling fashion and frequently interfered with their work.

Nonetheless, our advantage on the ground was a constant. Nativ, after all, had been active professionally in the Soviet Union for decades in many fields, especially contacts with Jews. The Foreign Ministry was simply not prepared to work with the Soviets and on Soviet territory. Most of its Soviet affairs buffs did not know the language or understand the country's culture or history, aside from what they learned from English-language works by Western "experts." Some of our diplomats had previously been posted to Ireland, South America, and Africa, and now they were being entrusted with the Soviet desk for two or three years! Nor did other specialized agencies have staff fluent in the language, at least not the modern spoken language. All too frequently, I saw retired Nativ staffers who had made *aliyah* from Poland in the 1940s and 1950s and were clueless about current idioms when translating material from Russian to Hebrew. Nativ had people with long years of mastery of the language and the material, in both the Soviet Union and in Israeli agencies—retired IDF officers we had recruited—all of them native Russian speakers, all *olim* from the Soviet Union, and most of them veterans of the Six Day War. And they had also expanded their knowledge and grasp of the situation after joining Nativ. For various reasons, including our close ties with the target countries and their people, we were the only agency that could draw upon our own sources of information and did not have to rely on foreign sources. As usual, like everyone who is successful in Israel, we aroused jealousy and opposition, particularly in the bureaucracy.

The Foreign Ministry saw all our endeavors as an affront to its standing. We often heard locals make unflattering comparisons between the Nativ operatives and the Foreign Ministry diplomats. Nativ never created a rotten and perverse organizational culture of the sort that prevailed in the Foreign Ministry. When an Israeli ambassador comes to blows with the security officer, it does not make the country look good. When people with emotional problems are chosen for jobs, without proper screening, it does not make a good impression on the host country and its population, particularly the Jews. An ambassador who "adopts" a local female staffer and makes her queen of the Embassy does not do honor to his country. Most of these ambassadors in the former Soviet Union, who knew no Russian, let alone other local languages, did not understand the countries in which they served and their mindset. The bureaucracy was poorly equipped to train people to work in the Former Soviet Union.

Russia and the Soviet Union had been no more than a sideshow in the Foreign Ministry for years and were never properly dealt with. How is it possible to speak about serious relations if our missions in countries like Russia or Ukraine were left without an ambassador for a year or a year and a half? On one of my visits to the State Department in Washington, a young Foreign Service officer in the Soviet Union/ Russia division, whose staff I used to meet twice a year, told me, "I have to tell you goodbye—I'm leaving." When I asked where he was going, he said that he had been appointed ambassador to Latvia. To my question as to when he would be taking up the post, he replied, "Next year." When I expressed my astonishment that he was leaving the division now, he explained that he was going to spend the year studying the language, the culture, and everything else relevant to Latvia. In the Israeli Foreign Ministry, this was unfathomable. No one thought that a post in the former Soviet Union demanded any serious preliminary study.

People of stature and knowledge, like Aryeh Levin, were an exception in the human landscape of the Foreign Ministry and its attitude towards Russia, and only got there by accident. Levin was born in Iran, when his family was en route from Latvia to Israel. He was fluent in Farsi, French, and English, not to mention being a native speaker of Russian. His service in other Israeli agencies before he came to the Foreign Ministry had honed his cognitive, analytical, and rhetorical skills. Another exceptional person was the late Meron Gordon, a Soviet-born expert in Russian poetry and culture, who died much too young. But even Aryeh Levin treated Nativ's successes and capacities with suspicion.

I remember a meeting in the Foreign Minister's office to discuss how Yakov Kedmi, the deputy director of Nativ, was interfering with the Foreign Ministry's work in Moscow. The minister at the time was Moshe Arens, who was blessed with healthy instincts, common sense, and a logical mind that was extremely rare in Israel, as well as both personal and professional decency. At the start of the meeting, Arens asked for an example of how Kedmi had obstructed the Foreign Ministry. Levin mentioned my meetings with political figures and other prominent persons. Arens asked for details; the reply was that I had met with Alexander Bovin, who at the time was one of the most important and influential journalists in Russia.

"And you don't have meetings with Bovin?" Arens asked. Levin admitted that he did. "If so, why does it bother you that Yasha meets with Bovin?" Arens wondered.

In response, Levin blurted out what really bothered him and many others in the Foreign Ministry as well as other agencies: "Bovin meets with me as an ambassador, but he meets with Yasha as a friend."

I plead guilty. Our ability to get people to open up and trust us, to develop personal relations so they would share their problems and thoughts with us, surpassed the wildest dreams of Foreign Ministry personnel.

The Foreign Ministry's neglect of Russia and the entire region, and general indifference generated large and unnecessary outlays. When I came to Moscow, I developed excellent relations with the local authorities. In general, we were on unusually open terms with the Russians, with the exception of their security services. To take advantage of the positive atmosphere, I proposed to the Foreign Ministry that we build a large new embassy that would suit all of our needs. At the time, it would have been possible to obtain almost any lot and put up a building quickly, which, I proposed, would include a residential complex, a school, and all auxiliary services. We spoke with the section of the Soviet Foreign Ministry that worked with foreign missions and with the relevant officials in Moscow City

Hall. They were all willing to sell us the apartment building next to the current embassy along with an adjacent plot. This would have allowed us to construct a full-service residential complex next to the Embassy, solving several problems, including security and social issues—and at a negligible cost. We would do just what the Americans and Germans had done. But the Foreign Ministry did not want to hear of the proposal. As a result, Israel is still stuck in Moscow with the old embassy building, which is quite unsuitable for our needs. An Israeli businessman even offered to pay for the construction of a new embassy if the Foreign Ministry would commit to renting the premises for a period of ten years, so he could recoup his investment, after which he would be happy to transfer the title to the State of Israel. We also suggested buying up apartments, which were available for next to nothing. The Foreign Ministry rejected all of these ideas. In the end, we were forced to lease a residential suite in a hotel for our ambassador in Moscow, at the astronomical price of $18,000 a month. Had our proposal been accepted, we could have bought a luxurious apartment in Moscow for the cost of six months' rent—but none of this seemed to trouble anyone too much.

Later, when we rented an apartment for Ambassador Aliza Shenhar, who had come to Moscow with her husband, we invested a fortune in a tiny two-room flat. I asked what they would do if her successor had a family, but no one cared. I won't even mention the folly of posting to Moscow of an ambassador whose academic expertise was Israeli folklore. She had no clue about Russia, its problems and its culture; or, for that matter, about international relations. Her appointment was not just an insult to Russia, but a disgrace to Israel itself, which extended this kind of treatment to the extremely complex and complicated relations with one of the most important countries in the world. But the selection was Shimon Peres' whim, and no one, not even Rabin, dared get involved. In the end, when the next ambassador arrived in Moscow, the Foreign Ministry had to spend a fortune to purchase and renovate a new apartment. The functionary responsible for this idiocy and the waste of hundreds of thousands of dollars received a promotion and was sent to the United States with a rank parallel to that of ambassador.

In anticipation of the increased volume of Russian Jewish emigration, we had to modify the layout of the Embassy building so that we could handle the large number of visa applicants. The ambassador and the Foreign Ministry dreamt fondly of tossing Nativ out of the Embassy altogether. I suggested constructing a prefab structure in the courtyard, like those I had seen at the Australian and other embassies. I spoke with the Australians and found out what was involved. Several companies in Finland did this kind of work quickly and cheaply. In the deliberations about the proposal, the Finance Ministry said, as it was wont to do, "Use your own regular budget." But our entire budget was earmarked for specific purposes, unlike the Foreign Ministry budget, which included discretionary funds that could be disbursed with a wave of the hand. And then a miracle happened. Minister Ariel Sharon came on a visit to Moscow. When he saw how the Embassy dealt with the public, he was appalled. Our people there told him that the only solution was to put up a separate building. When he returned to Israel, he pressured the government, and the Finance Ministry was forced to allocate the money.

I proposed adding another floor, which would have cost $50,000 (an extra 20–25 percent over the original sum), to make the building more appropriate for our needs. This time, I ran into opposition not just from the Finance Ministry, but from the Foreign Ministry as well. While I was studying at the National Security College, someone at Nativ decided to leave the choice of the contractor and oversight of the work to the Foreign Ministry and the Embassy. The Foreign Ministry gave the job to a local contractor. Within two years, the building proved to be unsuitable because of faulty construction and we were forced to undertake serious renovations. This time, we chose a Western company, paid double the amount that had already been spent, and came out with a proper building in which it was not disgraceful to receive the public.

We also had to handle the logistics problems of the Nativ branch in the Moscow Embassy. The first time I came to Moscow as the head of the organization, I discovered that for accommodations and services, the Embassy relied on a local Jewish organization and a private company owned by its director, one Mr. Roitman. I demanded that we immediately break all the leases with that company for Embassy staff apartments. I insisted that all logistics issues be solved with the authorities and that we not get mixed up with private individuals and companies. We would work exclusively with the government agency that provided services to foreign diplomats in Moscow. All the diplomats laughed and stayed in the apartments they had leased from Roitman, because the apartments provided by the Soviet Foreign Ministry were of inferior quality, although their rent was also much lower. For Nativ, though, it was important to work with the authorities, particularly because the apartments they provided were close to the Embassy.

I put an end to the practice of hiring workers through Jewish organizations and personnel firms. As a rule, I preferred to employ Gentiles, because Jews were a headache: If they weren't suitable, it was hard to fire them—how could you throw a Jew onto the street? And when local Jews work in an Israeli embassy, the authorities immediately grow suspicious of them or try to recruit them to work against Israel. With non-Jews, there were no such problems. Because the Jews had been hired during my absence, we continued to employ some of them, but we mostly relied on competent Gentiles who did a fine job.

I severed the links between Nativ and Roitman in all fields except for one—Hebrew language instruction. Roitman was one of the young Jews who had got involved in Jewish activity back in the 1980s, especially Hebrew classes. In the late 1980s, he set up and oversaw an organization of Hebrew teachers, which functioned for a number of years at the end of the Soviet era. It did excellent work, setting up Hebrew courses throughout the Soviet Union and its successor states—a great achievement in those days.

We made contact with many groups and individuals, some of whom later found work in various organizations. Nativ was also the first Israeli agency to develop ties with research institutes that studied Israel or the Middle East. It was only later that the Foreign Ministry sent out people who were even capable of communicating with these institutes. We provided them with material and explanations and hosted some of them in Israel during professional visits. For them, visiting Israel, a country they had only studied about, was an extraordinary experience. For us, it was important to get close to them, given the strong pro-Arabic foundation of Middle Eastern studies in the Soviet Union. We tried to identify, encourage, and support people who wanted to receive a more balanced picture of the situation and were open to a more objective approach. We wanted to strengthen pro-Israel attitudes and give them tools to see our side of the problem. These efforts were quite successful and some of our contacts are still active today. Some were promoted in the academic world or diplomatic corps and even received postings to Israel.

A very important focus of our work with government agencies in the FSU was to shed light on the issue of *aliyah* and the relationship between Jews and the State of Israel. We got everyone to accept that Israel's top priority was ties with Jews and *aliyah*, and that every other aspect of bilateral relations depended on openness on this issue. Although most of the functionaries in Israel, particularly the bureaucrats of the Foreign Ministry, ranked the priorities in the other direction, we managed to create the impression that our perspective represented the Israeli government position.

Chapter 40

Back in the early 1980s, I made sure to get my hands on every article by Alexander Bovin. I knew from my sources that Bovin was close to Andropov. I valued his writings because I surmised that his opinions were close to or representative of some of Andropov's views, or were at least floated for the latter's consideration. When I arrived in Moscow in 1988, I looked up Bovin and contacted him. I recall the first time I came to see him in his office at *Izvestia*, the official government newspaper. When I entered, the first thing I noticed was a photograph of Andropov on one of the side walls. It was the only picture in the room, and I smiled to myself when I recalled my interest in his articles. Bovin was wary throughout our conversation. Towards the end, I switched the topic to Andropov and his role in the Soviet Union. I discerned excitement on Bovin's face. When he spoke about Andropov, his eyes teared up. This was the icebreaker in our relationship, which over time developed into one of close friendship and mutual admiration. At his request, I brought him extensive Russian-language material about Israel. Whenever I visited him, he would half-jokingly ask, "Nu, did you read what I wrote? Did I understand correctly what I read in the material you gave me?"

I explained where, in my opinion, he had hit the mark and where he had got things wrong. This doesn't mean that I manipulated him or tried to make him into what is known in the professional jargon as "an agent of influence." Bovin was one of the most important shapers of public opinion in Russia, and just as he called for the restoration and improvement of diplomatic relations with Israel, he also recommended the establishment of diplomatic relations with South Africa and spoke about adjusting Soviet policy towards Japan. Israel fit right into his outlook, which was that of a Russian intellectual who loved his country, was pained by its problems, and was trying to repair the mistakes of the past. All of this without giving up his classic Communist worldview, at least not yet. What was most important for him was love of the motherland, its people, and its culture. To construe our relationship as some form of manipulation on my part is to insult Bovin's intelligence and the memory of a man who was a true and sincere Russian patriot, at a time when they were few and far between. Aryeh Levin hit the mark when he complained that Bovin treated me like a friend.

I invited Bovin to visit Israel and get to know it firsthand. In keeping with protocol, I informed the Foreign Ministry of his arrival and added that if it wanted to take advantage of the visit to meet with him, we were willing to cooperate. The Foreign Ministry agreed to split the visit 50/50—for half the time, he would be meeting with people the Foreign Ministry wanted him to talk with, and during the other half, Nativ would have him meet with whomever we thought appropriate and show him whatever we wanted to show him.

When Bovin came to Israel in 1991, I went to the airport to meet him. Due to the visitor's status and importance, Consul General Alexei Chistyakov, the senior Soviet diplomat in the country, was also there to receive him. When he saw me leaving with Bovin, Chistyakov's face contorted with anger and fury. I flashed him a sadistic smile and said hello. We both remembered the time in Moscow when I threatened him, and he also knew that despite his best efforts to stop me, I had gone on to conduct negotiations with the managing director of Aeroflot. I saw that just seeing me with Bovin was bad for his health. He barely managed to restrain himself while acting cordially towards

Bovin, a Soviet VIP in Israel. Afterwards, I joked with Bovin about Chistyakov's suffering and the difficult conditions he had to put up with in "diplomatic" encounters with characters like us.

Ignoring Chistyakov's recommendations and standard Soviet practice, Bovin wanted to visit the territories; his Foreign Ministry handlers asked me to deal with the matter. Suddenly, it didn't bother them that this had nothing to do with Nativ's official brief and was an activity that was patently political in nature. They simply said, "We don't know how to handle this. You must have contacts and acquaintances in the settlements."

They were right, of course, and I was glad to oblige. I set up a few meetings in advance and drove Bovin in my car. We began the tour in the West Bank town of Ariel, where I introduced him to its mayor, Ron Nachman, one of the most successful and energetic mayors in Israel. Many new *olim* from the former Soviet Union had moved to Ariel; some of them recognized Bovin and greeted him enthusiastically. Bovin was stunned by the warm regard and respect that people showed him. Afterwards, I asked if he wanted to visit a settlement deep in Samaria, perhaps Elon Moreh, outside Nablus, and he agreed enthusiastically. We drove towards Nablus like regular civilians, supposedly unarmed (I had a gun, but Bovin didn't know that). I passed the checkpoints without trouble. I showed the soldiers my ID as an employee of the Prime Minister's office and they let me pass right through.

We reached Nablus, drove up the road, and stopped in Elon Moreh. We continued through the Samarian hills to Ma'aleh Adumim, and then to the Etzion Bloc south of Jerusalem. In one day, I gave him a guided tour of most of the territories. We traveled in a civilian car with Israeli plates through all of Judea and Samaria, including the main cities, with no problems. At some point Bovin asked how it was possible for us to be driving and driving, with no weapons, no problems: Where was the Intifada? I told him that if he wanted to see it, I would step out of the car, tell the children that he was a journalist, give them fifty sheqels, and they would begin throwing stones—and voilà, the

Intifada! Later, Bovin told me that he had met one of the Palestinian representatives in East Jerusalem a few days after our trip. When the Palestinian began speaking about the Intifada, Bovin laughed and said that he had traveled all over Judea and Samaria and that the Intifada was a fifty-sheqel bluff. He had seen that with his own eyes, and they shouldn't tell him about any phony Intifada. I wasn't trying to mislead him, but this was one of the funny paradoxes that occurred. After he had been in Israel somewhat longer, he came to understand the situation in greater depth. He also understood that you can't judge a country and a situation so complex and tangled on the basis of a single excursion.

The Foreign Ministry put Bovin up in a hotel in Tel Aviv. When I went there to coordinate the rest of the visit, he asked me whether the Ministry could find him a different place to stay. He had been sent to a cheap hotel, frequented mainly by practitioners of the oldest profession, plus a few tourists and teenagers. I was utterly embarrassed. Bovin told me that some of the "ladies" who worked in the hotel were from the Soviet Union and they recognized him and said hello. The whole scene embarrassed him as well as the "ladies" and indicated the lack of consideration and sensitivity and just plain ignorance of the bureaucrats at the Foreign Ministry. To house one of the most important molders of public opinion in one of the most important countries in the world in a hotel of that kind risked creating antagonism and could have wrecked relations beyond repair. I promised Bovin that as soon as Nativ took over responsibility for him, we would move him to suitable accommodations. The new hotel was only 20 yards away and cost an extra $10 a day.

At the end of his scheduled visit, Bovin asked if he could extend his stay by a few days. Boris Pankin, the new Soviet Foreign Minister, was about to arrive—the first visit by a Soviet Foreign Minister to Israel—and for Bovin it was very important to be here during the visit, both as a journalist to provide coverage for his newspaper and as someone who was actively promoting better relations between the two countries. I notified the Foreign Ministry that Bovin would stay for a few more days to cover Pankin's visit. Neither of us could have anticipated what this would lead to. At one of the events during the visit, a crowd of journalists collected around Pankin. While he was speaking with them he suddenly spotted Bovin and called him over. When Bovin reached him, Pankin announced, "We are looking for a Soviet ambassador to Israel. Now I know who that ambassador should be." Bovin didn't take the remark seriously, although he told me about it immediately. When he returned to Moscow, he was summoned to the Foreign Ministry and informed that President Gorbachev had decided to appoint him Soviet ambassador to Israel. Bovin agreed on the spot to take up the job. He was the last ambassador of the Soviet Union to submit his credentials anywhere in the world, and then, a few days later, the first representative of the new Russian Federation to do so. It was symbolic of everything that had happened in Russia overall and to its foreign policy in particular.

I was truly touched when one night around eleven, Bovin phoned. "Yasha," he said with emotion, "I arrived by car from Cairo five minutes ago, to serve as ambassador. I'm at the Hilton Hotel in Tel Aviv. Please come see me. You're the first person I've called." He had of course told me about his appointment earlier. I drove over at once. We opened a bottle of wine to celebrate and stayed up half the night in the hotel. He spoke enthusiastically about what he had seen in Cairo, how he viewed his new assignment, and his perception of the relations between the countries. Afterwards, he kept joking that it had all been my Zionist plot to turn him into a diplomat, and that I "elevated him and made him an ambassador."

Bovin and I maintained our close relationship throughout his term in Israel and after he returned to Russia. I learned much from him about Russia, the regime, and the work. He told me a lot about his work both with Brezhnev and Andropov. He was a cultured man, a proud Russian who loved people and loved life. He was a true friend of the State of Israel and did a lot to bolster mutual understanding and close ties between our countries. I, too, lost a true friend when he passed away in 2004.

Chapter 41

The process of building Nativ's organizational infrastructure throughout the former Soviet Union lasted for two or three years; at their end we were operating regularly in more than 400 cities. Sometimes we were forced to call in the highest political echelon, the Prime Minister or Foreign Minister. Rabin and Peres were usually forthcoming with their assistance.

From the moment Yitzhak Rabin returned as Prime Minister in 1992, the Labor Party and the Jewish Agency (whose senior executives were affiliated with Labor) pressured him to clip Nativ's wings. There were also complaints against me personally: How could a man identified with the political right and its views, who was appointed to the post by Yitzhak Shamir, continue to head Nativ?! In one of our first working sessions, Rabin told me, "Pay no attention to what they are writing in the newspapers and to the leaks by party members. Don't worry. I won't let them get you."

In our initial talks, I called his attention to all of our quarrels and disagreements with the Jewish Agency and recommended that he appoint a team to study Nativ and define its powers on the basis of the situation and the needs of the country. I told him that in the past, the Dekel committee had conducted an inquiry of some sort, but its decisions, although very favorable to us, had not been implemented because everyone, and primarily the Agency, simply ignored them.

In short order, Rabin appointed reserve Maj. Gen. Yitzchak Hofi, OC Northern Command during the Yom Kippur War and subsequently head of the Mossad, to investigate the activities of Nativ and the State of Israel in the former Soviet Union and submit recommendations.

Hofi did a thorough and serious job and studied the issue in depth. In our early meetings, he told me, "The situation I found at Nativ is similar to that of the Mossad when I got there, and I will have to recommend various new practices."

Even before Hofi's inquiry, when I became director of Nativ, we began instituting formal work procedures which had not previously existed. This included drafting clear guidelines, defining methods for activities and operations, drawing up detailed plans, and writing summaries of meetings and programs. Until then, my attempts to modify the organization's work habits had been only partially successful, and over the years I had been able to effect changes only in the units that were directly subordinate to me. We had to delay the implementation of some of the procedures until Nativ's mission, powers, and areas of activity had been redefined.

It took Hofi a rather long time to complete his assignment. He told me that he wanted to consult with Rabin before he submitted his report, because the latter would have to accept it in principle. A few days later, he informed me that the Prime Minister had done so and that it was now possible to officially submit his recommendations. And then a different problem cropped up. Hofi recommended that Nativ remain subordinate to the Prime Minister, as it had been for years; but Shimon Peres had other ideas. He saw himself as one of the few people who was knowledgeable about both the Soviet Union and *aliyah* matters, and in many ways this was true. Peres had certainly made a major contribution to *aliyah*, particularly from the Soviet Union, and he wanted Nativ to fall under his jurisdiction. But Peres was now Foreign Minister, while the logic in Hofi's recommendations, which coincided with my own outlook, was that Nativ had to be subordinate to the Prime Minister because of the many problems and decisions that required integration among the various government ministries and because our work had an impact on political decisions that only the Prime Minister was authorized to make. A further consideration was that in the Israeli system of government, every minister represents a political party. Thus subordinating Nativ to some ministry would automatically identify it with the incumbent minister and his party, for better or for worse. The minister's political problems—and every minister has political problems—would be likely to affect both Nativ and its effectiveness, as well as *aliyah* in general, which was a national issue of the utmost importance. This assumption was confirmed in the next decade, when the transfer of Nativ to Avigdor Liberman's domain caused it to be identified with him and his political opinions and wreaked serious havoc on the organization.

Hofi's recommendation led to some friction between Rabin and Peres. Peres even complained to me and asked why I didn't want to work under him. I responded that it wasn't a personal issue and that I certainly recognized his contribution and ability to contribute to *aliyah*. I also noted that today he was Foreign Minister and all was well, but what would happen to Nativ and *aliyah* when he was replaced? "Suppose David Levy became Foreign Minister tomorrow. Just imagine what would happen to Nativ then!"

Peres ignored the argument, as he usually did when something was inconvenient for him. His ego and obsessive self-esteem got in his way and often ruined things that had begun well and were proceeding just fine. In this case, too, Peres saw the recommendation that Nativ remain subordinate to the Prime Minister as a personal insult. Because of his resistance, Rabin hesitated to conduct a joint discussion with the Foreign Minister, the intelligence community, and the Jewish Agency to officially approve the recommendations.

In the end, I found a way to overcome the problem. The Secret Services subcommittee of the Knesset Foreign Affairs and Defense Committee had to approve Nativ's budget. From the beginning of my tenure as director, we submitted annual work plans for the Prime Minister's approval before the corresponding budget was forwarded to the committee. In those days, the chairman of the Foreign Affairs and Defense Committee was reserve Maj. Gen. Ori Orr, one of the most honest and terrific people not only in the Labor Party, but in general. For me, he had another virtue—he had been one of the best tank commanders in the IDF. Hofi had just submitted his report and Orr would approve only a three-month budget, and rightly so, until Rabin made a decision on adopting the recommendations. But as already mentioned, the Prime Minister hesitated to convene a meeting on the subject and our budget remained pending for almost six months. Orr and I reached an agreement that his committee would not approve the budget for the rest of the year until the recommendations had been approved, and I asked him to send a letter to this effect to the Prime Minister. The trick worked. Rabin convened all the relevant parties and got them to ratify Hofi's recommendations verbatim, despite the objections raised at the meeting, including by Peres. No minutes were kept. Shimon Sheves, the director general of the Prime Minister's Office, took down only the part that related to his area of responsibility—coordination of the work with Israeli youth movements. Nativ relied on the youth movements to provide counselors for the summer camps and centers we ran in the former Soviet Union.

For us, one of the most important decisions was the definition of Nativ as the arm of the Israeli government that dealt with Jews in the former Soviet Union. Although this had been the arrangement for years, it had never been defined formally. Other matters were resolved, too, including Nativ's responsibility for assessing the situation of Jews and issuing warnings about dangerous situations. Various groups, including the Jewish Agency, were unhappy with the recommendations, but they were forced to accept them. As usual, the Agency leaked distorted information about the recommendations, which were classified and never officially published. In their version, as conveyed to journalists, Hofi had decided that most of the activities among Jews in the former Soviet Union would be the responsibility of the Jewish Agency rather than of the State of Israel. At Nativ we did not play the media game and avoided both leaks and denials.

We reorganized Nativ in accordance with Hofi's recommendations and also used them as the basis for our new procedures and work methods. We restructured ourselves to correspond precisely to the recommendations and the missions that had been defined for us— some of them public, others classified.

When I began working with Rabin as Prime Minister, I hardly knew the man. I had heard about him, seen him, and met him once or twice, such as our brief conversation during the affair of the hijacked Caucasian plane. My impression, based mainly on publications from the race between Peres and Rabin for leadership of the Labor Party before the 1992 elections, was that Yitzhak Rabin was dry and distant. I was surprised to discover a very sensitive, warm, but shy man. A serious and profound thinker, he was always agonizing whether his decisions were correct. But this didn't interfere with his ability to make decisions; it only motivated him to think things over soberly, again and again, to listen and examine the issue from all sides. I don't mean to suggest that Rabin was incapable of making incorrect or mistaken decisions—nobody is. But when Rabin thought things over, he examined them in depth with no extraneous considerations, to the best of his ability and the extent possible. When I discovered his personal warmth and sensitivity, I was furious with Peres. The rumors about Rabin that were spread before the party leadership primary, including his purported disdain for people, came from Peres' camp. As usual, Peres disclaimed responsibility and claimed that he didn't know anything about them. For some reason, Shimon Peres never knows anything. Things are always done in his name, both vile deeds and events in his honor, like his flashy birthday parties. It was clear to me, in any case, that Peres was behind the rumors and lies that had been spread about Rabin, and I was very angry with him.

Rabin's warm and sensitive attitude towards *aliyah* came as a great surprise to me. Our work meetings went on for an hour, sometimes longer, about once a month, unless one of us felt an urgent need to discuss some matter. Usually we met alone to address a specific issue, and only rarely were we joined by his military secretary. I was directly subordinate to the Prime Minister, so no other minister or the director general of the Prime Minister's Office dared interfere or come between us. In our meetings, we would go over twenty to thirty issues I brought up, along with others that Rabin raised, related to reports, problems, questions, suggestions, or authorizations. In essence, these were ongoing matters, most of them associated with Nativ. Sometimes, other matters on which Nativ had an impact or indirect bearing, or vice versa, came up. There was always a situation assessment about Russia and the neighboring countries. It was clear that Rabin paid close attention to our assessments and valued them highly. He was quick on the uptake and understood what I was talking about. He also remembered many details from prior meetings. Often he would say, "Wait a minute! At our meeting two months ago, you asserted such and such. How does that reconcile with what you're saying now? Isn't there a contradiction here? Please explain it to me." When I convinced him that something had to be done for Nativ and its activities among Jews, he would drop everything and see to it.

There was sometimes a need for the highest Israeli echelons to intervene to avert an international crisis triggered by activities among Jews or in order to promote those activities. In fact, these were the circumstances that prompted the first visit of the Israeli Foreign Minister to Ukraine. When Jewish Agency personnel began working in the Soviet Union in 1991, not only did they fail to coordinate with us or any other Israeli government agency, they did not bother to formalize their status with the authorities. They used the cover of private invitations from various and sundry organizations, or claimed to have permission for their work from the local echelons, which were easy to get along with, but this created problems. A serious crisis erupted in Ukraine, putting all Jewish Agency activities there in peril. Due to the fierce response by the Ukrainian regime and security services, Peres convened an urgent conference about the crisis. At the meeting, I proposed that he immediately leave for Ukraine to resolve the problem. I always favored a direct approach by the State of Israel and direct contact between Israel and other countries on Jewish matters. No one else at the meeting, from either the Foreign Ministry or the Jewish Agency, suggested this. Their ideas generally involved asking American Jewish organizations to intercede. But Peres accepted my proposal on the spot, and this is what led to his first visit. The Jewish Agency imbroglio was resolved while he was there. Although the Agency did not receive official status in Ukraine, at least the authorities stopped making its life difficult. They also agreed that until the Agency's status was defined, they would not interfere in its activities.

The Jewish Agency's problematic status was also the main reason for the delay in the signing of educational agreements between Ukraine and Israel. The Agency demanded that it be mentioned in the document, but the Ukrainians vehemently rejected the idea, on the grounds that the Jewish Agency was not a government body and they were signing an agreement between countries; the parties had to be only governments and government bodies. The Jewish Agency insisted, the Foreign Ministry surrendered to its importunities, and the foot-dragging went on for months. The Ukrainian negotiators told us openly, "The Jewish Agency is your hot potato. It's your problem. We are signing an agreement with the State of Israel. We see the State of Israel as a party to the agreement and responsible for it. We do not understand what you need the Jewish Agency for."

One of the important stages in the consolidation of the relations between Israel and Russia was Shimon Peres's visit to Russia, the first there by an Israeli Foreign Minister. In Moscow, he was put up in the Metropol Hotel in the city center. We reached the hotel late at night and I proposed that Peres go for a nighttime stroll in Red Square, a unique experience. We went out towards midnight—Peres and his entire entourage and the local security personnel—and walked to Red Square, a few hundred yards from the hotel. It was an amazing sight and we were all moved, particularly Peres, who was visiting Moscow for the first time. When we got close to the Lenin Mausoleum, who should we see but Uri Geller (Israel's most famous illusionist). He immediately recognized Peres, of course, and we all recognized him.

"Tell me," Peres said to Geller. "Can you really do all those strange things people say you can?" Geller smiled and asked for a key. He placed it in his hand, and the key grew hot and bent. A few minutes before Geller showed up, Peres had seen some statues behind the mausoleum, in front of the Kremlin wall, and asked what they were. I explained that those were the graves of the most distinguished heads of the Soviet regime, including Stalin. Peres asked if we could go there. I told him that at night the answer was usually no, but I would see what could be done. I went up to the Russian security man and asked him how we could get to the wall and the tombstones. The man replied, as I had expected, that he would check, but that it would cost money. I promised him that money would not be an issue. He called the duty officer of the Kremlin security guard and they agreed on $50. When we started walking towards the passage behind the mausoleum, in order to reach the Kremlin wall, Geller appeared and wanted to join us. Peres stopped short and told Geller, with a smile. "Stay here. You're not coming with us. We're going to be passing by Stalin's grave and you, with your tricks, the devil knows—you might raise him from the dead. You're staying here."

I don't think that anybody remained indifferent when we passed by the graves, particularly Stalin's. I remembered the last time I had stood there. I had visited the mausoleum many times on compulsory school trips and by myself, out of curiosity. I had seen Lenin's body there alone, then in company with Stalin's, and then again alone. The day before I left the Soviet Union for Israel, I went to Red Square. My mother came with me because she didn't want me walking around there by myself. When we passed behind the mausoleum and I reached Stalin's grave, my mother apparently felt something. She caught my arm and pleaded with me. "Don't do anything! Don't spit on the grave. Don't walk on it! Don't throw anything on it. I beg of you. You are leaving them for good." I restrained myself. I stood for a few minutes floating on air, proud of victory, as I looked at the stone face of Stalin. And now here I was, standing with the Foreign Minister of the State of Israel, whom I had brought to Stalin's grave. We had not come to show him respect (heaven forbid!), but to mark our presence here in Moscow, after Stalin's Soviet Union no longer existed.

Peres's schedule included a meeting with Jews at the Israel Center. David Bartov, who was now overseeing Nativ's activities in the former Soviet Union, made a major effort, and many Jews, particularly intellectuals, showed up to meet the Israeli Foreign Minister. For Bartov, the meeting with Peres in Moscow also bore personal significance. It was Peres who had appointed him director of Nativ, and they had worked together in the 1980s, during Peres's term as Prime Minister. When we left the business session before the meeting with the Jews, we were running late and I knew that the audience had already been waiting for more than half an hour. Suddenly I realized that we were driving in a different direction. When I saw the car turn towards the exit from the city, I told my driver, who worked for the Nativ section in the Embassy, to pull out of line and overtake the security car at the front of the convoy. I should note that in Moscow, government convoys with security escorts speed down the roads; all other traffic is stopped and no one dares pass or approach the vehicles. When we came up level with the lead car, I signaled to the security officer to pull over and stop. He looked at me in astonishment at first, but then he recognized me and brought the entire convoy to a halt.

I got out of my car and asked him where we were going. The security officer said that we were on our way to the Jewish Agency camp outside the city. I told him that according to our itinerary, our next stop was the Israel Center. The man replied that he didn't know anything about that and had been told by the Israelis to go to the Jewish Agency camp. I looked back and saw that the ambassador was peering out of his car. I did a slow burn as I walked towards him, but he quickly closed his door and rolled up the window.

I went back to the Russian security men and told them that I was giving orders now: "Everyone turns around and drives back to the Israel Center. No one moves until the event there is over."

The Russians obeyed, and so did everyone else. No one dared to argue and the instructions were immediately conveyed over their walky-talkies. The convoy turned around and we raced back to the Israel Center, while police officers quickly blocked the traffic in our new direction.

The attempt to thwart the Foreign Minister's visit to the Israel Center, which was affiliated with the Israeli diplomatic mission, just because the Center came under the purview of Nativ, was simply reprehensible. I was livid at the thought of how all those Jews would feel if Peres didn't show up; many had made their way to the Center from all over the vast metropolis, traveling for hours after work. I always put myself in their shoes and tried to understand what they were feeling. But the disgraceful trick was standard procedure for with the Jewish Agency, and we had grown used to them.

We arrived at the Israel Center in under ten minutes. It was an inspiring and emotional meeting, and went on for over an hour. Afterwards, we proceeded to the camp and saw the project that the Jewish Agency wanted to show off. It goes without saying that the campers were there the whole time, so it was completely meaningless what time we got there.

During a meeting with the most important Jewish activists in Moscow, Peres was asked what the point was of having both the Liaison Bureau (Nativ's public name) and the Jewish Agency. Peres had an excellent answer, one of his typically intelligent and brilliant formulations, which I never heard from anyone else, neither before nor since: "The Jewish Agency represents the Jewish people. The

Liaison Bureau represents the State of Israel. Each of them works for the same goal, but pursuant to its own authority and in its own sector, while coordinating the interests of the Jewish people and the State of Israel." The answer captured the problem and the roles of the two organizations in a nutshell.

I had a personal interest in the Israel Center in Moscow. It was located only a few hundred meters from the maternity hospital where my younger brother, Shurik, and I had been born, and about a mile from my house, where my Grandma had lived and my mother had grown up. Every time I visited the Israel Center, which was housed in a beautiful old building, I felt a twinge in my heart. I was going back to the scenes of my childhood. But I was going back not to live there, but as a representative of Israel to help other Jews make *aliyah* to the Jewish state.

To expedite the process of setting up the Nativ organization in Ukraine and cut through the red tape and problems, I decided to enlist the Prime Minister of Israel. On one of my business trips to Ukraine, I met with the head of the Ukrainian intelligence and security services. We were the same age and had grown up and been educated in the same country. For a certain period of time, we also had something of a shared interest—he got his start in the KGB as a young officer in the Fifth Directorate, which kept tabs on national movements in the Soviet Union, including the Jews, and dealt with my file from 1967 to 1969. We understood each other and had excellent work relations. In one of our conversations, the idea was born of arranging a visit to Ukraine by the Israeli Prime Minister, in order to advance relations between the two countries in all domains—political, Jewish, and cultural. The president of the new country, Leonid Kuchma, saw such a visit as a way to enhance its international status (and his own), and gave his blessing. All the countries that rose from the ashes of the Soviet Union were certain that good relations with Israel would benefit their ties with the United States, particularly in light of their perception of the Jewish lobby's influence in Washington.

I set to work with the Israeli bureaucracy to set up the visit. After it had been approved by both countries, I met my Ukrainian colleague, who told me, laughing, "I don't know which Foreign Ministry was more opposed to the Prime Minister's visit, ours or yours. You cannot imagine how furious people in your Foreign Ministry were with you and how much they cursed you during all their phone calls, because you were forcing their hand about the visit." Everyone knows that the phone lines of the diplomatic missions are bugged. The Ukrainian Foreign Ministry was opposed to the visit because of a few senior officials inherited from the Soviet Foreign Ministry whose attitude towards the Middle East and Israel was cold, to say the least.

In one of my routine meetings with Rabin, I mentioned that I was at odds with the Foreign Ministry—I wanted him to visit Ukraine, and those in the Foreign Ministry did not. Rabin asked me to present arguments in favor of my proposal. Most of them had to do with organizing and assisting Nativ activities among the Jews in Ukraine. When he asked why the Foreign Ministry was hostile to the idea, I responded that I preferred that he not hear its arguments from me, so that they could not blame me for distorting their position. Rabin called Eitan Haber, his bureau chief, and asked him if what I said was true. Haber confirmed my statement and explained why the Foreign Ministry was opposed to the visit. Rabin decided on the spot that he would go. He told Haber to inform the Foreign Ministry of this immediately and to begin preparations for the visit. To be fair, I should note that the resistance to the visit was stoked by the ministry bureaucracy and not by Foreign Minister Peres. It is obvious that my success in setting up the visit did not win me or Nativ any fans at the Foreign Ministry.

The visit was excellent and made a major contribution to improving relations between the two countries. This made it much easier for both government organizations and the Jewish Agency to work among the Jews in Ukraine. After the private meeting between Rabin and Kuchma, the former took me aside. One of the Israeli journalists (I think it was Shimon Schiffer) heard the beginning of the conversation, when Rabin said, "Yasha, let me tell you what we accomplished. I told the president exactly what you asked me to. Now tell me if I got it right and if it's really what you wanted?" Afterwards, Shiffer chased after me and kept asking, "Tell me, who is working for whom? That's the first time I ever heard a Prime Minister telling his subordinate that he wanted to report to him what he had done at his request."

I smiled to myself and thought what a special Prime Minister we had. Yitzhak Rabin, a sabra, a Jew born and raised in Israel, felt the Jewish issue with his whole being and was always willing to help. I remember that en route to the dedication of the Israel Center in Kiev, which Rabin officially opened, I was walking in the entourage with the head of the Ukrainian intelligence services, and Shraga Krein was behind us. Krein, who by then had joined Nativ, was conversing with a colonel in the Ukrainian Security Services. "Do you think," the colonel told Krein, gritting his teeth, "that we don't know why you're opening all these schools and Israel Centers? It's all to seduce our Jews to move to your country. We are aware of the whole problem, of all of your subversive activities."

The Ukrainians (and the others) knew the significance of our activities, but presenting the Jewish issue, including Nativ's work, as an arm of the State of Israel, as an essential element of the relations between the countries, forced them to agree to our presence, despite the security services' professional misgivings and realization that what we were doing would ultimately lead to increased Jewish emigration. The Prime Minister's visit to Ukraine was a great boon.

In anticipation of Rabin's visit, we held a series of discussions to coordinate matters with the Jewish Agency, which revealed the Agency's idiocy and malice in all their glory, at least as embodied by its then-emissary in northern Russia, a reserve brigadier general who had been awarded the Medal of Valor for bravery in battle. I have never thought that heroism is a guarantee of wisdom, and he afforded decisive proof of that. I didn't know him in the army, but as a Jewish

Agency representative in the field, his performance was atrocious, a true disgrace. In advance of Rabin's visit to St. Petersburg, this man demanded of Eitan Haber, who was planning the schedule, that the Prime Minister of Israel not take part in the inauguration of the new Israeli school there. When Haber asked why not, the emissary responded in total seriousness that, by his count, the Prime Minister was scheduled to visit a certain number of Nativ institutions and a certain number of Jewish Agency institutions. And if the Prime Minister attended the ceremony at the school, he would be making one more visit to Nativ institutions than to Jewish Agency institutions! This didn't surprise me. The man excelled at pressuring Jewish activists in his district to cut off all ties with Nativ and threatened to deny Jewish Agency funding to anyone who was in contact with us. It was pure extortion.

Overall, though, the visit was excellent. For us, the most successful part was indeed the dedication of the school in St. Petersburg. The school was housed in the building of the Prince Mikhail High School. Prince Mikhail had been a cousin of the last Czar, and the school was one of the oldest and best educational institutions in St. Petersburg. Rabin unveiled the plaque that stated that the school was operating as a collaborative venture of the Israeli and Russian ministries of education. The ceremony in the auditorium included some very emotional moments. Rabin's wife, Leah, could not control her feelings. "What are you people doing to Yitzhak?" she asked me. "Look at him. I have never seen him so wrought up!" Just then a teenage boy came onto the stage and announced in fluent Hebrew that he would soon graduate from the school and planned to make *aliyah*. He added that his dream was to serve in the IDF paratroop unit. Rabin was stunned and moved to tears. At least in those days, this was a truly surrealistic scene for Israeli eyes.

During his term, Rabin paid another visit to Ukraine and Russia. This time, the focus was on thwarting the sale of nuclear reactors and missiles to Iran. But Rabin met with Jews as well and visited both

Jewish Agency and Nativ projects. On the flight back to Israel, Rabin asked me why I wasn't running Nativ branches in countries outside the former Soviet Union. I told him that we did not work in the West.

"Everything the Jewish Agency does," he replied, "is one huge pile of bullshit and deception. Whereas you are doing the things that have to be done. I want you to work in the West, using your methods."

I told him that if I received instructions I would follow them, but only if they were coordinated with the Finance Minister. Rabin's response was that he was giving me the order, now, and that he would settle things with the Finance Minister.

He asked me to submit a plan for activity in the West and I drew up a proposal for an experimental project—opening schools and centers in the United States and Germany for a pilot and run-in period. Micha Goldman, who was serving as deputy education minister, forwarded the plan to him. One Friday in early November 1995, Goldman phoned to say that he had been to see Rabin, who had read through the plan and approved it. We agreed that we would speak at the beginning of the week. Yitzhak Rabin was assassinated the next night.

When I was appointed director of Nativ, I instituted an annual "Nativ Day," following the model of similar organizations in Israel. It was a conference to which we invited all our pensioners, employees, and emissaries, as well as heads of other organizations, to wrap up the year in a friendly spirit. I invited the Prime Minister, too. I remember that Rabin came to one of these conferences right after a seven-hour flight home from abroad. Yaakov Perry, the director of the GSS at the time, called me shortly before the start of the event and apologized that he would not be coming, because he was simply wiped out by the flight. But Rabin skipped in like a young man, walked up on stage, and delivered an extraordinary speech—not read from notes but spoken from his heart, personal and moving. I still get emotional when I recall that evening. The only thing he asked for was cup after cup of coffee, while chain-smoking cigarettes.

After the speech, he apologized to me. "Yasha, I can't stay. Not because I don't want to, but because I have other things to do in Jerusalem. I have to keep working. I've been away for too many hours." I followed him to his car and he was driven off to Jerusalem.

I was amazed by his capacity for work—a man over 70, in the harness twenty hours a day, he put in incredible physical effort, and was always alert and ready to keep on going. Since then, I have tried to compare Rabin to those who came after him, but there is simply no comparison, neither as a person nor in his attitude towards the issue of *aliyah* and towards Nativ.

Our last meeting was right before Rosh Hashanah in 1995. He visited all of the units that worked under him to wish the staff Happy New Year, and he came to us as well. We all assembled on the roof of our building. Rabin said that he had come for only half an hour, because he had to go on to other appointments. In his remarks he said something we had never heard from anyone before, and certainly not after. "What you are doing is the most important task there is for the State of Israel, second only to guaranteeing its security," Yitzhak Rabin told us. "Know that we trust you and believe in you." That was a moment of great satisfaction for Nativ. A wave of extraordinary emotion, enthusiasm, and spiritual exaltation washed over us all.

The allotted half an hour passed, and then an hour, and Rabin simply didn't want to leave. He mingled with our staff, talking and asking questions. His aides and security men urged him to leave. Even I told him, "Mr. Prime Minister, you have to go."

But he just smiled his sheepish grin and said, "Yes, I know. But I like it here with you." When he finally left, it was with sadness, as if he felt it was the last time.

A month later, he was murdered. The beautiful State of Israel that I had known was murdered along with him. So was that human, Jewish touch that he had given us. No one in Israel ever treated us that warmly, or anywhere near it—certainly not the Prime Ministers who came after him. Yitzhak Rabin was flesh and blood, and like every human being he had his weaknesses. But the good of the country and of the people was always his top priority—not in words, but in deeds.

Chapter 42

On the night of the assassination, I was sitting at home. I don't usually go to demonstrations, certainly not political ones. Suddenly the broadcast was interrupted by a news flash: Shots had been heard near Tel Aviv City Hall and Rabin had been taken to the hospital. The live feed switched to the plaza in front of Ichilov Hospital. And then I saw Eitan Haber's face and heard his words and I could not believe him. To this day, it is hard for me to accept. I was familiar with the Prime Minister's security arrangements and knew many of the people involved—we met often in various circumstances. Security is not my profession, but I am familiar with its basic principles. On various occasions and in various countries, mainly during visits by heads of state or government, I was exposed to the planning and organization of security measures. So I had many criticisms of the work of our VIP protection unit but didn't want to get involved. Nevertheless, my professional run-ins and arguments within the system were frequent enough.

I was particularly infuriated by one incident. One evening in mid-1995, Rabin phoned me at home and told me that the next day there would be an event in Jerusalem in memory of Sen. Henry Jackson. He asked me to prepare a few main points for his speech and come to the event. Arriving at the site somewhat early, I walked around and observed what was going on. To my surprise, I noticed a person who was very familiar to me—Avigdor Eskin. I knew him as a young man from the group led by Eliyahu Essas in Moscow, one of the first circles of Jewish religious activists there. I had heard about his political activities in Israel and his opinions, which were even more extreme than Meir Kahane's. I was aware of his provocative behavior and his identification with the radical right. I went over to one of Rabin's bodyguards, whom I knew, and asked him to keep an eye on Eskin. What surprised me was that the name of this extreme militant meant nothing to the people who were guarding the Prime Minister. I explained in brief who Eskin was and noted that he should be watched and kept a safe distance away from Rabin. The guard assured me that he understood and would take care of it. The hall filled up and Eskin took a seat about three yards from Rabin, a little off to the side. The bodyguard, it turns out, did nothing. He didn't say a word to the police officers posted at the entrance to the auditorium, along with the other security men, didn't move Eskin to the back of the hall or a different location, and didn't even assign a man to watch him, never mind body-search him. The bodyguard simply stood there, about two yards to Rabin's right. Only three yards separated Rabin and Eskin, with no one between them. In the middle of Rabin's speech, Eskin jumped up and began slinging accusations and insults. The security guard grew tense and edged closer to Rabin. After a minute or so, policemen came and escorted Eskin from the room. I thought to myself, what if words hadn't been enough for him?

That was the atmosphere in those days and the level of professionalism of the Prime Minister's security system. In this respect, the news of the assassination and the pictures on TV did not surprise me. But I was brokenhearted that we had lost our Prime Minister through such incompetence—and not just any Prime Minister. Particularly galling was that this was the system Rabin relied upon and believed in. The members of the team were good people, but there was a basic flaw in their approach and an exaggerated sense of self-confidence, which always leads to disdain and negligence.

The solution that the GSS introduced after the assassination was "security on top of security": inflated security margins. Today, the security arrangements for the Prime Minister have a significant element of CYA.

There was one case when I actually complained to Rabin about security, or, more accurately, raised the issue with him—the possibility that the GSS was operating in violation of his orders. Rabin was surprised and asked Danny Yatom, his military secretary, to look into the matter. In a letter to the head of the GSS, Yatom wrote: "In a working session with the director of Nativ, the latter raised such and such points. Your comments, please." When I received my copy, I knew that it was a lost cause. After all, the GSS would never admit that it was breaking the rules. Someone from the GSS contacted me immediately and asked me to explain what I meant and the circumstances I was referring to. Although I knew the facts, I said that it was only a conjecture on my part. The GSS agents had left tracks and signs of their activities, which I had spotted. I knew exactly what had been done, and how, but realized there was no one to talk to. I won't expose the people involved. If these are accepted practices, when everyone shuts their eyes, I won't go to war over them now.

Shortly before Rabin's assassination, the head of the VIP Protection Unit visited Moscow, on his way home from the trip to Ukraine. I met him at a social gathering. He said he had heard that I was on excellent terms with Ukrainian intelligence and perhaps would agree to help the GSS. Certainly, I replied, and asked what the problem was.

I found out that after a serious incident, the Ukrainian security services had confiscated the weapon of one of the security men who had been sent for a two-month hitch to guard the Embassy in Kiev. The GSS wanted to know if I could recover the gun. I was about to visit Ukraine anyway. When I arrived in Kiev, I met with the heads of Ukrainian security services and asked about the incident. Following the practice for most of our embassies, the GSS sent out "night staff" for two-month periods to protect the compound after working hours. This was a period of high tension in the region, with civil wars raging around Ukraine: the fighting in Chechnya, incidents in the Caucasus, a war between Azerbaijan and Armenia, bloody incidents in Central Asia, and the return to Ukraine of the Crimean Tatars, some of them brimming with the extreme religious zeal that Islamic organizations in the world were stirring up. The Ukrainians were worried that militant elements of various kinds would infiltrate their country. The overall situation gave the Ukrainian Security Services a serious headache—but the GSS was oblivious to this. It sent over a dark-skinned Mizrahi Jew who didn't know a word of Russian and apparently briefed him inadequately.

He was an energetic young man. Early one day, dressed in a track suit, he left the Embassy compound for his morning run. I heard the rest of the story from the Ukrainian security agents who were involved in the incident. The two of them, in civilian clothes, were patrolling the area when they noticed a swarthy young man running in the street. Nobody in Ukraine goes jogging like that, definitely not in certain areas or that early in the morning. The officers came up and asked to see his papers. The young man, who did not speak Russian, obviously didn't understand them. He replied in English with an Israeli accent, but they did not know English and did not understand him. Suspicious of him, the two agents began speaking sharply. When the Israeli suddenly pulled out a gun, the Ukrainians overpowered him. Later they told me that they didn't know why they hadn't killed him. They were sure they had caught a Caucasian terrorist who was trying to get away. Only after his detention did they find out who he was. The Ukrainians could not understand why our people were not better prepared or briefed before being sent out. After all, you can't work like this; it might cost someone's life and harm relations between the countries. I asked the Ukrainians to return the gun, and in the end they did so.

Chapter 43

The ugly relationship between the Jewish Agency and Nativ that prevailed throughout the 1980s escalated during the next decade when it came to activities among Jews in the former Soviet Union. The Agency's involvement there gained momentum when Baruch Gur, a one-time operative of Bar, the Nativ unit that worked in the West, joined the Agency. Bar had sent him to the United States, where his problematic performance led to his being recalled to Israel in the 1980s. But they didn't want him in the office here, either, so, because of certain personality traits, he was promoted sideways to serve as the head of the Council for Soviet Jewry. This was a public organization that Nehemiah Levanon, when director of Nativ, had set up so that Bar and Nativ could pull the strings of the campaign on behalf of Soviet *aliyah,* even though the council was supported by various philanthropies. Gur continued to receive his Nativ salary despite his marginal involvement in its activities. When David Bartov became head of Nativ, he relented and sent Gur to represent the agency in England. But we ran into problems with him there, too, and were again forced to recall him. Just then, Simcha Dinitz asked us to recommend someone to advise him on Soviet Jewish affairs. Bartov saw this as an excellent opportunity to get Gur out of our hair. The fact that he was a distant relative of Mendel Kaplan, the then-chairman of the Jewish Agency Board of Governors, didn't hurt. I had correct relations with Gur, although we had our disagreements, as colleagues always do. Besides, we were about the same age.

One day Gur told me that he had heard that I was drafting a plan for work in the Soviet Union and would like to receive an update. I saw this as a natural request, because he was still an employee of Nativ though on loan to the Jewish Agency. Moreover, I saw nothing wrong with a Jewish Agency official being aware of our activities in the Soviet Union. For three hours, I presented Nativ's entire organizational approach to him, including all the projects we were planning. Shortly thereafter, at a meeting of the Agency's Board of Governors or Executive, the program that Gur and Dinitz outlined for the unsuspecting American philanthropists was almost a carbon copy of Nativ's. They spoke about the need to work among Soviet Jewry and asked the Board to authorize the activities and associated budget. It goes without saying that they "forgot" to tell them that all these projects were being conducted by the State of Israel. The Jewish Agency, after all, was not subordinate to the State of Israel, as Dinitz often bellowed when we got into arguments: "I am not a functionary of the Israeli government and I have my own policies. I am not obligated to carry out the policies of the government."

This was followed by a new campaign of leaks, libels, and outright falsehoods in the media, which were intended to disparage Nativ's activities and provide excuses for complaining about us to the government. We had never interfered in the Jewish Agency's work and I had never complained about that organization. I asked for only one thing: that its activities be coordinated with us so that we could avoid missteps or inept and unprofessional actions and prevent damage to the State of Israel or trouble to Nativ or the Jewish people. But the senior echelons of the Jewish Agency wanted to take over the Soviet Jewry brief and replace Nativ and the State of Israel. The monster, now long past its prime, had turned against its master.

As director of Nativ, I developed good relations with the German ambassador in Israel, Otto von der Gablentz. Gablentz, a typical

German diplomat and scion of a family that had been in the German diplomatic service since the nineteenth century, was an outstanding professional. We kept in touch even after the end of his posting to Israel and appointment as German ambassador in Moscow. What interested me in our conversations was the issue of the immigration to Germany by ethnic Germans and Jews; these talks gave me a much better understanding of the forces at play in Germany on the issue of Jewish immigration. In those days, the main reason was Chancellor Helmut Kohl's desire to renew the Jewish presence in Germany and restore its Jewish population to what it had been before the Nazis rose to power (600,000). A majority of the German leadership did not share his opinion, but no one dared disagree or argue, given the sensitivity of relations between Jews and Germany. The strong Jewish influence in the United States also played a role.

Jews were receiving entry visas to Germany in disregard of all the rules on immigration and admission of refuges. It was enough for the visa-seeker to prove some connection to the Jewish people. The German authorities would accept confirmation of this from synagogues as well. A document market emerged, and one could obtain a certificate that was authentic, phony, or forged for a paltry sum. Germany's attitude towards Jewish immigration contained a large measure of hypocrisy. The official argument was that Jews deserved preference because of the Holocaust. But during the Second World War, the Germans also managed to annihilate half of the gypsies of Europe. Nevertheless, even as the country was taking in tens of thousands of Jews, it blocked the entry of the Roma, persecuted them, and even deported them. Not until the new century did the rules for immigration by other nationalities and citizens of other countries become equalized with those for Jews, on account of domestic German considerations and with no involvement by Israeli or Jewish elements. Another topic of interest I discussed with Gablentz was the immigration to Germany and absorption of ethnic Germans. Germany resembles Israel in that there is a government bureau within its Foreign Ministry that deals with ethnic Germans living outside the country and their return to the fatherland.

In one of our conversations, Gablentz told me about his meeting with Dinitz several days earlier. Dinitz had informed him that the Jewish Agency was in charge of the plan to extricate Jews from the former Soviet Union if they were in danger, and that the Agency was likely to ask Germany to help fly these Jews out on German planes. The ambassador wanted to hear my response. I was shocked at Dinitz's irresponsibility. His tendency to boast was well known, but in this case he had, quite simply, broken the law. Although the State of Israel was prepared for the possibility that those Jews might find themselves in danger and the Jewish Agency was involved in the plan, the operation would be run by the government. Worse still, the whole thing was highly sensitive and classified; its existence was known only to those who needed to know. Other than an impulse to brag, what reason could anyone have to expose such a sensitive state secret to a foreign diplomat? As for the plan itself, there was no intention or need to ask other countries for assistance with rescue flights, certainly not Germany.

We often found ourselves having to help Jews in hazardous areas because of the many armed conflicts that erupted in the former Soviet Union. Sometimes we asked the Jewish Agency for help, mainly with logistics and funding, but other than that, we kept them on the sidelines. We never published anything about these emergency campaigns and did our best to prevent information about them from getting out. The Jewish Agency tended to trumpet the incidents it was involved in, emphasizing that it, the Jewish Agency, was rescuing Jews. In addition to the personal glorification to which senior Agency officials were addicted, the publicity helped its fundraising (which had become its main purpose for existing).

I remember one incident during the war between Georgia and the breakaway republic of Abkhazia. I sent out Nativ representatives to the war zone to make preparations to evacuate Jews from the

Abkhazian capital, Sukhumi, which was at the heart of the fighting and liable to pass from one side to the other. We gave the Jewish Agency advance notice of the possibility that we would need to fly the Jews to Israel. The response we received was a derisive comment that we were making a mountain of a molehill. But when they learned that we were sending a delegation to the region, they asked to send two of their people along. We reached an agreement with the Georgian armed forces that our representatives could fly to Sukhumi on military planes, and we added the Jewish Agency representatives to the flight to the embattled city. In short order, we organized the Jews for evacuation from both sides of the front, with the aid of the local community. In the meantime, though, a temporary ceasefire was announced and negotiations began between the president of Georgia, Eduard Shevardnadze, and the Russian official who represented the Abkhazians.

My assessment was that if the talks failed, the fighting would resume, so I called for the immediate evacuation of the Jews from the city. The Jewish Agency, which, as noted, had originally accused me of making trouble for no reason when there were no special problems on the ground, told me that due to financial constraints, it wasn't convenient for them to send a plane just then and proposed deferring the mission. I went ahead and issued instructions. We obtained a plane through our own efforts and our own funds and it left for Sukhumi within a few hours.

In a panic, the Jewish Agency immediately convened its Executive to discuss a single topic: how to prevent Nativ from recording a propaganda victory. They demanded that we have our plane fly the refugees to Tbilisi and promised to bring them from there to Israel on a different plane. We agreed to the proposal because we thought that getting the Jews out without delay took priority over everything else. In the end, the Jewish Agency paid double for the flight. Before the plane landed in Israel, the entire Jewish Agency Executive assembled at the airport, where Dinitz told the journalists, who been alerted in advance, about the rescue operation. His cronies leaked to reporters that the heroic mission had succeeded despite Nativ's attempt to meddle in a matter outside its jurisdiction, because rescuing Jews was the exclusive province of the Jewish Agency. The Nativ operatives who had handled the affair got off the plane and walked to the side to report to me. Two Jewish Agency staffers who had flown with them came up to me and praised our people, who, they said had carried off the inconceivable. These staffers could hardly understand how we had managed to bring the operation to a successful conclusion, given the conditions in Georgia. I thanked them for their words and we left the airport without bothering about the press conference and Dinitz.

As already noted, the Jewish Agency initially operated in the former Soviet Union on the basis of permits they extracted from local officials in various and sundry ways, exploiting the unstable situation and government chaos typical of that period. Nativ's status, by contrast, was unassailable. As we had always done throughout the world, we worked out of the embassy in accordance with bilateral agreements. In the end, the Jewish Agency found a solution for its activities in Russia, although in my view this solution was extremely problematic. The Agency registered as a local organization with several Russian Jewish citizens listed as its directors—a sort of "Russian-Jewish Agency." That is the format in which the Jewish Agency continues to function in Russia to this day—as a local Russian organization subject to Russian law, including tax and currency-transfer laws. I am not sure that the people at the Jewish Agency really grasp the situation. Any slight change in the authorities' attitude could cause fatal damage to the Agency's operations. Worse still, local Jews involved in Agency activities could suffer severe consequences. The State of Israel refused to understand that both the state and the local Jews would pay the price for the Jewish Agency's irresponsible activities. Everyone who is familiar with the history of the Soviet Union knows this.

I proposed that our Foreign Minister visit Ukraine as a way to keep the Jewish Agency from being thrown out of that country. Later, though, I heard multiple complaints from the security services in Ukraine and other republics with whom I had excellent relations, about Agency personnel's illegal activities in their countries. There were references to financial irregularities or foolish and inept attempts to give bribes. Sometimes this related to currency transfers and sometimes it was an innocent incursion into sensitive areas. I always got involved and tried to solve the problem quietly, and we always managed to bring the matter to a close. Sometimes, when I concluded that the situation was beyond repair, I would contact Moshe Nativ, the Agency's director general and the only one I could talk to there, explain the problem, and ask him to transfer the emissary to a different city. This was always done quietly. We never reported these incidents or told anybody except for the Prime Minister and the GSS. The senior officials of the Jewish Agency, by contrast, were not content to complain about us; they also felt a need to attempt to torpedo almost all our activities. Some of its emissaries did not shrink from pressuring the local Jews to limit or break off contact with us; otherwise, they threatened, they would be deprived of Agency funding. Nonetheless, I must admit that most of the Jewish Agency emissaries in the field were amazing people. They worked hard and did their jobs with devotion, to the best of their ability, and we usually had good working relations with them.

One of the Jewish Agency's dirtiest wars was against the Na'aleh program that I had initiated. When it proved to be a great success, the Jewish Agency changed its tune and demanded that we transfer Na'aleh to their auspices. The Jewish Agency already had two programs of its own for teenagers, which I did not think very highly of, but we didn't get involved. Na'aleh was thriving, but left a large hole in the Education Ministry's budget. So the Jewish Agency Executive submitted a tempting proposal to Finance Minister Avraham Shochat—transfer Na'aleh to us and we will fund it in full. The Finance Ministry jumped at the bargain. Without giving too much thought to the matter, with no serious investigation or discussion, it was decided to move Na'aleh to the Jewish Agency. There was nothing I could do about it and we transferred the Na'aleh administration to the Jewish Agency. We were still responsible for the consular screening of applicants, but the rest of the admissions process was handled by the Agency. A few months after the transfer went through, Shochat confessed to me that "the Agency pulled a fast one on me when it promised to bear all the expenses of Na'aleh—now it's asking for money from the Finance Ministry and this will cost us at least as much as before, if not more." Shochat was seething, but it was too late to turn back the wheel.

The Jewish Agency placed Na'aleh under the Youth Aliyah Department. Youth Aliyah was a glorious enterprise in its day and worked miracles in the early waves of *aliyah*. But the department's setup wasn't suitable for Jewish teenagers from the former Soviet Union in the 1990s nor the essence of the Na'aleh program itself. The Youth Aliyah boarding schools, most of them on kibbutzim, were of low caliber, even by Israeli standards. The first crisis struck when they were confronted with high-achieving students. I remember that a group of about twenty students came from St. Petersburg, where most of them had attended special schools for physics and mathematics or foreign languages. In the Soviet Union, Jews always attended the best schools and were always excellent students. In Israel, Youth Aliyah sent them to agricultural schools, most of whose students were not even taking for the matriculation exams required for admission to university, and math was taught only at the lowest (three-unit) level. I was pained to see that within six months, fifteen of the students went back to St. Petersburg. The problems of the Israeli school system, with its inferior education, often caused grave damage to Na'aleh.

The concept we devised was that the Na'aleh kids would stay in Israel until the end of their first year at university, if they were transferred to the responsibility of the Student Authority, or until they enlisted in the IDF, with whatever support they needed until they were discharged. But the Jewish Agency funded them only until they completed twelfth grade, after which the teenagers were suddenly left high and dry, with nothing to live on—which would have never happened had the program had stayed in our purview. I received a report about a group of Na'aleh graduates who had simply been thrown into the streets with no way to support themselves; they had found their way to Lifta, an abandoned village on the outskirts of Jerusalem that was notorious for the drug-addicts and other low-life characters who frequented it. I asked Prime Minister Rabin to get involved and of course there was an outcry. The first to jump in was Avraham Burg, the Jewish Agency chairman, who accused me of fabricating the story. Many people have accused me of many things on many occasions, but no one ever dared accuse me of lying. Had someone tried to, he would not have been able to find the slightest inaccuracy, let alone a lie, in my reports. I was always meticulous in my reports, which were precise and grounded in solid facts. My knowledge of Burg and the Agency had led me to expect this response. So after I was accused of lying, I sent the Prime Minister, at his request, a list with the names of Na'aleh graduates who were living in Lifta, along with details of how long they had been there and when and where they completed their studies. Only later did everyone begin to run around in search of a solution. After all, it is standard practice in Israel—and the Jewish Agency is no exception—not to lift a finger until things blow up or turn into a scandal. Somehow, they found a solution to the problem and put an end to the incident, but the problems with Na'aleh graduates who had been left to their own devices after their studies continued for many years.

Na'aleh took on a totally different character after it was transferred to the Jewish Agency. It began to decline both quantitatively and qualitatively and became less attractive. In my original proposal, I had planned for Na'aleh to have as many as 5,000 teens each year, and with a suitable allocation of resources it could certainly have reached that goal. In practice, the program reached something like twelve or thirteen hundred students a year in its early years. Had we stuck to my plan, almost every Jewish teenager in the former Soviet Union could have been integrated into an Israeli education program and have tied his or her destiny to the State of Israel. But financial considerations and the "wars of the Jews" kept us from realizing the program's full potential. My assumption was that teenagers who attended Israeli high schools would not want to live in any other country, but this was Israel before Rabin's assassination and before Sharon and Netanyahu came to power. The Na'aleh program reached its distressing situation because of the collapse of the Israeli education system and the changes in the former Soviet Union. The Na'aleh that I had envisioned and fought for, which registered so much success under my jurisdiction during its first three years, has little in common with the Na'aleh of recent years—just as there is no resemblance between the Nativ of the early 1990s and until the day I left, and the organization that bears the name Nativ today.

In the end, Na'aleh was returned to the Education Ministry, where, despite it all, it has turned into the most successful program in the entire Israeli education system. During its first 15 years, it brought more than 13,000 Jewish teenagers to Israel. Na'aleh has even been expanded to accept pupils from other countries, as Yitzhak Rabin had wanted. All of this happened because of the administrators of Na'aleh, who worked with devotion and determination despite the many obstacles placed in their path.

My job again forced me to encounter and cope with bereavement. Early in my term as Nativ director, I established the post of internal auditor, even before it was decided that every government organization must have one. To fill the position, I recruited Henri Ariel, who had previously served as controller of one of the most serious and complex government agencies. At age fourteen, Ariel joined the Résistance in his native France and fought the Nazis. He made *aliyah* in 1949 and eventually found his way to the civil service, where he held diverse positions. I was enchanted by the man, his caliber, and his immense enthusiasm for his work at Nativ. One day I received a phone report that some of our people had been involved in a traffic accident on their way from Kazakhstan to Kyrgyzstan. Several had been injured and Ariel, who was visiting on business, was killed. We immediately obtained a medevac plane from a Swiss airline to fly the injured back to Israel, along with Ariel's body. The hardest thing was going to Ariel's home and giving his wife the bitter news. I went to see her with a few people. I remember that as I was approaching the front door, I saw her walking around happily inside and knew that, in another minute, I was going to tell her that her beautiful life had ended and she would never see her husband again. She opened the door with surprise and welcomed us joyfully, suspecting nothing—and then she started to realize the awful truth.

I didn't beat around the bush. "Henri was killed in a traffic accident. I'm sorry to be the bearer of such terrible news."

For me, Ariel's life and death are a symbol of the Jewish people and the State of Israel, and instilled me with strength and belief in them.

Chapter 44

One of the finest Nativ projects of all, one of which I am extremely proud, was its work to rescue orphans. After the Soviet Union crumbled and all the social and government systems collapsed, hundreds of thousands of children were left with no one to care for them. Throughout Russia, and particularly in the large cities, deserted children wandered the streets, without family or home. In the 1920s, in the wake of the October Revolution and the Civil War, there were seven million abandoned children—*besprizorniki*—in the country. Seventy years later, at the end of the twentieth century, the same visions of horror returned, as bands of hungry children in tattered clothing roamed the streets. The authorities estimated that there were a million such children in the worst years of the 1990s. We assumed that some of them were Jewish. Our inquiry determined that the orphanages did indeed house Jewish children who had been rescued from the streets.

We drew up a program to bring them to Israel and try to rehabilitate them. Aware of the political sensitivities that come up when one country takes children from another country, we classified the project as "top secret." At the time, the authorities in the former Soviet Union had not yet issued rules to govern the adoption of orphans by citizens of foreign countries. Working with the Russian Ministry of Education and later with the authorities in other republics, we drafted a plan to deal with the problem, as part of the new cooperation agreements with the Israeli Education Ministry. With the consent of the institutions in which they were living and the local child welfare agencies, it was decided that these children would be placed in Israeli orphanages, with oversight by the orphanages and agencies in the countries of the former Soviet Union, and attend Israeli schools until they were 18. When they reached 18, they would decide where they wanted to live. The children's legal guardians (the country or distant relatives) would be asked to consent to the children's transfer to Israel.

The work was Sisyphean. We scanned all the orphanages and all the slums of the former Soviet Union in search of Jewish children who had been abandoned, and then began hunting for their relatives. It was like looking for a needle in a haystack. We discovered many abandoned children. The first we located were very difficult cases; the sad stories we knew from novels paled in comparison to what we saw before our very eyes. We took children from age four to fifteen. With a few exceptions, we didn't take children over 15 because their integration in Israel would be problematic.

We flew in the first group of *besprizorniki* together with a Na'aleh group, to keep them out of the spotlight. Prime Minister Rabin and Education Minister Amnon Rubinstein came to the airport to meet the Na'aleh teens. I told Rabin about our project.

"Look there," I said, as he stood on the dais. "You see those little children? They're orphans." He was deeply moved and wanted to go over to them, but I stopped him. "You can't go there," I told him. "The journalists will see you singling them out, and will want to know who they are and to take pictures. Then the whole thing will blow up in our face. I promise that if you want to, we will arrange for you to meet them. But please be patient now and just look at them from a distance."

Rabin followed my advice, but I will never forget the look on his face that day. From time to time, he would ask me what was happening with the children and how the program was progressing. I gave him updates and saw his face glow.

The orphans' stories were painful, some of them quite horrific. First we brought the children to the Ben Shemen residential school. We wrapped them in as much kindness as we could. The children's first shock was when they entered the dining room and saw the selection and quantity of food. They didn't understand that they could eat as much as they wanted and asked for more. We gave them more. They ate that too and asked for more still. They couldn't stop eating. But the worst was what the counselors told us: that when they approached the children, some of them would hunch over and cover their head and body with their hands, as though expecting a slap or blow. It took about a year for the children to start opening up, thanks to intensive individual therapy. They had many emotional problems that were not congenital, but a result of the conditions in which they had lived for most of their short lives.

I will never forget one little boy of five. He was discovered at a train station in the northern Caucasus. For three days he had been sitting on a bench, next to the body of his dead mother. He didn't eat or drink, and he couldn't cry. He just sat next to his mother's body as people passed by and didn't understand what had happened. Eventually, they took him away. We found him in one of the orphanages and brought him to Israel. In another case, we found three children who could not be separated. We found a family in Israel who wanted to adopt a child—the Bitons of Kiryat Shemona, a Moroccan couple who already had children of their own, people with hearts of gold. When they realized that we were talking about three children, they were stunned, but when they went to the Ural Mountains and saw the children there, they said, "We'll take all of them." We arranged the documents and I stayed in touch with the family in Israel. The Bitons saved those children. There were countless problems—organizational, educational, and medical—but today, no one could distinguish those three from any other Israeli children.

When the counselors and employees of the adoption agencies with which we had agreements visited Israel to inspect the children's situation, they always told us, "You saved them." We continued to look for orphans and brought over new groups of children from time to time. Once, though, there was a glitch. The chairman of the National Council for the Child, Yitzchak Kadman, is a good man who does important work, but apparently has an uncontrollable urge for publicity. Without trying to understand the true situation, he raised a ruckus. He claimed that the State of Israel was stealing children, skirting the bounds of the law, forcing them to come to Israel and not upholding its commitments. His charges led the Knesset Aliyah and Absorption Committee to schedule a hearing on the matter. None of our attempts to prevent the session, for fear the publicity would harm the project, the children, or other children who might yet come to Israel, were of any use. On the appointed day, the committee room in the Knesset was packed with journalists. "Why are you doing this?" I asked them.

Their answer was, "Because the public has the right to know."

Kadman did not show up, despite being the one who had initiated the debate. He said he wasn't feeling well. I answered all the questions directed at me and turned the matter on its head. All the committee members, even those who had already prejudged the issue, left the hearing with nothing but praise and the sense that good things were happening in Israel. None of the journalists came to the follow-up session, probably because they knew it would be extremely positive. The public's right to know suddenly didn't matter anymore. Kadman himself was still sick and didn't come.

There was a postscript to the incident. Alexander Bovin, the Russian ambassador in Israel, phoned and told me that, following all the publicity in Israel, his superiors in Moscow had instructed him to look into the affair of the orphans. I sat with him for several hours, explained the situation, and emphasized that everything was covered by an international agreement, with the full cooperation and supervision of the Russian authorities. I added that we made sure that the children retained their Russian citizenship until they reached the age of majority, unless they were adopted by Israeli citizens in coordination with the authorities in their countries of origin. My explanation satisfied him and he wrote an extremely positive report. The issue was never mentioned again at any level.

Overall, we brought several hundred orphans to Israel. The residential schools and Ministry of Social Affairs did exceptional work with them. The Joint Distribution Committee funded the project and there were never any media leaks.

Journalist Nehama Duek came to me once and protested, "You don't understand. This is extraordinary publicity. It is one of the finest things being done in the State of Israel. Why do you want to keep it under wraps?"

I told her, "We must do everything possible to avoid endangering the project. I have already received enough publicity in my life. This won't do anything for me. But the children are likely to be harmed." To her credit, she never published a single word about the project.

One day, about twenty teenagers assembled in the offices of Nativ. They were the children of the first group that arrived, several years earlier—and now they were about to join the IDF. It is hard to describe the emotions that flooded me when I looked at their faces. Fine-looking young adults with the direct gaze of any ordinary Israeli child. I recalled some of their life stories and was full of pride in our country, which would perform superhuman deeds to rescue a Jewish child abandoned at the edge of the world. I also felt blessed to have been part of this work. Because we kept in touch with them during their military service, we saw them in uniform as well.

At my farewell party when I left Nativ, two young women in uniform got up on stage and sang a song in Hebrew, which they dedicated to me. This is standard fare at goodbye parties, but I didn't recognize the soldiers; they were not among those seconded to Nativ. Then the emcee asked me if I remembered two little girls with pig-tails who had been in the first group of orphans who flew with me from Moscow to Israel. Before I had time to answer, I began to sense something.

"Look at them," the emcee continued. "The little girls you brought over are now soldiers serenading you." Sometimes we have moments when we know why life is worth living. This was one of those moments for me.

Chapter 45

After the failed coup against Gorbachev, the situation in Russia changed swiftly. Yeltsin, president of the Russian Federation (the largest component republic of the Soviet Union), found himself the ruler of a giant independent country that had been caught up in a fateful whirlwind. As all the mechanisms of the State malfunctioned, the Soviet regime simply collapsed in late 1991. There was no revolution, but the old regime was no longer functioning and the legal system was no longer clear or functional in any sense of the word. So it had been in Russia with the revolutions of February and October 1917. The Czarist regime collapsed and was replaced, for a few months, by a provisional government that never managed to assert control over the country.

Yeltsin was no democrat. He was a typical Soviet apparatchik, like most of the Soviet leadership, quite indifferent to ideology, who had moved up the party ladder thanks to his skills, both positive and negative. In terms of his personal abilities, he was at most capable of running a provincial branch of the Party, or maybe a municipal branch in a small city. His worldview, thought patterns, and political culture were those of a party hack at the regional level; his position as head of state did not change him or give him any new skills that he was lacking. His sole advantage over others was his sharp and almost animalistic political instincts, and the determination and willingness to go for broke, letting nothing get in his way. He obsession with power was unbridled and his dominant trait was a willingness to trample over dead bodies, both figuratively and literally.

Like every Soviet Communist, Yeltsin was an opportunist, ready to make alliances with anyone who was momentarily suitable. Such was his alliance with Alexander Rutskoy, who bolstered his position; without Rutskoy as his running mate, Yeltsin would not have been elected president of the Russian Federation. Yeltsin later got rid of Rutskoy with the same ease with which he had welcomed him. He used a similar ploy with Alexander Lebed to win the presidential election in 1996. He had no interests other than his own welfare and his thirst for power. Everything that served his interests was permissible; everyone who got in his way had to be eliminated and destroyed. In the absence of a political party or force of any kind around him, he was obliged to make do with the people who happened to be around him, mainly for their own reasons.

Russia's great tragedy was that the long years of Soviet control had not allowed any constructive political thought to develop in the country. The dissidents were isolated individuals with liberal worldviews, mostly anti-Communist. But they had no serious organization, not even a skeleton of one. They were never united among themselves and didn't have a solid grasp of what needed to be done in their country. Most of the dissidents focused on criticizing the other side—the regime or its representatives. Their understanding of the world outside of Russia was almost primitively simplistic, distorted, and not grounded in reality. It is hard to blame them, because this was the result of the Soviet dictatorship. The isolation imposed on the Soviet people left them with no understanding of global processes, and of course, no understanding of their country's true and natural place in the world. Because of this disconnection from the world and refusal to acquiesce to the pitiful state of their country, they overly idealized the West, both with regard to Western ambitions against Russia and the moral, ethical, economic, and social institutions in the West. The warped political culture that prevailed in the Soviet Union for decades kept its citizens from acquiring the habits of public, social, and political thought and action that were standard in democratic societies. The worship of power and admiration of solutions based on force remained part and parcel of the worldview of Soviet dissidents and oppositionists.

Their idea of freedom and individual rights was also skewed: they believed that they were allowed to do anything, but their political rivals were not. They attributed freedom of thought and democracy only to themselves; whatever didn't serve them or their goals was considered to be reactionary and therefore could and should be suppressed by force. Intolerance and the rejection of alternative opinions were therefore typical of most of the dissidents and "neoliberals," and the same applied to most of the *olim* from the Soviet Union. Giving up old habits and developing tolerance for other opinions and pluralism is a long process. The Bolshevik worldview was deeply ingrained in Yeltsin and post-Soviet Russian society. The administrative apparatus was made up of clever people with sharp elbows who had caught Yeltsin's eye and been co-opted into this system. Some of them were also talented people, but almost all were extremely cynical and nearly devoid of ethical principles. They constituted the regime that tried to march Russia ahead in double time from the Bolshevik anachronism, its culture still peppered with elements of Czarist Russia, to the modern world of the late twentieth century.

The worst character trait of so many intellectuals and dissidents was arrogance and gross indifference about the people, their problems, and their fate. Most of these intellectuals and dissidents were completely isolated and aloof. Their talk about the people's welfare was nothing but lip service, just as it had been in Soviet society. For them, "the people" was an abstract statistic, a basis for arguments that were supposedly ideological and in fact demagogic. The Soviet worldview, that "it's not so terrible if the people are suffering, it's not so terrible if they are making sacrifices, as long as it's all on behalf of a better future," continued to reign. The architects of reform in Russia were not at all worried by the steps that had already been taken and that had hurt millions of people. With inhuman ease and indifference, they decided to leave everyone penniless, to throw the intellectuals out into the street, to produce hundreds of thousands of abandoned children, and to topple all the economic and social systems. Let the people pay the price. The people always pay the price for politicians' mistakes, and the people of Russia paid horribly for the criminal arrogance that conducted social experiments on live subjects. This approach is not compatible with the democratic or liberal perspective, even if supposedly done in its name. I remember the eyes of educated men and women standing on the streets, glancing down in embarrassment, their faces pale from hunger, trying to sell books so they could buy food and not die of hunger. This was the worst breakdown of the country I knew so well.

The key question was whether the situation would stabilize. If it didn't, what direction would Russia take? What forces would rise to power? How likely was it that anti-Semitic, anti-Israel forces would take the reins? What would their policy be? Their goals? How could we neutralize them or turn their weakness or other qualities to our benefit? How could we protect the Jews and rescue them from danger? And what was the nature and plausibility of the risks? Making all of these assessments was a very complex task. In the chaos that prevailed in the Soviet Union, almost everything was possible. In his face-off with the Duma, the Russian parliament, in 1993, Yeltsin proved his determination and lust for power. When the Duma would not pass legislation to implement his policies and rejected his illegal decisions, he solved the problem very simply—with military force. Although the army refused to support Yeltsin, his defense minister Pavel Grachev managed to assemble crews for three tanks at the very last minute, which then opened fire on the parliament building. Yeltsin's opposition was not much better, but unlike him it stayed within the law. That was the personal and economic level of the

Russian ruling elite during the critical period. In those days, Yeltsin's fate was really hanging by a thread. It was only the opposition's lack of popularity, crude mistakes, and weakness that saved his regime. The chief justice of the Constitutional Court ruled that Yeltsin had acted in violation of the constitution, but who cared? Yeltsin dissolved the Constitutional Court. Valery Zorkin, who was chief justice of the Constitutional Court then (and is again today), an outstanding jurist and an honest man with fairly liberal views, was sacked. Both the court and the Duma were dissolved.

Mention should be made of the role played by the Alpha anti-terrorism unit in Yeltsin's assault on the Duma. The unit received an order to liquidate the leaders of the opposition, but its commander in fact instructed his men to enter the Duma building and prevent any killing there. Essentially, he saved the parliamentarians' lives. In 1991, the leaders of the coup, wishing to avoid bloodshed, did not dare use force and refrained from issuing similar orders. Yeltsin and his "liberal" and "democratic" friends had no compunctions about issuing orders to open fire and kill their opponents. All, of course, in the name of freedom and democracy.

With a sad smile, I read the news articles and assessments about the victory of "democracy" in Russia, and was amazed. Had the world gone mad? Tanks firing on the parliament building? Dissolving the Constitutional Court? An order to kill members of the Duma? This was democracy? I wasn't on either side, not even emotionally, although I did feel compassion for the Russian people. But I couldn't stomach the pundits' unprofessionalism and lack of objectivity.

In the end, Yeltsin survived, but it was clear to all that his regime was unstable. He had no serious political power base. The Communist Party had fallen apart. His political infrastructure consisted exclusively of those who were close to the regime, and the regime was the basis for his survival. The government under Yeltsin was run like a Byzantine court—just as in the time of the czars, just as during the long years of Stalin, Khrushchev, and Brezhnev, but without the Party.

Chapter 46

Despite the chaos, the situation of the Jews continued to improve, as did that of some of the Gentiles. But most people remained mired in an economic catastrophe. The Jews, who have always been the most dynamic group wherever they lived, including Russia, found their place in the world of novel opportunities offered by the new capitalism, even in its brutal Russian incarnation. The Jews belonged to the intelligentsia and were concentrated in the large cities, so their situation improved much faster than did that of the rest of the population. They also adapted to change much more quickly. From the beginning, the majority of Jews, particularly of the younger generation, had more of the traits and skills needed to integrate into a progressive and dynamic society. Many Jews made *aliyah*; a few, more independent and patient, took advantage of the opportunity of direct immigration to the United States. The American quota for Jewish immigrants from the (former) Soviet Union was a maximum of 42,000 people a year, but you had to wait two years just to submit your application to the American Embassy, and then another year to get approval. In the wake of the slow improvement that was taking place in Russia, particularly in the cities, the number of Jews who decided to make *aliyah* or emigrate elsewhere began to decrease. This was a natural phenomenon, and we were conscious of it.

By contrast, a different phenomenon made *aliyah* and emigration easier and facilitated absorption in Israel and other countries. As the Soviet Union evaporated in the early 1990s, private ownership of apartments became legal. A significant number of people in the large cities, many of them Jews, were able to acquire real estate, which meant they had property to sell before leaving the country. For the first time, Jews who came from what the Israeli authorities defined as "countries in distress"—such as Russia, Ukraine, and Kazakhstan— could make *aliyah* with a full wallet. They had financial means that earlier *olim* from those countries did not. In short order, we realized that this was the most important factor that could help them integrate in Israel. In retrospect, I can say with certainty that the relatively successful absorption of *olim* from the former Soviet Union was less a product of the absorption system than of the small bankroll with which they arrived. This cushion kept them from falling or crashing in the first months and even years after *aliyah*. Some drew on it to purchase apartments in Israel.

Every year, the Israeli Finance Ministry took another bite out of the "absorption basket," a set of benefits given to *olim* to facilitate their absorption. In one discussion I attended, Finance Ministry officials asked me how much they could cut the funding for *olim* without dealing a body blow to *aliyah*. Their question reminded me of the story about the farmer who "trained" his horse to survive on an ever-smaller daily ration of hay—until the horse died of starvation. The Finance Ministry wanted to cut back the assistance to *olim* until *aliyah*, too, became a dead horse. The Jews' ownership of apartments and other possessions delayed emigration from the former Soviet Union, because of the need to sell at a good price. What is more, the end of the restrictions on emigration tempered the sense of urgency and allowed people to bide their time.

As I noted, most people, aside from a thin crust of *nouveaux riches*, were in a very bad situation. The regime crisis reached its peak before the 1996 elections. The new constitution of "democratic" Russia, enacted with the support of the new "liberals" and the quiet acquiescence of the "friends of democracy" in the West, gave Russian President Yeltsin powers that not even the czars had enjoyed. There is no president anywhere in the world today, with the possible exception of Zimbabwe, who has powers even approaching those of the Russian president. They were granted him on the assumption that a chief executive of Yeltsin's kind would be a puppet in the hands of the new "democrats," who would manage things as they saw fit.

Yeltsin didn't really control Russia. What was happening in the country did not interest him all that much. His health declined and his love of the bottle, encouraged by his "friends" and intimates, reached shocking and embarrassing proportions. What interested Yeltsin were the few pleasures that he had left, his family, and his status as ruler. Yeltsin's poor image, the rampant corruption of the regime, and the economic situation left him no real chance of winning the democratic elections in 1996. The problem was that the alternative was the Communist Party, headed by Gennady Zyuganov. I met him once. What I saw was a Communist who might have been considered progressive during the Soviet period. Despite his attempts to adjust the Communist worldview to suit the Russia of 1996, he was not cut out for the job. So despite the poor image of Yeltsin's regime, the possibility of the return of Communism rattled the new economic system, as well as the politicians who swarmed around Yeltsin.

In Nativ, our assessment in 1996 was that Yeltsin would not be re-elected unless he resorted to anti-democratic measures. And that is what happened. In March 1996, his inner circle decided that to perpetuate his rule, they would cancel the elections, use Interior Ministry troops to seize control of Moscow, dissolve the Duma, and outlaw all political parties. Yeltsin approved the plan and the Interior Ministry troops were ordered to begin deployment. I was in Moscow at the time and was receiving regular and immediate updates about all that was occurring. In fact, I received a copy of the orders and details even before the Interior Ministry paramilitary units that were supposed to carry them out did. In a discussion of the topic, the Interior Minister at the time said the army was likely to see this as a violation of the Constitution; he expressed his doubts as to the ability of his own forces to seize control in that case. Russia was liable to degenerate into civil war. At the last minute, several of Yeltsin's intimates, recognizing that the Interior Ministry forces were no match for regular army units, persuaded his daughter to get her father to rescind the orders at the last minute. At the same time, Boris Berezovsky and a few of the leading oligarchs rallied to Yeltsin's side. Yeltsin was persuaded that they had the power to ensure his victory in the elections, without the use of force. Those involved in this initiative knew that they were taking a risk, but they figured that if Yeltsin used force to hold on to power, he would find himself hostage to those implementing the violent plan—particularly Alexander Korzhakov, the head of the Presidential Security Service, and Mikhail Barsukov, the head of the Russian Federal Security Service (the FSB). As long as Yeltsin remained in his abysmal state of health, he would be a puppet manipulated by Korzhakov and his cronies. They would pull his strings and remake the country, particularly the economy, and almost none of the new oligarchs would survive after the election.

Russia was only five years past the fall of Communism. According to the criteria of Western democracy, there may well have been several crude irregularities during the election campaign. But by the standards of the Soviet Union or Communist Eastern Europe, these were so minor as to be negligible and perfectly acceptable. The government apparatus and the oligarchs who supported Yeltsin devised an extremely effective propaganda system. They threw a lot of money into brainwashing the voters, using Western techniques and breaching all accepted democratic principles. Three days after the first round of elections, two cohorts of former deputy prime minister Anatoly Chubais, who was serving as Yeltsin's campaign manager, were arrested as they left the Russian White House, allegedly carrying a briefcase that contained half a million dollars in cash. The money was to be used to pay off one of the media companies that was working on Yeltsin's behalf in the campaign. The whole thing was quite illegal. But Chubais and his colleagues took a brilliant step: They panicked Yeltsin's daughter and persuaded her that the arrests would cause her father's entire campaign to collapse. In the meantime, Chubais convened a press conference and spoke about another coup attempt—utter nonsense and with no foundation, but the story was enough to frighten at least a few people. Yeltsin was left with no choice. He had to decide what he preferred—to lose Chubais and his people or to sacrifice Korzhakov. Giving in to his daughter, he dismissed Korzhakov and Barsukov. The victory of the "reformist" oligarchs over the violent group around Yeltsin was complete, and they managed, with a minimum of the sort of fraud that had been standard practice in the past, to have Yeltsin win. Had the election been properly democratic, with an honest vote count, Yeltsin would certainly have lost.

Immediately after the election, Korzhakov and Barsukov's people were purged, in good Bolshevik tradition, but no longer with executions or long prison sentences. Yeltsin was on the brink of death, but the same people who rescued his presidency also managed to save his life. Were it not for them, and of course his physician, Yeltsin would not have lived much longer (he had a quintuple bypass early in his second term and spent months in the hospital recuperating). So he held the trappings of office, but the real power was usurped by his daughter and her lover (who later became her husband), whom Yeltsin appointed his chief of staff. The most prominent and strongest member of this group was Boris Berezovsky, but the other oligarchs who helped Yeltsin win reelection also helped themselves generously from the public purse. They demanded to be rewarded for their efforts to keep him in power. They knew precisely what they wanted: a healthy chunk of the country's national resources. Not everything had been divvied up yet. Berezovsky made no bones about it in a television interview: "We deserve it. We helped the authorities and now we deserve part of the government pie." So a new distribution of the spoils began. But as with every such operation, this led to a war within the president's inner circle over Russia's economy and its transfer to private hands. The erstwhile allies began to fight among themselves. They tried to translate economic power into political power, and vice versa. Defamatory "investigative reports" began to appear—"black" psychological warfare in all its hideousness.

The last years of Yeltsin's rule were marked by corruption of a degree that Russia had not known throughout the twentieth century. Because most of the oligarchs concentrated on dividing up the spoils, buttressing their position, and amassing capital, in the wars among themselves, they paid no attention to the processes that their country was going through. Berezovsky's strategy rested on the idea that his confidant, Railways Minister Nikolai Aksenenko, whom he had built up and groomed, would be appointed prime minister in the summer of 1999. According to his calculations, whoever was prime minister then would almost certainly win the presidential election in the spring of 2000. This was where Berezovsky's mistake lay—he had not properly assessed his power. The other oligarchs, appalled by the very thought of Berezovsky holding so much power in his hands, closed ranks to thwart Aksenenko's appointment. Thanks to court intrigues, Aksenenko was eventually sacked and Berezovsky's lust for power was dealt a fatal blow.

According to the Russian Constitution, Yeltsin could not run for a third term, and his precarious health precluded it in any case. The ruling "family" and its intimates reached the conclusion that it was better to appoint an heir rather than risk the uncertain results of the power struggle that would follow Yeltsin's sudden disappearance from the scene, for whatever reason. In this situation, its main goal was to ensure that the next president of Russia granted total immunity to its members and cronies and refrain from doing what every new ruler had always done—settling accounts with those who had their hands in the trough. In the summer of 1999, the prime minister was Sergey

Stepashin. The "family" and Berezovsky did not feel they could rely on him to keep his promise and not harm them and their intimates. They did not trust Stepashin's ability to withstand pressure and were not sure of his blind and absolute loyalty to the "family." Stepashin had served in several of the most senior positions, including head of the security services and interior minister (responsible for the police), so there had been ample time to realize that he had a mind of his own and would not always surrender and kowtow to the "family" and Berezovsky. I had met him a few times and shared this assessment of the man.

With no other choice, pressed for time, and in the absence of a carefully vetted candidate, the only realistic possibility was Vladimir Putin, who was head of the National Security Council and of the Federal Security Service. Putin did not stand out as a political animal and struck the "family" and Berezovsky as a man they could count on. He demonstrated his capacity for loyalty through his absolute support for St. Petersburg mayor Anatoly Sobchak, when he refused to cross the lines and join Vladimir Yakovlev after the latter defeated Sobchak in the 1996 elections. Putin was not identified with any political party or camp and was not involved in political intrigues. He had no independent power base, whether political, economic, or any other. He was considered an honest man, a man of action with no great political pretensions. Thus, he was seen as lacking the capacity to manipulate the regime. Almost by accident, a man who was scarcely involved in all the intrigues, the least touched by all the dirt and corruption, the least identified with the oligarchy or the apparatus that was controlling Russia, was chosen by the "family" to be the next president. Their hope was that he would be an obedient president, a puppet, compliant and controlled.

This was a huge mistake. Berezovsky and the "family" simply didn't understand the history and character of Russia or the nature of the regime. They fell under the illusion that they controlled everything and everyone, thanks to their ostensible hold on the government.

Their worldview was simplistic and primitive when it came to political concepts, policy, and running the country. They had never managed government agencies and weren't familiar with them. Berezovsky was a scientist, and a rather mediocre one at that, whose work in a senior position in a research institute did not qualify him for the job of running the country. As for the rest, their manipulation of people and participation in court intrigues, sometimes accompanied by sycophancy or predatory behavior, did not prepare them to run a country, even from behind the scenes.

They did not understand the cruel dynamics of government in the Russian political culture that had evolved over centuries. The history of Russia and the Soviet Union made it clear that the first rule in every regime, particularly in an absolutist regime of the kind they had re-established with their own hands, was that a new ruler must act speedily to eliminate the people who brought him to power. Moreover, the Russian constitution gave the president powers on a scale far beyond those granted the presidents of France or the United States. The president holds power by virtue of his office, but he can become the real and undisputed ruler only by shaking off the grip of those who put him there. Those who thought that Putin would remain the same colorless and submissive man even after achieving this position of immense power did not understand the man or the nature of the Russian regime. But Putin did stick to one thing without wavering: his honesty. He never allowed anyone to take revenge on Yeltsin's family and he never hurt the "family" and its intimates, as long as they knew their place. And they knew their place.

Putin didn't make any moves against the wealth that the "family" had amassed, against its economic power or the people who protected it. In one of my conversations with him, right after he was elected president, he told me that Russia would be different under his administration. There would be what was called a separation between money and power. "We're the government," Putin said. "Whoever wants to make money may do so, but on two conditions: First, they have to do so legally; and second, they have to pay their taxes in full. They are not to pass laws. They are not to get involved in running the country. Business and government will be separate. We are the government. Anyone who fails to understand that will have no place in the new Russia. And I don't think that either Berezovsky or Gusinsky understands this—so there will probably be no place for them in the new Russia." This was the policy he adopted when he first came to power.

As far as keeping the tycoons out of power, Putin was right; businessmen no longer interfered with the government. But as for the other side of the equation, he failed: politicians and officials did meddle in business. The new government bureaucracy amassed more and more influence and control of the economic domain, to the point that senior officials' personal involvement in business affairs began to pose a serious danger to Russia's future. The corruption in Russia today is shocking. It is the most massive and horrible in all the country's history. Government corruption is the main threat to Russia's future today, much more than any other danger, domestic or foreign. The spread of moral and ethical corruption is the worst result of Putin's ascendancy. It is the beginning of the degeneration and decay of the controlling elite, which has twice brought Russia to the edge of the abyss and almost caused its collapse in the previous century.

Putin was not a born leader and had no real executive or organizational experience until he became the head of the Security Services. Nothing had prepared him to stand at the head of such a complex country, in such a difficult situation, on the verge of collapse. To the surprise of many, he learned how to be president on the job, and fairly quickly. He learned how to make political decisions. He had no natural instincts for government, of the almost animal kind that came naturally to Yeltsin, who had been raised in the party system. But Putin learned the ropes and in most cases made decisions that almost restored Russia as the great power it wanted to be. Slowly, patiently, and without too much force, he purged the bureaucracy of Yeltsin's people. Today's Russia is completely different from that which Yeltsin left behind. Had Yeltsin's regime not come to an end and had Russia's government stayed in his hands or those of people like him, it is doubtful whether Russia would have remained intact. It certainly would not have achieved the economic power it has today, even with the rise in oil and natural gas prices. The social and political disintegration simply would have brought it to the brink of a new collapse. That was the price that Russia paid for the grave leadership crisis it underwent in the last stages of the Soviet regime, whose degeneration and internal decay left no one near the top who could take control of this country and make reasonable decisions.

During Yeltsin's two terms, the foreign policy system completely disintegrated, particularly in the early years, when Andrei Kozyrev was Foreign Minister. Russia's international status plummeted. The rest of the world paid less and less attention to Russia and its influence nearly vanished. The personal interests of private individuals or bureaucrats predominated, while the country's interests were ignored. Kozyrev's personal conduct as Foreign Minister was disgraceful beyond belief. For example, on his way back from a meeting with Yasser Arafat in Gaza, Kozyrev, half drunk, stopped the convoy, stripped off his clothes, and went swimming in the Mediterranean. I was frequently witness to outrageous behavior by senior Israeli officials abroad, but never at that level. The Foreign Minister's behavior was not much different from the primitive ways of his boss, Yeltsin, but the lack of foreign policy, simply because no one cared enough to make one, led to the total collapse of the Russian Foreign Service. It was only when Kozyrev was replaced by Yevgeny Primakov that a long and exhausting process of rehabilitation began, which continued with greater vigor when Igor Ivanov assumed the post. Today, the Russian Foreign Ministry functions very well, in professional terms. I measure that not due to the content of Russia's foreign policy, but by the fact that the foreign policy apparatus is functional and efficient, and carries weight among the other national decision-making forums.

Our chief interest—the reason we were there in the Soviet Union—was, of course, the situation of the Jews and *aliyah*. The Jewish problem always annoyed the Soviet regime, like the problems of the other nationalities, as a function of their size. Although anti-Semitism was certainly the birthright of much of the population, it didn't play a decisive role in Soviet policy about the Jews. I once had a serious conversation with an expert who knew this issue backwards and forwards—Filipp Bobkov, a four-star general in the KGB whose last post, in 1991, was deputy director. At first, he was surprised that I spoke Russian so well. But when I told him my original name and surname, he remembered me at once. "Yes! Your file was one of the first that landed on my desk in 1967, when the Fifth Directorate of the KGB was established." He was its deputy director then and basically built the Fifth Directorate from scratch. In our conversation, he told me, "You people defeated us. You broke us. With the help of the West, you managed to encourage and strengthen the refusenik movement within the Soviet Union, and used that same movement to pressure us until we lost the Jews of the Soviet Union."

It gave me pleasure to hear this from a man who, from a professional standpoint, bore the greatest responsibility for the attempt to curb the Jewish movement. He attributed his failure to the party leaders' refusal to accept his professional recommendations. Apparently even totalitarian regimes suffer from discord between the political and professional echelons, which aren't always satisfied with each other. The Party claimed that the KGB had failed to deliver the goods, while the KGB asserted, after the failure, that the political leadership had undercut its efforts. It all sounded familiar. I don't think that Bobkov was right. Even if, back in the 1940s, the Soviet regime had implemented his later recommendation to allow increased emigration by activists and senior members of the Zionist movement, it could not have won. Bobkov thought that if he threw out the troublemakers, all the others would calm down. The Soviets didn't understand that every Jew who received an exit visa encouraged a few more Jews to follow suit; and by the time they got the message, it was too late. The more people who left, the more who wanted to leave. This was an axiom of the Soviet and international reality of that time. No matter what the Soviet regime did, whether they adopted the KGB's recommendations in whole or part, they would have had to let the Jews leave for Israel in the end. Only in the early 1980s did the authorities hit upon the method that almost put a halt to emigration. But by the end of the decade, we managed to exploit the collapse of the Soviet regime to the benefit of the mass *aliyah*, which took place in parallel with the Soviet Union's disintegration.

One of the most interesting things about the work of the Fifth Directorate was the extent of its surveillance of various national groups. I heard from a KGB man who was assigned to the ethnic Germans that every fourth adult in that group was an informer, at least from time to time. I don't think that the Jewish department was any less efficient. When the Fifth Directorate went out of business, along with the KGB, many of these small-scale spies continued to submit reports to their handlers, who were also no longer on the job—at least that's what the head of the German department told me. Their recruitment had been so thorough that the informers felt a real emotional need to continue reporting. Later, the FSB (the Federal Security Service), which replaced the KGB, set up an office similar to the Fifth Directorate to keep tabs on subversive political activity.

Chapter 47

In three years, 1990 to 1992, more than 400,000 Jews made *aliyah* from the former Soviet Union. Almost all of them came through Nativ, with no loud publicity or bells and whistles. The Jewish Agency's role was limited to funding the operation, while we did the actual work with local employees whom we hired. But at the Jewish Agency's behest, and with the Israeli government's consent, we transferred the logistics to the Agency. The fact of the matter is that there was no need for that, because we did everything the Jews needed, and did it well. But the usual games of prestige, political squabbles, and fights over budgets were again at play. Because governments and prime ministers are enslaved to parties and philanthropists, it was decided to transfer everything related to *olim* flights to the purview of the Jewish Agency.

We thought we had solved the Jewish problem in the Soviet Union. The feeling at the time was that it was only a matter of time until almost all the Jews emigrated and most of them settled in Israel. Had the state gotten its act together, we could have taken advantage of the opportunity and our assessment would have been largely confirmed. But as usual, the Israeli bureaucracy thought that what is true today will always be the case. It imposed a drastic cut in the aid to *olim* and slashed the absorption basket. In reaction to the lack of enthusiasm and preparations in Israel, the number of immigrants declined. Officials in the Finance Ministry, along with other groups, wanted to slow the pace of *aliyah* in order to reduce expenditures. So what if all the *olim* don't arrive in five years? Ten years is fine! It was of no use for me to try to explain that we could not be certain that what was possible today would still be possible tomorrow. The situation, it turned out, was much more complex.

From 1994 to 1995, many Jews managed to find positions in the business world and civil service in the successor republics of the Soviet Union. Official anti-Semitism almost totally disappeared. Everyone, Jews and non-Jews, was gushing with sympathy and admiration for Israel. All of the Jews would have been delighted to visit Israel and get to know it from up close, but not everyone had reached the decision that the time to make *aliyah* had come. Their ties to their birthplace—Russia, Ukraine—were still strong. The opportunities now open in their countries, thanks to the changes that were taking place, beckoned to them. Thanks to the new availability and relative simplicity of emigration and *aliyah*, many decided that it was a good idea, at least for the moment, to try their luck in their own countries, because the opportunity for *aliyah* wasn't going away. They figured that if and when they decided to leave, they would have no trouble doing so. Under the pressure of circumstance, I admit, we failed to properly assess the dimensions of this trend before it began to develop. It was hard to predict how far the positive changes in the countries of the former Soviet Union would go. It was certainly plausible that the Jews would feel comfortable in their home countries, but so were much worse possibilities, and we focused more on risks and dangers and preparing for them.

We encouraged Jews to organize. We supported these activities and sometimes initiated them. Although they were not always wholly in line with our goal, we preferred that Jewish projects, whatever their form, be carried out in coordination with an official Israeli body. The Jewish community of the former Soviet Union, unlike Western Jewry, was poor and dependent on outside assistance, because it had few resources. Israelis and Jews in the West had the notion that their coreligionists in the former Soviet Union were poor and miserable, with no independent abilities, and in need of constant encouragement, support, and help. Most of the organizations and institutions assumed that "Soviet Jews are incapable of deciding their destiny on their own. So we'll go show them what to do, how to do it, and who to do it with." I disagreed and favored joint activities. Perhaps because I too was a Soviet Jew, I understood them better than the others did and could identify with their feelings. I had no problem putting myself in their shoes and seeing the situation through their eyes.

And then reality slapped us full in the face. Suddenly, it turned out that the new Russia (and the other countries that rose from the ruins of the Soviet Union) was allowing the Jews to organize, unite, and make their own decisions about what they wanted from their communities and from world Jewry. This was the background for the establishment of the Russian Jewish Congress. One day, when I was riding in a car with Zvi Alderoti, then the director general of the Prime Minister's Office, he received a phone call from the chief rabbi of Moscow who asked him to organize a meeting between a Russian Jew, Vladimir Gusinsky, and the Prime Minister. Gusinsky was about to come to Israel and wanted to meet with Prime Minister Peres to update him about the plan to establish a new Jewish organization. Alderoti looked at me, smiled, and told the rabbi that Gusinsky should contact Yakov Kedmi. Only then would a decision be made about the meeting.

I knew of Gusinsky—he was one of the new Russian oligarchs of those years. I also knew about his past problems with Korzhakov, the head of the Russian Presidential Security Service. In the wake of their confrontation, Gusinsky had been forced to flee Russia. He contacted Jewish organizations in the West and asked them for help and protection. Some of them asked us whether there was any basis to his claim that he was being persecuted because he was Jewish. My response was: Gusinsky is a Jew, but his clash with the authorities has nothing to do with anti-Semitism. The organizations are entitled to make their own decisions about whether and how to help him, but it is not a Jewish issue. By this time, though, Gusinsky was in a much better situation and back in Russia.

Gusinsky visited me to present his ideas about establishing a Russian Jewish Congress. The reasons behind his initiative were obvious to me. He saw the Congress first and foremost as a tool for bolstering his position in Russia vis-à-vis the regime and ensuring his safety. His last altercation with the authorities had made him painfully aware of the fragility of his position and that of other oligarchs. His abortive attempt to gain support from international Jewish organizations had taught him that it was not enough to be Jewish; you had to also be sufficiently involved in the Jewish world. The best way to do this was to become the head of a prominent Jewish organization. I didn't see anything wrong with his idea. All over the world, most of the leaders of Jewish organizations engage in Jewish activities for the same reason, at least to some extent. Involvement in Jewish activities is one element of their social, political, and frequently business standing. It doesn't matter to me how a person comes by his Jewish consciousness and involvement in the Jewish world. Nor can I offer a rational explanation of why, one fine day, I suddenly got excited about Zionism and the State of Israel, to the point that I became unable to live without this country and without a sense of belonging to it and its people. It is true that the vast majority of Jews who made *aliyah* did so because of the pressure of circumstances. But who am I to judge the motives of other Jews who want to help the Jewish people and their country?

Gusinsky's idea of establishing a Russian Jewish Congress strongly appealed to me. I quickly understood what I had not fully comprehended before—namely, that Russian Jewry was sufficiently mature to chart its own course. It had sufficient financial, human, and political resources to do so. I offered my own perspective on the idea of the Congress and on independent Jewish organizational activity in Russia. We had no major disagreements and quickly settled on the goals of the Congress and on the forms and plans for collaboration between the Congress and the State of Israel. I recommended to the Prime Minister that the country support the idea, assist the new organization and begin working to support and strengthen it. Not everyone understood this, even at Nativ. To this day, the attitude of most Israelis and Western Jews towards the Jews of the former Soviet Union is one of superiority, rather than partnership. Most functionaries still see their role as giving orders rather than working with these Jews. They have never understood that the Jews of Russia, Ukraine, and the other countries are members of vibrant and independent communities with minds of their own, and that they are able to think, make decisions, and conduct independent activities at home and in the international Jewish arena. When it comes to their national essence, these communities are no different from American Jewry or the Jews of Europe or Australia.

We gave as much assistance as we could to set up the Congress and strengthen its position vis-à-vis the authorities in Russia, Israel, and the rest of the world. It was important to me that the Russian government see the Congress as a representative body for Russian Jewry, one that reflected the broad diversity of opinions and social classes—including the authentic Jewish intelligentsia and Jewish business elite. It was not a religious organization; otherwise, it could not have represented a Russian Jewry that was overwhelmingly secular. It was important for me that the Russian leadership understand that Israel saw the Congress as the main Jewish organization in Russia, through which and on behalf of which it was willing to speak with the authorities, and also to frequently rely upon it to make the Jewish case on questions of bilateral policy. I wanted the authorities to understand that if they did not maintain correct relations with the local Jews, other facets of relations between the two countries would not move forward. Thus, I channeled bilateral relations through the Congress to the extent possible. I frequently had the Congress sponsor joint projects we initiated in order to build up its position. On more than one occasion I told Gusinsky and other officials of the Congress that I saw eye to eye with them on their goal of achieving a status equal to that of American Jewry. Russian Jews had their own interests in both domestic and foreign policy, and a role to play in the Jewish world just like American or European Jews.

For example, when Ariel Sharon, both as Minister of Infrastructure and as Foreign Minister, asked me to handle his visits to Russia, I involved the Congress in planning his itinerary. I could have organized it just as well without the Congress, but I thought it was important to show that every Israeli official who came to Russia met with the leaders of the Congress, which represented Russian Jewry. Gusinsky's success in co-opting many members of the Russian Jewish business elite to run the Congress, despite internal disagreements, was very important. During Sharon's visit, the Congress organized a meeting between the Israeli Minister of Infrastructure and more than 40 local Jewish businessmen. Sharon was astounded by these young Jews (the oldest among them were pushing 40), by the warm atmosphere, by their respect, and by their interest in him and the State of Israel. He addressed them with total candor and asked them to invest in and develop business ties with Israel. Many of them later did so, until the Israeli police and society, which saw them as the "Russian mafia," rewarded them with a resounding slap on the cheek. I saw this social consolidation with the Jewish Congress in the vanguard as the best way to build up close relations with the dynamic and growing Jewish community in Russia.

I was aware of all kinds of internal ploys and attempts to exploit the Congress to polish the luster of some individual or group, but this was legitimate and widespread not only within the Jewish world. What was important for us was to be able to influence the Congress's activities and collaborate with it to benefit Israel and the Zionist idea, and so it was. The Congress's financial independence and ability to act with full autonomy were fine and important qualities. The

Israeli Foreign Ministry made fun of the Jewish Russian Congress. In its eyes, it was inconceivable that Russian Jews, poor miserable wretches of an inferior culture, half European and half Asian, could act like Westerners. American and European Jewish organizations and the Israeli establishment, both political and professional, had and continue to have difficulty seeing Russian Jewry as their peers in any way. Only one theme influenced the Israeli establishment and public: money and economic power, and consequently the increasing wealth of Russian Jewry. For most Israelis, money talks. After all, the Israel establishment's attitude towards American Jewry was based mainly on worship of its economic and financial might.

At some point, the idea came up of bringing *olim* over by ship. I thought this was an excellent idea: because the voyage from Odessa takes four or five days, Jews would be able to load most of their cargo on the same ship and could complete most of the formal procedures, including the issuing of documents, while at sea. When they reached port in Israel, the *olim* could proceed straight to their new home, which would have been arranged during the journey, along with all their belongings. The fare would be less than that for a flight. The tens of millions of dollars, if not more, invested in storage warehouses for transshipment and storage of the containers with the *olim*'s belongings would have been saved, not to mention preventing the agony of waiting for up to a year for their belongings to arrive. The closure of the way stations in Europe would have saved tens of millions of dollars every year. But that was precisely what got the Jewish Agency to back away: Close the way stations and reduce the gigantic outlays, which came to hundreds of millions of dollars, with all the ramifications entailed? Needless to say, the Jewish Agency sank the idea before it set sail.

Chapter 48

In the early 1990s, Nativ began cooperating with the Israel Police. One day, I met with reserve Maj. Gen. Yaakov Lapidot, who had been commander of the National Security College when I began my studies there. Lapidot had retired from the IDF after his term at the NSC. Later, when I was already director of Nativ and he was director general of the Ministry of Internal Security, I invited him to my office for a friendly meeting. I proposed that he visit the former Soviet Union on our behalf and speak to Jews there. I saw him as an impressive man, and not only physically. He had another advantage for us: His parents came from Lithuania and he spoke fluent Yiddish. That was a rare accomplishment for an IDF general and I knew that it would make an impression on the Jews in the FSU. Lapidot, taken by surprise, asked me what he would say to them.

"Tell them about yourself," I told him. "Tell them about Israel as you know it and understand it. Tell them about the IDF as you know it and represent it. Speak Yiddish. They will understand you and we will translate whatever you say in Hebrew. A fine-looking Israeli general who fought in the wars and speaks Yiddish—you'll make a strong impression on the Jews."

My enthusiasm was infectious and he agreed. In the last briefing before he left, I recommended that he also get in touch with senior police officers there and offered to arrange the meetings. I mentioned that it was very important for us to have good relations with the police everywhere, in every republic he visited. For Nativ this was important, because the emigration offices were under the jurisdiction of the police and the Interior Ministry. Good relations with the emigration bureaucracies would allow us to solve many problems associated with *aliyah*. I saw the visit of the director general of the Ministry of Internal Security as an opportunity to forge and strengthen ties with the police in the successor republics.

There were other considerations as well. After the disintegration of the Soviet Union, many regions were swept by instability, insecurity, and violence. Their rulers had been higher-ups under the old Soviet regime, and it was unclear in which direction they would develop. Civil wars broke out in the new countries in the Caucasus, in central Asia, and in Moldova. Russia and Ukraine, too, were on the brink of civil war or submerged in internal armed conflicts fanned by nationalist tensions. This was before the start of the war in Chechnya, but we were already aware of the dangerous situation there. We were concerned for the Jews' welfare and saw that they were likely to need help—rescue or evacuation from combat zones. We often launched such operations, which depended on the local authorities, police and interior ministries to make Jewish emigration possible, organize it, and arrange passage through neighboring countries. I told Lapidot all of this in detail.

Lapidot visited several countries, including Russia, Ukraine, and Belarus. We notified the Interior Ministry in every country that the director general of the Israel Ministry of Internal Security would be visiting. Although he was coming to speak on Jewish issues, he would certainly be glad to meet representatives of the police. The response in every place was enthusiastic. The police and interior ministries in the new republics and the new regimes were looking for connections and recognition in the West. It was important for them to receive support and assistance from the police of a Western country, both to receive professional guidance and to buttress their standing and "purge themselves" of their image as vestiges of the Soviet police.

There were a number of moving incidents during Lapidot's visit. In Belarus, for example, hundreds of Jews gathered in a large auditorium in Minsk and greeted him enthusiastically. He had a meeting set for the same evening with the top echelons of the Belarus police. Towards the end of the program with the Jews, several uniformed police generals and other senior officers suddenly entered the hall and took seats of honor in the first row. For a Jew from Minsk, the appearance of the police was usually a traumatic event that evoked unpleasant memories, and they were stunned by the sight of the unexpected visitors. Lapidot greeted the guests and continued his dialogue with the Jews; the audience kept asking questions and showed no signs of letting up. Lapidot apologized and said that the heads of the Belarusan police were waiting, so he would have to cut the session short. And then the head of the Belarusan police, a three-star general, stood up. "Please continue," he told Lapidot. "You, an Israeli general, came from a Jewish country to speak to the Jews. We respect this. First complete what you feel you owe the Jews, your kinsmen. We will wait."

The audience was shocked by the respectful attitude of the chief of the Belarusan police—an entity that, until a few years earlier, had terrorized all citizens—towards them, towards Jews, and towards the visitor from the State of Israel who had come to see them, as members of his people. Lapidot, too, was very moved. This was one of the signs that things were changing and that new opportunities were opening.

The second incident took place the next day. When Lapidot arrived for his official visit to police headquarters, a review had been organized in his honor. Goose-stepping units of the Belarusan police were marching past the building. But the climax came when their orchestra played Jewish melodies and accompanied the police choir in Yiddish songs! It was utterly surrealistic. During Lapidot's visit, the countries concluded an agreement for cooperation between their police forces, which led to the posting of a representative of the Israel Police in

Russia, with responsibility for Belarus and several other republics as well, and another Israel Police representative in Ukraine.

Lev Kaplan was the first to hold the position in Ukraine. Kaplan, who had been a police officer back in Lithuania, served in the Criminal Investigation Division of the Israel Police and held the rank of superintendent. I first met him back in the 1980s during a joint operation with the unit run by the legendary police brigadier Binyamin Segal. Later, I asked Kaplan to serve as the Nativ emissary in Uzbekistan. And then I received a call from Lapidot, who asked me to return Kaplan to the police so they could send him as their representative to one of the former Soviet republics. I was glad to comply. Thus was the start of the collaboration between the Israel Police and the police forces of Russia and the other Soviet successor states.

Before the great wave of *aliyah*, I made several attempt to explain that the police, too, should be preparing for the new situation. I told them that the *olim* included people who had not exactly been law-abiding citizens of the Soviet Union and that it would behoove the Israel Police to learn how to handle people who were utterly different from what they were used to. Moreover, what I knew about the Israel Police led me to conclude that it was incapable of dealing with Soviet criminals, who were extremely cunning, brutal, and aggressive, and had managed to hold their own against one of the strongest police forces in the world. As usual, though, my recommendations were ignored, and when the wave of *olim* arrived, the Israel Police had no capacity to understand what it was facing. Many mistakes were made and much damage was wreaked upon the Jews, *aliyah*, the police and its image, and the country as a whole.

As part of their cooperation, the police forces of the several countries began exchanging information. Nativ had excellent connections with the police departments in the former Soviet Union, which helped us in our current and future activities. One of the most amazing things happened in Ukraine. Nativ organized a seminar for officers from all over the country who handled the issuing of exit visas to Israel. The weeklong seminar featured Russian-speaking lecturers from Israel, who explained the procedures for *aliyah* and absorption in Israel and the legal aspects. Essentially, Nativ taught the Ukrainian police how the State of Israel viewed the *aliyah* process and how the procedures that began in their offices ended in Israel. Our goal was to make the emigration process smoother, based on full cooperation with the local authorities. We also reached agreements to allow us to provide assistance to Jews in neighboring countries who ran into problems. This included issuing transit visas to Jews who arrived in the country without documents, if we vouched for them.

I submitted one of the first reports (perhaps the very first) to the Israel Police about how the Russian underworld could penetrate Israel. I summed up all the information we had collected from our sources and included descriptions of every person we had reason to suspect of being involved in the underworld. As was standard, I noted that most of this information was hearsay and generally not based on primary sources. I conveyed the material to the Police as it was, in almost raw form, with no attempt to evaluate it. Crime was not Nativ's affair and we did not bother to investigate or cross-check the information. We were interested in crime only insofar as it was relevant to Soviet Jews and their *aliyah*. We saw the information and the suspicions as merely an indication. We did not think the data were very reliable and never imagined that the Israel Police would treat it as virtual proof of the suspects' guilt, or that they would base their policy on reports that had not really been checked out. The Israel Police, like every other Israeli agency, had no understanding of or ability to deal with the Russian or post-Soviet bureaucracies. Although the Police representative in Moscow knew Russian from his childhood in Poland, he had no understanding of the developments in the Soviet Union or in Russia. It wasn't his fault, after all; that had never been his field.

During the Israel Police representative's stay in Moscow, he held frequent meetings with police officials and others, as a matter of routine. In these meetings, often held in restaurants, all sorts of strange rumors and gossip that were circulating in Russia were exchanged. You had to be intimately familiar with the country and its people to properly assess the credibility of all those rumors, which included a large element of vivid imagination and only a modicum of truth. This was exacerbated by the power struggles that were raging in the country at that time, which catalyzed the production of false and malicious rumors intended to destroy opponents' reputations. It was called "the war of *kompromat*" (compromising materials), or black psychological warfare. The Russian media dabbled in this frequently. Media outlets, both private and public, as well as many journalists, were willing to publish any item or report for money, including those that were fabricated or written to order. Some even turned this craft into their main source of income. Journalists and representatives of broadcasters or periodicals often contacted someone and demanded a payoff to bury a damaging story about him, whether true or fictitious. Most people paid up. There were also those who paid to insert a story that would hurt their competitors or rivals. These were the marvels and wonders of the new Russia as it cast off every restraint: there was no rule of law, no functioning government, and everyone did just as they pleased. Or, more precisely, every strong man pursued his own interests, in accordance with his power.

The corruption in Russia spread as far as the police and Interior Ministry and even penetrated the intelligence and security services (the latter more than foreign intelligence). This jumble of rumors came to the ears of the Israel Police representative, and as a disciplined officer, he put everything in writing, stamped it "classified," and forwarded it to headquarters in Jerusalem. The police were flooded with stories straight out of the *Arabian Nights*—about Russian crime, the new wave of criminals who were going to swamp Israel, and so forth. On top of this, when Russian businessmen began to appear in the West in the late 1980s and early 1990s, their operations involved removing vast sums from the country—billions of dollars. In an attempt to stop the flight of capital, the Russian intelligence services began to spread disinformation in the West that all this money originated with the KGB, that it belonged to the Communist Party, or that these businessmen were suspected of ties with the underworld or the KGB. The goal was to sow distrust and make it harder for these people, Jews and non-Jews alike, to transfer funds abroad and do business in the West. The tidal wave of slander had an effect; every businessman from the former Soviet Union was thought to be a KGB agent or mafioso. The monster came back to haunt its creator. To this day, Russia and its businessmen continue to pay the price for the foolish and irrational decision by a few intelligence officers in the late 1980s and early 1990s.

The West, including the United States and Israel, has never developed a deep understanding of Russia and the Soviet Union. The basic and traditional fear of Russia, that vast, half-Asian country in the East, was almost pathological. So these warnings fell on fertile ground. The authorities, police departments, and intelligence services quickly and willingly adopted an incriminatory attitude towards businessmen from the post-Soviet world. When the Soviet threat disappeared, the imagined threat of the "Russian mafia" provided a justification for these agencies to keep receiving their astronomic budgets. The Israel Police, too, were carried away by the fear that the Russian crime wave would flood the State of Israel any minute. In its efforts to prepare for the impending scourge, the best the police could do was to rely on the opinions and suggestions of a long-time Russian *oleh*. He was a somewhat extravagant and problematic character whose public appearances usually bordered on provocation. This man suddenly decided to help the police, or the police somehow decided to ask him for help, despite the fact that he had no connection to police work aside from a few interrogations to which he had been subjected in the Soviet Union and Israel. For several days, the man sat in the offices of the Serious Crimes Unit in Petah Tikva and regaled the police with stories and fabrications about the Russian mafia that was about to seize control of Israel. And the officers paid close attention to him, wrote everything down, and came close to taking this hodgepodge of fiction and gossip for gospel truth and the basis for operations to target the "Russian mafia."

Some of the police officers thought they could build their careers on this. One of the heads of police intelligence defined Russian crime as "a strategic threat to the State of Israel." He thought this had a fine and serious ring to it. Once, this officer returned from an international police conference in Europe and loudly announced that "Four billion dollars have already been smuggled into Israel by the Russian mafia." In one of our meetings, I asked him what that figure was based on: Had anyone ever investigated and checked the transfer of money through banks? Sums of that magnitude certainly had never yet been brought into Israel.

His response was amazing—he had heard it from a police officer in Budapest. I was stunned. The gossip of one Eastern European policeman had turned into an almost official datum of the Israel Police?! No one would have imagined that the source of such an earth-shattering piece of news was so unreliable. Everyone assumed that the police of the Jewish State would certainly have conducted a thorough investigation and done serious research before publicizing a figure that reeked of anti-Semitism. This "fact," based on arbitrary and made-up numbers that no one had bothered to check, featured prominently in many debates, political statements, and decisions by the police and even by the government. The excuse of the "Russian mafia" was even used to justify a brilliant idea hatched by the Israel Police: to place the central computer of the Bank of Israel under police supervision so that the police could keep tabs on every transfer of funds to and from the country. I can only imagine what the world would have thought and what businessmen would have done had they known that the computer that handled all movement of funds into and out of the country belonged to the police. Fortunately, this fond fantasy of the Israel Police never came true.

A meeting with Prime Minister Rabin about the possibility that organized crime might infiltrate Israel from the former Soviet Union led to the decision to establish a new police unit to track Russian crime in Israel. The intention was to investigate the phenomenon and only then to make decisions. At the same meeting, it was also decided not to define this unit as being directed against the Russian mafia, for "public" reasons. To camouflage its main target and primary reason for establishment, it would be designated the "Unit for International Crime." After the meeting, I told Rabin that I was worried by the attitude displayed here. I was concerned that the matter would lead to stigmatizing all *olim* and create a climate of anti-*aliyah* sentiment. His response was, "I am aware of that and will not let it happen. Don't worry, we will keep it under control." I trusted him and knew that he really would do so. I still believe that had he not been murdered, Rabin would not have tolerated the hysterical outbursts about the "Russian mafia."

Rabin was assassinated soon after that meeting, and Shimon Peres became Prime Minister. Leaving aside his shock at the circumstances that brought him back to the Prime Minister's chair, Peres' main goal was political survival. The police began to run amok. My unambiguous position contradicted the police's point of view, and I tried to debunk all their claims on the basis of facts. They did not like my position, even though they had no ability or information with which to counter it. Nor did they have any basis for suspecting that criminal elements were involved in Nativ activities. Despite all their efforts, the police never found a shred of evidence to ground that suspicion.

I remember a meeting with Prime Minister Peres that was attended by the heads of the intelligence community and police. Suddenly I heard the police representative tell a story that infuriated me: A Ukrainian gangster had purportedly been discovered in Israel. The representative said that the man had fled here with $300 million, but he would see to it personally that he was returned to Ukraine for trial. About a year after this meeting, I submitted a report to the Prime Minister, with a copy to the police, in which I wrote that anti-Semitic motifs were starting to infiltrate the political power struggles in Ukraine. In pursuit of that end, I added they were blaming the Jews for the harsh economic situation in the country. As an example, I noted that an anti-Semitic Ukrainian newspaper published by veterans of the Ukrainian Nachtigall Battalion (which had fought alongside the Germans in the Second World War), had printed an anti-Semitic article accusing the Ukrainian Prime Minister, a Jew, of fleeing the country with $300 million, and asserted that this was the reason for the economic crisis in Ukraine. When I submitted the report, I attached the comment that this was a good example of the use of anti-Semitic motifs. I never imagined that the Israel Police would take a malicious report in an anti-Semitic newspaper published by SS veterans and turn it into proof of Russian criminal activity and an indictment against a Jew. I knew that criminal files were opened and closed against prominent government figures every other day, usually as part of the political infighting. Someone who was charged yesterday could come out pure as snow tomorrow, and the whole ritual would be repeated two days later. I too had heard nasty remarks about the Ukrainian Prime Minister, but it was a far stretch from that to the claim that 300 million dollars were smuggled into Israel.

I met the man when he served as Prime Minister of Ukraine during Shimon Peres' visit as Foreign Minister. I discussed his case and others with Ukrainian security and police officials. To prevent false hopes, I made it clear to them that the State of Israel would not be dragged into their internal squabbles. If the prosecutor issued an arrest warrant against someone to settle political accounts, and the man was Jewish and escaped to Israel, we would not spring to attention and would not extradite him. As a Jewish State, we would protect Jews and not allow them to be turned into political pawns, either in their country or any other country. The Ukrainians accepted this position. Those who didn't accept it were the "wise men" of the Israel Police, in the Jewish State, who had been turned into a tool of the anti-Semitic forces.

I had reported this incident to Prime Minister Rabin and notified him of the Ukrainian publications and my conversations with the Ukrainians. Rabin supported my position and said in no uncertain terms that we would not be sucked into this nonsense and would never extradite this man or any other Jew in such a situation. In the meeting with Prime Minister Peres, I became very angry and said that it was a disgrace to hear a representative of the police repeating tales taken from anti-Semitic, pro-Nazi newspapers and propaganda. The story was resurrected about a year and a half later, when Uri Cohen-Aharonov, the Israel Television police affairs correspondent, "revealed" this incident as a shocking new scoop about the Israel Police's war on the "Russian mafia." Apparently, the police had not unearthed anything new for a year and a half, and to keep the issue of the Russian mafia in the public eye they decided to recycle an old fiction, with the help of a compliant police reporter. As for the object of the whole mess, he eventually returned to Ukraine. All the charges against him were withdrawn and he was again elected to a seat in parliament. On his eightieth birthday, he received one of the most important Ukrainian decorations from the country's president, and everything ended in a poof of nothing, like so many other fabricated scandals.

The Israel Police had so little ability to fight Russian crime that it was absurd. I recall a visit to Israel by the Russian Minister of the Interior, Gen. Viktor Yerin. He asked the Israeli authorities to locate a person suspected of severe criminal offenses in Russia. The Russian police handed over the details several times, including the aliases that the man had used and his addresses and telephone numbers in Israel. But the Israel Police declared that they could not find him. During Yerin's visit, the police hosted a dinner for him and his entourage at a hotel in Haifa. Imagine the disgrace when the wanted man was sitting in the lobby of the hotel waiting for the Minister's entourage to enter, in the hope of arranging his affairs with them.

Incidentally, during the same visit, Yerin asked the Israel Police for help in his contacts with the authorities in the United States. He said that the Russians had been unable to persuade the Americans to extradite Vyacheslav Ivankov (known as Yaponchik), allegedly a kingpin of organized crime in Russia. He arrived in the United States illegally and settled in New York. For three years, the police and FBI ignored both his illegal residence and the appeals of the Russian police. Only then, after two Soviet-born American businessmen accused him of extortion, was he tried, convicted, and, after nine years in prison, extradited to Russia. Several years later he was eliminated, apparently on the order of a rival crime boss. This is evidence of how seriously police forces around the world treated the issue of "Russian crime." It was usually exploited in the service of political or establishment interests and was never seriously targeted by law enforcement agencies.

One day I realized that our Interior Ministry had become a branch of the Israel Police and that every idiocy that emerged from the latter was taken as an order by the former. I could not accept this approach, particularly when it hurt *olim* in Israel. The police could have an opinion, but I felt that the Interior Ministry had to have the final say. One day, a Ukrainian Jew who had been in the country for a year and a half but had yet to receive *oleh* status got in touch with me. I went to the Interior Ministry to find out the reason for the delay. I was told that according to the Israel Police, the man was suspected of criminal activity and consequently barred from receiving citizenship. I contacted the police, who sent me the document they had received from the prosecutor's office in Ukraine. It stated (not word for word, but this is the substance of it) that the man had been the director of some sort of government fund, and it was possible that there had been serious fiscal irregularities in this fund, and it was possible that this man was connected to financial activities, and it was possible that these activities had criminal aspects. That was it. There was no word about an investigation against the man or an investigation of the entire matter, or any mention that he was suspected of anything. On the basis of this document, with its string of "it is possible's," the police had informed the Interior Ministry that they opposed his request for Israeli citizenship. They had already classified him as a wanted international criminal. I asked the police how long they expected the man to wait: Are you investigating the case or not? Their response was that the police had done nothing other than send the letter to the Interior Ministry. The man was convicted without knowing what he was accused of, without being able to defend himself, on the basis of a letter that even a cursory look revealed to be fabricated. I decided to look into what had happened.

When I was in Ukraine, I had meetings with many people, including the Prime Minister. I knew that he was acquainted with the man in question. I asked him if there were any suspicions of criminal activity by the man and whether any investigation was in progress. The answer was: "What on Earth? He's not being investigated. He isn't suspected of crimes. He is an honest man." When I returned, I wrote a report which I submitted to the Israel Police, with a copy to the Prime Minister, that no investigation was under way and that the man was not suspected of anything—according to the Ukrainian Prime Minister himself. The police had no choice. They wrote the Interior Minister that they no longer opposed his being granted citizenship. Because I knew who I was dealing with, I wrote my own letter to the Interior Ministry, demanding that they backdate his citizenship to the day he had submitted his application, more than a year and a half earlier, because he was not to blame for the delay and should not have to wait another year to receive a passport. Indeed, the matter was settled and the man received citizenship. The question is: Had the man not bumped into me by accident, had I not taken on his case and gotten to the bottom of it, exploiting my connections as director of Nativ, and had the Ukrainian Prime Minister not known the man, what would have happened? And even scarier: How many more cases like that were there and still are in Israel?

But that was not the end of it. Six or seven years later, by which time the man already owned an apartment in Netanya, he was in the practice of traveling abroad on business several times a year. One day, upon his return from one of these trips, his passport was confiscated. Why? Because six years earlier, the requisite year had not elapsed between the confirmation of his citizenship and the issuance of his passport. The Interior Ministry had decided to conduct a review of the records of all *olim* who had received citizenship. I had already left Nativ, but because of my personal knowledge of the case I contacted the Interior Ministry to try to straighten things out. The Interior Minister at the time was a well-known fighter for human rights, a hero of the struggle for *aliyah*: Natan Sharansky. I wrote a detailed letter explaining the mistake. After a month, I received a response that the man's file had not been found. I asked Nativ to locate all the documents on the matter and forward them to the Interior Ministry. A month later, I called Sharansky's office. No response. I called again, as usual through the Minister's office. I received the standard response of Israeli bureaucracy, as though none of the letters had been read: "Because the period between the granting of citizenship and issuance of the passport had been less than a year, we decided to confiscate his passport six years later." All my letters to Interior Minister Sharansky, the white knight of human rights, were of no avail. This was the straw that broke the camel's back and I assailed the Interior Ministry in the media for its inhuman treatment of *olim*. I said that even the Soviet bureaucracy had not gone so low when making up reasons to prevent Jews from making *aliyah*. I protested not only this incident, but many others as well.

I would contact the Interior Ministry in many cases that came to my attention or in response to special requests by *olim*. For example, I once met a waitress at a coffee shop who told me that she was one of the Na'aleh children and was now waitressing until she began her university studies. She couldn't receive a passport because while in Na'aleh, she had gone to visit her mother in the Soviet Union. We had made it a requirement of the program that the children visit their family at least once a year; it would have been inhuman to tear children away from their parents without making sure that they saw them regularly. But the Interior Ministry told her, "You left Israel, so we will restart the count of the year you need to be in Israel in order to receive a passport from the day you returned. A year will have to pass before you can receive a passport." Again I contacted the Interior Ministry. After several letters from me, and with the intervention of the Minister's office, this injustice was righted and her passport was returned to her. I intervened with every Interior Minister (except for those from Shas), but Sharansky's failure to include the Soviet *olim* in his "campaign for human rights" infuriated me, and others as well. He continued to fight for human rights in Russia, but not for the human rights of his kinsmen and in his country.

There were many cases in which I encountered the "professionalism" of the Israel Police and its "handling" of the Russian mafia. But the pinnacle was the famous list issued by the police of thirty-six organized crime suspects. I asked for a copy of the document for one reason—to see whether any of the names on the list were Jews with whom we had connections. The police were evasive about giving me the list. I heard from many people, including businessmen, that they had seen it. Half the State of Israel had seen the list—but all Nativ got were various excuses as to why the police did not send us a copy. Finally I went to the Prime Minister, and in response to a direct order from his office, we received the document at long last. Most but not all of the names on the list were familiar to me. I also saw almost verbatim quotations from my report of a few years prior about the risk of infiltration of Israel by criminals from the former Soviet Union. I decided to ignore the misuse of my report, although it is not exactly a sign of professionalism to turn unconfirmed suspicions or gossip into ostensibly solid intelligence material and use it as grounds for a bureaucratic decision. Nonetheless, there was one case I could not ignore: that of Vladimir Gusinsky. Gusinsky was the president of the Russian Jewish Congress and as such enjoyed the support of the government and Prime Minister of Israel. He used to meet with the Prime Minister and I could not reconcile myself to the idea that we were supporting a man whose name was on the list of organized crime suspects.

Even before we decided to support the Congress and Gusinsky as its president, I had checked with our sources in Russia to find out who he was, what his background was, and where he stood with the law. This investigation was the basis for my recommendation to the Prime Minister to meet him and set up meetings for him with other cabinet ministers. Suddenly, I saw him featured prominently in the ranks of the "Russian mafia" and didn't know whether to laugh or cry. According to the document, Gusinsky was a non-Jew who came to Israel by virtue of a marriage of convenience to a Jewish woman. In Russia, he was suspected of bank robbery, and, even worse, he was Grigory Lerner's partner. But as it happened, I had known Gusinsky's late mother, a kosher Jew, and he too was a fully kosher Jew—not only was his mother Jewish, so was his father. I knew this because I had sent our representatives in Moscow to the Population Registry there to find Gusinsky's birth certificate, which stated clearly that both his parents were Jews. Our representative followed standard Nativ practice and filed an official report of this. The truth is that Gusinsky's wife at the time wasn't Jewish. But how could the police turn a Jew into a non-Jew, with no factual basis, and even invent a story about a marriage of convenience?! Moreover, how could a marriage of convenience produce two children? Of course this made no difference, because no less a personage than the head of the Population Administration in the Israel Interior Ministry declared that for her, the birth of children was insufficient proof that the marriage was not fictitious. She laid down this rule in a general directive to Interior Ministry staff. Gusinsky's wife had received an *olah* status because of her marriage to a Jew. I have no clue where the police came up with this particular idiocy.

I wrote a letter to the police and noted that Vladimir Gusinsky was a Jew but his wife was not, so he could not have made *aliyah* on the premise of a fictitious marriage to a Jewish woman: quite the contrary. Regarding the alleged bank robbery, I wrote that his only connection to the bank in question was that he owned it, and that—at least back then—it was one of the largest banks in Russia. I added that the police report did not make it clear whether he was suspected of having robbed his own bank or robbing a different bank. And regarding Mr. Lerner, who was the boogeyman used at the time to frighten everyone in Israel, I noted that Gusinsky's line of work had nothing to do with Lerner's. Gusinsky was active mainly in the media and banking, and to the best of my knowledge, he had never had any dealings with Lerner, business or otherwise. We had investigated this matter, too, several times and via several sources. Gritting their teeth, the Israel Police were forced to take Gusinsky's name off the list, but the damage to the man and to the image of Russian Jewry in Israel had already been done and the police continued to defame him in all sorts of ways, spreading ugly hints and rumors. When Gusinsky asked for a meeting with the deputy Finance Minister, the latter made excuses because he had heard from someone in the police that perhaps not everything with Gusinsky was on the up-and-up.

The police reached the lowest depths in the case of Grigory Lerner. They turned him into the biggest and most frightening mafioso in Israel. When I visited Russia, senior police officials there were astounded. "Yasha, tell us, what has happened to you guys? Have you gone crazy? Grishka Lerner a mafioso? In the worst possible case he's a two-bit con-man. A mafioso?! How and why are you doing this?"

I told them that this was the police's doing and I wasn't going to get involved. Some twisted mind in the Israel Police decided to lock him up in the isolation cell that had once held the convicted war criminal John Demjanjuk. A cheap play had been put on by the SWAT unit, with helicopters circling above the courthouse, because of the claim that the "Russian mafia," which existed only in the sick mind of the police, was about to raid the building to release the defendant. What Russian mafia? There is no Russian mafia in Israel. There is organized crime in Russia, but what do the syndicates care about Grigory Lerner? Would they really send men to release him? It was all nonsense, but an impression needed to be made in Israel and they needed to use him to set an example. The head of the Serious Crimes Unit said openly, "I arrested him to set an example." I cannot understand a statement like this by a policeman or law-enforcement official. A man is arrested if he breaks the law. You don't arrest a man to show others. A democratic country should never have show arrests or show trials.

Lerner spent a year and a half in jail awaiting trial while the Israel Police kept getting the court to extend his remand. An Israeli judge received notes from the police with all sorts of intimidating statements that no one could examine or refute. Their content was more or less at the level of the examples I have already mentioned. Any normal Israeli judge would have been shaking in his boots after reading these notes and immediately approve his continuation in custody. I asked Lerner's lawyer, whom I happened to know from elsewhere, why Lerner accepted a plea bargain in the end. His response was that Lerner had sat in prison for a year and a half because judge after judge had extended his remand, leading Lerner to think that there was no judge in Israel who would acquit him. A plea bargain would get him out of prison sooner and he also wouldn't waste more money on useless legal proceedings.

Nothing in the charge sheet was ever proven, except maybe that he had given a box of chocolate to a bank clerk. He was accused of murder, of trying to defraud a bank in Russia. Russia had not asked for his extradition or submitted any documents on him. The man was tried and sentenced and did time on the basis of gossip. What really made my blood boil was not that he was imprisoned in

Demjanjuk's cell, but that the Attorney General refused to approve his request to study Hebrew with a teacher who would come to the prison, claiming the prisoner was dangerous. The Attorney General of a Jewish country, a man who wears a *kippa*, barred a Jew from studying Hebrew in an Israeli jail?! That same Attorney General, today a Supreme Court justice, had never barred terrorists and violent criminals from studying any subject they wanted to, working towards a high school or university degree. He only prevented one Jew from studying Hebrew in an Israeli prison.

Lerner's true nature came out in his second trial; he turned out to be, just as the Russians had said, at most a two-bit con-man. But, as I said, the Israel Police needed somebody they could use to put the fear of the "Russian mafia" into Israeli society. The fact is that aside from Lerner and the rumors the police spread about him through its favored journalist, they couldn't find even one other Russian gangster to save their soul. In Lerner's case, the behavior of Israeli society was no less grave. It doesn't matter what kind of man was subjected to a carefully scripted show trial and convicted of crimes he hadn't committed. Nobody in Israel uttered a peep. Of all those fighters for human rights or seekers of justice, not one raised a voice about the injustice done to Lerner and all Soviet *olim*, or against the disgraceful abuse of the Israeli justice system. Everyone saluted and was silent, including judges and public officials. This is a mark of Cain for Israeli society, which is steeped in unfavorable attitudes and prejudices against Russian Jews. Israelis were delighted, almost gleeful, to adopt a negative image of the Jews from the former Soviet Union. Even today, they are in no hurry to discard their false beliefs about the Russian mafia and Russian crime.

Something similar happened with Mikhail Chernoy. The Israeli government eavesdropped on his conversations for five years and had no compunctions about lying to Israeli judges when it submitted a request to approve the wiretaps. It justified the request by stating that the man was a suspect in no fewer than thirty-two murders in the Soviet Union. This claim was made by the head of the Police intelligence unit, who even repeated it on television. In the trial, which ended with Chernoy's full acquittal, the judge asked the police representative if they had looked into the criminal suspicions, including murder, of which they had accused him. No, replied the police representative, they never had. Luckily for him, Chernoy had the money to hire the best, most expensive lawyers in Israel. But what would have happened if he weren't rich? Before he agreed to take the case, one of his lawyers, Yaakov Weinroth, asked me, "Is this Chernoy fellow kosher?"

"I don't think he's one of the 36 Righteous Men," I replied. "I don't think he's a model citizen. But one thing I can say: there is no basis for the crimes in Russia that the Israel Police are accusing him of. As for the rest, I don't know." I could say the same thing with a clean conscience about Lerner. The charges against him in his first trial held no water.

One of the worst distortions in the Israeli legal system is that a defendant's confession is deemed sufficient grounds for conviction. Even in the Soviet Union under Stalin, at least according to the letter of the law, a defendant's confession did not constitute grounds for conviction without corroborating evidence of his guilt. The Soviets violated their own laws, but it never occurred to them to phrase the law in an unjust way, as in the State of Israel. In democratic Israel, if the police can get the suspect to confess—using blows, torture, or psychological pressure, they can end their investigation right there. And most Israeli judges accept this.

The same injustices perpetrated upon the Jews of the former Soviet Union were later wreaked on others, using the same method. In fact, it all started a long time ago. The stigmatization began the moment the Israeli public decided to stay mum about the discrimination and prejudices towards the Arabs, and continued with its apathy towards, or even applause for infringements of the law directed against Russian and Ethiopian *olim*. No one should be surprised if the legal system turns against veteran Israelis, the salt of the earth. But there is one difference: Those people have power and influence, whereas *olim* do not. One example is the case of Avigdor Kahalani. Kahalani (who had been the Minister of Internal Security) and several police officers were accused of the same crime. They were all offered a plea bargain, but Kahalani was made of tougher material. It was no accident that he won the Medal of Valor for his conduct in the Yom Kippur War. "I will not surrender," he said. "I will not be broken, I will sell my house, but I will not accept a plea bargain." The result is that he was acquitted, whereas the others, having accepted plea bargains, were convicted of the same crime. They were weaker and lacked courage, and the system broke them. Does that mean that to stand against the Israeli justice you have to be either extremely wealthy or a war hero? That is what I have to say about the Israeli system of justice today.

The Israel Police keep reviving their tales of the Russian mafia and Russian crime. The Anti-Money Laundering unit staged a highly-publicized raid on the Bank Hapoalim branch on Hayarkon Street in Tel Aviv. Years passed and nothing came of it, except that a few dozen Jews originally from Russia paid civil penalties to avoid criminal charges. What did the police do? They arrested people or questioned them after warning them that they were suspects. What was the basis of their suspicions? Nothing more than the account holder's Russian or other post-Soviet origins. The money transferred to his account by a new *oleh* or Russian tourist had turned him into a suspect. Suspects were made of people whose only "crime" was to be so stupid as to deposit money in an Israeli bank. And then they were threatened—pay a civil penalty (it's called "ransom" in Hebrew!) and we'll close the file; otherwise we'll launch a full-scale investigation. And how did the police investigate? They sent letters to police forces all over world: "We are investigating Joe Shmo on suspicion of membership in the mafia, drug trafficking, white slavery, running a protection racket, or murder"—or whatever else they could think up. "Do you have documents about that?" What were the police in other countries supposed to think about this? If the Israel Police write such things about some Jew, they assume there's something to it, and before you know it, the files of every police force in the world contain a mark against the man. What businessman would want this? So people paid; I know they paid. They paid whatever they had to, and then took the rest of their money and hightailed it out of Israel. An indictment was filed against Arkady Gaydamak, but his is a completely different story. If this isn't an act of government-sponsored extortion, what is?

The International Crime Unit, which swallowed up the Serious Crimes Unit, numbers almost a hundred persons, including dozens of senior officers—even though the police are supposedly collapsing due to a shortage of manpower. Tens of millions of shekels were spent on wiretapping, and the unit produced absolutely nothing. It found nothing serious or substantial, no case that justified its existence and the horrific waste of money by the police over a period of fifteen years. There is no Russian crime in Israel. There are a few *olim* who have found their way into the Israeli underworld, and the police have not managed to deal with them, whether in Netanya, Ashqelon, or Ashdod. There is no Russian mafia in Israel. There is a mafia in Russia, but it has nothing to do with Israel. It is all an invention of the Israel Police.

I was involved in one case that illustrates just how serious the police are about this matter. A Russian police officer with a rank equivalent to Chief Superintendent in the Israel Police had served for many years as the head of the Serious Crime Unit in a large Russian city, receiving many citations for his war on crime. He solved difficult and complex cases, notably those related to organized crime, murder, and drug trafficking. He is a man with vast experience. He also wrote several books on the topic. The entire Israel Police force doesn't have one percent of his professional experience and knowledge, particularly with regard to Russian crime. He came to me accompanied by the

Israel Police representative in Moscow. During the conversation, he told me that he had received an offer of a senior position with the Israel Police if he made *aliyah*. I asked who had made him that promise, and he said the head of the Unit for International Crime, who had met with him. I told him that although I didn't want to say too much, I would never rely on a promise by anyone in the police.

But the man told me innocently, "It was a general from the Israel Police who made the promise."

"Do as you wish. But I've said my piece."

The man told me that he wasn't even sure he'd be allowed to leave Russia, because he was a senior police officer. I agreed that this might be the case, so we settled that he would bring his whole family to Israel as tourists and then change his status here, as many others did. The man came to Israel. He contacted us as usual and we confirmed his eligibility for *oleh* status to the Interior Ministry. But more than six months passed, and the Interior Ministry refused to grant him *oleh* status. The director of the Population Administration (whom we've met before) simply ignored all our inquiries concerning him. In fact, they only got her back up. There was no reason to delay the process other than sheer malevolence. The man could not receive medical care when his son was sick. He couldn't even buy medication from the HMO. His children couldn't be enrolled in school. And what was he living on for more than six months? After all, he couldn't work. He went to the police and got the standard response: "We can't hire you."

I tried to intervene, but it was no use. I went to Sharansky, and he, too, tried to resolve the matter. In the end, the head of the Human Resources Branch of the police decided that the man was too old to be hired. The police, who hadn't the foggiest idea of what Russian crime was or how to investigate it, refused to employ this man. Instead, they simply abused him. First, they seduced him with empty promises—but in Israel, no government official or agency takes responsibility for its promises. Not only prime ministers, ministers, other politicians, and generals, but police generals as well. The Interior Ministry, too, mistreated him for more than six months, until after all his travails, he was reduced to near starvation. We spent a good deal of time and effort finding him a job, at a much lower level in the system. But what comparison can there be between an Israeli chief superintendent, who has barely completed one or two advanced courses, and this man, a graduate of the Soviet Police Academy, with a university education, a law degree, and a diploma from an advanced police academy? His job in Israel did not make use of even one percent of his skills, knowledge, and experience. And this after all the screaming about the strategic threat to the country posed by the Russian mafia and Russian crime.

The police and the Interior Ministry, in collaboration with others, introduced a regulation requiring *olim* to prove that they don't have a criminal record. What is a criminal record? According to Soviet statistics that were once submitted to the Politburo, five percent of all *olim* to Israel had criminal records—mainly for economic offenses. You have to understand Soviet society and how the Soviet economy worked to know what this means. Israel never checked into the criminal past of immigrants who came in mass waves of *aliyah* for one simple reason: The conditions in which Jews lived abroad are not necessarily those in Israel, particularly when we are talking about totalitarian regimes with an anti-Semitic atmosphere or policy. In fact, the vast majority of criminals in Israel fell into crime only after they arrived. There have never been as many Jewish criminals as there are in the Jewish State, which is the most prolific producer and supplier of them in the world. The Israeli mafia, with its various branches, is a well-known brand in the criminal underworld of every continent. But to annoy hundreds of thousands of people just to uncover one person with a formal criminal past—that is true Zionism! Lest we forget, the legal system in the Soviet Union was as warped as could be, with an anti-Semitic police and many judges with anti-Semitic prejudices. You must not assume that a Jew who was found guilty was convicted in a fair trial and was really a criminal. Sometimes yes, sometimes no. Before the 1990s, there was never a problem with *olim* who had a criminal record. They made no contribution to the Israeli world of crime, which swelled only thanks to "Made in Israel" criminals. People who use the excuse of Russian crime are just looking for a reason to restrict *aliyah.*

In a session of the Knesset Aliyah and Absorption Committee, the Minister of Internal Security said that he wanted more stringent investigations of immigrants' criminal pasts, the way the Americans do it, and the Justice Ministry representatives supported his request. I responded with my usual bluntness. "You should be ashamed of yourselves," I scolded them. "If you don't understand that we are a country of *aliyah* and you treat Jews like the United States treats immigrants from Latin America or Asia, you have no clue what you're doing and aren't worthy of being involved in it. As long as I am in this job, I won't let you do it." I won.

I remember one case when I intervened with Sharansky and asked him to approve the *aliyah* of the wife of a young Israeli who had gone to St. Petersburg and married there. My appeal worked and her *aliyah* was approved, but the matter dragged on for over a year, until the young woman was already in her ninth month of pregnancy. One day, she called me crying. "I was at the Interior Ministry and the clerk told me with a sadistic smile, "Great, you've been approved. Now we just have to wait for you to bring a certificate from the St. Petersburg police that you're not a criminal." The girl was all of nineteen years old. If this isn't criminal abuse, what is?

Chapter 49

It is a Foreign Ministry tradition, going back to the 1950s and 1960s, to oppose Nativ activities. Foreign Ministry personnel were always scheming against the rival organization, except for a short period when Golda Meir was Foreign Minister. There were objective reasons for this. Nativ worked outside Israel. It expressed and implemented the national interests of the State of Israel concerning Jews and *aliyah*. For the professionals at the Foreign Ministry, the essence of their activity is Israel's relations with other countries. Some of them come down with a typical Israeli syndrome, which strikes *olim*, too: The very fact of being Israeli allows them, consciously or unconsciously, to let go of their Jewish identity. They are ashamed to be seen as Jews by Gentiles. Abroad, they are Israelis, not Jews, perhaps with the exception of the United States, because of the special status of American Jewry. It is important for them to be perceived on the same footing as the French, the Americans, and the Italians, and to be distinguished from the Jews who live in those countries, with their Diaspora mentality that makes them inferior to Israelis.

Nonetheless, national priorities frequently determined that dealing with Jews and Jewish *aliyah* was more important than formal relations with any country. Even before my time, Nativ operatives frequently had more appropriate skills and abilities for working in certain countries than did Foreign Service officers. This was the case in Romania or Tito's Yugoslavia, for example. The Eastern European countries where Nativ worked were less attractive than the countries of the West, in terms of living conditions, salaries, and status. So there was less demand among Foreign Ministry personnel to serve—and when demand falls, so does quality. The skills of Nativ staff who worked in those countries were on a different level. Many of them had been born in those countries and were fluent in the language and culture. The nature of Nativ's activities was different, too. Nativ agents had operational goals; they were there to get things done. They frequently shook up the complacency of the Foreign Ministry and moved the Jewish issue to the forefront much more than professional Israeli diplomats thought was appropriate. And they often found themselves in conflict with various government representatives in the countries where they served.

Nativ's activities in the West focused on encouraging the campaign on behalf of the struggle of Soviet Jewry to make *aliyah*. Some individuals who represented Nativ in the West turned into first-rate diplomats and ambassadors, like Meir Rosenne, who later served as ambassador to France and the United States, Ephraim Tari, who served in Argentina, and others. The Foreign Ministry claimed that Nativ was meddling in other country's internal affairs and creating friction between those countries and the Soviet Union and Communist bloc. They also grumbled about why Embassy personnel who were Nativ operatives had to participate in this work.

In 1974, the Nixon Administration was strongly opposed to the Jackson-Vanik Amendment that linked the issue of human rights and emigration from the Soviet Union to the trade agreements between the two superpowers. But the Israeli Foreign Ministry, which many expected to support the amendment, was opposed to it as well. The Israeli ambassador in Washington who worked vigorously to scuttle the amendment was Simcha Dinitz, who later became chairman of the Jewish Agency. On the other hand, former ambassadors in Washington, like Abe Harman and Yitzhak Rabin, did support it.

Nativ operatives were posted to Israeli embassies under diplomatic cover. Although the ambassador was formally responsible for them, he could not interfere in their work. Moreover, throughout Nativ's history there were some classified matters that were concealed from the Foreign Ministry. For Nativ employees, their diplomatic status was just a work tool; but it was a thorn in the side of the Foreign Ministry.

In the 1950s and 1960s, Israeli ambassadors frequently complained about Nativ agents' excessive zeal in Poland, Romania, the Soviet Union, and Hungary. In those years, however, the Prime Ministers always gave Nativ their unwavering support, and this essentially determined how things went. When I joined Nativ, I found serious differences of opinion with the Foreign Ministry. They did not train people to work on Soviet issues and there were almost no immigrants from the Soviet Union within its ranks. So in the mid-1980s when the problems became more relevant and urgent, the Foreign Ministry was left utterly clueless, completely unable to handle the challenge of relations between the Soviet Union and Israel. When we heard what Foreign Ministry personnel who dealt with the Soviet Union had to contribute to our discussions, we didn't know whether to laugh or cry. I have already mentioned that all the Israeli agencies were weak on the Soviet issue, but as compared to Military Intelligence, the Mossad, and particularly the GSS, the Foreign Ministry stood out for its ignorance and amateurism.

The Foreign Ministry waged an undeclared war against Nativ. It endeavored to frustrate every Nativ project or initiative and to restrict or limit Nativ's activities on the ground. Even Zvi Magen, a Nativ man, tried to disavow his affiliation with the organization while he was ambassador to Moscow, acting like "a good Jew" in a hostile environment. He conducted discussions at the Embassy about ways to impose limits on the Nativ agents there, apparently thinking that this would earn him a place in the regular Foreign Ministry hierarchy—but he was, of course, disappointed.

Things got worse when the Foreign Ministry returned to the Soviet Union in 1988. Our agents were like fish in water. By contrast, most of the Foreign Ministry staff assigned to the country didn't know Russian and, at least at first, had no idea where they had landed and what was going on. Nativ field operatives had effective and good relationships with the locals; thanks to our ability to understand the situation and our access, we had earned their respect. The admiration Nativ staffers enjoyed and the status they had attained made the diplomats' blood boil; the more Nativ's activities expanded, the worse the conflict with the Foreign Ministry became. For example, when the Israeli ambassador submitted his credentials in Baku, the capital of Azerbaijan, he preferred to be accompanied to the ceremony not by the Nativ representative, the only other accredited diplomat at the Embassy, but by his local secretary. (The stories about his relationship with this woman are a disgraceful matter best left for another time.)

When I suggested the establishment of Israel Centers in the former Soviet Union, I naturally met with severe resistance from the Jewish Agency—but even before that, I had already experienced it from the Foreign Ministry. Only Rabin's enthusiasm for the idea, and his unambiguous statement that he saw the Israel Centers as the key to building an infrastructure for Israeli activities, forced the Foreign Ministry to "swallow the frog." They had no choice but to cooperate with us. In collaboration with the legal department of the Foreign Ministry, we drew up all the international agreements between the State of Israel and the Soviet successor states, relating both to education and to the Israel Centers. Most of the work was actually done by Nativ staff, with the help of attorneys in the target countries; the Foreign Ministry and its legal counsel provided only retroactive support.

In the mid-1990s, the Foreign Ministry, like all other government ministries, had its budget cut. The bureaucrats decreed that the saving would come from closing the Israel embassies in Belarus and Georgia. I was strongly opposed to this. At a meeting with Foreign Minister

Peres, I argued that both Belarus and the Caucasus had large Jewish populations and it was therefore ill-advised to close the embassies there. The Foreign Ministry dug in its heels and claimed it simply didn't have the money, so I proposed that Nativ fund the embassies. I said that we would send ambassadors, with the approval of the Foreign Ministry, and also carry out all the regular diplomatic and consular functions. Peres told the stunned officials of his ministry that he agreed: Nativ would provide the budget and personnel for the embassies in Belarus and Georgia. I informed Eitan Haber, Rabin's bureau chief, about the decision, so that he could inform the Prime Minister. Haber told me that I was dreaming and that it simply wasn't possible. A few hours later, he called back and apologized. He said that Peres had updated the Prime Minister and the decision accorded with what I had said. The Foreign Ministry bureaucrats soon recovered and managed to find money in their budget to keep the embassies open under their own control. The thought that the arrangement I had proposed would actually be carried out drove them crazy. For me, the main thing was that the embassies continued to function and that we could keep working from them.

One day, Yossi Beilin, speaking for Peres, offered me the job of Israeli ambassador in Russia. I thanked him but declined the offer, because I was not willing to leave my position as director of Nativ, which was much more important to me. When he kept pushing, I told him that I would accept the offer if I could also continue to serve as head of Nativ. Beilin was delighted and told me that he had no problem with the idea. A week later, though, he called back and told me that the arrangement would not be possible, because of the ambassador's diplomatic status and the standard protocols of the Foreign Ministry and international relations. I wasn't too upset.

Back in the early 1990s, I had proposed establishing a single computer database of all *olim*, shared by Nativ and the Interior Ministry, to which the Foreign Ministry and the Israel Police could have access. The goal was to collect all information about *olim* even before their arrival in Israel, to facilitate their absorption. The issue dragged on for years, in part because the Foreign Ministry and Interior Ministry proved incapable of overcoming their own computer problems. I persuaded Sharansky, who was head of the Ministerial Committee on Absorption, to hold a discussion on the matter. The Finance Ministry spared no effort to torpedo the idea, with the usual excuse that there wasn't enough money. Before one of the meetings to discuss the topic, the Foreign Ministry representative told a minister who was a member of the committee that they were opposed to the idea. When the minister asked why, the representative brazenly replied that the shared database would strengthen Nativ's standing—and the Foreign Ministry would not let that happen! At the meeting, the diplomat did not dare repeat this. Instead, he offered a new proposal. The Foreign Ministry had a budget surplus and was willing to fund the establishment of the new database, on one condition—that the right to determine eligibility for *aliyah* be taken away from Nativ and transferred to the Foreign Ministry. I can't deny that this was a creative idea. But was this behavior base, contemptible, an expression of ill will, or just a lack of comprehension? I don't know. The Foreign Ministry has a budget surplus? What is it—a foreign country? According to its warped logic, the Ministry would "buy" the right to undercut another "hostile" organization! A lofty goal, indeed.

Over the years, we encountered even uglier things. One was the case of Reuven Dinal, the Mossad representative in Moscow, who was declared persona non grata by the Russians. The Mossad and Russian intelligence agreed that the affair would not be made public. The Russians had their own reasons for this, but they also did not want to publicly undercut the relations between the two countries. Israel, for its part, also preferred to hush up the matter.

I had known Dinal since the 1980s; we were friends and held each other in high regard. After making *aliyah* from Lithuania in the 1970s, he served as an officer in the IDF. There were negotiations to bring him to Nativ, but the IDF was not willing to release him. Even my attempt to get Ehud Barak involved was fruitless. In the early 1990s, I finally got approval for his transfer to Nativ. One day, Shabtai Shavit, the director of the Mossad, called and asked my opinion of Dinal. He said they were considering his appointment as the Mossad representative in Moscow. I told Shavit that I wanted Dinal for myself, but would bow to the Mossad. It was easier for me to recruit people than it was for the Mossad, which had special requirements. Towards the end of his posting in Moscow, I asked Dinal what he wanted to do when he came back to Israel. He told me that he didn't want to work at the Mossad and didn't want to return to the IDF, but he would be interested in joining Nativ.

"Call me when you get back to Israel," I told him. I was interested in his skills, not his contacts. My contacts in the intelligence agencies of the former Soviet Union were much better than those of the Mossad and the GSS, particularly in the fields that were relevant for Nativ. When Dinal came back from Russia, he began working in Nativ, as per our agreement.

Some Foreign Ministry official, known for his constant unauthorized disclosures to the media, leaked the circumstances of Dinal's leaving Russia and dwelled on the fact that a man expelled from Russia was now working at Nativ. I learned about the leak from journalists. The man's goal was transparent—to damage Nativ. He did not consider whether he would harm Israel's national interests by doing so. The Foreign Ministry didn't care too much about his indiscretion, and the man was later promoted and served as an ambassador. But Nativ's status was not impacted, either. The Russians didn't care whether Reuven Dinal was working for us. They were fairly well acquainted with the organization, and the fact that Dinal had joined our ranks did not detract from their strong admiration for Nativ. But this devious move constituted a crude violation of the agreement between Russian intelligence and the Mossad, and the Russians were livid. Naturally, the relations between the two countries and between their intelligence services took a blow. I issued a clear directive: no sensitive materials were to be transferred through the Foreign Ministry's telecommunications system; they must go only through our separate and classified system, to which the Foreign Ministry had no access.

An even uglier affair connected with Dinal involved a senior Foreign Ministry official. A delegation headed by the police minister of one of the former Soviet republics visited Israel. Dinal was friends with the guests, whom he had met frequently by virtue of his positions at the Mossad and Nativ. When the visiting minister hosted a reception in Jerusalem, he invited several Nativ staffers who were involved in the visit, including Dinal. During the reception, several of the generals in the minister's party told me that a certain woman, a senior diplomat who was also there, had angrily complained that "they had invited to the reception the man who was expelled from Russia as a spy!" As might be expected, the guests, who did not understand such behavior, felt very uncomfortable. When they told me about her remark, I was embarrassed that my country was being represented to foreigners by people like her. I asked them to ignore her comment and did not spare them my opinion of her stupidity. Indeed, Dinal's prestige was unaffected and he continued to be invited to most of the events. Moreover, he was even decorated by the visitors' government for his contribution to the relations between Israel and their country. By the way, that bureaucrat continued to climb in the ranks of the Foreign Ministry and later served as an ambassador.

Chapter 50

On my way home on furlough in 1974, while I was still on active duty after the Yom Kippur War, I passed through Tel Aviv and, as usual, stopped off to say hello to Geula Cohen. I had met Geula through Herzl Amikam—both were veterans of Lehi. As mentioned, Geula Cohen and I shared a strong bond of friendship and esteem.

When I entered Geula's office at Jabotinsky House (Herut and later Likud headquarters), a young woman was sitting there. Judging by her appearance and dress, I concluded that she was a very recent *olah* from the Soviet Union. Geula introduced us: "I'd like you to meet Natasha Stieglitz. She is the fiancée of *aliyah* activist Anatoly Sharansky and is working for his *aliyah*."

That was how I met Avital (as she later Hebraicized her name) and first heard of Anatoly (now Natan) Sharansky. Later, during the course of my work at Nativ, I frequently reviewed our files on Sharansky. The copious and diverse material gave a picture of a very talented young man, a graduate of the best physics academy in the Soviet Union (and one of the best in the world). The Soviet scientific elite taught there: Lev Landau, the Nobel Prize winner in physics; Sergey Korolyov, the father of the Soviet space program; Sergey Sukhoi, the aircraft designer, and others. Most of the institute's graduates were employed in the Soviet defense and military industries, and almost every graduate had the security classification required for his field.

Jewish graduates of the institute who filed *aliyah* applications were rejected automatically, on security grounds. So Sharansky's status as a refusenik seemed perfectly normal.

Here I want to set to rest some of the malevolent rumors that were spread about Sharansky. At Nativ, we had received requests from two different young women, on two different occasions, to send an *aliyah* invitation to "her fiancé" Anatoly Sharansky. But there was no follow-up in either case. We didn't attribute great significance to this, because it was not really unusual. Requests to send out invitations were frequently accompanied by the mention of a close relationship, to expedite processing of the matter or make receiving an exit visa easier. Later, various nasty people tried to turn this into a juicy story and sully Sharansky's reputation. When Stieglitz began her campaign on Sharansky's behalf, we ignored the earlier applications. So far as we were concerned, she was the woman who fought for him. A few Nativ employees who did not look too kindly on Sharansky and what they saw as the excessively vocal struggle on his behalf spread tales, after his *aliyah*, perhaps in the secret hope that his marriage would be exposed as phony. But to their chagrin, and to Natan and Avital Sharansky's good fortune, theirs has been a true and deep marriage, of a kind that many do not merit to experience.

Our conclusion, based on the materials, was that Sharansky was among the several dozen most prominent activists in the Jewish movement, but not one of the top ten at the time. What made him stand out was his close relationship with Andrei Sakharov and his involvement with the dissidents of the Helsinki Watch Group, which was monitoring the Soviets' adherence to the Helsinki Accords on Human Rights. Sharansky became the group's liaison to foreign journalists, probably because his English was better than theirs. And thanks to his contacts with foreign journalists, he also frequently connected them with the Jewish movement.

Nativ and most of the important *aliyah* activists were wary of close collaboration with the dissidents, whose goal was to modify the Soviet regime. Some higher-ups at Nativ did not have a favorable view of Sharansky's involvement with the dissidents, and their attitude towards him was "very cautious," to put it mildly. The Soviet leadership decided to take drastic steps to suppress both the dissident movement and the Zionist movement. There were ample signs that they were planning harsh action, even to the point of putting major aliya activists on trial. An analysis of the material we had accumulated indicated that the main thrust of the KGB's efforts on the Jewish issue was directed against the scientific seminars and ties with the West. The influence on the scientific community and links with scientists abroad seem to have greatly worried the Soviet leadership. In my assessment, they had three main targets for arrest and trial: Prof. Alexander Lerner, the organizer and head of the scientific seminars for the refuseniks, whose name began appearing more and more in the vicious attacks on *aliyah* activists in the Soviet press; Vladimir Slepak, one of leaders of the Jewish activists and a prominent refusenik; and Natan Sharansky. The Soviet propaganda system began preparing public opinion for what was coming, continually hammering on these three names. But suddenly, almost overnight, the references to Lerner and Slepak disappeared. Soon afterwards, Sharansky was arrested, to the accompaniment of raucous publicity. I concluded that, at the last minute, the Soviet leadership had gotten cold feet about a show trial for Lerner, a famous scientist who had international connections and status. Moreover, Lerner's poor health meant that he might die in prison. There were also last-minute questions regarding Slepak, so in the end Sharansky had to bear the full brunt alone.

At the time, Sharansky was sharing an apartment with a Jewish physician, Sanya Lipavsky. Lipavsky's father had gotten mixed up in illegal foreign currency dealings. Under Soviet law, this was a capital offense. Apparently, the KGB pressured Lipavsky and offered him a deal—his father's life in exchange for cooperation. It was a cruel and inhuman choice, and it is hard to blame anyone who fell into this trap. Lipavsky broke. He served the KGB as an informer for years, in various parts of the Soviet Union, exposing mainly economic crimes. Then he was "retrained" and sent to infiltrate groups of *aliyah* activists. Not long before Sharansky's arrest, Lipavsky had invited him to share his apartment, which made it easier for the KGB to gather incriminating evidence about Sharansky's activities. According to Nativ sources, though I'm not sure how accurate they were, the CIA also tried to recruit Sanya Lipavsky.

It was problematic to be too close to Americans, including CIA operatives. Nativ asked every Western intelligence agency to keep away from Jewish activists. From its inception and throughout the years, Nativ received requests from British, other European, and American spy agencies to draw on its sources for their own purposes. We always responded with a categorical no. Moreover, we forcefully demanded that they stay at arm's length and not make contact with or try to recruit Jewish activists. Generally, everyone respected our request, but in the case of Sanya Lipavsky and Sakharov's group, the Americans went too far, due to a lack of discipline, understanding, or caution. The KGB hoped to get Sharansky to confess his crimes in short order and publicly declare his remorse. They thought he would break quickly in prison and that his show trial would resonate loudly. The interrogation team was headed by one of their best men, who had already questioned and extracted confessions and statements of contrition from several prominent dissidents, including Pyotr Yakir and Victor Karsin, but they grossly underestimated Sharansky and his staying power.

Articles full of defamatory statements and self-flagellation were published in all the media carrying Sanya Lipavsky's signature, although they had actually been written by the prosecution in concert with the KGB. Sharansky was arrested. Despite his stalwart resistance to his interrogators, it was decided to continue the efforts to break him. So his trial did not take place until two years after his arrest. It turns out that this young Jew, who looked so small and weak, was much stronger and more resilient than his interrogators had imagined. Every form of pressure they applied (physical pressure was not allowed in such cases) failed. When Natan Sharansky finally stood in the dock, he made a dignified appearance, which also brought honor to the Zionist movement. Sharansky bore no responsibility for the tempest in which he found himself. His emphasis on the Jewish and Zionist aspect of the case, which he did not confound with the dissident movement, was brilliant and proportionate, allowing all those fighting for human rights to stand by his side.

Pressure continued to be exerted on Sharansky in prison as well, both objective and subjective. He conducted himself with dignity. I totally reject the malicious slurs made by various people, including former *aliyah* activists and Prisoners of Zion. I do not want to go into the reasons for this behavior or the psychological problems that motivated them. Based on the information available to us, Sharansky's behavior during his trial and imprisonment was impeccable. But the years in confinement took their toll. I compare what he went through to the experiences of my army friends who were prisoners of war. Whenever I tried to speak with them about their experience, I saw how they closed up, how their expression changed, how the nightmare and terror took control of them. Being a prisoner of war in an Arab country may be more brutal than even a Soviet prison camp, but Sharansky's imprisonment lasted for nine years and was no picnic.

Two factors made the difference in the fight for Sharansky's release: the most important was his wife, Avital, who moved heaven and earth on his behalf. She is truly a woman of valor, who did everything possible and impossible. There was not a stone she left unturned, working obsessively and never allowing anything to deter her. An objective look at the struggle from a broad perspective suggests that the excessive focus and attention on Sharansky may have been ill-advised. Certainly it was not viewed positively by certain other Prisoners of Zion and their loved ones, who saw it as a factor that kept the overall topic of Prisoners of Zion from being presented in a fuller and more appropriate manner. But the shallowness of American public opinion, which does not delve into matters too deeply, turned Sharansky into the ultimate symbol. The awareness of the Jews' suffering and their struggle for *aliyah* was distilled into the persona of one man, and this served the goal very well. I am far from certain that the Americans could have coped with a more complex campaign.

The other decisive factor was the guilt feelings of the American administration, even though it never openly admitted to them. Its officials apparently realized that their incautious behavior was one cause of Sharansky's imprisonment. The United States mobilized on his behalf in an exceptional and extremely effective manner, almost as it would have for an American citizen, and this gave the battle the push it needed to succeed.

Because of certain reservations felt by the Israeli establishment, including Nativ, Israel did not enlist in the struggle for Sharansky at first, or with full force. No organization or agency, certainly not in the government, was willing to work under the baton of a private individual like Avital Sharansky, and there was certainly an objective gap between what she wanted and what the Jewish organizations and Israel felt was appropriate. The Israeli institutions and Jewish organizations saw Sharansky as one Jew in trouble, but not the one and only, as he was for her. Without support from members of Gush Emunim (the group that promoted Jewish settlement in Judea and Samaria), which rallied to help her, it is doubtful whether Avital Sharansky would have achieved her goal. In the end, Nativ and the Jewish establishment were quickly swept up by the tidal wave she generated and began working vigorously on Sharansky's behalf. Aside from the other arguments, they understood that his name carried immense power to persuade many more people to join the campaign. Their efforts, sometimes independent and sometimes in concert with the relentless toil of Avital and her friends, helped achieve the goal. Sharansky was released in a spy swap with the Americans and finally arrived in Israel in February 1986.

Sharansky met several times with Nehemiah Levanon, who tried to explain in his special way what Nativ had done on behalf of his release. Levanon managed to soften Sharansky's opposition to and reservations about the establishment, which he had absorbed right after his *aliyah* from Avital's close circle of friends who had assisted her during the struggle. The tendency not to trust anyone, an understandable legacy of his time in prison, caused Sharansky to rely solely on the small group that had gathered around Avital and to treat everyone else with suspicion. I invited him to Nativ headquarters, where, at his request, I let him look at all the files related to our activities on his behalf. After he read all the files, cables, and reports, he said that he realized that we had been doing much more for him than he had thought. He understood that many things he thought had been independent initiatives had actually been carried out under the auspices of the Israeli government.

We developed a good relationship. He often asked for my advice, not on his political path, but on matters where he thought I had gained knowledge and experience from my work in the Israeli establishment at senior levels. But it didn't go further than that. We never became real friends. We are different people with different lives, although we were born in the same country and fought, each in his own way, to make *aliyah*.

When Sharansky established the Zionist Forum, a voluntary organization that received funding from the West, I treated this project as normal and positive. *Aliyah* was going strong and I saw the Forum's assistance to *olim* as a positive development. Before the 1992 elections, Sharansky announced his intention to establish a new party and run for the Knesset. Eduard Kuznetsov, the key figure in the Leningrad plane hijacking in 1970, helped me explain to him that he was making a mistake. It was risky to jump into the waters of electoral politics without serious and thorough preparation. If he didn't win, things would be more difficult for him in future elections and it would also damage the image of *olim* and their ability to realize their political potential. Sharansky took our advice and did not run in 1992. When he did run, four years later, his new party "Yisrael ba'Aliyah" won seven seats in the Knesset.

When we met at his initiative right after the 1996 elections, one of the things I told him was that he should appoint talented *olim* to key positions, to demonstrate both to the *olim* and to the Israeli public at large that the *aliyah* had brought gifted, accomplished people to Israel, who were well qualified to run the country. I advised that he look beyond the ranks of his party to the entire Russian-speaking community. One person I recommended was Robert Singer, who was then head of one of Nativ's units. Singer, who wasn't yet 40, was a lieutenant colonel in the reserves. After serving as chief education officer of a regional command, he set up the Nativ education and public information system in the former Soviet Union. Later Singer was posted as our top emissary in the United States, where he gained experience working with the most important American institutions, both government and Jewish. I recommended him as director general of Sharansky's ministry, head of the Export Institute, or something along those lines. By way of example, I cited Ariel Sharon's appointment of Yossi Ginosar, a former senior official in the GSS, as director general of the Export Institute.

Sharansky showed no enthusiasm for the idea. He preferred to give jobs to Yisrael ba'Aliyah activists or to people who were close to him and whom he trusted, most of whom had stood at Avital's side during the long years of her struggle, some of them members of Gush Emunim. Most of his appointees, both in the party and in government positions, were failures, and this was no surprise. Sharansky was never an organization man or administrator and had never held a management position or even a steady job (though that, of course, was through no fault of his own). His conceptual world was rather simplistic, shaped by the Soviet reality and prison. He had a basic fear of contact with people and preferred to run things through a few loyal aides. Decision-making was not his forte. The adulation he encountered when he made aliya and his status as a hero had set his head spinning, and he began to believe in his own genius and universal skills, which unfortunately he did not have.

I did not look kindly on Sharansky's hesitation to deal with the real problems of *olim*. When he served as Minister of the Interior, the deterioration of the ministry's attitude towards *olim* caused me to vent my wrath in the media. I said that the Ministry had erected more obstacles for *olim* than the Soviet emigration offices ever had. In 1998, when the Knesset Foreign Affairs and Defense Committee and the Knesset State Control Committee held a joint session to discuss the State Controller's report on Nativ, Sharansky arrived thoroughly unprepared, without a clue about the report or what was to be discussed. I had sent him our point-by-point response to the State Controller's report well in advance, but he hardly mentioned the report during the session. At one point he mumbled, by way of excuse, "I didn't know that this was the topic of discussion—nobody told me. I had prepared for a different discussion."

I wrote a scathing letter to Binyamin Netanyahu about this fiasco, and an even more caustic letter to Sharansky. It has never been published and I intend for it to remain confidential. I will say only that I accused him of betraying the principles he stood for, of turning his back on the struggle for *olim* rights and for *aliyah*. I told him that what could be forgiven to Netanyahu, as a stranger to the issue, could not be forgiven to Natan Sharansky, who had become the symbol of Russian Jewry's battle for its rights. Sharansky never answered me. Apparently he had nothing to say for himself and was unwilling or incapable of confronting me on this issue.

I think that Sharansky did himself an injustice and displayed traits that are not appropriate for a political leader. This was also the reason for the swift downfall and fragmentation of his party before the 2006 elections and for his descent from the political stage. It pains me that Sharansky's political career ended in this fashion. Perhaps he should have assessed his true abilities more accurately, been more honest with himself, and not been swept away by the flattery of those close to him, who exploited him in a fairly cynical way in pursuit of their own goals. Despite his caution, he frequently failed in his judgement of people.

One example of how he was tripped up by his inner circle came on his visit to Dniepropetrovsk. Sharansky phoned me one day and asked if we could meet. He told me that he was going to Ukraine on an urgent matter. It turned out that he had decided to accept Lev Leviev's request to attend the inauguration of the new Chabad school in Dniepropetrovsk. For Leviev, who was then in the midst of efforts to fortify his position in Ukraine, it was important that an Israeli cabinet minister, and especially Sharansky, be present at the opening of a school affiliated with his network. The importance of the gesture went beyond the status of the new school, because he was then at loggerheads with other Jewish players in Ukraine and a minister's presence at the event would bolster his position. I asked Sharansky whether he was also visiting Kiev, and he replied that he would go only to Dniepropetrovsk. I explained that the Ukrainians would be insulted, and rightly so, if he, an Israeli minister, and a Ukrainian by birth, no less, failed to hold meetings with senior officials while he was in the country. Sharansky's answer was that Leviev was flying him in his private plane to Dniepropetrovsk and back. I warned him not to fly on an Israeli businessman's private plane. I suggested that he take a commercial flight and be sure to meet with representatives of the government in Kiev. I was happy that he took my advice.

A curious incident related to Sharansky was his KGB file. During a reception for Ariel Sharon, who was then Foreign Minister, I reached an agreement with Vladimir Putin, then head of the Federal Security Service (FSB), who was also there, about the technicalities of releasing these documents to Sharansky. Sharansky came to Moscow and we met with the senior echelons of the FSB. It wasn't the first time I had sat with the FSB director and his generals. Putin introduced his people, and Sharansky introduced his entourage. When he got to me, he didn't quite know how to introduce me or what to say. One of the generals sitting next to Putin said with a smile that there was no need to introduce Yasha Kedmi, whom they knew very well. We all smiled and got down to business.

We adjourned our meeting to the old KGB building, which was infamous throughout the world. Eleven cartons of documents related to Sharansky's trial were brought into the conference room. Sharansky thought that he was going to receive all his KGB files. I explained to him that there was no chance of receiving the files on KGB operations, with all their information about him—all the documents, all the reports, all the surveillance records, all the assessments about him, and so forth. No, he would be allowed to see only the legal file, which contained only documents relevant to his interrogation and trial. (The difference was that the interrogator was a KGB man rather than a police officer.)

Sharansky and his staff reviewed the index of every file and they noted the documents they were interested in receiving. He only had a few hours to get through the lot. I reviewed the index list of every file before them and saw that one file was of particular interest. I didn't say anything about it to anyone, but added its number to the list of documents I wanted to see. Then I gave it to the KGB general who was supposed to carry out our requests. He looked at the list and I saw him blanch. Quivering with emotion, he asked how that file had reached us. I said we had received it with all the other files. He looked straight at me and said we weren't allowed to see the file in question; there must have been a mistake. And then, in a trembling voice, unsure of himself, he asked me to give him the copy, too, of the list of documents that we had requested. I smiled and gave him the list. I told him that when I saw the file and its contents, I thought that they must be crazy to reveal it to us. I added that I wouldn't tell anybody about the slip. I saw relief wash over him. He had literally been sweating in fright at the thought of what would have happened had his superiors discovered that he had made such a grievous mistake. In the end, we completed our review and gave the FSB the list of the documents we wanted.

I could not suppress my excitement—and I'm certain that Sharansky and the others couldn't either—as we walked through the hallways and cellars of the old KGB building, with its hair-raising history. We stood in the office of the former KGB director and took pictures. The FSB man offered to take my picture sitting in the chair that had been used by Andropov when he ran the KGB. I declined and said that, in my opinion, sitting in Andropov's chair would be in bad taste.

The end of the affair was also interesting. It turned out that the FSB did not own a photocopier that could handle such a large stack of documents. I found money outside Nativ's budget and we acquired a copy machine and copy paper for them. This was my second "contribution" to the FSB, after the handcuffs of the plane hijackers. This time, though, I don't think they put up a plaque that the equipment had been donated by Nativ.

When we received the copies, we forwarded them to Sharansky. Because the material was given to the Israeli government, and its acquisition was paid for by the Israeli government, I am sure that one day, after Sharansky copies what he needs, it will find a permanent home in one of the relevant archives in Israel.

Chapter 51

After Rabin's assassination, the situation changed drastically. When Peres served as Foreign Minister in Rabin's government, he was often depressed, if I may put it that way. I remember an incident during his visit to one of the Asian republics, in which I was included. One morning when I left the guesthouse, I bumped into Peres, who taking a walk, and he asked me to keep him company. I joined him and he walked in silence. Suddenly he said, "Nu, what's left in life for me? To travel to all these Third World countries and tell them stories." He said this quietly, with sadness and pain, and a twinge of anger. I tried to reassure him that not everything was over and that the situation was not so bad, but inside I agreed with him. Before the assassination, he had almost made his peace with the fact that Rabin was Prime Minister and was running the country. Even though he saw that he was far from achieving his life's ambition and had apparently lost all hope of returning to the premiership, at least he was Foreign Minister. He was stunned by Rabin's assassination, both the murder itself and the way in which he returned to the Prime Minister's Office.

Being Prime Minister brought some of Shimon Peres's less attractive qualities to the surface. He was a weak Prime Minister. Mainly he suffered from an inner debility, as though he no longer believed in his abilities, and then suddenly the position he had yearned for so deeply was thrust on him without warning. Evidently, it was hard for him to make peace with the fact that he had to prove he was worthy of filling Yitzhak Rabin's shoes. Because he always suspected that everyone was looking at him as an accidental prime minister, it was very important for him to win people's admiration and then be elected on his own merits. His inner sense and the feeling in the Labor Party added to the pressure he felt, and pressure is not a good advisor. Because of the stress, Peres made several decisions that determined his fate—first and foremost, not advancing the date of the elections. He did not call a snap election, which he would have won, because he was concerned that a victory so soon after Rabin's assassination would be attributed to his predecessor's giant shadow. He was certain that as soon as it became clear that he was Prime Minister and he would do the job well, everyone would realize that he was the best person for the position. Peres's self-appraisal always exceeded his actual skills and abilities. In a number of areas, his abilities were truly exceptional, but overall they were poorer than his self-estimation and much poorer than others' assessment of him. People don't know how to judge him. They exaggerate in both the positive and negative direction, and this explains why their image of Peres was generally wrong.

Peres called elections for May 1996, about six months earlier than the latest date provided by law, and lost the premiership to Binyamin Netanyahu (it was the first time that direct election of the Prime Minister was in force). I am far from certain that Rabin would have defeated Netanyahu, had he not been murdered. The negative dynamic in the public was gaining rapid momentum, and every additional month was eroding the luster of Rabin's government. The public was looking for an alternative, and the only serious alternative was Netanyahu. Peres didn't take this trend into consideration and assumed that he would overcome it and win: After all, he was Shimon Peres. That is why he lost the election. As usual, he looked for excuses and people to blame. He has always looked for someone to blame for his failures; but he himself is never responsible and never guilty. This kept him from making an accurate, deep, and true assessment of the reasons for the failure and his mistakes and errors, so as not to repeat them.

His short period as Prime Minister between Rabin's assassination and his election defeat was not a good time for us at Nativ. We had been spoiled by Rabin's unqualified support. Despite Peres's strongly positive attitude towards *aliyah* from the Soviet Union and the importance he attributed to it, he disappointed us as Prime Minister. Nevertheless, I did develop a good working relationship with Peres during the months I worked under him. There was no need to explain what *aliyah* was or why it is important. But I did not have the close bond I had had with Rabin—he didn't have the same sharpness or brilliance, the same ability to pay attention, the same understanding of the broad diversity of problems we had to deal with, or the same loyalty, trust, and openness.

Chapter 52

In 1991, when David Bartov was still director of Nativ, he told me that the State Comptroller wanted to perform a review of Nativ's activities, but he had asked the Comptroller to postpone it. About a year later, by which time I was director of the organization, the State Comptroller's office contacted me and repeated its request to carry out an audit. I recommended that they wait for Yitzhak Hofi to complete his study of the agency and for Prime Minister Rabin to decide on implementing his recommendations regarding the nature and form of the organization, and they agreed.

When Rabin adopted Hofi's report, I raised the issue of the failure to formalize the definition of Nativ's brief, a situation that had lasted for years. His response was short and to the point. "You focus on your professional work, and leave the formal side to me." I trusted him; of course I couldn't know that he would not be there to handle things when problems arose. To conduct its review, the State Comptroller's Office assigned a reserve lieutenant colonel from Military Intelligence to spend eighteen months looking over our shoulders. During his military service, he had never handled any issues related to the Soviet Union and had focused solely on the Mediterranean arena. What was more curious, he never sat with me, the director of the organization, during the entire review—not even once—nor did he ask me any questions or submit any requests for clarification, aside from asking to see an occasional document. In December 1995, we received a draft of the State Comptroller's report for our comments. I have no intention of going into detail about the report, but must address the most important points because of its serious impact on subsequent developments.

When I read the draft report, I was shocked by the large number of mistakes, inaccuracies, and misunderstandings. Assuming that the auditors had not understood certain matters, we drew up comments and responses, supported by documents, for each section of the report and forwarded them to the State Comptroller's Office. It was not until March 1998, more than four years after the period under review, that the final report was completed. When we received it, we saw that the State Comptroller had almost completely ignored our responses and explanations, as well as the documents we had submitted. Moreover, when he did refer to them, the contents of the documents were frequently twisted and distorted, which I must assume was done deliberately. To the best of my judgment, it was an unprofessional, careless, utterly tendentious report, littered with mistakes and falsifications.

The main body of the report dealt with Nativ's purview and official status. It was asserted that most of the organization's activities were undertaken without proper authorization. The authors played what I saw as a filthy trick. They started from the thesis that Hofi's recommendations, which were the formal basis for our work, had never been approved. If they were uncertain about what had and had not been approved, they could have contacted Hofi himself or the Prime Minister's Office and asked for clarifications on this point. But they did not do so, and not by accident. As the formal basis of their report, they took the incomplete minutes of the discussion of Hofi's recommendations in the Prime Minister's Office. Because the minutes were taken by an aide to the director general of the Prime Minister's Office, they included only matters for which his boss was responsible, in accordance with the Prime Minister's decision.

Moreover, they ignored all the definitions and goals of the organization, as stipulated from the time of David Ben-Gurion through the Dekel and Hofi committees.

They concocted a vague definition, which was unprofessional, simplistic to the point of being primitive, and completely meaningless: Nativ's mission was limited to "winning hearts." I have no clue what "winning hearts" means; I am not an expert in hearts and I don't think that anybody can understand this nonsense. Moreover, these people, who had no clue where the Soviet Union was (except perhaps what they remembered from geography class) or what was going on there, who knew nothing about its problems, *aliyah*, or the Jewish people, arrogated to themselves the right to define the organization and its goals. The State Comptroller is supposed to examine procedures and the way they are implemented, not invent them. The State Comptroller may prefer one of several definitions provided by authorized agents, but he may not write them himself. In our case, though, he decided that anything that did not accord with his vague definitions was irregular and illegal. It was clear from the very first pages of the report that the reviewers' work had been superficial, biased, and slipshod. For instance, the report began by asserting that Nativ had never been audited by the State Comptroller. The fact was that over a period of nineteen years, between 1964 and 1983, the State Comptroller had audited Nativ six times. But the current staff in that office, who wrote or approved the report, failed to read or were unaware of the reports published by their predecessors. After we pointed this out to them in our responses to the draft report and gave them copies, they were forced to admit their error, but did not modify the statement.

I should note that at the joint hearing held by the Knesset Foreign Affairs and Defense Committee and the State Control Committee, the representatives of the Comptroller's Office explicitly stated that they had nothing to say against Nativ staffers with regard to ethical behavior and there wasn't the slightest suspicion of embezzlement, diversion of funds for personal needs, or corruption. They kept referring to uses of funds that were not in accordance with the agency's approved goals, and defined these expenditures as wasteful. In addition to gross errors in accounting, the report included items that simply begged belief. For example, the State Comptroller multiplied a single one-time expenditure in one month of a certain project by thirty-six months and asserted that he had found expenditures for three years. In this way, he arrived at an incredible figure and did not even bother to check whether this money had actually been spent. Had he done so, he would have discovered that it hadn't. After all, you can't spend money without leaving a trail.

Another nonsensical assertion about expenditures related to a certain periodical, the *Voice of the War Invalids*. An Israeli organization, the Invalids of the War against the Nazis in Eastern Europe, published a magazine in Russian. Because we felt it was important to distribute the publication to Jews in the former Soviet Union, where the issue of war veterans was very prominent and there was strong demand for the magazine, we purchased a large number of copies. The State Comptroller's Office alleged that the purchase was in violation of the regulations, because we had not published a request for bids. You would have thought that Israel was blessed with five or six organizations of invalids of the war against the Nazis in Eastern Europe and that each of them published a Russian-language periodical. Another claim about the same magazine was equally ludicrous: that our bulk purchase of the magazine was meant as thinly-veiled support for the organization, a subsidy that had not been approved in accordance with the relevant government-ratified procedures, and should be seen as exceeding our authority, a waste of money, and so forth. Since when do subscriptions to the periodical published by some institution constitute a subsidy? But this assertion was just one in a pile of similar claims about Nativ's alleged waste of funds, acts without proper authorization, and deviations from procedures.

I will offer only two more examples of the critical faculties and judgment of the people who wrote and approved the report. In the chapter on Nativ's exercise of consular functions, they wrote—and the Controller herself, Miriam Ben-Porat, a retired Supreme Court Justice, put her name to the document and this allegation: "The consular function of issuing *aliyah* visas should be revoked from Nativ, because since 1989, the issuing of visas is no longer a classified activity." How can this be said, even in jest? What did these people think? That before 1989, Nativ used all kinds of evasive maneuvers to locate poor Jews and hand them *aliyah* visas in secret, so that the authorities and KGB would be caught unaware? That until 1989, Nativ had issued *aliyah* visas clandestinely, and then suddenly began to do so above board?! But the pinnacle was the section that stated that Nativ's failure to maintain the volume of *aliyah* of 1990–1991 in 1992 and 1993 should be seen as a proof of its lack of professionalism and incompetence. In other words, Nativ was blamed for the decrease in the number of *olim* after the peak in 1990–1991! Not only were these charges an insult to intelligence, they are a mockery of the very concept of official audits.

When the Knesset committees held their hearing to discuss the report, Miriam Ben-Porat exploded: How dare we try to contradict every point in her report?! In response, I told her that we rejected it and all its allegations, as well as its strident style. For us, the bombastic, almost hysterical headlines, which were characteristic of Ben-Porat's term as State Comptroller, were unacceptable and inappropriate. I said that foolishness and nonsense written on the State Comptroller's letterhead and signed by her—even if she was a former Supreme Court justice—remained foolishness and nonsense.

In December 1995, a draft of the report was submitted to the Prime Minister's Office and other relevant agencies. Two days after we received their draft, Prime Minister Peres came to speak to our staff in honor of Nativ Day. Before going up on stage, he took me aside and told me that the draft of the report had been leaked to the press and all kinds of things would be published in the newspapers the next day.

"Another war," I told myself. "It's not the first time, and I will fight again."

Zvi Alderoti, a wonderful man who served as director general of the Prime Minister's Office during part of Rabin's term and stayed on the job for a few months under Peres, told me, "Yasha, don't react the way you usually do. People write reports, people read them, and then they move on. Bend a little bit, don't argue, don't resist. It's only a wind, it will pass. The tree that bows when the wind blows straightens up afterwards."

"I can't do that," I replied. "I will not bend and I will say my truth with all my might, no matter what. I will not bend and I will not let these statements go by without a response."

The worse part of this story is that the material was leaked to the press by someone in Peres's bureau. Journalists later told me as much. This certainly would never have been possible when Rabin was Prime Minister—neither the act itself nor certainly the response. The response was basically total silence. Peres gave no backing to Nativ—employees of his own office, his subordinates—and this was an unpleasant surprise for us. The GSS, after two total fiascos—the scandal following the #300 bus affair, and Rabin's assassination—received staunch support from Peres, as an organization. He said that he stood behind the GSS and its employees and would work to correct any mistakes or failures if and when they were revealed. But Nativ as an organization did not receive this show of support, nor did its staff. The Prime Minister simply did not support us, directly or indirectly, in any way. His only move was to convene a committee to look into the situation at Nativ, if and when the State Comptroller's report was published. The bottom line is that it was Yitzhak Rabin's Nativ, not his.

Peres had found it difficult to accept Hofi's recommendations—not so much the content as the fact that they ran counter to his view (and were in accordance with Rabin's). Apparently he could not accept my support of the recommendations that Nativ be subordinated to the Prime Minister and not to Foreign Minister Shimon Peres. Peres was obsessed with hyper-personalizing his job. When he was

Foreign Minister, he was the best Foreign Minister, and everything had to fall under his direction; when he was Prime Minister, it was obvious that everything should be subordinate to the Prime Minister. He took the same approach no matter what ministerial portfolio he held: Peres had to be at the center of attention, of all the work and the decision-making. And so it would be when he was elected president of the State and tried to make it the important position of all, at least in the public arena. Being in the limelight is an obsession with Peres. Everyone around him knew that on every flight, he would announce, "Don't take the seats next to me, I'm going to sit with the journalists"—which he proceeded to do for hours, feeding them juicy stories. In this way he drew them close and won their trust. Most of the journalists, of course, ate this up and repaid him with positive coverage. Peres's narcissistic need for publicity was disproportionate and went beyond all limits of good taste, almost to the point of being pathological.

I tried to counter the Comptroller's report in every way I could. In fact, the only means available was to be truthful in our response to the draft of the document. The Nativ staff did excellent work. Our response drew on documents and facts to refute almost every charge made against us. I expected that the discussion of the report by the two Knesset committees would treat it seriously. Once again I was deluded. The hearings did not even reach the level of a joke. Most of the committee members did not even show up; in fact, not a single one attended all the sessions, except for the chair of the State Control Committee. This was an indication not only of the seriousness with which they took their job, but also and most importantly, of how the country's political elite related to Nativ's reason for existence. In my view, the hearings were slapdash and bordered on irresponsible. I did not know that the sort of superficiality shown by most of those who took part in them was possible, and I was certainly not used to it. One of the most embarrassing performances was by the director general of the Foreign Ministry and his aides. He read from a printed page that contained a list of the incidents where his ministry felt that Nativ's activities had caused damage to the ministry's work. I will address two of them.

The first case involved a Nativ emissary who'd had direct contacts with diplomats stationed in foreign embassies in one of the former Soviet republics. According to the director general of the Foreign Ministry, this was a breach of the correct work procedures and relations between the Israel Embassy and other missions. The director general did not go into detail about either the substance of the contact or the circumstances. I replied from memory, because I knew all the cases by heart. I had investigated each case and each misstep alleged by the Foreign Ministry. The truth was that the Nativ representative, the director of the local Israel Center, had sent an invitation to every embassy in the city where he served, as well as to those cities' authorities and public institutions, to attend an evening marking the anniversary of Yitzhak Rabin's assassination. It goes without saying that the Israel Center was affiliated with the Israel Embassy. The ambassador who complained received advanced notice of the event. How could a Nativ emissary have dishonored the State of Israel and harmed its international relations by inviting people to honor the memory of the assassinated Prime Minister?

The second case was a serious one: a male Nativ staffer slapped a local female employee. He was a placid and disciplined man who had served many years in the GSS as a researcher before being seconded to Nativ. He had indeed slapped the woman. She enjoyed a "special status" with the ambassador, whom she accompanied to diplomatic receptions, official meetings, and every event scheduled by the local Foreign Ministry. I have already related how this ambassador chose her to participate in the ceremony at which he submitted his credentials, in preference to a Nativ employee who held diplomatic status. Once, when the woman was arguing with the Nativ representative, she called him "a filthy kike." The man in question was a native-born Israeli and the son of Holocaust survivors. I investigated the case myself and issued him an extremely stern rebuke. I told him that regardless of the circumstances, he had to control himself. He apologized about the slip. But was the woman fired? No—she kept her job as long as the ambassador served there. It was only when he was called back to Israel that she, too, was dismissed.

All of the director general's complaints were more or less on the same level. He and I had always been on good terms until then and still are today. He was simply parroting materials prepared for him by the Ministry. I was always disappointed, to say the least, by the caliber and quality of these materials, whenever Nativ was involved.

The testimony by the deputy director of the Mossad was no less wretched. She showed up for the hearing totally unprepared, ignorant of even the most basic facts about the relationship between Nativ and the Mossad. To almost every one of my questions, arguments, and counter-arguments she replied, "I don't know," "I didn't know," "I haven't heard," "I'm not familiar with the material." I was embarrassed by this pathetic presentation to a parliamentary committee by the representative of such a respected organization.

Ami Ayalon, the director of the GSS, made some sensible comments in his testimony. "Define the organization however you think right, and we will organize ourselves accordingly and give suitable instructions to the organization," he said. In a discussion of the classified section of the report, the GSS asked me not to raise the only point that contradicted one of their main arguments. The matter was very sensitive and, in fact, it was the GSS men who violated procedures and made a mistake, not us. But I agreed to their request out of concern that the affair would leak out.

In general, there was no substantive discussion about the content of the report or our response to it. Even at the first session, the chairman of the State Control Committee interrupted the discussion every five minutes to ask me what conclusions I would draw to rectify matters. After the second time he did this, I cut him off rather rudely. "Study the matter, listen to the evidence, and only then, at the end of the deliberations, ask your questions. Don't ask me questions without knowing what you're talking about."

Right after the first session, he came out with a bombastic declaration questioning whether there was even any need for Nativ. It was clear that the only thing that interested him was making headlines and exploiting the issue to advance his personal political fortunes. When his statement was published, his friends, both in his own party and other parties, came down hard on him. They explained he was talking about matters he didn't understand and would be well-advised to "climb down from the tree" before he damaged his reputation even more. In subsequent hearings, he sat quietly. Shortly thereafter, when we ran into each other by chance in the Knesset, he apologized in a fashion. "Don't be angry with me. You know, our job is to draw attention. That's why I said what I said." I reassured him that I wasn't angry with him, because I knew what politicians were like.

Prime Minister Netanyahu said what prime ministers have to say: "We will look into the matter, do our homework, draw conclusions, and so forth and so on." Like everyone else, he did not address the content of the report, all the accusations and vilifications and their refutation. I took note of one point in the Prime Minister's remarks: "There is no argument that Yasha and his people may be able to provide superb materials about the former Soviet Union and about Russia. Perhaps even the best materials available in Israel, and not only Israel. But I don't need that. For what I need from Russia and about Russia, the materials I get from the Americans are enough."

This was precisely the essence of our disagreement. Was the State of Israel working, or at least trying to solve and cope with its problems on its own? Or was it enough for us to go to the Americans, for the Americans to solve our problems for us? I categorically rejected the latter approach in every matter, all the more so with regard to *aliyah* from the Soviet Union and relations with countries in the post-Soviet area, and did not agree with him. I told the Prime Minister that the State Comptroller's recommendations about Nativ and its mission had harmed the organization, its goals, and its ability to function, and would continue to do so. I went on to say that if it were accepted, I would quit on the spot. I would not lend either my name or my experience to such an act, which would damage the organization and deprive the Jews and the State of Israel of the capacity that only the organization in its current form could provide.

In response, the Prime Minister, the members of the committee, and even the staff of the State Comptroller's office clarified that they had no intention of forcing me out. Everyone, including the Prime Minister, underscored their hope that I would stay on and continue the work I was doing. The State Comptroller's people insisted that "the report is not aimed against you personally. Wherever it says, 'the director of Nativ,' we mean every director of Nativ, including those who came before you. After all, you're not the one who created this unclear situation."

I recalled these words when Elyakim Rubinstein, then Attorney General, told Finance Ministry officials, "We always viewed the status of the organization and its employees as having the same status as other organizations and their employees. We never imagined that matters were not formally defined. Had we been aware that they weren't, we would have settled the matter." With this, he essentially contradicted everything stated in the State Comptroller's report about Nativ's status—but this was already several years after the report.

In the atmosphere of all-out attack on Nativ during that time, what hurt me the most was the silence of its former directors, Nehemiah Levanon and David Bartov. Neither of them called, came to visit, or even offered a suggestion or help of any kind—neither during the audit itself nor after the draft report was issued. After the Bus 300 affair, after Rabin's assassination, and after the various fiascos of the Mossad, the former heads of the GSS and Mossad turned out to defend their organization and help it through the crisis, probably because they still felt a strong connection. We got through the crisis on our own, without Levanon and Bartov. Ariel Sharon was right when he said, a long time ago, "You will be forgiven for your failures, but you will never be forgiven for your successes."

Chapter 53

Nativ's problems with the Finance Ministry got worse when David Brodet resigned as its director general. The ministry bean counters who supervised the finances of other government agencies launched an all-out war against Nativ. They had grown used to running the country. They were young and ambitious, with good technical skills they had acquired in their studies and in previous assignments in the ministry. They knew everything. They had no god; nothing was sacred to them. They tended to see the law as an obstacle, although they did try to work within its bounds. There were many examples of this, such as a dispute that embroiled the Civil Service Commission, a Nativ staff member who had formerly worked for it, and the Finance Ministry. To settle some mysterious score with the Nativ employee, the Commission attempted to downgrade her pension rights. As head of the organization, I attended a number of meetings with representatives of the Commission and the Finance Ministry. At one session, a Finance Ministry bureaucrat proposed a procedure that the ministry's legal advisor opposed, out of concern that it would not stand up to legal review and would be overturned by the courts. The response of a senior Finance Ministry official stunned me, though it certainly epitomized the ministry's theory and ethical principles: "We are saving the country's money, so we can do whatever we want."

They were fighting a Holy War against everyone, so everything was permitted them.

I recall a discussion by the Knesset Aliyah and Absorption Committee about compensation for Prisoners of Zion who had made *aliyah* and found themselves in financial straits. The Finance Ministry was opposed, of course. Their representative at the hearing suggested that any moneys paid them be deducted from their National Insurance Institute allowance for senior citizens. I couldn't hold back and yelled at her that perhaps they should start by denying National Insurance allowances to the millionaires in Savyon, Kfar Shmaryahu, and other ritzy places who didn't really need them.

Her response again reflected the warped perspective of the people at the Finance Ministry. "What are you talking about?" she retorted. "Do you know how much those people have contributed to the country?" She was talking about the millionaires, many of whom had grown rich at the expense of the country, and not, God forbid, about the Prisoners of Zion. Those who had suffered and spent years in prison to fight for their country, some who had lost not only years of their lives but also their health, were seen by the Finance Ministry as a burden and a nuisance.

In the deliberations about the budget sometime in the mid-1990s, one Finance Ministry official said there was no need for Nativ and they didn't care what the government decided. The bureaucrats at the Finance Ministry tried to take advantage of the draft State Comptroller's report on Nativ, many of whose distortions and falsehoods had originated with them. In our discussions with Nir Gilad, the Accountant General, we laid out our work program, needs, and the entire situation. Gilad listened and asked questions. After two hours, when we finally reached the question of costs and the budget, he said quietly, with a sadistic smile, "We need to make cuts in the Intelligence community. We've decided that the entire cut will come from Nativ and will not be divided up among the other agencies. This has been approved by the Prime Minister."

He was talking about nearly half of Nativ's budget at that time.

"Why didn't you start by saying that?" I asked him. "Why have we been sitting here for two hours? If that's the situation, we have nothing to talk about. These cuts are unacceptable to me. I'll see you at the Prime Minister's office."

I went straight to the Prime Minister's bureau and asked the economic advisor, military secretary, and director general of his office whether the Prime Minister had agreed to cut Nativ's budget. Everyone was taken aback and said that the matter had never been discussed, let alone agreed upon.

By chance, a meeting about the Jewish Agency had been scheduled for that same hour in the Prime Minister's Office, and Finance Minister Avraham Shochat and Nir Gilad were going to be there. Before the meeting, I went to the Prime Minister and asked whether he had decided on any cut in Nativ's budget. Peres responded with an absolute no. Next I asked whether the work plan he had approved and the budget based on it were still valid. He confirmed that there had been no change. Before the Jewish Agency representatives arrived, I told Shochat, while pointing to Gilad, "Your man is a liar and a fraud. He slandered the Prime Minister, as if he had decided on and approved the cut in Nativ's budget. The Prime Minister says it never happened."

Later that day, in my work meeting with the Prime Minister, I showed him the draft budget and the cuts demanded by the Finance Ministry. I explained that the budget was a function of the work plan, and that cutting the budget would entail dropping programs that he had approved. I asked him directly what activities he was instructing me to cancel or reduce. Peres was not willing to eliminate programs. He worked rapidly to remedy the situation and soon made it clear to the Finance Minister that Nativ's budget would be cut proportionally to the budgets of the other agencies in the intelligence community.

Chapter 54

On May 29, 1996, Binyamin Netanyahu was elected Prime Minister. I was glad he won. I knew Netanyahu, albeit superficially, and had a good opinion of him. My impression was that he was a young, native-born Israeli, the son of an old-time and well-known Revisionist family, dynamic and charismatic, well educated, sharp, intelligent, and eloquent, and an expert in the inner workings of international politics. But when I got to know him when he served as Deputy Foreign Minister (1988–1992), warning lights began flashing for me. His aide, Avigdor Liberman, called and said that Netanyahu wanted to meet with me. Because the door of Foreign Minister David Levy's office was closed to Nativ staffers (we were considered to be Shamir's men—and there was a fierce rivalry between the Foreign Minister and the Prime Minister), I was glad for a meeting with his deputy. At our meeting, Netanyahu asked me a question and I started to answer. I had not got beyond my second sentence when he cut me off and began to explain something to me. The conversation lasted ten minutes, and Netanyahu spoke for five of them. He had no patience to hear a full response to any of his questions, which were fairly superficial to begin with. When I left the meeting, I could not understand why he had called me in. He had demonstrated a shallowness I had not encountered for a long time. I figured that is was probably because he was pressed for time.

Shortly after he became Prime Minister, in 1996, Netanyahu came to an evening reception for Nativ. One of the things I told him was that we had problems with his predecessor, Peres, who did not back us strongly enough. Netanyahu was astonished. "That is unthinkable. The organization must have the Prime Minister's support. The subject is too important, and that won't happen on my watch." I was delighted and trusted him.

I was also glad that Ariel Sharon was given a ministry, despite Liberman's pressure to exclude him. Many saw Netanyahu's failure to include Sharon in his original list of ministers as mean and nasty. Aside from Liberman, I doubt whether anyone contributed more to Netanyahu's victory over Peres than Sharon did. And this was David Levy's finest hour. He demonstrated a nobility that is rare in politics, announcing that he would not join the government if Sharon was not included. At that moment, I was ready to forgive him for everything. He showed his true humanity and loyalty, despite all his past friction with Sharon, and even endangered his political position. Sharon himself would never have done for David Levy—or anyone—even one tenth of what David Levy did for him. In those days, however, I still harbored illusions about Ariel Sharon.

After Netanyahu got into the groove as Prime Minister, though, I saw that nothing was moving. We no longer held work meetings. Throughout Netanyahu's term as Prime Minister, we had no more than one or two such sessions a year. He totally ignored what Nativ was doing. I remember one such meeting, which was attended by representatives of other agencies, where several problems were raised and decisions made. The Prime Minister's military secretary kept the minutes. The next day, when I received the summary of the meeting through internal mail and saw that the conclusions were different from those we had reached, and in some cases the exact opposite, I went straight to the Prime Minister's bureau. I entered the military secretary's office and asked him why his report differed from what had been agreed on. He told me that Netanyahu had changed the conclusions after the meeting was over. I told him that this was impossible. It is the Prime Minister's right to change his mind, but in that case he must hold another meeting and explain his position. The military secretary looked at me sorrowfully and said that this was Netanyahu's style. Another warning lamp lit up for me, one of a series that was to keep blinking from then on.

Chapter 55

In 1997, Ariel Sharon, the Minister of National Infrastructures, asked me to help organize his visit to Russia and invited me to accompany him. He said that the Foreign Ministry was having difficulties organizing the visit and the crucial meetings. I took the matter in hand and got the Russian Jewish Congress and its head, Gusinsky, to do most of the work setting things up. I also included Gusinsky in the agenda. I informed the Prime Minister's bureau of my involvement in the trip and received a note back that I could not accompany Sharon. When I asked why, it was hinted that Liberman had persuaded Netanyahu to keep me at home. In fact, it wasn't really important for me to go with Sharon, because everything was already settled; and I usually did not travel to the former Soviet Union with ministers, except for the Prime Minister and the Foreign Minister. I informed Sharon that I would not be joining his retinue, in keeping with the Prime Minister's instruction, but that everything was arranged and there was no cause for concern. Sharon was livid and contacted Netanyahu, and I received word that I could go after all. Nonetheless, Liberman made sure to call and tell me that I could not participate in any of the meetings on economic matters. I told him that I never attended such meetings. I didn't tell him that I didn't care what he said anyway. After all, the director of Nativ is not subordinate to the director general of the Prime Minister's Office.

Sharon wanted to have a private meeting with Russian Prime Minister Victor Chernomyrdin. Although Chernomyrdin was on vacation, we managed to get him to agree to host Sharon at his summer home in Sochi. He would have his official plane fly us there from Moscow. Because he didn't want Russian Foreign Ministry personnel to take part, Chernomyrdin decided that the Israel Embassy would not be represented either. He also decided that no Russian interpreter would be there and that I would perform that function instead. One doesn't need a particularly vivid imagination to picture the reactions of our ambassador and the Russian Foreign Ministry when they discovered who would and would not be at the meeting. Sharon and Chernomyrdin discussed projects for cooperation, including the supply to Israel of Russian petroleum and natural gas, avenues for economic collaboration, and Russian weapons sales to Syria and Iran. The Russian Prime Minister promised Sharon that Russia would not provide certain weapons and components to either Syria or Iran, as his visitor requested. To the best of my knowledge, Russia has continued to abstain from providing these categories of weapons to these two countries to this day. Aside from the meeting with Chernomyrdin, we arranged other interesting and important appointments for Sharon, including one with the head of Gazprom, in which I was not included.

One day I told Sharon that I would not be joining him for lunch, because I had an important and interesting meeting with some Russian official. My meeting would take place at the same restaurant where he was eating, in his hotel, but at a different table. It was an interesting, frank, and serious encounter. I was impressed by my lunch partner, his earnest attention, and his completely non-Soviet approach to the problems we were discussing. The man's appearance and speech gave away his past affiliation with the Soviet secret services, but I had known about his KGB career even before our lunch. Our conversation covered many topics having to do with the relations between Russia, Israel, and the Middle East and the opportunities for cooperation between our countries. We discussed our mutual interests and the common risks we were facing. Our meeting, which lasted for more than three hours, laid the foundation for good chemistry between us later on. My lunch date that day was Vladimir Putin. I knew him from when he had worked with the mayor of St. Petersburg, Anatoly Sobchak. When we set up Sobchak's visit to Israel, Putin attended the meeting, in his capacity as the person responsible for the city's foreign relations. I knew Sobchak, and I had a few interesting meetings with him. After he was defeated for reelection, Putin refused to work with his successor and moved to Moscow.

While we were planning Sharon's visit, I proposed that he visit a Russian Army unit. I always aspired to build a good relationship between the IDF and the Russian Army. I suggested that he visit the General Staff College and the Tamanskaya armored division, one of the most famous units of the Soviet and then Russian Army, and he agreed. Sharon was strongly impressed by the college, the caliber of its commanders, and its curriculum. It was just as we were about to leave the college en route to the Tamanskaya Division's base that things started going wrong. The entire convoy came to a confused halt. When I asked what the problem was, I was told that no one knew where they were going. Sharon asked the IDF attaché in Russia, who had come along that day, whether he knew—and only then did they find out that the attaché not only didn't know the address, he hadn't even spoken with the division's headquarters to arrange the meeting. He hadn't contacted the college either, and didn't know its address, but that didn't matter because he got there with us in the convoy. Even though I had arranged the two visits through my own connections, I could not understand how an attaché could avoid responsibility for contacting our two destinations. Sharon didn't hide his anger and said that as a retired major general in the IDF, he was affronted by the attaché's negligence, which was unbefitting an officer.

The appointment of IDF attachés to Moscow in those years was one of the major scandals in our relations with Russia. Only the first attaché, Mikhail Stieglitz, was a combat officer, an artillery group commander. He was Avital Sharansky's brother and came to Israel before her, in the early 1970s. Before *aliyah*, he had already graduated university in Moscow and served as an officer in the Red Army. But he was followed in the position by a series of mainly political appointees, such as a lieutenant colonel in the military police, a one-time senior noncom who had been made an officer after completing a special course intended to turn sergeant majors into majors, of the sort that the IDF liked to run from time to time. What could a regimental sergeant major, whose job was to impose discipline in the ranks, possibly know about military affairs, even if he did wear the insignia of a lieutenant colonel? I once met the British naval attaché in Moscow who held the equivalent rank and had commanded a nuclear submarine in the Falklands War. He said that he himself didn't know Russian, but the members of his staff were fluent in it. By contrast, our attaché knew none, and the only person on his staff who did was his secretary, an Israeli woman. How were the Russians supposed to understand these shameful and insulting appointments, other than as displays of Israel's disdain for their country?

I told everyone to follow me and led the convoy to the division's base. Sharon was very impressed with what he saw there as well, but was particularly amazed by the commanders. The division commander, a major general (equivalent to brigadier general in the IDF), was forty-one. Sharon was surprised to learn that this was the second division he had commanded—he had been given his first divisional command at the age of thirty-eight. Sharon said that he had never imagined that the Russian Army had such young generals. The man came from a Siberian village, and Sharon said with pride that he too was a farmer from a village. He was even more impressed by the level of education of the officers he spoke with, and muttered that they had spent half their military service in studies at the highest levels. Like all division commanders in the Russian Army, this man was a graduate of several academies, including the General Staff College.

Sharon spoke about this with envy and expressed his hope that one day, IDF officers too would devote time to serious military studies.

In St. Petersburg, his hosts invited him to tour one of the Czar's palaces outside the city. As usual, we traveled in a convoy with escorts. Later, the hosts laughingly told me what had happened on the way. The team from the Russian Security Service that was escorting us suddenly identified an unknown vehicle that was trailing behind us. They forced it to the side of the road, hauled out its passengers, showed them their Security Service IDs, and demanded that they identify themselves. The travelers were not at all ruffled and calmly pulled out their own Security Services IDs. The official escorts wanted to know what these other operatives were doing behind the convoy when they themselves were providing security for the Israeli minister. The agents from the car that had been pulled over explained that they didn't care about the minister; their man was Yakov Kedmi. Then they told the local squad to continue its assignment of watching the Israeli minister, and they would go on tracking Kedmi.

When we returned to Israel, police investigators looked into the visit. I was called in by the Serious Crimes Unit. I knew the personnel and commanders of the Unit from joint meetings. They questioned me for hours, employing all their best tricks, which I knew very well and sometimes thought were funny—but I didn't react. Why should I insult people who were just doing their job? The interrogators wanted to know who paid for what meals during Sharon's trip, and they were particularly interested in what meals Gusinsky paid for. I said that I never worried about who paid for meals during ministerial visits. It was none of Nativ's business and we left it to the Foreign Ministry. They asked who owned the plane that flew us to the meeting with the Russian Prime Minister.

"The Russian government."

They demanded that I prove this, and I replied, "It was obvious from the plane, the crew's uniforms, and what they told me when I asked them whose plane it was."

This entire show irritated me. It was obvious they were trying to dig up dirt to use against Sharon. I asked the interrogators why they gave certain people preferential treatment: I had flown with Peres more than once in a private plane that had been placed at his disposal by an American billionaire, and I knew that he frequently traveled on private planes that were loaned to him by international tycoons. Shimon Peres's fondness for private planes was well known to affluent Jews around the world. Whenever he was invited to an event, they went on alert for a hint that it would be a good idea to send a private plane to fly him there. It was not an attractive habit, but journalists who enjoyed the same privileges stayed mum about it. As far as I know, Shimon Peres's passion for private flights provided by various rich men has never been given serious public attention.

"If Shimon Peres can do it, why can't Sharon?" I challenged the investigators. Most ministers are invited to hundreds of meals by local Jews when they visit the West, and nobody was ever interrogated or suspected of criminal behavior for this. Why should something done all the time by American Jewish millionaires be a problem when it's done by a Jewish millionaire from Russia?! Of course I didn't get an answer, nor did I expect to. I just wanted it to be written in the protocol.

Chapter 56

Prime Minister Netanyahu was about to visit Russia. The visit was important for his public and international standing and for that of the Israeli nation as a whole. As usual, Nativ prepared a kit ahead of the visit and sent the materials to the Prime Minister's bureau. We also prepared information booklets about Netanyahu, which was standard practice for state visits by a prime minister. We planned our part in the visit as we always did.

In the meanwhile, the public commotion about the Russian mafia and Russian crime reached alarming proportions. The Prime Minister's staff did everything possible to keep him away from anyone who was the subject of rumors, gossip, or hints by the police that they might be involved in the Russian underworld—not even chance meetings could be allowed. The names of these people were struck from the lists of those to be invited to events. It even reached the point of threats: "If this man is present, the Prime Minister will not attend the event." Netanyahu certainly knew nothing of this; it was a decision made by his bureau, or, more precisely, by Avigdor Liberman, the director general of the Prime Minister's Office, who had absolute control over the bureau, and implemented by Ruhama Avraham, the bureau chief, who blindly obeyed every order Liberman issued. Liberman was frantic about his boss's image, not to mention his own, for many reasons. Among other things, he was concerned about the not-so-subtle hints about his purported relations with the Russian underworld that his political rivals had begun to spread. There was a racist undertone to these rumors. Liberman's grotesque image certainly played a role in the campaign of intimidation, and people began tagging him with every negative quality, to the point of caricature, and blaming him for almost every possible crime. I often told people, including journalists, that the Israeli media loved to hate Liberman and to make him loathsome to the Israeli public. Liberman was apparently concerned that he would be accused of introducing people with a criminal past or mafia connections to the Prime Minister. I disagreed with his approach. I tried to intervene wherever I could, and kept insisting that keeping so many people away from Netanyahu was wrong, as a matter of substance, fact, and ethics; but Liberman won out.

This approach reached an absurd level during Netanyahu's visit to Moscow. Mayor Yuri Luzhkov hosted a reception in honor of the Israeli Prime Minister at the Metropol Hotel, one of the most luxurious in the city. Everyone who was anyone was invited, including prominent Jewish Muscovites like Iosif Kobzon, a very popular Jewish singer who was close to Luzhkov and was one of the leading fighters against anti-Semitism. In the Soviet era, he actually dared to perform Jewish music and Jewish songs, despite the authorities' manifest displeasure.

A very shameful incident took place during the reception. The whole affair could be traced back to Peres's term as Prime Minister. Once, during a work meeting I had with Mossad personnel in their office, they received a phone call from the Russian Embassy. After they hung up the phone, my hosts told me that the SVR representative at the Russian Embassy (the SVR is Russia's foreign intelligence service, parallel to the Mossad) had been on the line. He said that the singer Iosif Kobzon, arriving in Israel, had been detained at the airport and was about to be deported. My Mossad colleagues asked me to intervene and see what I could do. They put through a call for me to the Prime Minister's bureau, over a secure line, and I asked to speak with Peres urgently. When I was told that he was in a meeting, I asked that he be informed without delay that a certain person had been detained—and that if he wasn't released immediately there would be a huge scandal and hell to pay for the State of Israel. About twenty minutes later, I was informed that Peres had been notified of the matter and had ordered that the visitor be released and allowed to enter the country. When I looked into the incident later, it turned out that the Israeli consul in Moscow, a good man on loan from the GSS, had given Kobzon a visa so he could perform in Israel. In his report, the consul mentioned the press reports that defamed Kobzon for his purported involvement with the mafia. However, he added, he had issued the visa because he saw no reason not to. When Batya Carmon, the head of the Population Registry in the Interior Ministry, saw the cable, she issued instructions to detain and deport Kobzon, without bothering to find out who the man was, without thinking. That time, things were set right by Prime Minister Peres's intervention; but if the episode had taken place under Netanyahu-Liberman's term, I doubt they would have dared to get involved.

At the reception in Moscow, I suddenly noticed a commotion in the hall. Kobzon came up to me, shaking, and told me in a broken voice, with tears in his eyes, that he had been told, in the name of the Prime Minister's entourage, that he would not be allowed to perform. When I asked who had said that, he pointed to an Embassy staffer who was standing off to the side. I went over to her. When she saw that I was fuming she immediately understood what the problem was and started stammering. "It's not me. I ... I ... I'm only carrying out the ambassador's orders, I don't know anything more about it."

So I went over to the ambassador, who was sitting on the podium next to Liberman, and asked her, "What's going on with Kobzon?"

Before she had time to answer, Liberman intruded. "Don't get involved. Let it go."

I replied angrily, "I will not let it go. You've created a scandal. You should not have done this."

Suddenly I saw that Luzhkov had turned to Netanyahu. "You see?" I told Liberman, "It's already begun."

Liberman capitulated as if he had retreated into a shell. He wasn't the only one. Suddenly, no one was to blame, no one knew anything about it.

I hurried over to Luzhkov and Netanyahu, who asked me, "What's the matter? Why is the mayor upset?"

I told Netanyahu that everything was taken care of. I turned to Luzhkov and apologized, saying there had been a misunderstanding but everything was fine now and there was no reason to trouble the Prime Minister. Kobzon would sing in a few minutes. Then I went back to Kobzon and apologized. I told him that he could sing as much as he wanted and no one would bother him, and that we genuinely respected and appreciated him.

There were other mishaps and incidents, but this was one of the most distressing, one that exposed Israel's stupidity and ignorance in all its fullness and showed that even the highest echelons were not immune. Netanyahu had no hand in the affair and I was sure that had I gone to him, he would have set matters straight at once.

There was an even more serious and embarrassing incident at a reception hosted by Russian Prime Minister Chernomyrdin in honor of the visitor. The reception was supposed to start at six in the evening. Twenty minutes before the appointed time, all of us, including the Russian security detail, were standing outside the hotel, waiting for the Prime Minister and his wife. Five minutes passed, ten minutes ... and the Netanyahus still had not appeared. The organizers called me and asked what was going on, why the Prime Minister wasn't there yet. No one knew anything. Five to six, and still no sign of him. I went up to our security men and asked where the Prime Minister was. They replied that his wife wasn't ready yet. I was in shock. Should the Prime Minister's wife be allowed to cause a diplomatic incident? The Russians called me again, reporting in a hysterical tone that the Prime Minister of Russia was offended and wanted to leave. I asked them to stall him at any cost and said that we were about to leave the hotel. I knew that the Russian security detail called in constantly and that Chernomyrdin's people knew very well whether we were on the way or not—and other things, too. Just short of 6:30, about a half an hour after the reception was to have begun, the motorcade finally started moving and raced to the hall. When we entered, all the who's who of the Russian government and society, as well as important Jews, were milling about. It was a disgraceful public scandal but there was nothing to do about it—this was my Prime Minister and this was how he represented the country.

But my mortification wasn't over yet. An official from the Prime Minister's bureau approached me. His official title was "Diaspora Affairs Advisor," but I knew that he was actually Sarah Netanyahu's aide. He whispered that his boss wanted me to make sure that the Russian Prime Minister mentioned Netanyahu's wife in his welcoming speech. I gritted my teeth and went over to Chernomyrdin. I addressed him in a friendly but respectful manner, which I permitted myself only because he called me by my first name. "Victor Stepanovich, I have a strange and unusual request that embarrasses me no end, but please understand me. Binyamin Netanyahu would very much like for you to mention Mrs. Netanyahu in your remarks."

Chernomyrdin looked at me, refusing to believe what he was hearing. "What?" he said, "That's contrary to protocol. Things like that just aren't done."

"That's true," I replied. "You're right. But we have to rise above it. We are about to patch up the relations and ties between our two countries after a long and difficult period. We appreciate everything you're doing, and even if the request is unjustified and against protocol, we don't need a scandal. Let's let them have their way."

Chernomyrdin responded with ridicule and scorn. "What kind of a man is he? What a wimp! How can he let her do that?"

"He was raised in the United States, and didn't get the education we're used to. Let it go. Please—I beg of you."

Chernomyrdin sighed. "All right, I'll do it."

Embarrassed, I went back to my place and thought that the people who were running my country saw the entire world as a larger version of the Likud Central Committee, which, when ordered to do so, cries out in unison, "Hail Sarah!" The staff of the Prime Minister's bureau waited, trembling, for a sign from me. I reassured them that everything would work out. During his speech, Chernomyrdin glanced at me with a smile and gave Sarah Netanyahu her moment of glory. And thus a diplomatic incident between the two countries was averted—all to satisfy the whim of the spoiled wife of a weak man.

Overall, the visit was routine. On the flight back, the Jewish Agency, as usual, embarked a group of *olim* in the Prime Minister's plane. No one cared if this cost more money or meant that the weary *olim* with their sleepy children had to wait several extra hours. The main thing was the photo opportunity it provided. The Prime Minister brings Jews with him on his return to Israel, and as he speaks with them on the way, Jewish Agency staffers are photographed next to him and everyone is happy. The satirist Ephraim Kishon and his immortal creation, Salah Shabati, were smiling in astonishment and mournful comprehension.

A few months after Netanyahu's visit to Russia, I went to St. Petersburg on work matters. At one of the events, Chernomyrdin called me aside. "I don't understand," he said. "Your Prime Minister was here and gave me a sea of promises—but nothing, not a single thing, has been implemented. We know all about promises by prime ministers, but never has it happened that not even one detail was carried out. Aren't you ashamed of yourselves?"

I promised him that I would look into the matter and take care of it, but I knew there was nothing to be done. This was the new political culture of the Israeli leadership.

Chapter 57

One of the issues I had to deal with was Russia's assistance to Iran in the development of missiles and nuclear weapons. Technically speaking, such matters are not part of Nativ's brief. I was aware of the issue of Iran's nuclear aspirations only from my exposure to documents on the topic, both classified and unclassified, that crossed my desk. During my interesting life, I had become familiar with the story of Iran's nuclear weapons development and had formulated a clear opinion of the Iranian regime and its ambitions. Like many others, I believe that Iran defines a nuclear capability and missile development as a strategic goal, independent of the nature of the regime. The idea was born while the Shah was still in power, as part of the country's regional and strategic perspective and view of the threats facing it. In the early days, at least, Israel maintained strategic cooperation with Iran, primarily with regard to missiles.

The subject was a priority during Rabin's second visit to Russia and was actually the main reason for it. I was not involved at the time and did not pay any attention to the matter. In 1997, the issue took on a much more serious and dangerous dimension with implications for Russia-Israel relations. Any disruption or deterioration of the relations between the two countries was liable to have a serious impact on Nativ's work. As director of the agency, I saw myself obligated to place our work with Russia on the proper footing, in light of the new developments in our relations and their ramifications for the situation of Russian Jews and their *aliyah*.

The new attitude towards Russia was initiated by IDF Intelligence, and primarily the two men who served successively as the heads of its Research Division in those years, Yaakov Amidror and Amos Gilad. At one meeting, I heard Gilad express a position that took me by surprise. He claimed that Russia saw Iran as its most important strategic partner in the Middle East and was accordingly interested in giving Iran a nuclear capability and the capacity to design and manufacture advanced long-range missiles. I couldn't hold back and said that only ignorance and a total misreading of the situation could allow him to assert that Russia wanted to provide nuclear weapons or capabilities to anyone. Why would Russia do this? I asked. The reply was an argument that was even more ridiculous: Russia would make it possible for Iran to go nuclear because it was afraid of Muslim Iran's influence on Russia's large Muslim population and the possibility it would foment unrest among them. I said that this was nonsense. I asked whether there were any reports of subversive Iranian activities in Russia at all or specifically among Muslims; no one had an answer. I understood that, as usual, we had formed a conception that was not based on facts or competent research.

I challenged Gilad to reconcile his statement with the fact that the Soviet Union, with its ambitions for ideological expansion and involvement in violent conflicts all over the world, had never provided advanced military technology to even its closest allies. The Soviet Union had never given anyone even the smallest detail that might further the development of nuclear weapons. So why should Russia, which had no ambitions for expansion and no ideology it was trying to spread throughout the world, engage in nuclear and missile-technology proliferation? This was completely illogical.

No one had an answer to my rhetorical questions. Instead of a carefully thought out and professional explanation, I again heard hemming and hawing about how Russia was providing advanced technology to Iran in order to prevent Iranian activity among the Muslims in Russia. I didn't let the matter drop and pointed out that Russia had never been afraid of Iran. On the contrary, Iran had always been afraid of Russia, which in the past had harbored designs on its territory. Russia's concern in the south was Turkey, because of its membership in NATO and the centuries of armed conflict between the two countries. The Russians had always seen Persia not as a menace, but as potential prey. The Iranians weren't making trouble for Russia, but for Azerbaijan. In geographic terms, a large part of Azerbaijan was under Iranian control—the political border did not coincide with the geographic or demographic one. All of northern Iran west of the Caspian Sea was populated by Azeris, and in fact there were actually more Azeris living in Iran than in Azerbaijan. Iran had launched various religious activities in Azerbaijan, but they were of low intensity and the Azeris had nipped them in the bud.

I never did get an answer to my question about whether there was any information whatsoever about Iranian attempts to work among the Muslims in Russia, and at what level. My contacts in the Russian Security Service told me that Iranian intelligence agencies conducted almost no operations in Russia, and certainly not among the Muslims. There were intelligence-gathering activities, of course, but they were not very professional; their focus was limited to science and technology, visits to exhibitions, acquisition of patents, and the like. I tried to explain this to the other people at the meeting, but no one wanted to listen. In the Israeli tradition, you do not undermine the conception. From my acquaintance with Amidror and Gilad, I knew that they were not accustomed to listening to others or letting rational arguments persuade them. A former head of IDF Intelligence, one of the best among them, told me that he had once told both of them that, in his opinion, they were not suited to serve in intelligence. When they asked why, he replied, "Because you are always sure you know everything. Someone who thinks he knows everything cannot be in intelligence." Skepticism and reexamination, mainly of antitheses, are essential for intelligence personnel, particularly those engaged in analysis and assessment.

When I saw that things were growing more complicated and harming bilateral relations, I asked for a meeting with Prime Minister Netanyahu. I told him that I disagreed with the assessment by IDF intelligence and thought it mistaken. I emphasized that I was very concerned that actions taken on the basis of that mistaken assessment were liable to damage relations between Russia and Israel and stressed my concern that there would be undesirable ramifications for both the Jews in Russia and our work among them. I proposed that he allow me to investigate a few cases that pointed to ostensible Russian-Iranian cooperation on nuclear weapons or missiles, which I would probe through my contacts in the Russian intelligence apparatus. I also noted that our intelligence people said they had no reliable contacts in Russia, so my intervention would be to our benefit. Netanyahu treated the matter without irrelevant considerations and in a mature and appropriate way. He agreed with me about the potential for damaging relations with Russia. He accepted my proposal and within a few days sent me a list of incidents to look into.

I left for Russia, where I met with Prime Minister Chernomyrdin, among others. I told him that there was a problem here, and that if our relations were important to both countries, we had to find a mutual solution. I noted that there were two ways to do so—to debunk all the claims on the basis of solid facts, or to immediately rectify the situation if the assertions were correct to any extent. Chernomyrdin emphasized that Russia viewed good relations with Israel as very important, so he was willing to do everything in his power to prove that the claims were false and to remedy the situation. He suggested that I stay for his meeting with Defense Minister Igor Sergeyev and ask him what was going on. I told him that I could not meet with the Minister of Defense. I answered to Netanyahu, who had tense relations with Defense Minister Itzhak Mordechai; a meeting between Netanyahu's subordinate and the Russian Defense Minister was liable to spoil the delicate fabric of relations between Netanyahu and Mordechai. As a subordinate of the Prime Minister, I must not make problems for him. We decided that I would have additional meetings to investigate the problem—one with the head of the Russian defense industries and another with the head of the Security Services. Chernomyrdin said that he would issue the appropriate instructions. He regretted that I could not meet with the Defense Minister and promised to raise the matter with him after I left.

So as Chernomyrdin requested, I met with the overseer of the defense industries, who explained some of the cases that Netanyahu had asked me to look into. The explanations surprised me, and not pleasantly so. One case had to do with the supply of raw materials—a rare metal needed to build missile engines. The information I received from Netanyahu stated that the metal was being supplied to Iran by a Russian company. The Russian was astounded. "There is no way Israeli intelligence could be that negligent. Two university students, one Russian and one Azeri, decided to con Iranian businessmen and told them that they had access to defense plants that built missile systems. How is it possible that your intelligence never checked up on the company?"

Even if I had wanted to, I couldn't have replied to his question. He would not have believed me if I said that the Mossad and IDF Intelligence had no operatives in Russia. But I did receive the answer: There was no such company and the sensitive metal was never supplied to Iran. This dubious and unchecked story was made into the basis for an amateurish argument with significant national ramifications!

The second instance was more serious. It dealt with assistance in the design and manufacture of missile engines, purportedly provided by a large and well-known Russian factory. The case was really intricate and urgent. My Russian contacts told me that this was a case of dual technology that had both military and civilian applications. When the Russian agencies realized this, they acknowledged that there had been a mistake. Neither they, nor anyone else in the world, had been aware of the issue. There had been no conscious cooperation between Russia and Iran in the development of missiles. They promised to expedite the passage of a new law to make sure there would be no future supplies of dual-use technology. Indeed, the law was passed almost immediately.

The third case dealt with Russian academic institutions where Iranians were studying nuclear physics and related applications. The people I spoke with admitted as much and promised they would try to restrict the Iranian students' access to nuclear technology with military uses and ramifications. But it was obvious that a nuclear physicist would have no problem switching to the military side. Still, there was a paradox in this entire issue: a majority of the nuclear physicists in Iran had studied in the West, mostly in the United States and Europe. Even at that late date, the number of Iranians who had studied nuclear physics in Western Europe and the United States far exceeded those who had studied in Russia. Throughout the Shah's regime and into the 1980s, when Iran was rolling in dough, American universities pursued Iranian students, and several thousand were invited to America by universities to study nuclear physics. These people now constituted the main infrastructure for the development of nuclear weapons in Iran. The number of students who got their training in the Soviet Union or Russia was negligible in comparison.

According to my agreement with Chernomyrdin, I was also supposed to meet with the head of the Federal Security Service (FSB), Nikolai Kovalyov. But a day before the scheduled appointment, I received an apologetic phone call from his office: Kovalyov was not feeling well and the meeting would have to be postponed. If I couldn't stay, they would let me know in a few days when it could be rescheduled. I said that I had to go back to Israel but would return immediately when they set up a new meeting. I wanted to get home quickly and catch the Prime Minister before he left for the United States, so I could update him on the answers and proposals I had received from the

Russians. It was important that he have this information when he visited Washington. The Russians' operative proposal was to establish two joint teams to examine two aspects of the suspicions about Russian aid to Iran. The first would look at the flow of equipment and technologies; the Israeli side would be authorized to visit any factory or research institute suspected of providing aid to find out what was really going on and to take steps if necessary. The second team, which would include representatives of the FSB, would make sure that experts in nuclear physics and missile technologies did not work for the Iranians.

Because my plane from Moscow was to land in Israel only a short while before Netanyahu's was to take off, I jumped into a car as soon as I landed and drove straight to the Prime Minister's plane (naturally after advance coordination with the military secretary). I boarded the plane, took Netanyahu off to the side, and gave him a concise report on the results of my trip and the proposals I had heard. Once again, his response was quick and to the point. He asked me to report on the trip only to the head of IDF Intelligence, Moshe Ya'alon, and to Defense Minister Mordechai.

My first meeting lasted for about an hour—it was with Ya'alon and the head of the Research Division, Amos Gilad. Before he heard even a single word from me, Gilad said that I had committed an extremely grave act and caused unimaginable damage to Israel's security. According to him, the Israeli strategy was that the issue of cooperation between Russia and Iran be dealt with exclusively by the Americans; Israel was forbidden to bring up the matter with Russia directly. The assumption was that the Americans had more leverage and could deal with the issue better than we could. Were Israel to talk to the Russians directly, the Americans would tell us, "If you want to negotiate on your own, that's fine with us. Handle it yourselves and we'll stay out of the picture." In other words, according to Gilad, I had breached a basic principle of Israeli strategy. But he had another argument, which was even more brilliant: "The Russians will lie to us anyway." I didn't want to argue with him. I knew it was a waste of breath. And what could I tell him, that he was talking nonsense?

One thing I heard from the people I met with in Russia was, "Many come to us with various claims about our alleged aid to Iran in developing nuclear weapons and missiles. We hear it from the Germans, the French, the Americans. And when we ask them, 'Where did you get this?' they answer, 'It doesn't come from our sources; the Israelis gave us the information.' We are surprised at how the Israelis beat around the bush and don't talk to us themselves. Sit down and talk to us. We are willing to talk to you, but stop sending others to attack us while you remain silent. This is no way to work, sheltered behind other people. We can talk face to face."

But Gilad had decided that the Russians would lie to us. I told him that I didn't have such a terrible opinion of our abilities. After all, the Russians didn't manage to deceive me. They knew that it was hard for them to mislead me and that if they tried, I'd catch on sooner or later. Moreover, in talks between intelligence agencies anywhere in the world, one of them is always deceiving the other to some extent to serve its own interests, even if they are partners or allies. I told Gilad, "If you are smart enough and professional enough, you'll know how to deal with it."

Afterwards, Gilad delivered a forty-five minute lecture, more or less of the caliber of one intended for a delegation from the Hadassah chapter in some American suburb, about the danger Israel would face if the Iranians had nuclear weapons and missiles. I listened only out of courtesy. Ya'alon did not intervene. The head of the Research Division did not want to hear about the outcome of my visit and inquiries or about the Russians' proposals. "It doesn't interest me," he said flat out, and the meeting came to an end.

When I informed the Defense Minister's bureau that the Prime Minister had asked me to report to him about my meetings in Russia, the response was that first I should sit with the Minister's military secretary, Yaakov Amidror. David Ivry, the Defense Minister's aide for strategic affairs, was also present, although he barely spoke and didn't ask any questions. I was asked to present my findings, and at least they listened to me, unlike the heads of IDF Intelligence. Amidror said that they would forward the minutes of the meetings to the Minister, but I noted that the Prime Minister's instructions were otherwise. The response was: The Minister would decide. Of course, I was surprised and didn't think that this was appropriate. To this day, I don't think Mordechai received my report in a serious and full manner, and that is too bad.

A few days later, I was notified by the FSB of the new date for my meeting with its director. I informed the Prime Minister's bureau and our staff in Moscow. In the car on the way to the airport, I received a call from Danny Yatom, the head of the Mossad.

I first met Yatom when he was military secretary to Defense Minister Moshe Arens. We met again when he was OC Central Command and, along with the other students of the National Security College, I visited his command, as we did with all the other commands. Subsequently, I got to know him well when he served as military secretary to Prime Minister Rabin. The military secretary is the liaison between the Prime Minister and the Intelligence community. We got along and worked well together, thanks in part to Rabin's positive attitude towards each of us. When Peres became Prime Minister, he appointed Yatom to head the Mossad. I wished him luck. At Yatom's behest, we talked about his new job and I expressed my opinion about the organization, its people, and the Mossad's activities, based on what I knew.

Now, as I was being driven to the airport, Yatom told me that he had heard that I was going to Moscow to meet with the head of the FSB. I confirmed this.

"Relations between the agencies are under the Mossad's jurisdiction," he reminded me.

I assured him that I knew the rules and that the goal of my visit was not to discuss the relations between the Israeli and Russian intelligence communities. I was going to talk about a specific issue, with the Prime Minister's permission. If he wanted, I said, I would be glad to include the Mossad representative in Moscow in the meeting.

In a menacing and angry tone, he said that his representative would not join the meeting and that he was warning me that he would see it as a declaration of war if I went to the meeting. I told him that I had heard him. Yatom went on, "I will fight you with all my strength."

I replied in a cold and dry tone, "À la guerre comme à la guerre (in war as in war). If you think I'm scared by the dirty methods and schemes you learned from the infighting on the General Staff, you're wrong. Threats are the last thing that can help in an argument with me." My fury was plain.

But he went on and asked anyway, "Are you going?"

"Yes," I replied curtly, "I'm going and I'm going to hold the meeting."

Now Yatom was angry. "Fine," he said, and hung up the phone.

When I reached Moscow, the Nativ representative there said that the Prime Minister's military secretary had called him with the message that Netanyahu forbade me to meet with the head of the FSB. I told him that, even so, he should keep all the arrangements in place.

When I reached the hotel, I called Brig. Gen. Shimon Shapira, the military secretary, and asked him to explain my new instructions. He said that Danny Yatom had called Netanyahu, who had then issued the ban. I asked him where the Prime Minister was and Shapira said that he could not be reached. I would have to wait until late at night, when he would be available at home. I said that I would handle the Prime Minister.

At two in the morning, I called Netanyahu in his official residence, and he told me that Danny Yatom was opposed to the meeting. I told Netanyahu, "You cannot let some internal pettiness damage our relations with Russia. The Russian Prime Minister had a hand in arranging the meeting. The Russians are treating this meeting as an attempt by the Israeli side, at the highest possible level, to solve the problem. No matter what excuse I make, they will interpret it as Israel's intent to stop discussing the problem. They will not look at it as if I had wounded the Mossad's pride, as it were. They will see it as a political maneuver that you, the Prime Minister, are responsible for. We cannot cancel the meeting. It is too late."

Netanyahu was persuaded. "All right. Go to the meeting and present the problem as you did to the Russian Prime Minister." It was with great relief and joy that I responded that I would carry out his instructions.

The next day, I met with the head of the FSB, Kovalyov. On one side of the table was the head of the organization, flanked by the generals who ran its departments. A small Russian flag sat on the table in front of them. On the opposite side, I sat all alone, with the Israeli flag in front of me. For a minute, I was swept away by a flood of emotions. Thirty years earlier, in Moscow, I had confronted the KGB on my own. Now, again alone, I was representing the State of Israel to its successor. But the adrenaline rush of the assignment had already hit, and within a fraction of a second, I tensed up. The head of the FSB introduced his people to me. When I asked whether I needed to introduce myself, one of the generals replied with a smile. "No, we know you very well indeed." We all broke out in laughter and then got down to work. We spoke about two topics—Nativ's operations in Russia and the specific subject I had come to discuss.

With regard to Nativ, I said that, as they knew, we were working in all the countries of the former Soviet Union, and regardless of what each of us thought about the other, we were all working in the interests of our own countries. I said that although there might be occasional foul-ups, I thought that Nativ's activities offered a wide field for cooperation and understanding without harming the interests of our respective countries. I said that if there were mistakes, or if they sensed that Nativ was infringing their security in some way, we should straighten things out between ourselves, just as I solved problems with the other former Soviet republics. I continued somewhat arrogantly. "After all, you know me. You know the organization that I head. You know Israel. You can be sure that we will achieve our goals just as we have done in the past, time after time. I would rather do this without complicating the relations between the two countries. The ball is in your court, but I repeat: We will achieve our goals." They smiled, some out of courtesy, some in response to my frank, if not indeed rude language.

On the Iranian matter, they had done their homework and coordinated their positions with Chernomyrdin and the other government agencies. They repeated the proposal that we establish two joint teams to deal with transfers of nuclear technology and personnel to Iran, both intentional and innocent. I said that I would forward their proposal to the Prime Minister and thanked them. I came home and reported on the meeting to Netanyahu.

The meeting, of course, did not impair the relations between the Mossad and the Russian agencies in the slightest, and the whole war of prestige was completely unnecessary. But my efforts came to naught. The State of Israel, steered by its intelligence community and piloted by IDF Intelligence, continued to make accusations against Russia on the Iranian issue, although the statements that part of the Russian strategy was to supply the country with a nuclear capacity came to an end.

The sequel to the story took place when Ariel Sharon was Foreign Minister. During the last visit to Moscow by Netanyahu and Sharon, in 1999, I sat in on the meeting they held with Prime Minister Yevgeny Primakov and Foreign Minister Igor Ivanov. The Russian repeated the same proposal I had conveyed a year earlier—to have joint teams handle the issue. Netanyahu looked at Sharon and said he accepted the proposal and would have Sharon determine the composition of the Israeli side. When we left the meeting, Sharon told me, "You will coordinate the teams."

I said, "Fine. We'll settle the details when we get home."

But back in Israel, everything was swept away by the election campaign. The teams were never established, the agreement between Netanyahu and Primakov was never implemented, and that was the end of the matter.

An amusing incident related to my confrontation with the Mossad took place when the head of the Russian National Security Council, Andrei Kokoshin, visited Israel. I was seated next to him at a dinner in his honor. "I heard you had a fight with the Mossad," he said. "What's wrong with you? Who dares go to war against an organization like the Mossad?"

I looked him straight in the eyes. "You forget that when I was young I took on another organization."

Kokoshin laughed. "That's right," he said, "What is the Mossad for you, after the KGB?" As they say, every joke contains a grain of truth.

When I reviewed the whole affair in my mind, I reached some rather harsh and distressing conclusions. The intelligence community, defense establishment, and political echelons had produced a faulty assessment of Russian aid to Iran, and worse, of the ostensible reasons for that aid. A lack of proper understanding, bordering on total ignorance, of everything about Russia had caused Israeli intelligence to make a mistaken assessment. But it wasn't just ignorance; it was also methods of analysis that were not sufficiently clear or professional, conducted with arrogance and real contempt for everything and everyone that did not fall in line with its conception. Because it did not understand Russia, Israeli intelligence was incapable of identifying Russia's interests—not with regard to Iran and not on other global issues, including Russia's relations with the United States and Israel. It was all part of the risk of misunderstanding Russia that I had warned about back in 1993 and tried to correct then. But then, too, the entire Israeli intelligence community was opposed.

Due to a simplistic view of Russia, the intelligence community recommended a steamroller solution to what it defined as Russia's aid to Iran. The political echelon, which is never really equipped to handle the assessments supplied by the military and the intelligence agencies, and which did not understand Russia very well either, adopted the assessment and recommendations it was fed. The view was that because Israel lacked sufficient means to impose its will on

Russia, the United States should be pressured to turn the screws on Russia for us. This was another mistake. No one took into account the fact that the United States might have its own considerations and interests with regard to Russia.

I remember trying to explain to Netanyahu that there were limits to how much pressure the United States could exert on Russia. In 1998, Yeltsin and his regime were very weak. There were elements in the United States that wanted to weaken Russia further and perhaps even dismantle the country, but the administration feared that Yeltsin's fall or removal was liable to lead to a regime ruled by radical forces that would be even more hostile to American interests. This meant that the administration could not pressure Yeltsin's Russia too much. Netanyahu dismissed what I said; all we had to do was get American Jewish organizations to exert pressure on the administration, just as they had done in their demonstrations on behalf of Soviet Jewry. I disagreed and told him that the American government had mobilized to assist the struggle for Soviet Jewry not because of pressure by the Jews, but because doing so coincided with its interests at the height of the Cold War. The administration and the Jewish organizations differed only as to what measures would be most effective for achieving their respective and overlapping goals. But Netanyahu, trapped in his simplistic American worldview, was incapable of digesting my explanation. It didn't fit in with the Hollywood notion of the world in which the good guys always defeat the bad guys.

So Israel wasted time trying to use the Americans as a proxy to coerce Russia. Over the years, the clashes between the United States and Russia about the Iranian problem intensified, and considerations of a global rivalry between them, which had not existed previously, also entered the equation. Eventually Israel began to understand not only that Russia's role in providing nuclear and missile technology to Iran was much less important than it had thought, but that without Russian cooperation there was no way to prevent Iran from acquiring nuclear weapons. Israel's tone with regard to Russia has changed somewhat, but its understanding and ability to work with the country have not improved, and the situation is not much better today. What was possible a few years ago is no longer possible today. Sharon's attempt to change the Israeli approach was not pursued, not even after he himself became Prime Minister. The idea that Russia must be coerced still holds sway; only the rhetoric has changed. When he served as head of the National Security Council, reserve Maj. Gen. Giora Eiland concluded that the policy about Russian involvement with Iran must be changed. He admitted that we had made a mistake when we overstated Russia's assistance to Iran in developing nuclear weapons and missiles, and the bang turned out to be a whimper. He regretted that we had done so and that our stubbornness had damaged bilateral relations and undercut our ability to deal with the problem. But when he tried to raise his proposals, formulated in concert with the Russians, the entire establishment rallied against him, just as it had done against me five years earlier. Even Sharon adopted the traditional position. My only consolation, if it can be called that, is that even the head of the National Security Council could not win out over the intelligence community and political echelon. It was quite literally a hopeless war.

I did not rejoice in others' misfortune when, a few years later, my position was confirmed. No, I am sad that the system made such gross mistakes on a question of such fateful import for the State of Israel. Because of a mistaken conception and bad work habits by those making the assessment, the other alternatives—Pakistan and North Korea—were paid scant attention and in fact ignored altogether. Intelligence agencies have limited means, and when they focus too intently in the wrong direction, they cannot allocate sufficient resources and attention to other possibilities. It seems likely that had the intelligence apparatus functioned more professionally from the outset, developing knowledge of and familiarity with the countries and their political interests, the mistake would not have been made and the outcome would have been better. Mistakes keep coming back, and when I heard the bombastic declarations before the American invasion of Iraq, the characteristic presumptuousness of statements like, "The world will tremble when it discovers how many nonconventional weapons Saddam Hussein had acquired," I smiled sadly. I was concerned that we would achieve the same results once again, and my apprehensions were confirmed. Some of the same people continue to shape Israel's Iranian policy today and, even worse—the same unprofessional approach, replete with faulty ideas and conceit, which usually go hand in hand—continue to characterize Israel's intelligence and political establishments.

As a result of my involvement in the matter, the head of the Research Division of the IDF Intelligence demanded that Nativ be banned from making situation assessments and distributing them. I could not hold back and warned that were such a decision made, I would not continue in my post. It is impossible to work and to decide on goals and methods without information and assessments. This recommendation was the main issue of my quarrel with Prime Minister Netanyahu, but it, like others, was not implemented as long as I remained the director of Nativ.

Chapter 58

One day in 1998, Foreign Minister Sharon, who was about to leave for the United States, called and asked me to come to the airport urgently so we could talk. He wanted to talk about our deteriorating relations with Russia. He mentioned Defense Minister Yitzchak Mordechai, who had cancelled the visit to Israel by the Russian Defense Minister and Chief of Staff. In Sharon's opinion, this was unnecessary and seriously damaged our relationship with Russia. Now he was looking for any way to improve relations or at least to cut our losses. He asked me to go to Moscow and arrange a visit for him on a very tight schedule, so he could stop off in Russia on his way back from the United States. He also asked my opinion about Mordechai's action. I told him that I thought the root of the problem was our Defense Ministry's wrongheaded attitude. This, I added, was the work of Amos Gilad, the head of the Research Division of IDF Intelligence, and a few other officers, whose views the Defense Minister had adopted. I told him about my intervention to rectify matters, in coordination with the Prime Minister, and of its result—which spoke for itself. But Mordechai, accepting the recommendations of his staff, had demonstratively ignored my achievements—that is, of course, assuming he had even received a competent report about them. I said I thought it was still possible to repair the damage and improve relations.

I told Sharon I was willing to help him, but things had to be done through the proper channels. First and foremost, he should obtain the Prime Minister's consent for me to be involved with issues that he dealt with as Foreign Minister; second, I had to be given an official status authorizing me to handle the matter. I was no longer willing to hear charges that I had exceeded my authority as director of Nativ and meddled in affairs that were none of my business. Sharon asked what I meant by "official status." I explained this meant my being appointed, in addition to my current post, as "regional coordinator for the countries of the former Soviet Union on behalf of the Prime Minister and Foreign Minister." This title was analogous to that held by Dennis Ross, President Clinton's special envoy to the Middle East. Sharon agreed immediately and gave instructions to his staff to proceed accordingly. I soon received a diplomatic passport with the new title. The permanent staff of the Foreign Ministry was no doubt thrilled by my incursion on their turf.

I flew to Moscow and arranged the outlines of the visit. Sharon arrived directly from the United States in the evening and told me that he needed to see Russian Prime Minister Primakov in the morning. In the diplomatic world, this kind of action is impossible. First of all, the Prime Minister is not always available for a visiting Foreign Minister—such meetings are not required by protocol and take place only in unusual circumstances; second, meetings like this require advanced planning, and there had been none. Nevertheless, I told him I would see what I could do. I contacted a senior official at the Russian Foreign Ministry—we had known each other for many years and had a good relationship. I apologized and said that we had an urgent problem: Sharon had come straight from the United States, after important meetings, and there were matters of the utmost urgency that he absolutely had to discuss with Primakov. The man told me that he didn't think he would succeed, but he promised to try. At midnight, he called back and said he didn't know what had happened, but Primakov had agreed and the meeting was set for the morning.

When we reached Primakov's office, Sharon asked for time alone with him. Primakov's bureau chief said that this was out of the question, utterly impossible. Sharon asked me what could be done—he had to have a private meeting. I told him that this was my problem and that I would solve it. Primakov arrived, visibly ill and in pain. He had been staying home for several days, but because of the importance of the matter and his respect for Israel and its Foreign Minister, he had got up from his sick bed just to hold the meeting that Sharon said was so important. Indeed, he went back to bed right after the meeting, at his doctor's orders.

Only someone with a good understanding of the complex and thorny relationship between the Soviet Union (and later Russia) and Israel can appreciate the radical change in Russia in its relations with Israel. I am not sure many other Prime Ministers would have acceded in similar circumstances to such a request, even if it was from Ariel Sharon. Only three Israeli Prime Ministers would have made a similar gesture—Yitzhak Rabin, Ehud Barak, and certainly Ariel Sharon. (I know this for a fact, unfortunately.) When the meeting began, Sharon was somewhat tense, because the private meeting had not yet been arranged. As usual at meetings of that nature, I sat at the table, not handling the translation because there was an official interpreter. Usually, I was more interested in the people on the other side—studying them, taking notes for myself, trying to detect things that the people doing the talking don't usually notice. Most of the time, the same old topics are addressed and I listen with only half an ear. It isn't worth focusing and wasting time on them. It is more interesting and more important to follow the people and what they say, and to understand what they are not saying or trying to hide.

After the standard exchange of greetings, Sharon opened with his introductory remarks. It was the routine introduction that every Foreign Minister makes in every meeting. I got up from my chair, walked around the table towards the Russian party, passed behind Primakov, and leaned over to the man sitting next to him. I had known him since 1988, when I first came back to Moscow. He had worked for Primakov, who was then the director of the Institute of World Economy and International Relations. We had met then and he had passed on to his boss the substance of our conversation. Since then, the man had served as ambassador to Syria and was then given a senior position in the Foreign Ministry. I knew that he was one of Primakov's closest associates. I whispered to him that Sharon needed to have ten minutes alone with Primakov. He replied that he would look into it. Primakov noticed our conversation. We had met before, in both Russia and in Israel, and he knew who I was from his prior posts as Foreign Minister and head of the Foreign Intelligence Service. Primakov asked if there was some problem. When he learned of Sharon's request, he said that he would call a recess in fifteen minutes and hold the private meeting then.

Fifteen minutes later, when a break was called, Sharon stayed for his meeting with Primakov. I stayed with him, and Primakov kept Viktor Posuvalyuk, the deputy Foreign Minister responsible for the Middle East, in the office. The first question Primakov asked was, "Tell me, please, Mr. Sharon, why is Yitzhak Mordechai doing this to us? There's no justification for it, you know."

Sharon looked at me. I told Primakov, "You remember your last visit to Israel? You remember that you asked me about Mordechai, and I told you exactly what kind of person he is?"

Primakov sighed. "Yes, I remember. You were right and it's too bad. But now we are here to try and fix things up."

I will not go into the details of the conversation, except to say that Primakov and Sharon both tried very hard to take steps in the right direction to improve bilateral relations. Sharon certainly devoted all his energy to this attempt and began moving things in a positive direction, both on this visit and on a later visit with Netanyahu, in which he took the lead on diplomatic issues.

That evening, Sharon hosted a reception. I made sure that Putin, who was director of the FSB at the time, was invited. I got there a bit early and saw Putin waiting, standing off to the side. I came and talked to him about several matters, including technical details about Sharansky's visit to the FSB to review his file. I introduced Putin to Ambassador Zvi Magen. When Sharon arrived, I introduced Putin to him. It was obvious that Putin held Sharon in high regard. Sharon suddenly began to tell Putin how beautiful our country is and that he really ought to visit. Putin looked at me mischievously and told Sharon, smiling, "In Israel, you have a 'special service,' a small agency, but one that is very active and effective. They have already made a point of taking me around Israel."

I explained to Sharon that Putin had already visited Israel, with our help, as well as on his own. This acquaintance between Ariel Sharon and Vladimir Putin served Israel well later, when Sharon became Prime Minister and Putin became President of Russia.

Chapter 59

On one of my visits to Moscow, an officer of the Federal Security Service (FSB) requested that I meet with him on a matter of great importance for both countries. He was a short, thin man with a Caucasian appearance. His Russian was fluent and standard, but not Muscovite. He cut right to the point and introduced himself as an officer in the anti-terrorism unit of the FSB, from the department that dealt with Islamic terrorism. From his last name, I guessed that he was Armenian, which he confirmed in response to my question. He said that his unit was having difficulties holding serious exchanges with Western intelligence services about radical Islamic terrorism. According to him, his people had amassed a great deal of important information about Bin Laden and his Al Qaeda organization, which led them to believe that he was one of the major players in international terrorism. He also told me that they had excellent information about the relationship between international Islamic terrorism and Chechen terrorism, including training camps in Chechnya funded by Bin Laden and run by Omar Ibn al Khattab, a Jordanian. These camps trained people from the Middle East, Europe, and even the Far East to stage terrorist attacks around the world. The man claimed that even though the Mossad had a representative in Moscow and his agency had a representative in Tel Aviv, there was no serious dialogue on the matter. The situation with the Americans was even worse. They had tried to talk to the Saudis, following the Al Qaeda attack on American troops in Saudi Arabia, but to no avail. His wanted me to help the Russian security services establish a useful communications channel with Israeli intelligence and perhaps with the Americans and Saudis as well, through us. I thanked him for contacting me and said I would convey his message to the appropriate authorities in Israel.

When I got back to Israel, I reported on the meeting to Prime Minister Netanyahu. He listened attentively and told me to inform his advisor on terrorism, Meir Dagan. I knew Dagan from his service in the IDF. After he heard my report, Dagan asked for my assessment. I told him that I thought we should get examples of the information from the Russians. If it was important enough, I thought we should meet with their representatives to decide on a course of action. That was our agreement. I returned to Moscow and met with the commander of the Islamic Terrorism Unit, a young major general. I received various explanations and information and passed them on to Dagan. We decided to have a follow-up meeting. After I had several more sessions with the FSB, we set up a visit to Moscow by Dagan and myself. The discussions were serious and thorough, including assessments of Islamic terrorism. Dagan drafted a report on the meeting and we went to submit it to the Prime Minister.

The report recommended moving ahead on this front—a recommendation that was fundamentally correct. I told Dagan that in my opinion, and on the basis of my experience, our intelligence officials would not be thrilled about the idea for a thousand and one reasons, some justified but most not, and the opportunity was likely to be missed. This was the end of my involvement in the matter.

Some time later, I received a call from a general at the FSB. He had come to Israel for talks and had asked his hosts to put him in touch with me, but they kept putting him off. Could I meet with him at his hotel? I went and we talked until the wee hours of the morning. He thanked me for my help and told me that more serious exchanges were finally under way. But he added that his impression was that the Israeli side was not all that interested and he was afraid that the process would not lead to the desired outcome. I told him that I couldn't get involved and influence the situation, because this wasn't my field of responsibility. We met a few more times in Moscow, at his behest, and I received a detailed update about intelligence relations with Israel, the information and proposals that we had been provided. Things started moving slowly but surely, but I still felt it was not fast enough.

Sometime thereafter, the Armenian officer who had made the first connection supposedly committed suicide by jumping from the sixth floor of a sanitarium. Our reading was that he had simply been eliminated by the Chechens. The year was 1998, three years before 9/11.

Chapter 60

Towards the end of Binyamin Netanyahu's first term as Prime Minister, shortly before the 1999 elections, he visited Russia again, accompanied by Foreign Minister Sharon. On Friday morning (Netanyahu was to start his visit on Sunday), Sharon called and asked about a technical matter regarding his visit.

"I don't know the details," I told him. "I am not going this time. The Prime Minister's bureau didn't invite me or send any instructions regarding this visit. I know there is a visit and we submitted briefing materials about it, but no one told me that I have to come along."

Sharon was furious and contacted the Prime Minister's bureau at once. Two hours later, someone called me from the bureau, mumbling an apology. I knew it was no accident. The director of Nativ had never been left out of the official party when the Prime Minister or Foreign Minister visited Russia or any other country of the former Soviet Union. Every such visit includes not only political meetings but also encounters with Jews. If the head of Nativ is not part of the entourage, this is an indication that the Jewish issue has been dropped from the agenda and is no longer important. I had already decided that if the plane took off without me, the Prime Minister would find my letter of resignation on his desk when he got back to Jerusalem. I had no intention of being a "poster child" for something that was really meaningless. It is the Prime Minister's prerogative to replace the head of Nativ, but he has no right to ignore the organization and deprive it of its essence. Thanks to Sharon's unsolicited intervention, though, I did take part in Netanyahu's second visit to Russia.

It was clear to everyone that this trip was mainly for show as part of the forthcoming election campaign. A meeting was set for Netanyahu with the top echelons of the Russian government. I asked Sharon if our ambassador, Zvi Magen, a former Nativ operative, could attend the meeting as well, even though the list of participants was restricted. They included Russian Prime Minister Primakov, Foreign Minister Ivanov, and two of their advisors. Our side was represented by Netanyahu, Sharon, me, the military secretary, and the ambassador. The official topic was the Iranian issue, but when we finished talking about that subject, Netanyahu, who had been silent almost the entire time, said that we had another request: that the Russians hand over to Israel the archives of the late Lubavitcher Rebbe. He went so far as to ask whether it would be possible to take the archives back to Israel on his plane.

I looked at the Russians and wanted to fall through the floor. Primakov had no idea what he was talking about, and Ivanov whispered him the explanation. The response was as expected: The issue is complex and not something we can talk about now. It was obvious even to the Russians that Netanyahu was hoping to obtain the Lubavitcher archives to win the full support of Chabad; in 1996, the Chabad slogan "Bibi is good for the Jews" had helped him defeat Peres. It was so transparent, so cheap and humiliating—to introduce his own election propaganda needs into a sensitive and confidential meeting on an existential issue for the State of Israel. Of course the Russians realized this. They had not held much esteem for Netanyahu before that, but this conversation lowered the status of Israel and its government to rock-bottom.

On our way back from Moscow, we made a stop in Georgia, a visit of no importance whatsoever. Correction: it was important for the campaign. This time, the Jewish Agency outdid itself and flew in *olim* from Russia to Georgia to fill up the plane. The *olim* were forced to endure a twelve-hour flight just to create a photo opportunity and a press release about how Israeli Prime Minister Binyamin Netanyahu had brought *olim* back home with him.

Chapter 61

In early September 1998, the Prime Minister's military secretary, Brig. Gen. Shimon Shapira, sent me the report of Brig. Gen. Yom-Tov Tamir's committee, the latest in the endless round of committees established to examine Nativ, with his recommendations. All the committees that investigated Nativ's role and operations, including the committee that wrote the State Comptroller's report (and excluding the Hofi "committee," which really consisted only of Yitzhak Hofi himself) had a common factor. They were not interested in what was good for the Jews or what was good for *aliyah*. All the reports, summaries, and recommendations—which, to our great good fortune, were not implemented as long as I was head of Nativ and were consigned to their deserved oblivion—were intended to serve the extraneous and bureaucratic goals and interests of those who sat on the committees. The fate of Soviet Jews and their *aliyah* has not seriously interested any Prime Minister since Rabin. It was an issue to be manipulated for political advantage, a cynical and demagogic tool for election campaigns.

I set down my response to the committee's recommendations in a letter to the Prime Minister—seven pages, thirty-five sections—in which I explained why the recommendations were unacceptable to me and why their implementation would not only be misguided, but would also cause irreversible damage to the country. I added by way of conclusion that should my opinion not be accepted, I would no longer remain as director of Nativ. Two weeks later, I received a letter from Shapira: "There is no response to your letter to the Prime Minister." To say that I was angry is an understatement; this was a formula similar to what millions of Soviet citizens had received in response to letters they sent to Comrade Stalin, mainly to request the release or re-evaluation of the files of their family members who had been sent to the Gulag, where most of them died or were murdered: "There is no response to your letter to Comrade Stalin." Shapira had no way of knowing that, of course. But it angered me that the Israeli government bureaucracy of the late twentieth century had reached the level of "no nonsense" replies and a wording that was identical to that of the Stalin era more than fifty years earlier. I didn't take it as a personal insult, but I was angry and sad that the Prime Minister's bureau was being run in such a way. A petty functionary was arrogating authority to himself and had the insolence to decide a matter of this import instead of the Prime Minister? I had no doubt that Netanyahu had never seen my letter and had not dictated the response. But how could a Prime Minister permit matters to be run in this way in his name?!

Shapira's very appointment as the Prime Minister's military secretary was an embarrassing story. After Maj. Gen. Zev Livni left the post, his replacement resigned after only a short time on the job and the bureau did without a military secretary for a duration. Brig. Gen. Shapira, who was deputy military secretary, took over "temporarily." From what I understood from my sources in the bureau, this was a scheme engineered by Shapira and Danny Nevo, the Government Secretary, to prevent the appointment of a military secretary of serious stature. In the end, their plot worked and Shapira was named military secretary to the Prime Minister.

Now I wrote a short and scathing letter to the Prime Minister. I reviewed the most important points in my original response to the recommendations and added that if they were not accepted, I would submit my resignation. This time, the letter was forwarded to Netanyahu and he actually read it. I was invited to a meeting with him, at which, I was told, Natan Sharansky would be present as well. Shapira was also there. Netanyahu began by saying, "I received your short and furious letter. I want to reply to what you wrote and tell you my opinion."

I interrupted him. "I'm sorry—that was the second letter. There was a letter before that, the original one, and it was much more detailed."

Netanyahu was surprised. "What letter?" he asked. "This is the only letter I received. I didn't see another letter."

I looked at Shapira, but he was concentrating intently on the ceiling. This confirmed my assumption that he had not shown my letter to the Prime Minister.

Netanyahu went on. "The decisions I took were made in concert with Natan, and with his approval."

I cut him off immediately. "Leave Natan out of this. You're the Prime Minister and you're responsible for your decisions. I will sort out my relationship with Natan on my own, without you. Don't hide behind him. Take responsibility for your decisions. You're the Prime Minister and, with all due respect, Natan has nothing to do with this."

Netanyahu was taken aback. His eyes and body language gave away his humiliation. "I am taking your letter very seriously," he replied. "But the American Secretary of State will be here soon and I will be completely occupied with the visit. I'm asking you to give me a week or two to rethink the matter. In the meantime, please stay at your job. I want you to continue."

Netanyahu's situation and sudden about-face were totally transparent to me. Shortly before that, the Government had found itself in a crisis and early elections were about to be announced (which they were, two weeks later). He and his close associates knew that, ahead of the elections, it would not look good if I quit and this scandal hit the headlines.

So I told him I had no problem with his request for an extension and would wait one week. As expected, I received a letter from the Prime Minister's bureau. It stated that the Prime Minister was suspending any decision about the future of Nativ and would return to the matter in six months. The exercise was transparent—to get through the elections. And after the elections, who knew what would happen?

Both Sharon and Sharansky phoned to tell me that Netanyahu was retreating and would not implement the Tamir committee's recommendations. I thanked them and told them that I was withdrawing my letter of resignation. Basically, I had no choice, because the decisions I opposed had not been accepted. I replied to the Prime Minister in writing that in the wake of his letter, I was suspending my letter of resignation and asking for a signed statement that Nativ's functions would remain unchanged. I drafted the most important points of the letter I wished to receive and forwarded it to the military secretary. A few days later, I received the same text back, verbatim, signed by the Prime Minister.

Our work continued as usual. One evening in April 1999, my wife phoned unexpectedly to say that I had just been mentioned on the evening news. I threw down the receiver and tuned in just in time to catch the end of the item, in which commentator Amnon Abramovitch was reading from my last letter to the Prime Minister. Within a minute or so I received a call from Geula Cohen, who asked if the report was true and what she could do to smooth things over. Could I say that the report was inaccurate?

"No," I told her. The letter was authentic, although I had written it a few months earlier. In any case, it was an official document on file in several places.

Sharon also phoned and asked what could be done to set things right.

"I can't deny the letter," I told him. "My suggestion is that Netanyahu's bureau announce that there were disagreements in the past, but that they have been resolved and we are continuing to work as usual. If I am asked, I'll respond that yes, there were problems, but we've found a way to work together and the letter is no longer relevant."

When the journalists called, their approach was different. "Yasha, the Prime Minister's bureau is preparing an assault against you, because of the letter. What do you have to say?"

I told them that I wasn't going to respond. The next day, the Prime Minister issued a response that savaged me. When I reached my office, I immediately wrote a letter of resignation and sent it with the driver to the Prime Minister's bureau. I wrote that I considered what was said in the Prime Minister's name to be an expression of no confidence. I could not continue working with the Prime Minister in the situation that had been created. I was submitting my resignation, effective immediately. I called in my staff, read my letter to them, told them what had happened and what the disagreements were, and thanked them. That was my last day at Nativ, after twenty-two years.

I received dozens of phone calls from journalists who wanted an interview. I called Shmuel Hollander, the Civil Service Commissioner, and asked whether, having resigned, I had to wait a specific period before I could have contact with journalists. Hollander said that I was authorized to give interviews starting the next day. I told the journalists to call back tomorrow.

This was the end of the Nativ chapter of my life, a most fascinating chapter that brought me much satisfaction and pride. During those years, I managed to see all my desires come to fruition, both personal wishes and those related to the country. It was a chapter brimming with activity and decisions that I had to make every day. Some of them were fateful choices that changed the country, affected the destiny of over a million Jews, and influenced the fate of my people. And that is basically what I aspired to—to take part in determining the destiny of my people and my country.

The immediate question was who would succeed me. My preferred candidate was Robert Singer, a talented man with excellent organizational skills, honest, fairly tolerant in dealing with people and institutions, and good at developing contacts. In addition to his background in the IDF, he had run the Nativ unit responsible for public diplomacy and educational work. He had a warm feeling for Jews, unlike Zvi Magen, who tended to be uncomfortable with Jews and Jewish affairs. Singer also had excellent experience serving in the United States and good contacts among American Jews. But although he would have accepted the challenge had he been offered it earlier, by now he had grown tired of waiting. Even before I resigned, he had applied for the position of director general of World ORT and was now unavailable.

I called Sharansky. "Natan, do you want Netanyahu to appoint Liberman's candidate to head Nativ?"

Liberman had already hastily established his own political party, as a rival to Sharansky's, and it was clear that Sharansky had no interest in promoting his interests.

"Who are you thinking about for the job?" he asked.

I told him that in the situation that had emerged, it was necessary to appoint someone right away. There weren't many choices. The best one was Zvi Magen, ambassador to Moscow and a Nativ man.

Sharansky phoned Netanyahu, who, as usual, was susceptible to pressure. Bowing to Sharansky, Netanyahu named Magen to run Nativ. But he would have to stay on in Moscow until a new ambassador was appointed. Netanyahu lost the election, so Magen took up his post under the new Prime Minister, Ehud Barak.

When I first met Magen, he was a lieutenant colonel in Military Intelligence. Born in Czernowitz, he had made *aliyah* as a child in the early 1960s, but his Russian was good. He had done his compulsory military service in Military Intelligence. Magen belonged to a category of officers whom I don't think highly of as military men—the classic staff officers who always serve at headquarters and never smell the battlefield, whether in combat or support units. Although he was an intelligent man with a good mind, he could not escape the bad habits of staff officers. Like many of his kind, his thought patterns and behavior were shaped at his desk, surrounded by intrigues, petty rivalries, conflicting loyalties, and betrayals. His greatest lack—far worse than his timidity—was that he was a total stranger to Jewish matters. Even worse, he was always trying to avoid dealing with Jewish issues and contact with Jews. Although he worked within the parameters I set and made a strong contribution to Nativ, the negative aspects of his personality sometimes came to the fore. Nonetheless, I had always found a way to keep them in tow.

When the Foreign Ministry was looking intently for candidates for ambassadorial positions in the former Soviet Union, I found out that Magen had submitted his candidacy without notifying me or asking for permission. This is unusual in the government bureaucracy, especially in units like ours. Had an employee in any other organization done that, the director would have summoned him, fired him on the spot, and informed the Foreign Ministry that he would not consent to his appointment.

I had a different approach. I knew that the Foreign Ministry was on the ropes in terms of finding suitable persons for service in the former Soviet Union. With all his shortcomings, Magen was several notches above any career Foreign Service officer who might have been considered for an ambassadorship, in terms of his knowledge and grasp of the region. When the Foreign Ministry asked for my opinion, I said that if he wanted the job and they found him suitable, I had no problem with it. I was also aware of the fact that, like a typical Jew in a Gentile society, trying to show that the Jewish aspect didn't influence him (say, the Jewish policeman in New York who treats Jews with greater severity than does his non-Jewish colleague), a Nativ graduate like Magen would try to be "more Catholic than the Pope" when it came to us. I knew that our staff would have a difficult time on the ground, but relied on his timidity and distaste for frontal conflict, certainly with me. I figured that I would be able to prevail over all his tricks, if he emulated his new bosses at the Foreign Ministry and tried to interfere with our work. As ambassador to Ukraine and later to Russia, he had made cautious attempts, which he thought I was unaware of, to restrict Nativ. I received reports of his discussions with Foreign Ministry staff about ways to hobble Nativ. This didn't bother me and I overcame it. Moreover, when the embassy in Moscow was left without an ambassador for over a year and the situation was worsening, I urged Sharansky to get Netanyahu to transfer Magen there from Kiev.

I saw Magen's appointment to head Nativ as the lesser of two evils. The alternative, that some political hack promoted by Liberman or Netanyahu would get the job, was much worse. Because I knew how Liberman thought and ran things, I saw the installation of his man as a catastrophe. There were no pleasant surprises in Magen's work as head of Nativ. As a born coward who never stands up for his own opinion and generally lies low until he knows what his superiors think, he shrank from responsibility. Because he could not withstand the pressures, the organization was powerless by 2007, with no budget and almost no professional staff. Nativ's continued existence and operation were a mere formality. It no longer had any standing among the Jews or authorities in the former Soviet Union, let alone in Israel. It was transferred from the purview of the Prime Minister, who showed no interest in it, to that of the Government secretary, and the Prime Minister almost never held working sessions with its director. I sadly recalled Yitzhak Hofi's recommendations: "Neither the Director General of the Prime Minister's Office nor any official should stand between the Prime Minister and the director of Nativ."

Under Prime Ministers Sharon and Olmert, the organization quickly turned into a shadow of its former self, devoid of power and content. Nativ's subordination to Liberman, when he served as Deputy Prime Minister and Minister of Strategic Affairs (2006–2008), did not help matters. It was Liberman, after all, who had said a decade earlier, "Nativ should be closed by December 1998." His many political and personal problems impacted Nativ. When Liberman left Olmert's government, the overseeing of Nativ was shunted back to the Government secretary. He left it in even worse shape than he found it.

Back in 1997, when Liberman, then director general of the Prime Minister's Office, recommended the dismantling of Nativ, I asked Netanyahu about it. His astonished reply was, "What on Earth? That's not my idea. I didn't know about it and have no such plans."

Netanyahu dismissed Liberman's strange decision to close Nativ in 1998. Liberman was the only person in the Israeli establishment who officially proposed shutting the organization and the only one who actually tried to do so. But less than a decade later he was given responsibility for it! Why Liberman, who wanted to close Nativ, demanded that it fall under his jurisdiction ten years later is a whole other story. It just goes to show the nature of the people who make decisions in Israel and how decision are made, somewhere in the space between personal caprice and irresponsible government.

Chapter 62

In 1996, I published a situation assessment in which I wrote that if the percentage of Jews emigrating from the former Soviet Union to Israel and other countries remained stable, the number would plummet to 20,000 or fewer *olim* per year by the end of the century. If so, this *aliyah* would no longer be of strategic importance for Israel. In such a situation, I was not sure there would still be a need for Nativ, at least not in its current format. The barrage I received in response came from within the organization as well: how dare I say such a thing, sawing off the branch I was sitting on? I responded that the truth was the truth and nothing could be done about it. These were my estimates and I was duty-bound to pass them on to my superiors and the organization.

History bore me out. *Aliyah* from the former Soviet Union collapsed; today it stands at fewer than 10,000 people a year. In other words, the "strategic resource" component no longer exists. In 1997 and 1998, the main problem facing Nativ was the instability and uncertainty of the situation in the post-Soviet sphere, especially Russia. But that no longer exists today.

At the time, it was uncertain what would happen in Russia after Yeltsin. His administration was clearly on its last legs, whether he would be thrown out of power or forced out by medical problems. In 1996, he was on the verge of death. The possibilities for the next chapter were many and diverse. Pro-Communist elements left over from the Soviet regime, ultranationalists, and even neo-Nazi groups were gaining increased clout. I knew all about Russian Nazism, having studied it back in the 1970s. We didn't know where Russia was headed—back to a Communist state, whether of the old style or in a new form, to a new dictatorship, or to a nationalistic or clerical nationalist regime. We didn't even know whether Russia would remain a single country or fall apart. It was obvious to me that until the situation clarified or stabilized, whatever the current scope of *aliyah*, Nativ's analytical abilities as well as its unique operational capacity would remain essential.

Things began to even out when Putin came to power and the threat to the Jews or *aliyah* evaporated. When the situation stabilized in 2000, there was certainly a need for a serious re-examination of Nativ's raison d'être: Was there any difference in the situation of the Jews in the former Soviet arena as opposed to the rest of the world? The Jewish problem and *aliyah* were no longer a political issue in Russia. Manifestations of official anti-Semitism and persecution of Jews were squelched and almost disappeared. The Jews' status improved to a level unprecedented anywhere in the world, with the possible exception of the United States today.

I remember the case of Russian nationalist and anti-Semitic politician Vladimir Zhirinovsky. Baruch Gur, the Jewish Agency official responsible for activity in the former Soviet Union, called me once and asked whether Zhirinovsky had ever been sent an *aliyah* invitation or applied for an *aliyah* visa. I checked and replied that he had not requested a visa, but he had been sent two invitations. Our database included all sorts of names, including Brezhnev, whom some clown had entered as requesting an *aliyah* invitation from Israel. And because these requests were processed automatically, the hundreds of thousands of invitations included one for Brezhnev.

Two days later, articles appeared in Israeli and Russian newspapers, claiming on the basis of sources at the Jewish Agency that Zhirinovsky had applied to make *aliyah*. This was at the height of the 1996 presidential election campaign in Russia, in which Zhirinovsky was running, and constituted a cheap and ugly swipe right out of the book of Soviet propaganda methods. It's true that Zhirinovsky had a Jewish father. So what? To use the Jewish motif for a political attack, with the help of Israeli agents? I saw this as an offensive paradox. We were the last people who should have been exploiting his Jewish origin to impugn the man, regardless of his worldview. This incident was not appropriate for the Jewish state and Jewish organizations. But Zhirinovsky's Jewish ancestry didn't harm his popularity or reduce his support among Russian nationalists—and this was a mark of honor and maturity for Russia. Similarly, Andropov's Jewish origins did not prevent him from rising to the pinnacle of power in the Soviet Union, and Primakov's did not prevent his appointment as Prime Minister of Russia. All kinds of possibilities emerged for the rebirth of Jewish culture and the development of cultural and religious connections with the entire world. Given the new situation, the reasons for Nativ's existence, which had been relevant until the end of the twentieth century, no longer applied.

Chapter 63

When I resigned, I returned my official car and waived the nine-month adjustment period to which I was entitled, because I would not have been allowed to write or be interviewed in the media during that time. My goal was to make the public aware of what I knew about Binyamin Netanyahu, who was running for re-election in an increasingly fierce campaign. I had expressed my opinion of him to family and a few close friends on various occasions, and now I felt it important to share it with the broader public. I said that, if re-elected, Netanyahu would pose a danger to Israel. He had a tendency to make rash decisions and could not stand up to pressure, and this made him liable, particularly in issues of fatal consequence, to bring disaster upon the State of Israel. I thought that it was my civic responsibility to speak up.

Netanyahu's style of thinking and decision-making was confirmed by his behavior with regard to the Mossad's botched attempt to assassinate Hamas leader Khaled Mashal in 1997. I am not talking about the failed execution of the plot, which was a professional matter and does not concern me here. My focus is the Prime Minister's authorization of the operation, which demonstrated the ignorance and rash adventurism of the person responsible for the country's fate. Later, there were other indications of Netanyahu's lack of discretion, of the intolerable ease with which he made public statements and revealed State secrets when he thought it would serve him. The frequency and regularity of such incidents were astonishing and worrisome.

As noted, the election campaign was already under way and I came out in favor of his opponent, Ehud Barak. I admit that after everything we went through together, Barak and I have a special relationship. The difficult and emotional experience of combat naturally forged a special bond between us. But in our first conversation after I decided to support his run for prime minister, I told him that I was not doing so on account of our wartime comradeship or because of the fairly complex and special relations between us, but for another reason—that he was much more suited for the job than Netanyahu. I added that this was not an absolute and fixed opinion and that I would always judge him against the alternative. Should the alternative to Barak ever strike me as the better choice, I would support that person without hesitation.

A few months before the elections, I emerged from the meeting of a Knesset committee. When I passed the cafeteria, I saw Barak sitting with a few close friends and said hello. Almost no one at the table knew me, but Barak replied, "Tell me, why don't we join forces?"

I was a little bit taken aback by the question. "You know me well—you can answer that question yourself."

Barak looked me in the eye and responded slowly, "You, with me, but not with the party."

The others followed our exchange with amazement; it was obvious they didn't understand my style of addressing the leader of their party.

I smiled. "Very good. You see that you know the answer." And that was indeed my motto: I wanted Barak to be prime minister, but could not see the Labor Party, as it was then, as my political home.

I have never belonged to any party. Not to Herut, despite my closeness to its positions, nor to Tehiya, with whose original platform I identified. The parties' opportunism and phoniness disturbed me. I saw how Begin and his colleagues in Herut behaved when they were in power and after Begin left the political stage. My first crisis with Tehiya was when it entered the Government and sought the Science Ministry for its chairman, Yuval Neeman. I knew him well and esteemed him highly, but with all due respect for science and for Neeman's scientific abilities, a party whose motto was "the People and the State" should have concerned itself with more important matters. It could have requested the Absorption Ministry, for instance. Herut didn't want it. Tehiya's up-and-coming young men and hopes for the future, Roni Milo and Dan Meridor, whom I had known for years and hoped to see in the most senior positions, preferred other, more technical portfolios. The Environment Ministry was apparently more respectable and more important than Absorption. The head of this right-wing government was Yitzhak Shamir, a dear and very honest man, both personally and politically, whose devotion to Israel and the Jewish people knew no bounds. Nevertheless, he gave the Absorption Ministry to Shas, a party that I would call non-Zionist, if not anti-Zionist. None of the illustrious Zionists wanted that portfolio.

Shas, a party whose principles, foundations, and leadership structure I do not accept, is, however, absolutely loyal to its principles. The man that Shas placed in the ministry was Yitzhak Peretz, who, though he may have been far removed from the issue of *aliyah* and *olim* and from the mentality of the new arrivals—was a good Absorption Minister. He really tried to solve problems and get to the bottom of them. He was 100 percent devoted to his portfolio and attempted to make the Absorption Ministry more efficient. Even if he did try to apply his own worldview, Peretz did so in a manner free of the vulgarity and crudity of others. I note with joy and satisfaction that during his term as Absorption Minister, *olim* were treated humanely, as they were when Yair Tsaban and Yaakov Tsur held the portfolio. This was different from the way it became later, even under ministers who were *olim* themselves.

It was the attitude of all the parties to the issue that was dearest to me and to which I had dedicated my life—*aliyah* and the Jewish people—that made me recoil from partisanship and have no confidence in them. I remembered the travails of Rabin, who was disgusted by dirty politics. He suffered almost physically when he had to engage in political games. This was one of the deep differences between him and Peres and one of the reasons for his contempt for Peres the politician, the expert in political schemes and manipulations. I knew the situation and had no desire to enter the partisan and political whirlpool. But I had to speak my truth and bring it to public attention. I could not remain silent about what I knew.

After I left Nativ, I met with Barak and said I would help him. I wouldn't join the Labor Party, but I would say what I had to say about him and about Netanyahu. I said that I was willing to appear in election broadcasts, but only on condition that I could speak from my own prepared text and convey only the message that I wanted. I was willing to hear what his advisors recommended, but the decision about what I said must be mine. And so it was. For my television spot, I determined the content and form, leaving only production matters to the professionals, who did an excellent job. During the campaign, I expressed my view about the two parties that were competing for the votes of *olim*—Sharansky's and Liberman's. More than once I said that I knew these people better than they knew themselves. I never took advantage of information that had come to me as part of my job or leaked it to promote personal or political struggles. But I could evaluate the candidates' personalities and toughness and certainly took that into account.

It was obvious to me that Liberman had put together a party at the last minute to be a satellite of the Likud. He had decided to take that step, which he had been weighing for some time, because he was fed up with being the lackey of politicians; he felt, and rightly so, that he had the ability and right to be an independent player on the political field. After all, he had catapulted Netanyahu to the top of the Likud through his own extraordinary skills, political maneuvers, and machinations, in which he has few peers in Israel. Liberman, the newcomer, routed David Levy on his home court, employing Levy's own methods. He proved to be more cunning, nasty, scheming, and aggressive than Levy's people. And thanks to him, Netanyahu became party leader and then Prime Minister.

Of course, the background for this success was the collapse of the party old guard, the electoral defeat in 1992, and Yitzchak Shamir's weak hand in running his party. With all his virtues, Shamir was too ethical, honest, modest, and cautious to control the Likud of the 1990s. There were not enough cunning intriguers around him who, like Liberman, had flexible principles and could run the party for him. Loyalty and honesty, the two qualities that made him successful in Lehi and the Mossad, were not so important in Israeli politics, particularly not in his camp at that time. In fact, they were disadvantages.

The devastation of the Likud was a byproduct of Begin's leadership style. His dominance, his egocentricity, his intolerance of other views within the party, his obsessive need for admiration and worship—all these neutered the party and chased out anyone with independent opinions and potential. Begin's despotic leadership of the party did not enable anybody of real caliber to thrive. No one could set foot in the party unless he saluted the "leader" and fulfilled his instructions without question. But Begin broke down at a critical moment for the country and his party; when he packed his bags, Shamir was the only underling with a deep-rooted Revisionist outlook who could step in to lead the party. Moshe Arens was too direct, too intelligent, and too ethical for the Likud. The competition, Ariel Sharon and David Levy, were opportunists. It would have been a joke to call them the ideological heirs of Herut.

Shamir tried to hold the party together, to continue its ideological line and adapt it to the new and changing reality. It was hard for him because he was a conservative. But Shamir, unlike Begin, didn't break and toss in the towel. He fought to the end, even though the party sank and almost disappeared. Today's Likud has no link to the historical Herut, to the truth of Herut. The only person who perhaps expresses this link, in a grotesque way that is all the same the closest to Herut's ideology, is Moshe Feiglin. Netanyahu's opportunism long ago triumphed over his own father's ideological principles.

The first time I encountered the name Avigdor Liberman was in 1986, when David Bartov was appointed director of Nativ. I saw a short article in the internal Likud paper, complaining that the position had gone not to a loyal party member but to a man identified with the Labor Party. No relevant or professional arguments were made, only party affiliation. The byline was "Avigdor Liberman." I inquired about the political commissar who wanted to preserve ideological purity in the civil service, in primitive Bolshevist style. I was told that he was a young man who had made *aliyah* from the Soviet Union (Moldova) and was active in the Young Likud group. A few years later, friends who had made *aliyah* contacted me to tell me about a small organization that was trying to help Jews in the Soviet Union, but was not being allowed to work there because its members were identified with Likud.

I always had been disgusted by the insertion of narrow partisan considerations into the struggle on behalf of Soviet Jews or *aliyah* in general. I agreed to meet with these people, who included Liberman. I smiled to myself, thinking that he had fallen victim to his own pettiness, but I didn't say a word. My impression was that there was a healthy element in their activities and I agreed to collaborate with them. I thought it important that *olim* work with the population from which they had come. They enjoyed the trust of the locals, who had only recently been their neighbors, and this was an extremely important and effective asset for us.

A few months before the 1999 elections, Liberman threw his hat into the political arena. He had excellent connections and control of the Likud activists who were *olim*, providing him with his initial power base. There was no way I could support Liberman's party, Yisrael Beiteinu, because I saw it as a one-man band to achieve his own goals, most of which I rejected. By contrast, Natan Sharansky chaired his party, Yisrael ba'Aliyah, but did not completely dominate it. Objectively, the *olim*, with their many unresolved problems, had matured to the point where they could create a political force to represent them and address their problems. Sharansky—the most prominent figure among the Soviet *olim*, a man with outstanding public marketing abilities, with an economic and organizational basis that had been built over the years, who enjoyed support among American Jewry—was the only possible choice to head the party. With all my concerns about Sharansky's conduct in Netanyahu's government and my reservations about the people in his party and some of its problems, I supported Yisrael ba'Aliyah against Yisrael Beiteinu because I felt that only the former truly represented the *olim*. Out of desperation in the last days of his campaign, Netanyahu betrayed Liberman by announcing, rather crudely, that he supported Sharansky and trying to identify with him. To the best of my knowledge, Liberman took this hard, but he knew better than anyone who Netanyahu was. By contrast, Sharansky dismayed his supporters with his reticence to explicitly name Netanyahu as his candidate for Prime Minister, despite their personal friendship.

After my public criticisms of Netanyahu, I read Shimon Schiffer's interview with him in *Yedioth Ahronoth*. Schiffer wrote that Netanyahu had taken the State Comptroller's report on Nativ, which was marked "top secret," out of his drawer. He then read aloud an excerpt that accused Yakov Kedmi of bribing a Russian official in exchange for information—information that was not essential for either the Mossad or the GSS. "See what kind of man is this Yakov Kedmi, who is criticizing me!" As hard as it was to believe, the Prime Minister had exploited extremely sensitive and classified material to vilify an Israeli citizen who had criticized him. There is nothing more despicable—and obviously illegal—than the exposure of state secrets, in general and especially to serve political ends. Schiffer had long since become the mouthpiece of prime ministers, who used him to reveal things they wanted to make public. That is a black mark against a journalist, and certainly for one of his stature.

What was conspicuous in the section Netanyahu quoted from the State Comptroller's report was the unbridled zeal of the Comptroller's office to uncover any detail of Nativ's work that could be represented in a negative manner, and especially to prove that Nativ was recruiting and running spies. In an investigation that went on for a year and a half, the State Comptroller's office could not find a single shred of such evidence. So the authors of the report seized on this one instance, misrepresented and distorted it, and pawned it off as an example of my running a spy network. I recalled a passage in one of the internal reports that the Russian Security Service (FSB) wrote about me: "Kedmi collects information in an unconventional manner—without recruiting people." The truth was much simpler, and it was presented to the State Comptroller; but who needs facts if they interfere with the goal of the report?!

The "bribe" was a payment made as part of an agreement with one of the public agencies in Russia. This organization, with which we cooperated, advised us and made it possible for us to receive and read archival information that was supposed to be available, according to the law, but that in practice could not be accessed. It asked to be paid in cash, which was common practice in Russia in those days for various reasons, including the dysfunctional banking system. I approved the payment and we received the material. By the way, the money didn't even come from the State budget and the payment was made by people on the ground, including David Bartov. Bartov, who initiated this extremely important and successful operation, was the former head of Nativ and a lawyer who had served as the registrar of the Supreme Court and as secretary of the Agranat and Kahan commissions of inquiry. Would someone so consistently law-abiding and so cautious have undertaken or authorized illegal activity or deviated from standard procedures?! The information we sought related to the complex relationship between the Jewish people and the Soviet regime. We received documents about the "Doctors' Trial" in the early 1950s, which were naturally of no interest to either the

Mossad or the GSS, which do not deal with the history of the Jews in the Soviet Union and Russia. The materials about which the Prime Minister defamed me were intended for the Jewish people and the State of Israel. A few years later they could have been obtained more easily, but in the mid-1990s this was the only way and we feared it might be a one-time opportunity. We certainly never paid a spy or recruited an agent to obtain it.

But Netanyahu revealed sensitive material and blamed a senior official of his own office, who was subordinate to him, for paying an agent in a foreign country for classified documents while serving and representing his own country. In essence, he was publicly stating that Nativ had collected materials in a foreign country by bribing state officials and then forwarding the documents to the Mossad and the GSS—but he also disparaged me by saying that the material we collected was not good enough for the Mossad or the GSS! In utter contradiction to the true situation, he pretended that Nativ was an arm of the Mossad or the GSS, for no reason other than to defame and vilify someone who had criticized him. In a civilized country, such behavior would never have been allowed to go unchallenged. In Israel, however, there was no public response. When a senior aide to the United States President disclosed that the wife of one of his critics had worked for the CIA, he was tried, convicted, and sentenced to prison. He protected the President with his own body; otherwise, the President might have faced charges as well. Nothing like this happened in Israel; what happened was far worse.

I asked Attorney General Elyakim Rubinstein to open a criminal investigation of Prime Minister Netanyahu for revealing State secrets. But Rubinstein decided to protect the Prime Minister and left my letter unanswered for a whole year! Instead, I received a request from his office that I respond to the complaint submitted by the Movement for Quality Government, alleging that the former head of Nativ had made political declarations while still in his post. Rubinstein's office forwarded all the material to me—which included a statement by Shmuel Hollander, the Civil Service Commissioner, to the effect that the head of Nativ had appeared in the media only after leaving his post and in accordance with the law. Never mind that the Attorney General hadn't bothered to read the material—Rubinstein actually wrote that he intended to investigate the two complaints together. After a year elapsed, I submitted a petition to the High Court against the Attorney General for his delay in responding and failure to open an investigation. The High Court dismissed my petition on the grounds that it did not see the Attorney General's action as an extreme deviation from his authority. It did not address the essence of the matter.

One of Rubinstein's arguments was that perhaps the Prime Minister thought that he was authorized to reveal State secrets, so that this should not be seen as a crime. This interesting and creative argument may perhaps have been appropriate for the defense, but not for the head of the prosecution. It contravenes all the rules of the intelligence community and the need to protect state secrets. Only those who classify materials are authorized to modify their status. The Prime Minister certainly lacked the authority to do so. In addition, the Attorney General relied upon the Prime Minister's letter to the State Comptroller's office and suggested that "perhaps it can be seen as a form of apology?" In my opinion, this is arrant nonsense. Netanyahu's letter included no apology, but the Attorney General was determined to save the Prime Minister from a criminal investigation and offered whatever explanation was conducive to this end.

I cannot accept this approach to the concepts of secrecy, sensitive security information, the public's right to know, and what is important for the people and the country. But the Israeli public didn't respond or demand an investigation of Netanyahu's leak. The American public would never have let such a matter slide. A public sensitive to ethical conduct and good government would not have remained silent. The main culprit in the decline of the Israeli leadership's system of ethics and morality, which accelerates every day, is the Israeli public, which accepts this and even bows down to its rotten leaders from time to time.

I recalled the time Elyakim Rubinstein responded sharply after I exposed Netanyahu's attempts to obtain the Chabad archives from the Russians during sensitive conversations about Iran's nuclear ambitions. Sources close to the Attorney General told me that he had tried to represent my criticism as a leak from a secret meeting I had attended. If this is true, then Rubinstein, who was Attorney General at the time and is now a Supreme Court justice, sees things very differently than I do. I believe that personal matters and cheap political gains should not be mixed with extremely sensitive national interests. Confounding the two is unseemly and should not be beyond the pale for the prime minister.

Chapter 64

Ehud Barak defeated Netanyahu and was elected Prime Minister in 1999. I was happy to have played a part in his victory and was glad that Israel was on the verge of a necessary and desirable change. I felt almost as I had in 1977, when Begin came to power. I expected that everything would be different and better now and hoped that I would not be disappointed, as I had been then. The morning after the election, I met with Barak in his home, at his invitation.

"Thank you," he said. "You did a lot for me." Then he asked what he saw as a natural question, but one I wasn't happy to hear. "What do you want?"

"I don't want anything from you. I don't want a job. Neither in politics nor in government. If you need my help, my skills, I will help you. But not in an official role. And on one condition—I don't want a salary or reimbursement of expenses. If you agree, tell me what you want."

And that's what happened. I did what Barak asked. I flew to Russia. I met with people and spoke with them. I conveyed messages. A few days after our conversation, I spoke with Ariel Sharon. Sharon and I were old friends. I first met him in 1969, at the home of Geula Cohen, who had invited a few officers to hear from two young *olim*, Dov Sperling and myself, about the Jewish struggle in the Soviet Union and our criticisms of what the Israeli government was and was not doing. Sharon was one of those officers, highly decorated. Back in

Moscow, during the Six Day War, I had kept several photos on my desk—Menachem Begin, Levi Eshkol, Moshe Dayan, and a number of generals—Sharon, Yisrael Tal, Yeshayahu Gavish, and Chief of Staff Yitzhak Rabin. I was excited to be shaking the hand of a man whose picture had graced my desk, where on difficult nights, I could look at it and mutter stubbornly to myself, "If they can, so can I." For many years, my relationship with Sharon was influenced by that picture from the Six Day War and his image then. I was a frequent visitor to his home, where I got to know his wife Lily and his sons when they were still young. I also encountered him in the army, and when he went into politics, I wanted him to succeed.

At the time, however, the slot for a retired general in Herut was already filled by Ezer Weizman. So Sharon joined the Liberal Party, which was aligned with Herut in the Gahal bloc. With his energy, assertiveness, and cunning, Sharon entered a dormant party of petty bourgeois and "wimpy intellectuals" who had not found their place in the socialist parties but viewed Herut as too extreme in the other direction. As part of Gahal, the Liberals had no influence on decisions, but they gave Begin legitimacy and moderated his party's extremist image. The next step in the legitimization process came when Gahal joined the National Unity Government just before the Six Day War. After that, Begin was no longer an outcast, as he had been in Ben-Gurion's time. In the 1973 elections, held in the shadow of the Yom Kippur War, the Alignment held on. But four years later, it lost power for the first time since the establishment of the State, and Begin and the Likud formed the Government.

Sharon was very creative, particularly when it came to intrigues. It was only thanks to his capacity for hard work, his ability to speak with people, win them over, promise them the world, and lie to them that the Likud came into being.

A party does not come to power because the people have adopted its political and social positions. It comes to power because the previous administration falls apart completely or weakens to the point that it can no longer hold the reins. To a great extent, this was why Ehud Barak defeated Netanyahu in the direct election for Prime Minister. Netanyahu simply failed to win re-election. He had made every mistake possible and was weak, like the Likud in 1992 and the Alignment in 1977. My relationship with Sharon grew much stronger during Netanyahu's last year in office. When Netanyahu quit politics after losing to Barak, Sharon filled in as chairman of the Likud and then ran for the position against Ehud Olmert and Meir Sheetrit. Sheetrit was never a serious rival, and Sharon felt it was insulting to run against a man like Olmert. There are very few people about whom I heard Sharon use the insulting and derisive expressions he aimed at Olmert during that campaign. But one thing about Olmert astonished Sharon. "He has so much money for the campaign! Where did he get so much money?!"

When I spoke with Sharon right after the 1999 elections, I asked him if he didn't think that this was the time to unite ranks and whether he would agree to join Barak's coalition. Sharon was very surprised by the question and asked whether I had discussed the matter with Barak. I said that hadn't yet; but if Sharon agreed I was willing to sound out Barak. Sharon gave me a green light. I knew that joining the coalition right after losing the election would rehabilitate the Likud in the public eye. That night, I called Barak and told him that I had an idea regarding a unity government and had already had a conversation on the subject with Sharon. Barak asked me to come over immediately, so I did, and outlined my proposal to him. Barak had a lot of respect for Sharon, bordering on adulation. He knew him well from the army, and like any real military man, he appreciated another professional soldier. In particular, as a veteran of special commando units, Barak esteemed the former commander of the legendary Unit 101. But he was also well aware of Sharon's weaknesses, much more than I was.

He listened to me, asked questions, thought out loud, and said I could speak with Sharon about a unity government. I carried messages

back and forth and set up a meeting between the two. At one o'clock
in the morning, I picked up Sharon and we continued to Barak's
home in Kokhav Yair, without being recognized. This was the first of
several meetings attended only by the three of us. My participation
was minimal. It was important for me that these two men find a
basis for a unity government. First of all, I thought and still think
that a collaboration between Sharon and Barak, with the latter as
Prime Minister, would have been the best team to run the country
and tackle its many problems. Second, I saw the Likud's inclusion in
the coalition as a guarantee that Barak's government would serve its
full term. Moreover, I hoped that having the Likud in the government
would leave Shas on the outside, returned to its proper dimension as
an ultra-orthodox Sephardi party with no serious political influence.

Barak and Sharon quickly reached common ground and it was an
almost done deal that the Likud would join the government. At the
same time, I worked vigorously to bring Yisrael ba'Aliyah into the
coalition. The party had won six Knesset seats—quite an achievement,
given that its rival Yisrael Beiteinu had won only four. During the
campaign, I was already pressuring Yisrael ba'Aliyah to demand the
Interior portfolio for Sharansky. Its campaign slogan, thought up
by the talented adman Motti Moral, was "*nash kontrol*" (Russian for
"our control"), meaning that its prime goal was to receive the Interior
portfolio. I participated in a few meetings between the Labor Party
and Yisrael ba'Aliyah. The latter's representative was a member of
Gush Emunim, a resident of the Old City of Jerusalem, who was
part of the group that had supported Avital in her campaign for her
husband's freedom. Sharansky apparently trusted him more than he
did other people. I very much wanted Yisrael ba'Aliyah to be the first
party to sign the coalition agreement with Labor. I was somewhat
worried by the fact that both Barak and Sharansky probed me to
find out whether Yisrael ba'Aliyah absolutely had to get the Interior
portfolio. I knew that each had reasons not to want this. The night
the agreement was signed, I pushed and pressed, and the first party

to sign off to join Barak's coalition was indeed Yisrael ba'Aliyah, which received the Interior portfolio. The National Religious Party signed next and received the Housing Ministry. Its leaders were furious, not because they weren't the first to sign the coalition agreement, but because they didn't get Interior. I sat with them for an hour to calm them down and try to convince them that the Housing Ministry held many possibilities, which coincided with the party's worldview and would allow it to serve its constituency.

I was worried that even though everything was settled with Sharon, including his appointment as Finance Minister, nothing was moving. Sharon had really wanted to be the first or second to sign the coalition agreement with Labor. Looking at Barak, I began spotting a baffling evasiveness, hesitation, second-guessing, and reservations. Barak never said so directly, but I knew, from certain tell-tale signs—his tone, his questions, his delay in making decisions and refusal to speak plainly—that he was under tremendous pressure from the dovish wing of the Labor Party, which preferred Shas to the Likud. The argument that Shas, with seventeen seats in the Knesset, could not be ignored was pure demagoguery. But these "righteous men" saw Shas, an ultra-orthodox, non-Zionist party, as a much more expedient partner, which could be bought off with budgets and not make too much trouble. I saw that Barak was about to surrender to these pressures.

Barak was no less wary than Sharon, and he too attached great importance to personal loyalty, though not as obsessively as Sharon did. They were both former generals, and one of the most malignant ailments of the IDF is the culture of cliques and loyalties between commanders and their subordinates. Too many people advance in the IDF not due to their skills and abilities, but because of their loyalty and closeness to a more senior officer. The opposite is true as well; qualified officers are frequently held back and not promoted because they aren't close enough to their commanders or are on bad terms with them. Barak was much more certain of himself, more confident of his skills and abilities than Sharon was. It can be said of Sharon that he was on the brink of a total lack of self-esteem, as strange as this sounds. Ehud Barak's problem was just the opposite—he often had an inflated estimation of his powers. His extraordinary intellect was not always fully translated into execution.

Sharon rashly met with members of the National Religious Party and Yisrael ba'Aliyah, which lit a red light for Barak and increased his suspicion. Barak began to fear that Sharon was trying to form a bloc consisting of the Likud, the National Religious Party, and Yisrael ba'Aliyah, which would serve as a counterweight to the other coalition partners. He saw this as a danger. Nonetheless, I don't think that's why he backed out of his agreement with Sharon; rather, it was the pressure in Labor to include Shas.

In every meeting with Barak, Sharon emphasized that they must establish a unity government without Shas in order to disconnect Shas from the spigot of the national budget and cut it down to size. He believed, and rightly so, that much of Shas's support came from natural Likud voters, who switched to Shas because of Netanyahu and because the two-ballot system (one for the Knesset and the other for Prime Minister) made this easy. Now he wanted to bring them back home. Barak made a mistake, but not because he didn't think about or understand the matter. On the intellectual plane, he probably sketched out all the scenarios; but even though he was the chairman of the Labor Party and the leader that brought it back to power, he was captive to the strong dovish wing of the party. He tried to find a way to connect to that sector, and that was the main reason for his appointment of Yuli Tamir, a representative of Peace Now, as absorption minister. Barak thought that out of loyalty to him, she would help him win support from the party doves. But that didn't happen. The government he established was dependent on the doves in his party, Shas, and Peres loyalists, who had never accepted the latter's defeat and engaged in constant subversion. Thus Barak's fate, and that of his government, were all but sealed right after his victory.

Barak was also mistaken about his ability to achieve a quick diplomatic breakthrough on the Palestinian or Syrian fronts, a move he thought would ensure his control of the Party and keep his government in power. Instead of first consolidating his administration, drawing on his election victory, he bet on the future successes he believed he could chalk up quickly. Insightful politicians and professional military men take advantage of their successes to fortify their position. After you occupy an objective, you prepare to defend it against a counterattack and only then organize and build up your forces for one last, decisive assault. Anyone who fails to learn this pays a hefty price, whether on the battlefield or in politics. Because of his excessive self-confidence, Barak did not take the future situation into account, did not prepare for it, and did not plan how he would function and stay in office if his diplomatic attempts didn't pan out. A government including Sharon would have buttressed his position, but he turned down that option repeatedly due to pressure from his "friends," who never fully accepted his leadership and were aware that a government with Sharon would have given him what they saw as excessive power.

I observed that there were no serious disagreements between Sharon and Barak on the issue of the Golan Heights. I knew Sharon and had not forgotten the destruction of Yamit as part of the peace agreement with Egypt and his support for Begin then, despite his own declared position. I knew that Sharon was capable of shifting gears easily if he thought some policy no longer served him. The evacuation of the Gaza Strip when he was Prime Minister offered the strongest possible proof of this. I wasn't afraid that Sharon would tie Barak's hands in reaching an agreement with the Syrians or the Palestinians, unless he felt that he could replace him. A stable coalition would have made it possible for Barak to move forward in negotiations.

In one of our first talks after Barak's victory, he asked me what I thought about the state of our relations with Russia. I explained my perspective and recommended that he visit Russia right after his visit to Washington. Given the snag in bilateral relations, I saw this as an opportunity to put things right (a move already begun by Sharon). I saw such a visit as conveying a very important message to the Russians and to the entire world, as well as to groups within Israel, namely that Israel viewed improved relations with Russia as a vital interest. Barak accepted my opinion and gave instructions to begin urgent preparations for the visit, which started an uncontrolled frenzy. The Foreign Ministry and practically everyone who was anyone in Israel, including some of Sharon's own confidants, were up in arms that he would go to Russia before Europe. They all knew it was my doing, which only increased the critics' tension and jealousy. But the visit took place nonetheless.

Barak was the third Prime Minister I accompanied to Moscow. When we landed and looked out the window of the plane at the honor guard waiting to receive the Israeli Prime Minister, I was deeply moved, because this time, the Prime Minister, Ehud Barak, was my former commander. I recalled one of our conversations. "You know," he said, "I doubt there is anybody in the world who knows me as well as you do, after all we've been through together."

"You're right," I replied.

We had shared many difficult experiences, and emotional times that made us show what we were made of. When we reached the Embassy, Barak said he wanted to be photographed with me at the spot where I had broken into the compound. This time I was not alone. I was standing there with the Prime Minister of Israel, my wartime commander and comrade in arms, at the very place where I had begun my way to Israel thirty-two years before. It is hard to describe this feeling. During those few seconds, it all flashed before my eyes: my break-in to the Embassy, the battle on the Tartur Road, the divisional assault on the western side of the Canal to sever the Suez–Cairo road, Barak's victory in the elections. All these emotions coalesced as one and carried me away for a brief moment.

During the visit, we met with Russian Prime Minister Sergey Stepashin. When we left the meeting, I told Barak that I was not sure that Stepashin would be around for long and that Russia was facing interesting changes. I said nothing more, because we were still in the building of the Prime Minister's Office. Our next meeting was with Yeltsin in the Kremlin, where I had already been many times. I felt excitement when I passed through the offices that had been occupied by Stalin, Beria, and Lenin—not out of respect for those men, but out of a sense that I was touching history, which was partly my own history.

The meeting with Yeltsin went well. I noticed one interesting detail: a binder on the table in front of Yeltsin, with the background materials for the meeting—standard practice going back to the Soviet era. Next to him sat a man from the Foreign Ministry with an identical binder. Yeltsin never even opened the binder, but he spoke to the point, clearly in command of the issues. I looked at his aide and saw that he was following what Yeltsin was saying, page by page. I understood from his face that Yeltsin had not deviated the slightest from the predetermined format and the topics that were to be raised. Yeltsin presented the Russian position in a clear and carefully reasoned manner, as though he dealt with the problems of the Middle East on a daily basis. Afterwards, I told Barak that this man, constantly vilified as an alcoholic, a grey Soviet functionary, a peasant, had surprised me with his professionalism on the diplomatic issues. I told him that this was the Soviets' method. The leader always comes prepared for a meeting and knows what to say, just as well as his aides.

In this context, I recalled the Ukrainian president's visit to Israel. As usual, we submitted a factual report with assessments and recommendations to the Prime Minister. We listed the topics that should be covered, including both general and Jewish issues. President Ezer Weizman hosted a reception for the visitor. I attended with my wife, according to custom. As usual, the host chief of state and his wife stood with the visiting president, the Prime Minister, and their wives in a reception line, greeting the guests with a handshake and a few words. I moved down the line of dignitaries, exchanged a few words with Weizman, whom I had known since 1969, his wife Reuma, and President Kuchma of Ukraine, whom I also knew. I then continued to Netanyahu, greeting Sarah first and shaking her hand. When I moved on to Netanyahu, he held me back. "Wait a second. I have a working session with the Ukrainian President in a few minutes. Tell me what the four main topics are. What do I have to talk to him about?" I was so ashamed, I wanted the ground to swallow me up. But I kept smiling, as though we were chatting about nothing special, and began reciting: "One-two-three-four … These are the four main points. Try to remember them."

Later, the journalists fell on me. "Yasha," they said, "what were you and the Prime Minister talking about for so long, with such congenial smiles?"

It goes without saying that I couldn't tell them that I had just given the Prime Minister a crash course in advance of his meeting with a foreign leader. Israel was never at the top of national and political priorities for any Russian president, including Yeltsin, but he was prepared for us. Ukraine and the Jews of Ukraine are important for Israel. Ukraine is also a country with rather advanced nuclear and military capabilities. As I listened to Yeltsin, I recalled Prime Minister Netanyahu and his woeful lack of preparation. Unfortunately, Netanyahu was not unique in this—and certainly in comparison to his successors a few years later, the "seriousness" of his attitude towards political problems wasn't even the most offensive.

I made two later attempts to bring Sharon into the government. The second time, Sharon was hesitant, and no progress was made. Sharon hadn't heard the promises he wanted from Barak. Barak didn't make those promises not because he thought it was wrong to do so, but because he wasn't sure he could get the Labor Party to assent to them. The third and last attempt was after Camp David. Barak no longer had a coalition, and I saw this as an excellent and final opportunity to keep him in office. When Sharon agreed to join the government, I thought everything was settled. All the details were settled. I remember that I went to see Barak in his official residence one night, at his invitation. I heard him wrapping things up over the phone with Tomi Lapid, the head of the Shinui Party. He told me with satisfaction that Lapid supported a unity government including the Likud and everything was fine. When I left his workroom around midnight, after we had discussed the details of the agreement for over an hour, I saw Yossi Beilin in the living room, along with several other members of the Labor Party, who were waiting to talk with Barak. I greeted them and went on my way.

The next morning, I heard about the "Shas safety net." Barak hadn't called to say that he had changed his mind; I'm not sure that he had called Sharon, either. This was Sharon's third slap in the face from Barak. Barak broke their agreement because of his own considerations. The last time was the worst: the whole "safety net" was a wretched joke—a Shas "safety net" instead of a unity government?! Even a political rookie should have realized that this simply wouldn't work and that the days of Barak's government were numbered. But he could not withstand the pressure on him from the dovish wing of the Labor Party. He once told me, with sorrow and concern, "If we have to call early elections, they are the only ones who will go out to the streets and support me. All the others, all the intellectuals, will sit home and read newspapers. I must keep them with me."

But the truth is simpler and uglier. The people who pressured Barak to preserve what remained of his coalition, relying on the Shas "safety net," never wanted him as Prime Minister and didn't believe in him. They wanted Shimon Peres, and to achieve their goal, the "genius" intellectuals devised a plan reminiscent of the "dirty trick" political scandal of 1990, hoping to have Peres replace Barak.

They dreamed that Peres might be able to return to the premiership if there were early elections and Barak dropped out of the running. So a festival of polls "that predicted victory for Shimon Peres" was organized. The hope of those behind these polls was that Barak would break, bow to the will of the party, and hand over his position to Peres. Then the party, headed by Peres as incumbent Prime Minister, could hold on to power by "buying" Shas or call and win early elections. Peres, as usual, "didn't know" who was behind the polls. The people wanted it, the party wanted it; but he wasn't involved. He was never involved in anything that was done on his behalf. He "wasn't involved" and would run for president only if asked; he "wasn't involved" in the cheap festival to celebrate his birthday—he knew nothing about it. If he wasn't involved, he could have gone on television and denied his part in the stratagem. But he did just the opposite.

The pressure by the dovish elite and Peres's supporters in the party didn't help, and Barak didn't relent. In fact, Peres would have had no chance running against Sharon, given Israel's situation in 2001. In the race for Prime Minister only (the only time this ever happened), Ehud Barak was resoundingly defeated and Ariel Sharon became Prime Minister. I wanted to ask the "wise men of Chelm," the inventors of the "Shas safety net" who dragged the country into that election: What harm could have befallen Israel had Barak remained Prime Minister for another year or two, with Sharon a minister in his government? Did Israel gain anything from this second "dirty trick"? By preventing the establishment of a unity government, they made Sharon Prime Minister and thus became indirectly responsible for all the evils of his administration—the failure to build the separation fence earlier, more than a thousand dead in terrorist attacks, the near-destruction of the Palestinian Authority—all the ugly phenomena that shook the country.

This series of events reminded me of how the Tehiya party had quit Shamir's government in 1992, forcing early elections. Tehiya thought its maneuver would serve its goals. In fact, it boomeranged and led to the Oslo Accords. I say this not as a criticism of Rabin's policies, but as a criticism of the wisdom of those who play politics without insight or responsibility. And the smarter and more experienced they are, the more disastrous their actions prove to be. It will be many years before Israel recovers from Sharon's administration, from all the wrongs committed then and the devastation wrought later when Ehud Olmert was Prime Minister.

Chapter 65

During the 2001 campaign for Prime Minister, Sharon called me. "Yasha, please, don't work too hard for your friend."

"I don't betray my friends, Arik."

"I didn't mean that," he replied. "Just don't exert yourself too much."

I couldn't accept this. I wasn't supporting Ehud Barak because of our friendship, but because I didn't want Sharon as Prime Minister. I was concerned about many things that might happen, and unfortunately I was correct. His administration was much worse than anything I could have imagined. I certainly thought that Barak was better suited to be Prime Minister. Barak warned me that Sharon was vengeful. I told him I didn't care and continued my work on Barak's behalf.

I interrupted a family vacation to make campaign appearances on behalf of Barak. One idea he floated was to announce that he would appoint me Interior Minister. I opposed this. I thought it would look so cheap, so primitive and artificial, that it would have the opposite effect. The voters simply wouldn't believe him. If he thought that it was necessary, he could have done it already. Such a declaration of intent during the campaign would be seen as an ineffective and ridiculous gimmick. Barak didn't listen to me and let it slip to journalists that he wanted to appoint me Interior Minister in his new government. When the media asked me, I told them that I wasn't a partner to his plan. I agreed to appear in the media and talk about only one issue—the civic revolution that Barak had promised to launch but had not implemented. As usual, the clip was carefully scripted. I wrote out the text of what I wanted to say. Barak's PR staff tried to soften the wording and persuade me not to make clear and unambiguous statements. They were concerned that I might reduce his support among religious voters or his ability to forge an alliance with the religious parties after the election. I stuck to my guns, refusing to change a single word, and the clip was filmed as I had wanted. But they didn't dare broadcast it. I was certain that people could not be persuaded to make a "light" or "pseudo" social revolution, and that if he formed a coalition with the religious parties, we could forget about the civic revolution and I would certainly withdraw my support."

I recalled that before the 1999 elections, which Barak won, I had proposed that he declare that he would remove the nationality entry from Israeli identity cards. He listened and promised to look into it, but he consulted with his advisors and told me that they didn't think it was a good idea. In the end, the nationality entry was abolished by an interior minister from Shas. After the High Court of Justice ruled that non-Orthodox converts had to be listed as "Jewish," he instructed that the field be left blank for everyone. As the old saying goes, the work of the righteous is performed by others. Barak didn't take this step because he paid attention to his advisors. As expected, he lost resoundingly in the 2001 election, "earning" his defeat fair and square.

Barak made his worst mistake, and the one that caused me the most grief, after the election. Sharon, who thought highly of Barak as a military man and as a statesman, wanted him in his government. Sharon once told me that Barak was the only politician he could speak with, the only one who understood things. Everyone who knew Sharon's derisive opinions of his "friends" in his government and his party could understand this, and this explains why he wanted Barak to be his Defense Minister so badly. What harm could possibly have come to Israel had Ehud Barak become Defense Minister in Sharon's government? All the ugliness and failures of the Second Intifada might have been averted, the government would have functioned better, and the separation fence would have been built sooner. In 1981, the Labor Party was not part of Begin's government, so there was no one in the cabinet to put the brakes on the First Lebanon War. Twenty years later, Barak repeated the same mistake. Barak surrendered to Haim Ramon, the architect of both the "dirty trick" and the safety net.

I congratulated Sharon after the election. I also told him not to delude himself—it wasn't that he won, but that Barak crashed because of his mistakes. I recommended that he avoid the same mistakes if he wanted to stay in power. I didn't think that Sharon would listen to me—I knew him and his personality—but I couldn't hold back from speaking my mind. We spoke only once more after that. We really had nothing to discuss, because what interested me didn't interest him; we had different priorities.

What saddened me was the fate of Nativ. I remembered one of Sharon's visits to Russia, when I took him to visit one of our Jewish schools in Moscow. Sharon was very enthusiastic and asked if there were problems. I told him that we could set up many more Israeli schools like this, which would be much more effective and influential, with a stronger curriculum and higher enrollment. The only obstacle was money. I remember how furious he was, how he raged that it was a national crime that Jews were prevented from having this opportunity because of a few million dollars. At the time, his words encouraged me to believe that not everything was lost and that there were still politicians in Israel who cared about Jews and *aliyah*.

During Sharon's term as Prime Minister, Nativ was completely neglected. He didn't hold work meetings with its director, except for one pro forma session. Nativ was transferred to the purview of the government secretary and sunk to its lowest point ever. But worst of all was the slashing of its budget. Sharon forgot his declarations and lost all interest in Nativ. The educational network in the former Soviet Union was transferred to the Jewish Agency, and, like everything else taken over by that organization, deteriorated in every sense.

The network lost all value and became a pale shadow of what it had been before. Its essence changed, too. During Shulamit Aloni's term as education minister in the early 1990s, she said that she didn't understand why her ministry should oversee Jewish education in the former Soviet Union, rather than the Jewish Agency. But when she studied the matter, she understood the implications of the fact that the Education Ministry of one country was active in another country, as part of international agreements, and realized her error. Aloni, like her predecessor and successors in the ministry—Zevulun Hammer, Amnon Rubinstein, and Yossi Sarid—understood the importance of its involvement in the former Soviet Union as a stage in the integration of the children into Israeli society and schools after they made *aliyah*. Limor Livnat, Education Minister under Sharon, was very creative in her demagoguery, with its national and nationalistic tone, but when it came down to the issue itself, she did what no previous education minister had dared—she abandoned the ministry-run network to the Jewish Agency. Like Sharon, she simply didn't care. In Livnat's case, this didn't surprise me, but I had expected more from Sharon.

Chapter 66

After I left the public service, I continued to travel to Russia and other countries, but only for private and business reasons. I stayed away from political issues. I took my two children, Revital and Sefi (Yosef) to Russia just before each of them was inducted into the IDF. On the trip with Sefi, we had an emotional experience. The Russian Foreign Minister, Igor Ivanov, with whom I was on friendly terms, came back to Moscow from a work visit. When he learned that I was in town, he asked me to come meet him. It was already late in the evening and I went with Sefi to see him at the Foreign Ministry. When we entered the minister's suite, Sefi stayed in the waiting room while I went into Ivanov's office. During the conversation, Ivanov asked why I was in Moscow. I told him I had brought my teenage son to see his roots before he joined the IDF. Ivanov invited him into his office, asked him several questions, and suddenly excused himself for a few minutes. When he came back, he told my son excitedly that he was from the Caucasus, where it was the custom that a boy who comes of age receives a dagger as a symbol of his manhood. "You are going into the army and becoming a man," he said. "This dagger belongs to my family. I am giving it to you with my fond wishes that you will be a good soldier. Protect your people and your country, and let your devotion to your motherland make your father proud."

I was deeply moved. The Foreign Minister of Russia was giving his blessing to my son upon joining the IDF! And I attached another profound and important historical element to this occasion. Although Ivanov had never told me, I knew that he had Russian, Georgian, and Assyrian ancestry, and the King of Assyria once conquered Jerusalem. Such are the wonders of human and Jewish history.

One fine day, I landed in Moscow. When I reached Passport Control, I saw the face of the woman in the booth go pale when she looked at her computer screen. She asked me to step to the side and called over a major from Border Police. The officer told me cordially that he had to clarify something and asked for my passport and flight ticket. He came back about 20 minutes later. "Mr. Kedmi, you have been banned from entering Russia. Your visa has been canceled. You'll have to leave on the same plane you came on."

So I flew back to Frankfurt. From Frankfurt, I called Ariel Sharon, who was then visiting Moscow. I was put through to him immediately and told him what had happened. This wasn't a private matter, I told him, but a problem between the two countries. It was completely out of step with the relations between Russia and Israel and must not be allowed to go unchallenged. I asked him to speak to President Putin and emphasized that there was no point in talking to anyone else.

Sharon consented, but he never actually spoke to Putin. Instead, he asked the Russian Foreign Minister to see to it. But the Foreign Minister was the wrong man—the director of the FSB was not his subordinate and didn't give a damn what he said. Only President Putin could have solved the problem.

I knew that this was not the first case of an Israeli being barred from entering Russia. Over the past year or so, several other Israelis had been kept out "for reasons of State security," the same reason the Border Police officer gave me. The FSB accused Israelis involved in joint projects in the hi-tech and electronics industries of espionage and revoked their visas. I knew that these people had absolutely nothing to do with intelligence activities. When they asked me for help, I advised them to contact the Prime Minister's bureau and ask the staff there to take up their case with the Russians, because this was an extremely charged matter that absolutely had to be dealt with. As far as I know, nothing was ever done, certainly not at the right level. I knew that this was a growing phenomenon and said as much to Sharon. But there was no response and no serious action was taken. I also contacted Zvi Magen, my successor at Nativ, and told him that as head of the organization he should raise the matter with the Prime Minister. No country in the world would have let this go by unchallenged. I also discussed it with the head of the GSS, Avi Dichter, and the head of the Mossad, Meir Dagan, because the Mossad is responsible for inter-service relations. My impression was that I was speaking with people who hadn't the foggiest notion of what I was talking about. Magen did understand, but I knew that his personal capabilities and courage were negligible, and certainly on this matter. I nonetheless expected the system would at least respond the way systems should—but in vain.

I looked into the matter on my own. It turned out that what Netanyahu had told Schiffer in an interview during the campaign had found its way into the Russian press. After publication, a member of the Duma submitted a parliamentary question to the head of the FSB, asking whether the story published in the name of the Israeli Prime Minister is correct and whether this man, Yakov Kedmi, who bribed a Russian official for information, was continuing to visit Russia. The reply was provided by the deputy director of the FSB: The agency was aware of the publication, and Mr. Kedmi and his activities during his tenure and afterwards were also well known to them. According to him, I had gathered information about Russia both as a civil servant and in my private life. My activities were against the law and I would henceforth be denied entrance to Russia. I have a copy of the response. It was obvious that someone had put the parliamentarian up to asking the question and that the FSB had decided to take action against me without prodding by the Duma.

All the things they attributed to me, even if partly true, were done in service of the country, on behalf of Israel and in its name. But Israel didn't want to respond. This was true of other cases, not just mine.

I recalled other instances in which the State of Israel restrained itself. The worst case was the expulsion of the Mossad representative from Moscow, which I have already related. When the Russians notified him that he was persona non grata, the representative of Russian Foreign Intelligence in Israel began packing his bags. Neither he nor his superiors could imagine that he would not be expelled—quid pro quo. This is an unbreakable rule: Regardless of what your man did, if he is expelled, you automatically expel his counterpart if you want to be respected and taken seriously. But Israel didn't respond, any more than it had to Nehemiah Levanon's expulsion from the Soviet Union in 1955 or that of Nativ's David Gavish in 1966. After the Russians recovered from their shock, they realized something about the character of Israel, its officials, and its leaders: They still haven't gotten used to being a sovereign state; they still have the mindset of Diaspora Jews who need to curry favor with the Gentile policemen and landowners, as they had in Poland and Russia. Russia decided that Israel was a pushover in this respect and it could do whatever it wanted. The Israelis would only wipe the spit off their face and wonder why it was raining.

There was nothing I could do now. I didn't want to use my own contacts in an attempt to have the ban lifted as a private affair. I stuck to the position that this was a national affair and not an individual matter, and I would not deal with it until the country did. After all, there were other people, including a former Nativ emissary, who were barred from Russia.

In my time, it was customary for the Prime Minister to come to our annual Nativ Day to greet the staff, as he did for the Mossad and the GSS on their days. The first Prime Minister to break this custom was Ariel Sharon. And it wasn't just any Nativ Day—it was our fiftieth anniversary celebration. Yet the event wasn't as important for Sharon as the circumcision of the grandson of some member of the Likud central committee. I published an article in *Ha'aretz* about Sharon's absence and the insult to the organization and its employees over the years. I added that this disrespect reflected his attitude not only to the organization but to the issue as a whole and the people who had dedicated their lives to it. The Prime Minister's bureau issued a faltering apology about how the Prime Minister certainly respected the organization and had sent a representative and his blessings.

This was at the height of the second Intifada. Terrorist attacks followed one another in quick succession and the casualty count grew almost daily. It was obvious to me that the main reason for the success of the attacks was the lack of a security fence—a physical barrier between Judea and Samaria and Israel proper that would deny terrorists uncontrolled passage to their targets. It was also obvious to me that the reason the security fence had not been built was Sharon's fear of political embroilment. In the conditions that prevailed, a potential terrorist would have to be very lazy to call off his mission. Few of the attackers had gone through professional training. Most of them were young men and women, who obviously had never served in an army, most of whom had never received military training or explosives drills. All they had to do was to get up, go a few kilometers, and hitch a ride or hire a cab to reach the heart of Tel Aviv. In the 1950s, when there was a similar situation and a porous border, the easiest and best solution to stop the infiltration by the Fedayeen would have been a fence. But the idea wasn't accepted then, either. The "wise men" of Israel had, as usual, preferred the demagogic argument that "Jews should never have to live behind barbed wire again." They traded in words and profited from the memory of the Holocaust in the service of their "ideology." They had always preferred reprisal raids, and Ariel Sharon was one of the commanders who had carried them out back then.

Israel is an absolute virtuoso of euphemisms. We don't say "withdrawal," we say "tick." The first tick, the second tick. It sounds much better. We don't say "evacuation," we say "disengagement." So of course we didn't refer to the reprisal raids as "revenge." "Reprisal" sounds so much more aesthetic and civilized. After all, we aren't primitive tribes, barbarians who engage in blood feuds. And even if we do, we do it with class. At the end of the day, it's all the same. Private individuals who conduct blood feuds are put on trial; but when a country turns a blood feud into a "reprisal raid," it is legal and justified. Instead of exercising political prudence, Israel lowered its policy to the level of basic animalistic instincts, which have no place in civilized society. Israel preferred a tribal blood feud to a barrier that would have prevented infiltration. In the end, though, the reprisal raids of the 1950s achieved nothing. They did nothing to reduce terror; they only improved the combat skills of several dozen guys in Unit 101, which excelled all IDF units in its prowess. But there were much better ways of enhancing the IDF's capabilities.

This custom of shooting from the hip instead of thinking seems to be encoded in the military and political genes of Israeli society and continues to this day. In 2001 and 2002, there were reprisals again, but under a different guise. They were the unsuccessful response to terrorism. Sharon never wanted or reconciled himself to accept Arafat's regime or the very idea of a Palestinian state, even though he was forced to agree to it out loud. And just as in 1982, when he took advantage of the attempted assassination of the Israel ambassador in London for a war against the PLO, launching the first Lebanon War, he exploited the terrorism of the second Intifada and essentially declared war on the Palestinian Authority and Arafat in order to destroy the Palestinian Authority.

It was obvious to me that the lack of a fence was the main factor inviting terrorism. There is nothing more encouraging than success. I could barely restrain myself, until one day when I met with Ehud Barak and we spoke about the situation. He told me he had seen Sharon and tried to convince him to build the fence. He had warned Sharon that he would later be condemned for this failure. I asked what Sharon had said and Barak replied that he had listened but remained silent. I knew Sharon and I knew that he had nothing to say. As a military man, he knew in his bones that Barak was right and the fence was essential. No one had to explain it to him. Had he had any relevant arguments, he would have used them

When Matan Vilna'i was OC Southern Command, he had a fence built around the Gaza Strip on his own initiative, using his own command's budget, and contrary to the opinion of the Chief of Staff. This fence has saved the lives of hundreds if not thousands of Israelis. Vilna'i's fence was far from state-of-the art, but it was good enough to shut down terrorism from Gaza into Israel

After I heard this from Barak, I could no longer control myself. My feelings for Sharon amounted to adulation. My love and admiration for him had blinded me to his problematic behavior for a long time. I simply repressed it. This was probably because Sharon symbolized for me some of the basic elements of the State of Israel; in my subconscious, I was afraid that debunking his myth would detract from my feelings towards Israel. Fortunately, it didn't. I suddenly sobered up from my delusion and began seeing his behavior in a clear and objective way, in its full seriousness. It pained me greatly, but I could no longer stay silent. Sharon betrayed everything that was dear to me in the State of Israel.

Journalist Shelly Yachimovich, who had heard from someone what I was saying about the fence, called and asked to interview me on Israel Channel Two. In the interview, I castigated Sharon for neglecting Israel's security and not building the fence. I said it was criminal negligence and blamed him for the deaths it had caused. He could have prevented most of the terrorist attacks by building the fence, had he not been driven by considerations of maintaining his coalition and avoiding a clash with the radical nationalist and religious groups, which were more important to him than the lives of Israeli citizens. I didn't spare the rod from the extensive influence of Sharon's family, either. I compared it to Yeltsin's regime, when "the family"—he, his daughter, her husband, and a handful of close cronies—dominated Russia. I said that Sharon was controlling the country through his sons and his sons were determining the national priorities. These were very harsh statements, uncouth but absolutely true. Until then, no one had dared call a spade a spade in such a clear and unambiguous manner.

Sharon's bureau responded just like Netanyahu had a few years earlier. They couldn't find anything bad to say about me, so his underlings recruited Shimon Schiffer, who was once again the dutiful servant. Relying on leaks by Sharon's cronies, Schiffer defamed me. "Look what kind of man, what kind of unsavory character this Yakov Kedmi is. Even Russia doesn't let him enter." Schiffer wrote that people at Nativ said that I was barred from Russia because of my connections with criminal elements! That an organization that was once such a magnificent symbol of professionalism on the issue of Russia and devotion to the cause was now providing filthy services for failed and corrupt politicians, was for me the lowest of the low.

After the Disengagement from Gaza, many of those who had reproached me for attacking Sharon in such a vulgar manner said the exact same things about him themselves. I snickered about my friends in the right-wing camp who had attacked me for daring to speak that way about Ariel Sharon, but now swooped down on him after he acted out of line with their political worldview. Before that, Sharon's corruption was acceptable; only when his political actions no longer suited their ideas did they discover his "sins." Everything about Sharon was clear to me now; I had lost my last illusions. It pained me to see how the country was sinking and declining day after day, in every sense—ethically and morally, administratively, nationally, militarily. The collapse of all systems applied to every domain in Israel, including the most sensitive and important area of all—security.

Afterword

Throughout my whole life, I have wondered time and again whether I chose the right direction, one that would lead me to the proper goal. Were all my wars justified and right? I still ponder those questions today, but I am less confident in my answers than I used to be.

My qualities as a person, which ensured my successes in many struggles but also caused failures, were formed in Soviet Russia, in Moscow. My personality and my ethical and moral foundations were consolidated in Russia, as was my respect for human dignity, regardless of a person's religion and ethnicity, and my sharp sense of justice, both social and general. In Russia, I learned about love for one's homeland, love for my people, and personal sacrifice on their behalf and for the ideals you believe in. Russia was where I learned to fight until the end, never to surrender, even if the battle was against everyone and against all odds.

When I came to Israel, the concepts of perseverance towards the goal and endurance were already branded in my personality and my consciousness. In Russia, I was taught to value literature, culture, education, and art. From my childhood, I developed disgust for cheap and primitive political demagoguery and phoniness, particularly on the part of rulers and party members, of the commercialization of principles and that whole lifestyle. It was there that I developed scorn for people who dedicated their lives to making money, despite the cruel and tyrannical regime, despite the hypocrisy and lies that spread throughout Soviet society and in the end destroyed it. I developed these characteristics in Russia and I don't regret that for a moment.

The knowledge and experience I acquired in Israel—in the IDF and in the intelligence community—only improved and refined both my character and my analytical and cognitive skills. I learned many things I had not understood before or had deluded myself into believing were true. I'm proud to say that this process of constant learning, delving deeply, and arriving at new understandings never paused for a minute, and I hope it will continue the rest of my life.

At first glance, one can say that I largely succeeded in achieving self-fulfillment and realizing my goals. I was able to stand alone against all odds and face down a superpower. This achievement still gives me great personal satisfaction. My children and grandchildren were born in a Jewish state, in the country I dreamed about and fought for the right to live in. It is their country and their people. My nieces and nephews, the children of my sister Vera and my brother Shurik, and the rest of my family, have enjoyed the same boon. I rejoice to see my mother glowing with happiness as she chatters away in Hebrew with her eight grandchildren, whose ancestors came from all over the Diaspora: Romania, Turkey, Tunisia, Ukraine, and Russia.

When I look at the *olim* from the former Soviet Union who now live in Israel, I am filled with tremendous satisfaction. I remember how, during the hard times I endured at Nativ, I used to go to the airport at night, drive my car out to the plane, and watch hundreds of *olim* descending the ramp. I tried to catch the moment and catch their expressions when their feet first touched the ground of their homeland. The faces of *olim* when they landed in Israel gave me the strength and confidence to go forward, despite all obstacles and adversaries.

But the thousands of cases of humiliation, disgrace, exploitation, racism, and discrimination against *olim* that I encountered over the years pained me and aroused intense fury and shame. I too was involved in hurting them, not only because I bear much of the "blame" for their being in Israel, but because this is how the Jewish country, my country, treats Jews who made *aliyah*. At these moments, I am struck by a horrible thought: did I take too much responsibility on myself when I decided their fate and prevented them from emigrating to other countries? From the perspective of what is best for the country, I have no doubts; but what about the human perspective? I don't have a clear-cut answer. I no longer have the same confidence I once had about this difficult question.

I look around me at the "thriving" Jewish country and harsh thoughts race through my head. Is this the state our people deserve? I recall my grandfather of blessed memory and what he said about the inhuman exploitation of Jews by other Jews. I see this every day, on an increasing scale and with growing cynicism. I look at the children of the *olim*. Most of the *olim* came to Israel to give their children a better future. Most of these children are among the best and brightest, and had they stayed where they were born or moved to other countries would certainly have completed university. But here, in their own country, most of them do not complete their matriculation certificate. Many end up involved with crime and drugs, as happened to earlier groups of *olim*. Is this what we fought for? In our Jewish country today, a Jewish child receives an education worse than that of almost any Jewish child in the world.

In my view, the state is not a goal, but only a tool. Its purpose is to serve its citizens, and not the other way around. For me, a Jewish state is the only means that can ensure the existence of the Jewish people and its future outside of the religious framework. Religion maintained the Jewish collective for more than 2,000 years, because there was no other kind of Jewishness. Jews who observe the Torah and the precepts will stay Jewish forever. But what can we do when most Jews are not religious, and the non-religious Jewish collective has no future without the State of Israel as our nation-state? Every attempt to drag the country and Israel's citizens back to the religious ghetto endangers the country's future. In today's world, and even more so in tomorrow's, nonreligious Jews will not be able to live within the same system of clerical laws that existed for centuries. And without a solid majority of secular Jews, the State of Israel will not survive for long. The religious sector alone, with all its factions, cannot maintain or protect the country.

The Jews have lost three states. The monarchies of Israel and Judah fell, as did the Hasmonean kingdom centuries later. The State of Israel is the fourth attempt, and, I believe, inevitably the last. We will not have a fifth chance. Our people managed to take advantage of international and regional developments in the twentieth century and establish a state, against all odds and historical logic. But founding a state and defending it are not enough to ensure its survival. Over the last hundred years we have seen many states collapse and disappear. Most of them fell because the regime failed, because they could not maintain the systems of government, and because of the irresponsible policies of their rulers and leaders.

Look around and try to imagine what Israel would look like today without the million Jews who made *aliyah* from the Soviet Union and its successor states in the last several decades. The economy would have been at least 25 percent smaller, without most of the high-tech sector, without 30 percent of the soldiers in the combat units, with a very different political system and demography. Would that much weaker country have possessed the same resilience as Israel has today? But a million Jews came here, almost by chance, and odds are that under other circumstances, most of them would not have come to Israel even had they left their countries of origins. Without that million, Israel would now be facing the worst crisis of its history. In other words, we were on the brink of an existential crisis in the late 1980s, even though we didn't know it.

And today? The most precious human capital in the world is being wasted in an appalling manner. The *olim* included more than 60,000 teachers, but the Israeli education system, which is deteriorating and locked in a perpetual crisis with a severe shortage of teachers, rejected most of them. Tens of thousands of physicians made *aliyah*, but the country is facing a terrible shortage of doctors. More than 100,000 engineers came, but we are on the threshold of a grave shortage in that arena as well. Thousands of scientists of the highest international standing made *aliyah*, but we are on the verge of an acute shortage of scientists. For most of its existence, Israel has benefited from the *aliyah* of the human and professional elite of the Arab countries and Europe. But more than sixty years later, we still have not learned how to use their skills and talents to build schools and other systems that are appropriate for the abilities and needs of the Jewish people in the twenty-first century and ensure the development of the Jewish state that the Jewish people can produce and deserve.

By contrast, what is thriving here are personnel companies, the Israeli form of modern slavery. Workers have no rights. Employees who won basic rights in civilized countries a hundred years ago are being exploited shamelessly in Israel and earning starvation wages. These "slave contractors," otherwise known as "human resource companies," hired thousands of teachers, engineers, and scientists and turned them into slaves, with the blessing of their new country.

Israel is in the throes of the broadest and most severe systemic crisis in its history. The events described in this book are merely a few expressions of this crisis. And if the Jewish people does not launch a basic and thorough rehabilitation of the entire system, it is doubtful whether the country will survive until mid-century to see its centennial. The *aliyah* of slightly over a million Jews in the last decade of the twentieth century will go down in history as merely a postponement of the end rather than as a tremendous resource that helped strengthen and restore the country's foundations and ensure its existence for the ages.

We, the Jews of the twentieth century, the century of the Holocaust that devastated our people, decided that the establishment of the Jewish state was the most important thing for us and the most vital need of the Jewish people. Were we right? For us and our generation, we were. Every generation has its truth. Our children's and grandchildren's generations will decide for themselves what is best for them. And if their decision is not the same as ours, that is their prerogative. We, too, decided differently than our grandparents. We decided our future and they will decide theirs, and, thereby, the future of the Jewish people. My hope is that they too will perceive the State of Israel as our most precious possession. And should they not, God forbid, the world will probably perceive that as the Jewish people's renunciation of its need for a state. If that is the future that awaits my beautiful and amazing people and the State of Israel, I am glad that I will not be living then.

Israel, August 2008